Red Hot

Alice Springs in the Seventies

Non Fiction / Autobiography

Mien Blom

ISBN 095816120-8
National Library of Australia Cataloguing
August 2002

Printed by Asprint
Tel: (08) 8952 8877
Alice Springs NT, Australia

Red Hot Soup

Alice Springs in the Seventies

Non-fiction - Autobiography
by
Mien Blom

Published by Centre Press
P.O. BOX 4072
Alice Springs NT 0871

Ph: 08-89550064
Fax: 08-89550214
Email: mienblom@bigpond.com

'Father Forgive Us...'
Coming to terms with my tears
Copyright © Wilhelmina J. Blom, March 2001
ISBN 0646-41301-5
March 2001

Red Hot Soup
Alice Springs in the Seventies
Copyright © Wilhelmina J. Blom, August 2002
ISBN 095816120-8

ABOUT THE AUTHOR

MIEN BLOM was born in Holland in October 1939 where she grew up on a small farm. In 1971 Mien emigrated to Alice Springs in Central Australia with her husband Fred and six young children, where she still lives today. She has worked as a nursing aid at the local nursing home for five years before starting their picture-framing/leadlighting business in 1980.

While recuperating from a nervous breakdown following the death of her mother, Mien joined the FAW in 1990 to obtain help with writing her family history. *'Father Forgive Us...'* the first part of her autobiography, was launched in May 2001. It describes the influence the lives of her grandparents, her parents and her own upbringing had on her married life.

'Red Hot Soup' is about the family's first ten years in Central Australia. Mien is now planning her third book about her lifelong interest and involvement in elderly care.

Dedicated to our children and grandchildren
Australia's future

Acknowledgments

Red Hot Soup is my honest recollection of what happened during our first ten years in Australia and how it effected our family and me personally. I am well aware that others involved would remember things differently and that, by writing about my own experiences, I also put my family and the many people I encountered into the public eye. I apologise for any inconvenience this may cause them.

I started writing my family history in 1990. I was fifty at the time, recuperating from a nervous breakdown after the death of my mother. I had the feeling that life was passing me by, trapped in our picture framing and leadlighting business. The last of our six children had left home two years earlier and I saw my dream of ever doing nursing again go up in smoke.

On a six-week trip to the Kimberley's in 1990 we met an elderly couple from New-Zealand. Like many other people we talked to, Beth and Allan Anderson were very interested to hear our stories and the reasons we left Holland, our home country, to settle in Alice Springs of all places. They urged me to write a book, preserving our stories for future generations. I started immediately, writing about our emigration. However, I soon realised that I first had to get rid of the crippling emotional baggage I was still carrying with me. The result *'Father Forgive Us...' Coming to terms with my tears*, published in May 2001, has truly freed me from the past. Whenever my emotions got the better of me I went back to writing about my happier experiences in Alice Springs in this book; *Red Hot Soup*.

The help and encouragement from my friends at the Fellowship of Australian Writers in Alice Springs throughout the years has been invaluable to me. My heartfelt thanks especially go to Marjorie Gook, who at eighty-five is still devoting her life to teaching proper English to people like me, who never learned grammar properly, correcting my work, time and again. I thank my family for their patience while teaching me the use of the computer, their valuable comments and their sometimes-painful criticism. Special thanks to our youngest daughter Regine for scanning the photographs and preparing the text for the printer, and to our son Eugene for designing the cover.

I am grateful for the valuable comments of Mr Dick Kimber, our local historian who checked my work for accuracy. Many thanks also to

Wabe Roskam the editor of the Dutch Weekly for his continuing enthusiasm and support. I also appreciate the many bookshop owners for giving a self-published author a go and my readers for their stimulating responses. I am very grateful for the financial support of my anonymous sponsor. His belief in me is very touching. I am happy that the printing of this book again could be done locally, by Max Kleiner of Asprint. I don't know what I would have done without them and all those other wonderful people who helped me, one way or another, along the way.

Last but by no means least, my love and appreciation goes to my husband Fred. Without his trust in me, and his willingness to accept that I needed more out of life than being a housewife and mother, I could never have written our story as honest and complete.

Mien Blom,
September 2002

Index

Red Hot Soup

Farewell – 3rd September 1971

It was close to midnight when I watched the lights on the coast of Holland slowly disappearing into the distance. My husband Fred's arms were comforting around me. We hardly spoke as the realisation sank in that we might never see our families and friends again. I shivered. What have we done? We were on our way to England. There was no turning back. What if it was all a big mistake?

It had all happened so quickly. We didn't get the chance to say good-bye properly, not even a hug for Mum but just a quick kiss through a hole in the wire fence as we hurried to the ferry. She had not cried at all. On the contrary, she was happy that we were going to join her two bachelor sons, Sam and Henk, in Australia. With me there too, she had a better chance to visit them, she had said.

During the first couple of years my two brothers had worked and travelled together. After living in Alice Springs, a little town in the middle of the Australian desert for some time, Henk returned to Melbourne. He could no longer stand the heat and flies in Alice, he wrote. That's where we were heading now.

Sam left Holland in May 1961, more than ten years ago. When Henk left eight months later, I had been away from home and married nearly four years. Like Sam, he could hardly wait to finish his compulsory service in the army to leave for Australia. Henk was only twenty and Sam twenty-two when we said good-bye. I hardly knew either of them.

Sam promised to build a house for us, but in his last letter he said that there was no way he could do it before we arrived; he was still waiting for the plans to be drawn up.

"But that won't matter," he wrote. "Bring your tent; you love camping don't you? The Aborigines here live happily in the dry river."

I shivered again. Sam had always been the odd one out in our family, and we were about to invade the privacy of his single-man's life with six lively children...

"Come, let's go," Fred said softly, leading me away from the railing. I had not noticed how cold it was. Everybody else had already gone inside.

We stepped carefully over the sleeping bodies on the main deck of the ferry. People of all ages hung in chairs or lay on benches filling every available space. Some were trying to read by the light of a torch. We wondered about all those hundreds of people who had come on board with cars, motorbikes and in buses. Most of them were on holiday and did not have a cabin for the overnight trip.

Grateful to have a proper bed after the long, emotional day I crawled into the narrow bunk bed in the tiny, eight-berth cabin. We had all been up since

1

five o'clock that morning, and I had not slept much the previous night. Our children, aged four to twelve went to bed before the ferry left the harbour and were asleep as soon as their heads had touched their pillows. But sleep did not come for me as the events of the last months kept flashing through my mind.

Eight very stressful months had passed since we walked arm in arm through the snow on the evening of New-Years-Day 1971, to mail our letters to Henk and Sam, asking them to help us create a better future for ourselves and our children. It had not taken them long to reply. Unemployment was becoming a problem in Melbourne too, Henk wrote. Jobs were not as easy to come by as they used to be. He couldn't do much for us as he and two other young men were boarding with a childless couple. He said that if we could stand the heat and the flies, it would be better for us to go to Sam in Alice Springs, because there was lots of work there.

Sam's letter was very optimistic. Oh, yes, there was plenty of work and heaps of space there. The prosperous little town could use people like Fred who were not afraid to get their hands dirty. Six months ago he had bought a block of land at an auction but he could not make up his mind whether to make a start on the house or go to Queensland 'to play with the old dozer on his thirty-acre block for a while'. With us coming he had a reason to build the house first, he wrote. That was eight months ago, now there would be no house for us and we might have to live in the tent after all... Fred's sister, Bep, blamed me for making her favourite brother leave his homeland where he had a good job and a comfortable house, to face an uncertain future in a country he'd sworn he never wanted to live in.

Fred had spent eighteen months, from October 1953 until April 1955, in Dutch New Guinea (now West Irian Jaya) with the Royal Dutch Navy. From there they made a trip to Australia for an overhaul of the engines of their landings-craft. After a dangerous journey in with one of the engines out of action, the Australian Navy had towed them into Cairns where the engine had been repaired temporarily. The engine later failed again in heavy seas near Mackay causing leaks in the fuel tanks and the engine room. Luckily, the Australian minesweeper 'Wagga' was in the area and towed them into Brisbane this time. Australians as well as fellow 'Dutchies' had given the sailors a fantastic time, inviting them to parties and into their homes.

"The homes of the Australians were very bare too," Bep said, reminding us time and again how horrified Fred had been to see the poor living conditions of the immigrants. Although most of them had been in Australia for many years, they were still sitting on fruit crates and sleeping on mattresses on the bare floor because they could not afford to buy decent furniture.

The truth was that Fred had become very frustrated with his job, in charge

2

of several troublesome, mentally handicapped young men in a small factory making machine-made furniture. He had worked there for the past six years and wanting to quit for quite some time but, because we lived in a house that went with the job, he had no option but to stay. There was little or no chance of finding other, suitable work as well as a house in Holland.

Ever since we married in April 1958, but especially during the last years, we talked off and on about emigrating. At first we were living with Fred's father, a lovely man who was a diabetic and needed us to look after him. Plans were made again four years later after our fourth child was born and my father-in-law moved in with Fred's eldest sister when she became a widow. But, being good Catholics, I got pregnant again and we had to forget about emigrating for a while. When we talked about leaving after our youngest child was born in May 1967, more seriously this time, Fred's father cried saying that it would break his heart if we took his grandchildren away. At that time Fred's boss offered him the much bigger house, closer to the job. So, instead we "emigrated" from the council home in Velp to the boss's house - which tied him to the job - in Oosterbeek on the other side of Arnhem. When Fred's father died in July 1968 we were free to go, but six months later I needed major surgery which put a stop to our plans yet again.

In the summer of 1970, we were forced to make a final decision as Lilian would be twelve the next spring and would be going to High School the following summer. We had heard how devastating it was for teenagers to leave their friends behind; some of them had run away, hidden until their family had gone. By that time I had recovered from my operation, my strength had returned and there was no risk of me having any more children. Fred would turn forty-one in November. If we wanted to leave, we had to do it soon or he would be too old to take such a big step.

We kept agonising about it until one day, shortly after his birthday, Fred came home from work at an unusual time, boiling over with anger. He'd had an argument with one of his older colleagues "who was as stubborn and selfish as the half-wits he had to work with all day" he fumed. Fred was an easy-going fellow most of the time; I had never seen him so worked up. The doctor said he needed a week's rest and change of scene. That's when we decided to write to Henk and Sam asking them about the possibilities for us in Australia.

A few weeks after we received my brothers' letters, an informative evening about Canada, South Africa, New Zealand and Australia was held by the Department of Emigration in Musis Sacrem in Arnhem. The big hall was packed. After a lengthy opening speech, films were shown about each of the different countries. Because of Fred's experience in Australia, Canada had been our first choice. My mother's two younger sisters went there in 1948 but when we realised how cold it was there in winter, it was no longer an option to

3

either of us. Australia, the most popular country according to statistics, was last. In the film everybody worked happily together either in friendly, spacious offices, in clean factories or in the well-organised building industry, under a beautiful blue sky. Brisbane, Sydney, Canberra, Melbourne, Adelaide and Perth each city seemed even more prosperous than the other. At the end of their working day, people would go to their lovely big homes, pick up mother and the kids and head off to the fantastic beaches. Children splashed around in the clear blue water of the ocean until they were rounded up for a 'barbie', eaten under a canopy of millions of stars before they headed home again in their roomy station wagons. While the sounds of the last film ebbed away, the public was invited to ask questions. We sat bolt upright when a middle-aged man at the back of the hall stood up at the end of question time and said: "In the documentary about Australia, only the big cities are shown. My wife and I have recently returned from Alice Springs, in the heart of Australia where we have lived for a year. The opportunities there are excellent for young families; why is it that the inland has not been mentioned here?"

The two officials answered that not much was known about Alice Springs. They said that many places were being developed in central and other rural parts of Australia but, because there were no roads and no immigration centres in any of those places, it was too risky to send people there. The emigrants usually went to a Government hostel from where they made inquiries and moved into the country.

Fred and I looked at each other. "We must try to speak to him!" Fred whispered. But when the program resumed with another documentary, the man stood up and left the hall.

That night I wrote to Sam about it. A week later he wrote back to say that the man's name was Jurrian Guth. His younger brother Henk, a well-known artist in Alice Springs, had given Sam his address. Jurrian was on the phone; I would find his number in the book, Henk had said.

Not many people in Holland had a telephone in 1971, but our next-door neighbours let us use theirs whenever we needed to. Along with thousands of other country folk, the 'Floortjes' had fled Indonesia when the former Dutch colony became independent in 1948. Floortje was very upset about us leaving.

"I should refuse to let you use the phone," she said. "You have no idea what you are letting yourselves and your poor children in for!"

We met with Jurrian Guth and his lovely wife Cor several times. They lived on the edge of the forest, not far from us, in a beautiful big farmhouse which they had rebuilt themselves after the war.

"Please call me Jurrian; there's no need to call me *meneer (Mr.)*," the friendly smiling gentleman said when we met him for the first time. "This is my wife, Cor."

4

"They don't bother with those unnecessary formalities in Australia!" *mevrouw* (Mrs) Guth, a tall dignified lady, laughed as we shook hands. During our later visits Jurrian showed us lots of slides and they both told us enthusiastically about the people they had met and the many possibilities there were in Central Australia for people like us.

From the beginning, the Department of Emigration worked quickly. In the first week of April, two weeks after we filled in the application forms, we were invited for an interview and medical examinations at the Australian Embassy in The Hague. There was barely enough time to have our passport photos taken and for Fred to arrange a day off from work.

We were both very nervous about the interview, mainly because Fred did not have a 'proper' trade. He had wanted to become an artist when he grew up but that was only for rich people in those days. After he finished school at the age of fifteen, just after the war, he had worked in a leadlighting workshop, mainly repairing church windows. Most of the churches had been repaired and leadlight in peoples' homes had gone out of fashion by the time he was twenty-one and had to go into one of the services. He had joined the navy for six years, hoping to learn another trade. Unfortunately, Radar operators were not needed in civilian life at that time.

It had been very difficult for him to find a job when he left the navy in 1956, four months after I met him. He worked in a men's clothing shop for a year, bored out of his wits most of the time, studying business-management at evening classes for which he got a certificate. He later had a job in a paint and glass warehouse, which was more in line with his artistic nature. About a year later Fred was asked to help make part of the paint shop into a pharmacy. Impressed with Fred's woodwork skills, a colleague's brother offered Fred a job as a foreman in his furniture factory in 1964.

There had been no need for us to worry about Fred's lack of formal qualifications. Our concern about the health of our eldest son Raymond, who suffered from bronchial asthma proved also unfounded; the clear Australian air would take care of it, the doctor assured us.

After the interviews we had taken the children to the big sea-aquarium in Scheveningen. I had been to The Hague once before but it was the first time most of our children had seen the sea. Even though it was cold and windy they had a ball on the beach.

Two weeks after our visit to the Embassy there was a letter in the mail with the gold-embossed Australian emblem on it. With trembling fingers I opened the envelope, reading the news through my tears; we were accepted... we would soon be leaving our home and family for good. We were advised to engage a travel agent, get the compulsory injections against malaria and other tropical diseases as soon as possible and prepare ourselves for the long trip.

We only had to pay two hundred guilders (fifty dollars) towards the cost of travelling and would be advised of our date of travel in the next couple of weeks. That was when the seemingly endless wait had started!

The travel agent gave us a list of items we could take with us: two cubic metres for Fred and me, and half a cube for each of the children. The crates had to be packed and ready to be collected for shipment ten days before we were travelling, as that was the time it took to take the containers via Rotterdam to Southampton in the south of England. We had to buy the wooden crates, which had to be made to order, and pay for the transport of those to the harbour in Rotterdam ourselves. The cost of that turned out to be the equivalent of four week's wages, more than we got for the furniture we had to sell at the last minute.

Because we did not have a telephone, and the agent expected to have the final arrangements any day, he advised us to ring his office every Friday afternoon. Nothing happened for weeks. According to the agent the problem was that nobody had ever gone from Holland directly to the centre of Australia. It was a question of which country was footing the bill of the additional transport costs.

We grew increasingly anxious. We could not make any plans or pack or sell anything. If we had to pay those costs ourselves the whole idea would fall through. Fred felt very uncomfortable at work. His boss had hardly spoken to him since he told him that we were leaving. The people that lived in our house before we moved in three years earlier had also left for Australia and nobody had ever heard of them again. His colleagues and some of our friends said that we were crazy and irresponsible. Like our Indonesian neighbours they said that it was cruel to take our children away from their environment and friends but others admired us for our courage. Some envied us, saying that they would be off in a flash if only their spouses were willing. When our neighbours, a young couple with four small children heard that we had been accepted at the end of May, they immediately applied for emigration too. Their application went smoothly. If they had not postponed leaving for eight months, they would have left a month earlier than we did.

When the approval finally came at the end of July, we were booked on a boat that left England a mere ten days later! The travel agent was annoyed when I said that that was ridiculous. It would take that long to have the crates made! A few days later he phoned to say that he had managed to change our bookings to the Southern Cross, which gave us another three weeks. I don't know how we managed to get all our belongings sorted and packed, the surplus sold, given away or taken to Saint Vincent and the house emptied and thoroughly cleaned, in such a short time. In our hurry we had sold our boys bikes that we had bought for them on their birthdays the previous year, only to find that there

6

was ample space left in the allotted crates to take them. The little money we got for them proved not to be near enough to get them very plain bikes, in Alice Springs.

Another thing that broke my heart was the dozens of boxes of material. I had taken them to Saint Vincent knowing that they would end up in the rag-bin. Because I always made all our children's clothes, people had given me their coats, suits and dresses, which I had carefully unpicked. I had washed and ironed the pieces and put them away to be used later. I had also pulled out and washed the wool of dozens of old jumpers. At least some of that may have been used even if it were only for craftwork at school. To think of all that work I had done for nothing instead of reading a good book!

I switched the light on and looked at my watch; two o'clock and sleep still would not come. Closing my eyes again I pictured the crowd on the quay in Rotterdam, waving and shouting their good-byes. Standing between the crowds my eldest brother Wout had entertained everybody on board the ferry as well as in the harbour, whistling well-known tunes on his fingers. Cheered on by the crowd on shore he was in fine form. When we were children Wout and I could not stand each other yet he cried the most when we said good-bye.

During the last three weeks our children had stayed with my mother at her *boerderij* (farmhouse) in Hooglanderveen, a small village in the centre of Holland where I was born, while Fred and I packed up the house in Oosterbeek. We spent the last three days with my family until we left for the harbour near Rotterdam on Wednesday the third of September 1971, shortly after lunch.

The trip from Hooglanderveen to the harbour was an absolute nightmare. The ferry to England was not leaving until seven at night, but we had to be there two hours before. We also wanted to be there early so that we could have a cup of coffee with the family before we boarded.

Fred and I and our two youngest children, Richard and Regine aged six and four, went in the back of my younger brother Bart's big station wagon. Mum and our two other girls, twelve-year-old Lilian and Simone who was eight, crawled into Wout and his wife Tony's little sedan. My youngest brother Ties and our eleven and ten year old sons, Raymond and Eugene, went with Wim, my younger brother. My only sister, Jopie, did not come to see us off. She lived with her husband and two children in Arnhem, sixty kilometres from our village. We had said good-bye after the big party in the attic of Mum's boerderij, the previous Saturday.

Because Bart had been to Rotterdam several times before, he led the way. Fred squeezed my hand when we drove off. With a big lump stuck in my throat I waved to the neighbours who stood beside the road to see us off, looking back at the farm through a mist of tears. When we swung onto the highway leaving our village behind I wondered if I would ever see it again. The tall, pointed towers of our neighbouring villages sped past the windows of the car. The hundreds of black and white cows kept grazing peacefully in the lovely lush-green countryside, unaware of the turmoil in our hearts.

The sickening tension in my stomach increased again when we got trapped in a traffic jam. Bart decided to take a different route. It would take longer but at least we were moving. I became even more anxious when I caught the worried look on Bart's wife Janny's face in the rear-view mirror. She was expecting her first baby in a week's time. Because my waters had broken before I had any other warning signs of the approaching birth several times (our two eldest sons were born three and four weeks early!) I was panicking.

Mum's favourite saying, "soup is never eaten as hot as it has been served", calmed me down a bit. A first baby usually took its time...

Sometime later Bart had to admit that he was lost. Wout and Wim's cars were nowhere to be seen.

"It can't be far off," he said when he stopped the car on the side of the road. After studying the map, he realised that he had gone too far at a busy detour. It took a while to turn on the busy road. Still scolding himself for being so stupid he drove back, taking no notice of the speed limits. When we finally got through the busy city and stopped in the huge car park near the quay, we were met by an aunt and uncle who came from The Hague to see us off.

"You'd better hurry!" they said. "Your names have been called for immediate boarding; all the emigrants are already on board. What took you so long? Wout and Wim have already been here for an hour!"

Fred rushed us through the crowd into the office buildings where our children were anxiously waiting for us. It took quite a while to have our tickets and our hand luggage checked. When we finally came out on the other side of the building, I raced off to the rest of our family, standing behind a high wire fence. Hands grabbed mine and we kissed as well as we could through the holes in the fence, biting the wire when we missed.

None one of Fred's family were there. We had said good-bye to them at the party the previous Saturday evening too. He was one of the youngest in his family of seven children. I had never met his mother who must have been a lovely lady. She had died in February 1956, three months before we met, when Fred was still in the navy. One of his four older brothers had lived in an institution in the south of Holland since he was nine years old. A high fever brought on by mumps when he was three had caused severe brain damage. I had never met him and we had lost contact with Fred's youngest brother who was at sea with the merchant navy. Fred's two sisters were nine and ten years older than he was. They all lived in and around Arnhem, sixty kilometres further from the harbour than my family.

Everyone, except Fred's youngest brother had been at the party. With the help of my brothers Wim, Bart and Ties, who were still living at home, we had cleared the big attic above the pig sty's and the empty cow stables at the back of Mum's new farmhouse. We moved a hundred bales of straw creating plenty space to dance in the middle of the wooden floor. Bart, who was a truck-driver for a feed and fodder supplier at the time, brought a huge sheet of canvas home, which we hung over the bales of straw. With long strips of yellow crepe paper and glue we made a picture of a big ocean steamer on the black canvas that made the reason for the party very clear.

Everyone had a great time dancing with and talking to aunts and uncles, neighbours and friends who had come from every direction to say good-bye and wish us well. Like most of our guests we had had a little too much to drink in the end that had softened the pain of our final good-byes. Fred did not want his favourite sister Bep to come to the harbour, as she would have been too upset to see him leave. Only his eldest brother Henk and his wife Gijsje had come all the way from Arnhem to see us off and Fred had not even been able to say good-bye to them.

Struggling with a heavy bag and his hands full of papers he yelled at the kids to stay together. I had to run to catch up with them.

"Come on! Hurry up!" he shouted impatiently.

By the time Fred stopped scolding me we had reached the ferry where a long queue of travellers was still waiting to be checked in. A young Belgian couple in front of us said they had been drinking coffee with their family when they realised that everyone had already left the restaurant. Another hour passed before our passports and tickets were checked again and we got through customs. Via steep stairs and endless passages, we went to one of our cabins in the bottom of the ferry. After we stored our belongings in the lockers we hurried back onto the deck. We had not noticed that the anchors had already been pulled up and the ferry was moving. Dusk was slowly setting in. Cursing ourselves for leaving our binoculars on the bed in the cabin, we frantically searched for our family. We heard Wout whistle a popular tune on his fingers. Then we spotted them waving and shouting. When Wout started whistling a song about keeping up your spirits and doing away with sorrows and sadness, the people on the quay joined in singing. Their voices grew stronger with every line until they formed a big choir. The crowd cheered when the song ended. A well-known waltz brought tears to every emigrant's eyes; "The stars will be shining wherever you are..."

The clear, sharp tones of Wout's whistling trilled over the still water when he started whistling the tune of an English song that was made popular by Vera Lynn during the war. We stood motionless on the ferry, with tears streaming down our faces while our families and friends on the quay sang the words:

It's time to say good-bye...

We will meet again...

Don't know where...

Don't know when...

But we'll meet again... one sunny day...

An Unforgettable Journey

It seemed as if I had only just closed my eyes when there was a knock on the door and we were told via the intercom to get ready for breakfast. It was still dark outside, five thirty am, and an hour before we would be landing in Harwich, England. The children were instantly awake when they realized they were aboard a ship.

Because we had been late at the ferry the night before, we missed the briefing of the emigration officials telling the emigrants what to expect on the journey. We had been given tickets for breakfast but after standing in a queue for ages waiting to be served, we were sent to another restaurant. Making sure the children were holding hands, we inched our way through the crowd to the other side of the ferry. Again our tickets were refused. All emigrants were supposed to go to the restaurant on the upper deck. When we finally reached the right place, there was no time left to eat.

In the meantime, the sun had broken through the thick morning fog. Most people were on deck, standing at the railing watching the ferry being towed into the harbour. We rushed the children back to the cabin to get our luggage, and then waited in line for the next hour to get through customs.

It was the first time I had ever set foot in another country. Even though we lived only twenty kilometres from the German border, I had never been there because I did not have a passport. There was no time to get excited as we hurried the children on shore. Presuming that we were going by train from Harwich to Southampton where we would board the Southern Cross, we followed a stream of travellers into the railway station, a short distance from the ferry. But the only train that was expected was going to London, not to Southampton.

Not knowing what to do, we were glad to hear an elderly couple speaking Dutch. While we were talking we noticed a man, standing on his own at the start of a broken-up road, holding up a board, which read: 'Southern Cross, Southampton'.

"You are late," the man grumbled. Then he directed us to an open area where two buses were waiting. The emigrants had apparently been the first to be let off the ferry; four other buses had already left. The friendly driver of our bus did not seem to be worried or in any hurry when he closed the door behind us and slowly swung onto the highway to London. I took a deep breath; we were on our way!

Talking non-stop, the driver showed us some beautiful mansions in the countryside and many, very impressive buildings in London, blackened by soot and smog. He made people laugh with his comments but Fred understood little of what he was saying.

During the few English lessons I had before we left, there had only been time to learn some of the most necessary household and travel sentences, and to speak with a 'hot potato in our mouths'. The driver not only seemed to have a hot potato in his mouth, but he swallowed the end of every word as well! Our children were most impressed by the big, red double-decker buses, while I marvelled at the many public toilets, most of them set in small, beautifully kept gardens. Why didn't we have them in Holland?

Leaving London behind, we went on to Buckingham Palace and Windsor Castle, the residences of our new Queen. Pity there was no time to stop and watch the famous 'changing of the guards' I had heard people talk about. There was so much to see that I temporarily forgot the rumbling in my stomach. The children did not complain when we didn't stop for morning coffee either and I only had a roll of peppermints to pass around until we finally stopped at a huge restaurant on a busy double-lane highway for a 'quick lunch'.

Half an hour later we looked at the cashier dumb-founded when he told us that he could not accept the Australian twenty dollar note Fred offered him to pay for the simple meals we had selected. He pointed to Heathrow Airport in the far distance where we could exchange money. Fred looked white with worry. We had been unable to get English money in our village before we left. The bank manager told us not to worry about it. Every big place in England would accept Australian currency as the two countries were closely related.

While everybody else was happily filling their bellies with delicious-looking food, we took our hungry children outside, trying to answer their questions. They could not possibly understand why they did not want our money when the face of the Queen of England herself was on the notes! Our friendly bus driver came over to see what was the trouble.

"There is no way I can take you to the airport," he said, "I'm pressed for time as it is. But hold on, I'll see what I can do."

It seemed ages till the other passengers, most of them Dutch, German and Italian came into the bus. When they were all seated, the driver explained what had happened to us. Within a few minutes, Jolanda and Kees, the couple with the Belgian accent, collected sandwiches, pieces of cake, bananas and apples, a can of coke and even a half-finished carton of chocolate milk. They became our best friends with whom we still have a close relationship today.

It was nearly three o'clock when we arrived in Southampton where an enormous ship, the Southern Cross, was waiting for us. Above the noise of the engines and shouting orders the bus driver was scolded for being late. He was supposed to have driven straight through instead of showing us half of England. He should have been there before midday.

After checking in, we were rushed along for afternoon tea before the dining room closed at three-thirty. While we were shown our cabins in the lower deck of the ship the boat rocked a little. We did not linger long but hurried to the deck to see what was happening. We could not believe our eyes when we saw that we were already at sea, soon passing the white cliffs of Dover, leaving England behind.

It was to be the last voyage for the Southern Cross, a world cruiser for holiday-makers. It was due for the scrap yard. The two hundred and forty unsold places were filled at the last minute with emigrants from several different European countries. The gigantic ocean liner was six hundred feet long and seventy-six feet wide, approximately hundred-eighty by twenty-three metres. It had six hundred cabins for the passengers alone. An enormous number of staff did their best (most of the time) to keep nearly two thousand passengers happy.

We already knew before we left Holland, that our family was to be split up during the trip, as there had been no cabins available next to each other. It was a great relief to see the four large suitcases we had handed in at the booking office in Rotterdam the previous day waiting for us in the first cabin on 'A' deck. I would share a cabin with our three girls, Lilian, Simone and Regine. Raymond, Eugene and Richard were in a cabin at the far end of the long passage with Fred. There were two single bunk beds, a wardrobe and a rack for suitcases in each of the tiny cabins. I had been disappointed that there was no window in our cabin until I saw through a porthole in the passage that our room was under the water line. The dark water, sloshing against the window at the water line, gave me the creeps.

Fred and the boys took their suitcases enthusiastically to their own cabin. While I helped the girls shower and dress for our first and only dinner together as a family aboard, Fred took care of the boys. Later in the evening we kissed each other goodnight in front of my cabin door before he went 'home' to his own place to sleep. It was rather romantic. There was no romance in the mornings though, as Fred soon got into the habit of letting the boys go to my cabin as soon as they were awake, so that he could sleep in.

On our first morning I thought that I was dreaming when I was woken up by a very gentle male voice. A perfectly groomed steward with olive skin, black curly hair and beautiful dark brown eyes bent over me saying softly: "I've got this lovely cup of tea for you M'lady. Shall I put a pillow behind your back so that you can drink it before the girls wake up?"

Curiously, I watched him leave, wiggling his neat little bum. I had heard about those men 'who weren't sure if they were a man or a woman' but I'd never met one before. Andrew, my young steward-waiter was always attentive and pleasant. He cheerfully cared for me and the children like a mother hen for her chicks. Fred's steward was completely the opposite; a surly, sour looking old seaman, often too drunk to be bothered with his duties.

It did not take us long to settle in and familiarize ourselves with life on board the big ocean steamer, a posh little city, surrounded by water as far as the eye could see. Mealtimes were the highlights of the day for me: no cooking for at least five weeks! The kitchen and dining rooms were directly above our cabins. A special tune, played on a xylophone announced the meals and coffee breaks: "Tedele tedele tedel-le-tom, tedele-tom, tedele-tom. Tedele-tom, le-tom!"

All meals were served in two separate sittings. The children ate first; then, while our stewards kept an eye on them, the adults ate their breakfast, lunch or dinner. Children over ten were to sit with their parents, which was extremely boring for Lilian and Raymond, especially when they heard about the fun the others were having with David, their young waiter. On the third day, they could join the younger children too. Knowing that Lilian would take care of her younger brothers and sisters, Fred and I happily had our meals in peace, enjoying the company of the holiday-makers from England and New-Zealand who shared our table.

The children always came back excited with funny stories about their waiter, except one morning, when David was too drunk to serve them their breakfast. Eugene came back first, soon followed by the others.

"We got nothing at all to eat," he complained.

"David does not want to give us anything," the little ones echoed.

"We will see about that," Fred said angrily, taking them straight back to the restaurant to see the headwaiter. Having been in the navy he knew very well what those young sailors could be like...

David was severely reprimanded and ordered to serve our children a big bowl of cereal immediately. They hated cereal, the slimy muck. David always gave them fried eggs and *patat frites* (hot potato chips) and, because Raymond could not stand eggs, he had ordered fried fish for him every morning. With long faces they sat looking at their plates, saying that they were not hungry anymore. Fred scolded them, in Dutch of course, telling them to eat it all now that he had stuck his neck out for them.

He had not been able to watch them for long. "Next time, they can go without," he fumed when he came back in my cabin.

As soon as the boat had reached the open sea every one of us, except Fred, was seasick. Along with half of the fellow travellers that had joined the ship in Southampton we lined up at the doctor's office. The children were given an injection but the doctor refused to give me one in case I was pregnant. Somehow, he did not seem to believe or understand that I had had an operation and I could not have children any more. I had no scar to prove it. The professor had done a vaginal prolapse repair the previous year, one of the first that had ever been done that way.

14

The children's seasickness improved rapidly, but I suffered for days and I was sick after every harbour we visited. One day, during the first week aboard, six year old Richard was as white as a sheet when he came down from the movies. The movie had made him sick, he said. He had thrown up on every one of the five flights of stairs, all the way from the cinema to our cabin. When I went up a little later, two stewards were cleaning up the mess. Still recovering from seasickness myself, I was extremely grateful that I did not have to do that horrible job.

The children were never bored during the four and a half weeks at sea. There was a lot to explore, especially for the boys. In a very short time they seemed to know every detail of the ship. Friends were made easily in the confined spaces. At the beginning a variety of games were organized for them every day. They loved Bingo until they discovered that the prize was nearly always the same, a roll of Lifesavers. Playing bowls and 'eight-ball' while the ship was slowly rocking, was also a lot of fun, but their favourite was the cinema. When the novelty of watching films wore off they played 'cowboys and Indians' or 'cops and robbers', crawling under the seats in the big, dimly lit hall. They sat for hours in our cabin, rolling scraps of paper into small balls. I later learned that they were used as bullets, shot off with the aid of a rubber band. The endless passages, staircases and lifts were another ideal place for them to play, and of course, teasing Fred's sour steward and the 'cranky old man' who attended the lift, telling them that the lift was only for adults.

Because the Southern Cross was a holiday cruiser there were a lot of elderly people on board. Some of them complained continuously and bitterly, scolding the children and chasing them away instead of making friends with them like most of the elderly folk did. I could not blame them. They had expected peace and quiet on their trip, for which they had paid a lot of money. Instead, they had to put up with emigrants who got their trip for almost nothing. Unfortunately, some of the emigrants were often as noisy and rude as their children were.

In spite of the fact that we had very little money to spend on board, and worried continuously about the uncertainty of our future, we had some very happy times during the trip. We both loved dancing, something we rarely had a chance to do in Holland. Because dancing did not start until ten at night and the children's breakfast was served at seven in the morning the nights were awfully short. On top of that, the clocks were regularly put forward during the night, to keep up with local times. We soon found a way around this by going to sleep with the children after dinner, then waking up at ten or eleven to go to the tavern for a couple of hours. It was always great fun for me to be taken 'home' to my 'apartment' by Fred afterwards. Occasionally I let him in but making love in the narrow squeaking bed, afraid that the girls would wake up, was not much fun for either of us.

Big parties were organized regularly. When we crossed the equator, King Neptune came on board with his big-bosomed wife to let us know that we were passing through his territory. It was a very rough spectacle, with some hilarious moments, put on by the crew and volunteers from the passengers. A certificate was given to anyone accepting King Neptune's challenge to be dunked in the pool by his chocolate-coloured warriors. The icy-cold water of the pool had turned into a dirty brown, chocolate-tasting mess in no time at all. The King's scruffy servants later pricked the balloons that were put inside his wife's costume, at the front as well as the back.

Another time we were invited to meet the captain of the Southern Cross dressed in our best clothes, for which we were ill prepared. Dress-up contests and parties with themes like pirates and mid-summer-nights were major events. It was amazing what people could do with towels, a few sheets of wrapping paper, scraps of material, glue and makeup. For one contest we had made Dutch costumes for ourselves, and the doctor, nurses and patient's outfits for the children from whatever materials we could lay our hands on. We later heard that we did not get a prize because one of the judges thought that we had brought the costumes in our suitcases.

Exercise classes, or a brisk walk around the deck with or without the children, were also part of our daily routine. Then there was the dreaded DRILL, which never failed to scare the living daylights out of me, especially when there was a storm brewing. Whenever the sirens went off everybody hurried to the lifeboats, ready to be evacuated, hoping it would not be for real.

At the beginning of our trip, an eager young man took on the job of teaching emigrant children English in the library for an hour every morning. Unfortunately he soon lost his enthusiasm. Because there were no other volunteers, Fred and our new friend Kees decided to take it on themselves. It was a case of the blind leading the blind, with the little English they knew. Their pronunciation was terrible. Their pupils, who were picking up an amazing lot of new words every day, often corrected them. Other library users obviously enjoyed the lessons too; they were often killing themselves with laughter behind their books and newspapers.

We saw nothing but water for a week or more between ports. We were fortunate to have good weather so that the sea was calm and we could enjoy watching the seagulls and flying fish for hours. Occasionally, a small group of dolphins would follow the ship, entertaining us with their antics. But sometimes when the sea was rough, we watched enormous waves rolling by. On those days, swimming in the pools on board became too dangerous. The two pools on the sun deck, at the very top of the ship, were always over-crowded when the sun was shining. Below 'B' deck, at the bottom of the ship, was a large indoor pool, filled with seawater. Our three youngest children all learned to swim there. Like many people in waterlogged Holland I had learned to swim later in life. I still can't bear to put my head under water. Although Fred had been in the navy for six years he could not swim until we took lessons after our fifth child was born.

Swimming when the water was wild was very exciting for the older children. I held my breath when they were sometimes sucked from one end of the pool to the other by an unexpected wave. One day the sea was so rough that the pool was empty at one end while the water went over the edge at the other side. Of course, the pool was closed but we could watch it from above, holding firmly onto the railings.

One night there was a terrible storm. Tormented by the terrifying thoughts going through my head, I lay rigid in my bunk bed, anxiously waiting for the sirens to warn us of impending disaster. Even the biggest ocean steamer was a matchbox on a wild sea like that. If only Fred was with me to comfort me. The thought that he probably wasn't worried at all because of his years in the navy, calmed me down. He might even be asleep, I thought, looking at our girls sleeping peacefully in the soft glowing night-light of our cabin. I got up and tucked them in tightly with their blankets, so that they could not fall out of their beds. Back in my own bed, praying for our safety I finally fell asleep.

The storm cleared as suddenly as it had started, leaving many passengers, including me, with another bout of seasickness. The next day Eugene had an extremely painful ear infection, which kept him in bed with a high fever for more than a week. It was the end of swimming in the deep seawater pool for all of us, as that was the cause of the problem, according to the doctor.

It was just after two o'clock on another night when I sat bolt upright in the cabin. It was pitch black. A deafening noise came from the kitchen above us and the ship was rocking violently.

"Mama! What's happening?" came the anxious voice from one of the bunk beds in the dark. Regine started to cry.

"Mama, I'm scared!" she sobbed. While I comforted the girls, the light came on again. A few minutes later Fred came in to see if we were all right. Apparently, the boat's course had been altered. Waves hit the broadside rocking the ship so much on the high waves that it had caused the pots and pans to fall out of the racks in the kitchen and crash, along with the crockery, onto the floor. We later heard that there had not been a glass, plate or cup left on the tables in the two dining rooms, and a lady had broken her arm when she fell out of bed.

Several stops were made on our way along the coasts. The first was Las Palmas in the beautiful Canary Islands. Coming down to the shore, I was puzzled by the attention we were getting from the dark coloured men who worked around the harbour. Shouting remarks at us, they pointed to our children counting them one by one, then to their own foreheads.

"They are telling us that we are crazy to have so many children," Fred said. The scene was repeated everywhere we went that day which made me feel very uncomfortable.

The following stop was Cape Town, the big African city of apartheid: a very different world! For some reason I had expected black and white people to walk on opposite sides of the streets, but they seemed to be happily mingling together. They were not all poor either; most of the black women wore modern, bright coloured clothes and lots of makeup and jewellery. It felt strange to see benches on the side of the streets with signs on them saying 'Blacks Only' or 'Whites Only' and to see a double-decker bus with white people seated in the bottom and blacks in the top.

Because we had no money to buy anything but a few children's books, the well-stocked rather luxurious shops soon lost their appeal. Walking through the huge meat-market the nauseating smell made us feel sick to our stomachs. After a few hours of walking aimlessly, we returned to the ship where it was very quiet. Sitting on the deserted sundeck, we listened to the radio, laughing about the way Afrikaans sounded to us. Being Dutch, we were fascinated with the language, a mixture of English and very old fashioned, back-to-front Dutch. While Fred recorded some children's songs and happy local music to remind us of a pleasant day in Cape Town, he also taped the melody of the xylophone to announce that afternoon tea was being served. One afternoon a few days later we were listening to the tape when the music stopped and the meal call suddenly resounded over the sundeck. To my embarrassment several people headed for the dining room but, as Fred and the children were doubling up with laughter, I soon joined their merriment.

After several days at sea again, we came to Durban where we decided to spend the one hundred dollars our friends and family had given us at our farewell party 'to have a good time on the trip'. Together with Kees and Jolanda we chose a bus trip to 'The Land of a Thousand Hills' in Zululand. There were no brochures about the day's outing and we had understood little of the oral information, so we had no idea what to expect when we boarded the big, rattling old bus. Just outside Durban the narrow, pot-holed road wound along the edges of very steep and rugged mountains with incredibly sharp corners. The two hundred kilometre trip was scary and often hair-raising, but the views were breathtakingly beautiful. Several picturesque villages dotted the open spaces in the lush-green countryside. They consisted of circular huts with pointed roofs made of twigs and straw and smooth whitewashed walls. There were no windows, only small openings for a doorway and one at the top of the roof, which let out a thin plume of white smoke into the bright blue sky.

18

When we came close to a village, there were always groups of friendly waving people laughing and dancing on the side of the road, hoping that the bus would stop and people would buy their art. Wearing bright clothes and heavily decorated with beads around their wrists, necks, heads and ankles the women held up their wares, mostly strings of beads and carved ornaments. It was fascinating to see how gracefully and freely they moved, carrying full baskets on their heads and a child on their backs, their heads held up high by the wide bands of beads tightly wound around their long necks.

Higher and higher we went, stopping at some fantastic lookouts. Although it was quite hot when we left Durban in the morning, it got colder as we got higher in the mountains. By the time we reached our destination, we were all shivering in our summer clothes. The bus stopped in an open field on the outskirts of a small village. First we visited a snake pit where a man demonstrated that even an enormous python could be our friend, as long as we handled it properly. The creatures slithered and wound themselves around the owner and some very brave volunteers. Some of the more adventurous children went up to run a wary finger over the snake's beautifully patterned skin, but I urged ours to keep at a safe distance.

On our way to one of the huts our six-year-old, Richard, suddenly stood still, gaping at half a dozen young women coming towards us.

"Mama! They have no clothes on," he whispered. Then, with glistening eyes and a cheeky grin on his face, he said admiringly:

"Look at their boobs! They're huge!"

The chocolate coloured girls were all solidly built and looked happy. Their heads were shaven and they wore short, plain coloured skirts with large, beaded accessories round their waists, wrists and ankles. The chief of the village, a handsome looking warrior with a black beard, was the only man to be seen anywhere. Apart from the young girls there were several older women, most of them carrying children on their backs. When we were all standing in a semi circle, the chief, who would have been in his early thirties, welcomed us to the village. In very clear English, he then introduced his eighty-two year old father, a tall skinny man, also dressed in warrior attire, who came dancing from one of the huts into the 'kraal'. The chief told us that three of the older women were his father's wives.

"He is still looking for a fourth one," he said, "but this time he wants a white one." No smile came from any of the older women; in fact they all looked cranky and annoyed. The chief himself had two wives, both young ones of course, he assured the onlookers, pointing at the happy, solid looking girls with the shaven heads. They were only fourteen, the marrying age, and obviously well fed. The men liked their women fat, a sign of wealth, the chief explained.

After some traditional dances and warrior demonstrations, we were invited to join the group to take pictures and inspect some of the huts to see how they lived. The huts were a lot bigger than I expected and seemed quite comfortable. With their whitewashed walls, a two feet wide black tarred edge at the bottom and the thatched roof, the huts reminded me strongly of the old farmhouse in which I was born and grew up. The main difference was that ours was rectangular and had one tall window at the front, with a small one on either side, with lace curtains. Our old 'hut' was divided into a small bedroom and a living room while the cows were kept at the back under the same roof. I tried to imagine what it would be like for those women to share a husband with two or three wives all living together in an open space like that. In one of the houses was a shop where we bought a statue carved out of black wood, which still reminds me of a day that made a big impression on all of us.

Six years after our visit, in August 1977, we were stunned to see several pictures of the Zulu chief in the Australian Woman's Weekly. He happened to be King Goodwill, paramount chief of the Zulus marrying his third wife, Princess Mantfombi, daughter of King Sobhusa ll of Swaziland. No wonder the chief spoke English perfectly; he had been educated at a top university in England! The two-page story showed the spectacular wedding festivities that had lasted for days. Thirty-five thousand people had attended his wedding, consuming twenty-five thousand litres of beer and two hundred and twenty head of cattle!

The photograph in our album with our youngest daughter sitting between the Zulu King and his elderly father is now treasured even more. Regine brought another memorable souvenir from that visit; on our return to the ship we found a tick embedded in her skin; a 'Royal Tick' I suppose!

Tension was building during the last and longest stretch at sea, eleven days from Durban to Perth.

What lay ahead of us? Would we be all right?

Arrival in Fremantle

When we came back to the Southern Cross from our trip to Zululand late in the afternoon, there were several letters from family and friends waiting for us. Disappointed that there was again no letter from Sam, I eagerly opened my brother Henk's letter first. We had not heard from Sam for more than six weeks. Maybe he had not received my letters and didn't know that we were coming. Or had he not taken our plans seriously?

My hands trembled when I unfolded Henk's short letter. Even though his writing skills had improved greatly, it would undoubtedly have taken him ages to write it.

Until he had stayed with us for a couple of days before he left Holland, I had not known that Henk could not write anything other than his name. He hated school and seldom had a pen in his hand since. When I had asked him if he had written to Sam to let him know when he would arrive, he said: "Oh, no! There won't be any need for that. I'll just rock up at his address in Melbourne."

Horrified, I had handed him a piece of paper and a pen, urging him to write. I still see him sitting in our bedroom upstairs, sweating for ages over a few words.

"I don't know what to say," he protested weakly when I looked in to see how he was getting on. I had brushed his argument away impatiently, saying:

"But its Sam; your brother. You can write whatever you want; just pretend you are talking to him." After several hours, he had produced half a page, which he proudly showed to me.

My spirits lifted when I read that Henk's American church, which he had joined a few years earlier, was holding a conference that he was expected to attend in Perth. He would be waiting for us when we arrived in the harbour at Fremantle instead of waiting in Melbourne!

That evening we left Durban for the long haul to Perth. On an afternoon a few days later, a film about Alice Springs was shown in the cinema. By that time every Dutch emigrant on board knew that we were going there, and they all came to see what the centre of Australia was like.

In the film, cowboys were riding through the main street which was still a dirt road, and there were none of the houses we saw on Jurrian Guth's slides. Our fellow emigrants were horrified. Saying that we were out of our minds to go to such a God-forsaken place. They urged us to change our minds and go somewhere else before it was too late.

Even though we knew that the film was old, we felt uneasy. We had no idea of the emptiness of the inland shown in the film. Not a tree or a blade of green to be seen for miles! Adelaide, the nearest city, was fifteen hundred kilometres away. The road was atrocious; just a narrow dirt road with enormous potholes. Huge trucks with two or three trailers had swirled up tons of dust behind them in the film. Like people said, once we were there, there would be no way out for us.

Kees and Jolanda were very worried about us.

"It's bad enough to go to a strange place with so many children," they said. "Try to stay with us in Melbourne. At least there will be more people there and you won't feel so isolated."

Kees was very concerned about his own future. The trip was no holiday for him. He seldom went dancing with us, spending all his time learning English and reading everything about Australia he could lay his hands on. He had been a policeman in Rotterdam and would have no chance to get into the protective service in Melbourne without knowing the language.

Our tension grew with every day we came closer to Australia. Dancing no longer appealed to us and we could not relax. Tired of seeing nothing but water day in day out, the days were dragging on. During the last week on board, the children became very restless too. We tried not to show them how tense we felt inside, but they always seemed to be around, listening in to our conversations with fellow emigrants. They all seemed to have accommodation waiting for them on arrival, even if it was only a government hostel, which would be nothing to write home about, they had heard. Some of our fellow Dutch and many British emigrants would leave the ship in Fremantle but most families would go on to Melbourne or Sydney. From there they had to travel by train to Adelaide, Canberra or Brisbane. A few people, including a family with seven children from Amsterdam were going to the mines in Whyalla where a house as well as a job was waiting for them.

Everyone aboard, even the holiday makers, seemed to be relieved when the coastline of Australia finally came into sight. Our worries about our future were temporarily forgotten when we stood, shivering from our pent-up emotions, at the railing of the Southern Cross to catch a first glimpse of Australia, our new homeland! It was the early hours of a clear, chilly morning, the third of October 1971,

Standing beside me, Fred soon became restless again. He had seen so many harbours around the world that they had lost their appeal for him. His responsibilities weighed heavily on his shoulders. He could not wait to see us settled. The previous evening there were several letters for us in the mail but again not one from Sam.

The sun shone brightly in an incredible blue sky when the big ocean-steamer, our home for five and a half weeks, reached the mouth of the Swan River and was slowly towed into the harbour at Fremantle. We craned our necks, taking turns to look through the binoculars. Would Henk be there as planned?

It took us a while before we spotted him, standing aside from the crowd in front of the big woolshed. Suddenly, everybody disappeared from the deck, hurrying to get through customs. Just as in the other harbours we visited, we were given a temporary boarding pass and the customs officials checked us thoroughly to make sure that we had nothing illegal with us when we left the ship.

It was as if time had fallen away when I hugged my brother. I had not seen him in nine years. He looked very healthy, had put on some weight and he was very brown, "from working in the sun all day," he laughed. After working with Sam for several years, laying bricks, Henk now worked in a market garden again, as he had done before he had left Holland.

Our three eldest children were too small to remember their uncle but all six felt at home with him immediately, laughing about the funny way he spoke. Because Henk had hardly spoken any Dutch since the day he arrived in Australia, he had to search for words continuously. No, Henk had not heard from Sam either he said when I asked him the burning question. There were very few telephone connections between Melbourne and Alice Springs and they seldom wrote to each other...

We stayed on board most of the day as Henk was allowed to join us on the ocean liner and, as most people had left the ship to explore the city, we had the entire place almost to ourselves. The weather was perfect; the sun shone all day in a cloudless sky of the brightest blue we had ever seen.

After we had shown Henk the Southern Cross from the swimming pool at the bottom to the sports-deck at the top, we settled into a corner of the sundeck. We had so much to talk about and so many questions to ask but Henk first wanted to know what had happened at home, and what life was like without Pa, our troublesome stepfather, who'd died of a stroke in 1968, three years ago.

Hooglanderveen where we grew up is a close-knit farming community near Amersfoort in the centre of Holland. I was nearly six when my father died of diphtheria and blood poisoning in October 1945, five months after the war ended. Mum was expecting her seventh child at the time - her eighth including my stillborn sister - and Wout, my eldest brother was only eight. After struggling to make ends meet for six years with the help of a twenty-five year old farmhand, Mum suddenly married a man from near the German border she had only met twice. I was eleven at the time. The young farmhand had wanted to marry Mum himself, and as he predicted, life became a misery for all of us. When I was twelve my 'new father' sexually abused me which greatly undermined my self-esteem while I was growing up.

In his old-fashioned ways, Pa demanded that we give him every penny we earned without ever wanting anything for ourselves. In 1927 his brutal father had disowned him, his eldest and only son, because he had made his girlfriend pregnant when he was twenty-seven years old. When his father died in 1950, a year before my stepfather married Mum, he had willed his substantial farm and market garden to Pa's two youngest sisters.

Every one of us except Wout, who expected to take over the boerderij according to tradition, could not wait to leave our unhappy and often violent home. I was at the edge of a nervous breakdown when I married Fred at the age of eighteen. When it had finally become clear to Wout that he would never inherit the farm, he too had left home, two years after I married and left.

The grand new farmhouse Pa had dreamed of was finally built in 1967. The following year, when he turned sixty-five and was entitled to an old-age pension, he had sold all the cows and most of the land to have an easy life with Mum. He died after several strokes a year later.

My youngest brothers Bart and Ties, who was born three years after Mum re-married, were the only ones left at home when Ties' father died. Wim, who was two years older than Bart and still single, came back home to live too when Pa had his first stroke. When Bart and Janny married at the beginning of 1971, Wim and Ties were the only two at home with Mum. After the initial shock of Pa's death, Mum enjoyed a freedom she had never known existed before, playing cards with neighbours and friends and visiting people on her pushbike. Life had never been so good for her.

When it became clear that we were leaving Holland my sixteen-year-old brother Ties was heartbroken. He had begged us to take him with us and not leave him behind with his old mother. Mum was forty-seven when Ties was born. Fred had carefully explained to him that we were heading for a very uncertain future, saying that we had our hands more than full with our own children.

"In two years time you will be eighteen and you can go to Australia under your own steam," he said.

I felt terribly sorry for my 'little' brother. When he was young, Ties had several 'fathers' and 'mothers' as we all adored him, but when he grew up we had left him one by one.

Henk could hardly believe his eyes when I showed him the latest picture of our handsome, dark-eyed brother who had written a letter asking us again to let him join us as soon as we were settled.

Our children were hanging onto Henk's every word when he told us about what happened to him in the army, and when he arrived in Australia on that hot day in January 1962. He had wanted to go with Sam the previous year, and his compulsory eighteen months in the army were the longest months of his life, he said.

Because he had joined the army six months early, Henk had been the youngest in his entire battalion, and like Sam, he found the army discipline very hard to take, often ignoring silly orders. Late one evening, Henk had gone home while he was supposed to be on watch. The following morning, fifteenth of August, the Holy Mary's Visitation and a Sunday for Catholics, the Military Police raced with screaming sirens through our village and into our driveway. One of the officers ran up the narrow ladder and got Henk out of his bed in the tiny room above the cow stables at the back of our old house. Mum was horrified to see the other two standing at the back door with guns in their hands, as if he were a dangerous criminal. She didn't even know that Henk was home!

A few minutes later the MP's had raced away again, with my brother in the back of the open jeep, handcuffed between the officers. The sirens had scared the living daylights out of our neighbours, who hurried to church on foot or on their bikes for the ten o'clock mass as usual. At the edge of the village the jeep had become stuck in the middle of a church procession, a large group of schoolchildren and parishioners behind a statue of the Madonna. The incident, which was the talk of the village for a long time, had cost Henk an extended three months in the army to make up for the time he spent in jail. He had left for Australia within a week of his release.

On the day before Henk's departure, our brother Wim, who was a carpenter, fell through the rafters of a six metre high shed. Wim's head had split open when he crashed onto the concrete floor below. He had been rushed to hospital and was still unconscious when Henk visited him briefly before he went to the airport. He had found Wim tied to his bed, swearing and cursing at whoever came near him which was completely the opposite of Wim's happy nature. Henk had not been able to forget the sight of his brother, foaming at the mouth like a mad man.

Wim had been unconscious for several days. In our worries, nobody had written to Henk or Sam to let them know that our cheerful brother's brain had not been damaged and that he was all right, until many months later... I also felt terrible to learn that Henk had gone to the airport in Amsterdam on his own; there had been nobody to see him off...

While I am writing this I realise how different things were at that time. I had not visited Wim, who had been in hospital for over six weeks, either. When you were married and had left home you had your own family to care for. The old saying 'if you burn your bum you have to sit on the blisters' was still very much in use. We had three children at the time, the eldest not yet three and the youngest six months. There was no telephone in those days and we had no car. Until we owned our first car in 1966, we only went home once or twice a year. Although we lived only sixty-five kilometres away, it would take nearly four hours to get from Velp to Hooglanderveen by train or bus. Mum seldom wrote to anyone and, as I couldn't do anything for Wim anyway, she had waited until he was about to be released from hospital before she wrote to me about the accident.

The temperature in Holland was below zero when Henk left in a Dakota for the three-day flight to Australia where it was midsummer. Although it was early in the morning when he arrived at Melbourne airport, it was already hot. Like most young immigrants in those days, Henk had only a few dollars in his pocket, did not speak a word of English and carried all his clothes and possessions in a small suitcase. He wrote his letter to Sam too late to expect him to be at the airport to meet him. Still wearing his winter suit, carrying his suitcase in one hand and his heavy overcoat over his arm, Henk set out for Sam's address in the Dandenongs where he finally arrived late in the afternoon. The temperature had gone up to a sweltering hundred and two degrees, over forty-one degrees Celsius, during the day and the air was full of smoke and dark clouds obscured the sun. Sam was just about to leave with a work mate when Henk arrived.

"The fire is getting close to a friend's house," he said after he greeted his brother. "We're going to move some furniture to a safer place. Wanna come?"

Henk had quickly changed into a pair of Sam's old shorts, a shirt and a pair of boots and gone with Sam in his old ute.

"What's a ute?" we asked simultaneously.

"A normal-size car that looks like a small truck," Henk explained. "You can use it for anything. Sam is still driving it now."

Henk must have read my mind when he said: "I wonder how he is going to drive all of you around."

Cold shivers ran down my spine when Henk told us about the terrifying bush fire that had nearly incinerated both of them on his first day in Australia. A ball of fire had suddenly rolled across the road in front of them, missing the car by only a few centimetres. Burning leaves had flown in one window and out through the other. A little further on, flames came from the back of the ute; a double mattress had caught fire. They had been lucky to extinguish the flames before the petrol tank could explode. Glad to be alive and looking like chimney sweeps, they had celebrated Henk's arrival with plenty of beer, late that night.

Like Wout and Sam, Pa had hired Henk out to a farmer as soon as he turned fifteen and could leave school. He too, left the farm where he had to work from dawn to dusk, six days a week, with one Sunday a month off from feeding and milking, when his eyes opened to the fact that most of their friends could keep their own money. Wout had returned home where he continued to work on 'his' farm without pay, Sam had gone to trade-school to become a bricklayer and Henk got a job in the local market garden until he too, had to go into the army.

Sam's boss, a married English man with two children with whom Sam boarded at the time, invited Henk to stay with them and, as he could use another labourer, Henk went to work with him the next day too. When, after a few weeks the work had run out, my two brothers had decided to go to Tasmania to try their luck there.

"All we built in the six weeks we were there was a *schijt-huisje*, a public toilet in a park in Hobart," Henk laughed. "It was midwinter and very cold. When we finished the job we decided to drive to Darwin in the Northern Territory, another fifteen hundred kilometres further north of Alice Springs, 'a small place in the middle of nowhere'.

"Only about three thousand people were living in Alice at the time," Henk said after he told us about the horrendous trip over the dirt road, which was still the only way to get there by car. "But there was plenty of work and a number of great pubs. So, we stayed for a while."

They had worked long hours and made a lot of money that was nearly all spent on drinks in the pubs.

"When my twenty-first birthday came in July, I decided to have the biggest party the town had ever seen," Henk laughed a little later.

"Did you want to make up for the forgotten birthday when you turned nine?" I asked.

Every year on his birthday since, I remembered how guilty I felt when I found Henk crying his heart out in bed that evening, telling me through his sobbing that 'no one in our whole family had remembered that it was his birthday. He had certainly made up for it on his twenty-first.

"We were drunk for three days running," Henk grinned. "I was so drunk that I had not even noticed that I had fallen through a big window."

Sam had not been there when the accident happened on the third day of Henk's party, held at the Stuart Arms, the biggest hotel in Alice Springs. He had kept working during the day and gone there in the evenings.

"I got to the pub late that evening," Sam told us later. "Some fellers showed me the hole in the window. They told me how they had lifted Henk's head out of it. You should have seen it! It was unbelievable that there wasn't a scratch on him. A couple of guys had stood him up but he had fallen to the ground like a rag doll, so they put him in a corner to let him sleep it off. He was unconscious for thirty-six hours."

"Eighty-eight dozen beers were only part of the bill," Henk said, shaking his head when he recalled the event to me recently. "Silly to spend so much money on a party, when you don't even know you're there."

Being winter, the weather had been beautiful when Henk and Sam arrived in Alice Springs at the end of April in 1962, but Henk found the summers unbearably hot. After working through the long summer months in Alice and on Aboriginal settlements in the bush, Henk had had enough of the isolation, stinking heat and millions of sticky flies. He no longer wanted to spend all his hard-earned money in the pubs either. They had gone on to Darwin via the fifteen hundred kilometre long, narrow bitumen road, made during the war to transport troops from the railway station in Alice Springs to the most northern tip of Australia, in case the Japs attacked the country. They had not stayed long in Darwin, the only other substantial town in the Northern Territory, because they could not find work and did not like the humidity. Driving back south, they had taken a short cut to Queensland, a hazardous track of thousands of kilometres. At one stage, Henk had fallen asleep while driving a particularly boring stretch. With one of his sporadic letters Sam had sent a photo home, showing his ute against a skinny tree in an almost completely empty landscape. On the back he had written: "There are hundreds of kilometres of absolutely nothing on the way, but Henk managed to hit the only tree there was."

On the coast they had both fallen in love with the lush green country. Because they both wanted to invest some of the money they had saved before they spent it on grog, and land was cheap, they had each bought a big block near Nambour, a hundred kilometres north of Brisbane. They had 'played' on one of the empty blocks - still Sam's beloved thirty-three-acre playground today - for the next three months. They bought an old bulldozer and built a dam in the middle of the rough piece of natural bush. Then they selected the tallest tree on the block and pushed it across the dam so that they could dive into the water before the mozzies had a chance to carry them away. Sam had sent an entire roll of photos home about it.

Because they could not find much work on the coast either, they had gone back to Alice when they ran out of money. After another summer of working non-stop in the exhausting heat, and some dangerous adventures, Henk had truly had enough.

"Sam is not easy to work with," Henk warned Fred. "He is very slow and incredibly fussy; a perfectionist in every detail, no matter what kind of a job he is doing."

"Just like our father," I said, laughing away the uneasiness I felt. "Remember how *Ome* (uncle) Hannes (Mum's favourite brother) told us about the way Papa was setting up a fence to keep the cows in with a spirit level? The beds in his vegetable garden were not a millimetre out of line and the weeds never had a chance to grow."

After a fiery argument my two brothers had decided to go their separate ways. Henk had gone back to Melbourne "Chasing the girls," Sam said later, while Sam divided his time between working in Alice Springs and 'playing' on his block in Queensland.

During the last year, Henk had felt lonely and depressed to the stage where he did not find life worth living any more. That's when he came in contact with the American based 'World Wide Church of God', which had saved his life, he said. His writing had improved tremendously because of his Bible studies and writing about his new religion to me.

Henk was amazed when he first saw me with our children. Eugene, our third child was only six months old when he had left Holland.

"Look at you," he said. "Six beautiful kids, already grown up. I'm nearly thirty and I've got nothing, not even a girlfriend!"

"That can change quickly enough," I reassured him. "This time next year you might be married."

That was exactly what would happen; three days within the year, Henk married Robin whom he had met at earlier church meetings.

Late in the afternoon we walked Henk to his hotel in Fremantle where we had our first encounter with Australian culture. The thing that struck us most was the huge, brightly coloured advertisements, screaming from shopfronts, car-yards, service stations and other buildings wherever we went. Our older children read the words out aloud, guessing the pronunciation and asking Henk what they meant. They were all killing themselves with laughter when Eugene, the cheekiest of them pointed to an advertisement for pies, yelling out: "They are selling *pies* (piss) in that shop!"

Henk stayed for another two weeks in Fremantle, a lovely place. In the weeks to come we would wish time and again that we could have stayed there...

Alice, Here We Are!

I felt sad when I said goodbye to Henk in front of the hotel in Fremantle. He had given us a lot to think and talk about and we had no idea when we would see each other again. Sleep did not come easily that night. Although Henk said that we would be all right with Sam, we were worried. The distance from Alice Springs to Melbourne was even further than from Amsterdam to Moscow! Sam was easy going, Henk had said. What was that supposed to mean if he was so hard to work with? What if he turned out to be impossible to live with? Suddenly having a sister with six children around, when he was used to being on his own for so long, was not going to be easy for him...

We could always live with the Aborigines in the Todd River, Sam had said in his last letter. We had seen in the old movie the previous week how the natives lived in the dry river. Jurrian Guth's slides had only been taken a year ago and they had shown very much the same. Those black people had no tents or cooking facilities. They just cooked their animals, skin and all, and bread called 'damper', in a hole in the ground. I was glad we had taken our big tent. It would at least provide a roof over our heads. We loved camping, didn't we? Did we? In his last letter, Sam presumed that we would travel from Melbourne to Alice Springs by train. A lump stuck in my throat when I recalled his words:

"I don't know what I'm going to do with you lot if your luggage does not get here before you arrive. Best thing would be that the railway goes on strike when you are halfway to Alice Springs; that way the government can look after you for a bit longer."

Both Jurrian Guth and Henk told us about the crippling strikes in Australia and they said that the railway line and the dirt road from Adelaide was at times washed out by floods for weeks. What if we would get stuck on the way for several weeks? It could already be stinking hot in October, Henk said. I had no idea what Sam would be like now. He left home when he was fifteen, hired out to a farmer at Hoogland, a neighbouring village. He only came home occasionally on a Sunday afternoon. When he was nineteen, Sam had gone to trade school and lived at home again. There had been some ugly fights between him and Pa, our stepfather. It made me shudder to think about them... We were all glad when Sam had gone into the army after that dreadful year. Soon after he left Fred and I married and we had only seen him briefly a couple of times before he left for Australia. At least Henk said that there was plenty of work in Alice Springs and Fred was prepared to take on anything to provide for us. And perhaps I could do some sewing for other people to supplement our income...

Bright white clouds drifted along the stark blue sky, forming huge castles at times, during the two-day trip from Fremantle to Melbourne. We spent nearly all our waking hours on deck, taking turns looking through the binoculars, pointing out lighthouses, mountains, cliffs and other points of interest on the sunlit coast. With Kees and Jolanda we identified the towns and cities, which were few and far between, on their map. When, at three o'clock on Tuesday the fifth of October, the Southern Cross was towed into the harbour in Melbourne, I waited anxiously for the mail to arrive but again, not a word from Sam...

Even before the boat had been anchored people hurried with their luggage to the main deck. Most immigrants were leaving the ship in Melbourne, from where they would be travelling by bus or train to other places. We still had no idea how and when we were going on to Alice Springs. While Fred lugged the four heavy suitcases to the exit I made sure that each one of our children took care of his or her own bag in the chaos of people rushing in all directions. A long queue had formed by the time we arrived on the main deck to check out, as progress through customs was agonisingly slow. People around us complained bitterly about the poor organisation and the long wait. Our nerves were on edge, and we too scolded our children for being restless. Our friends Kees and Jolanda were nowhere to be seen. We had not even said good-bye to each other. As we were only allowed to bring one radio per family Fred was still worried sick about the new one he had brought for Sam, while our own twelve year old radio sat in the crate at the bottom of the ship.

When it was finally our turn to be checked out, it was after five. A Dutch-speaking customs officer told us that our crates would not be released until customs had inspected them during the next couple of days. They would then be sent on to Alice Springs by train. Nothing was said about the extra radio after all.

When our stamped passports were handed back to us, the officer directed us to another table where an Australian and a Dutch officer of the Department of Immigration welcomed us into our new country. While Fred signed some papers, the Dutch officer said:

"You will be taken to a government hostel where you will stay the night. At 5.30 tomorrow morning you will be taken to the airport for your flight to Alice Springs where you'll arrive sometime in the afternoon."

Flying? We would be in the middle of the desert tomorrow? It was as if a cold hand had grabbed my heart; I suddenly did not want to leave Melbourne. The officials were not happy with my decision but I was adamant that I was not going inland until I had heard from my brother.

"We can't just show up there with six children without him expecting us," I exclaimed to the officer who had welcomed us to Australia. Fred agreed with me that we could not take the risk not to be welcome. After arguing back and forth for a while, with the help of the Dutch officer who translated what was being said, they agreed to allow us to stay in Melbourne for a week. In the meantime, they would send a telegram to Alice Springs to ask Sam to ring us at the hostel.

It was well after eight in the evening when the chartered bus dropped us off at the Midway Hostel in Footscray. We were the only people left in the bus. The manager, a friendly middle-aged man, showed us to our apartment. After we deposited our luggage, he took us to the canteen where the kitchen staff had just about completed the cleaning up.

As we hadn't had anything to eat or drink since lunchtime on the ship, we were all starving. The women who served us spoke with a strange accent, and we couldn't understand a word of what were saying, but the way they slammed the plates with food in front of us spoke for itself. The brown, slippery mess on our plates they called 'lamb stew' smelled revolting and tasted even worse. It made me shudder every time I swallowed a mouthful. We encouraged the children to eat at least a little of it, as there wouldn't be anything else. Saying that they were not hungry any more, they picked out some of the soggy potatoes, pulling faces at each other. In the end we bought a packet of dry 'bush biscuits' and left the table, the food hardly touched. If the looks of the women in the kitchen could kill, we would never have reached our apartment.

It was close to midnight by the time the children were in bed. Completely exhausted from the long, emotional day, I crawled gratefully into my own bed hardly aware that this was the first night in our new homeland. The following morning we were all awake early. After more than five weeks in a tiny cabin without windows on the ship, we were greeted by the Australian sun, shining brightly through the gaps between the dark curtains. The apartment, one in a block of half a dozen, was new and surprisingly roomy. It had three spacious bedrooms, a lounge and a small kitchen without any cooking facilities except an old-fashioned electric kettle to boil water for a cup of coffee or tea. Every room had two narrow windows from the floor to the ceiling, overlooking the well-kept gardens between several identical buildings. The children dressed themselves in record time to go outside and explore their new surroundings. Not knowing how to get to the separate shower block we washed their hands and faces at the kitchen sink.

It was already very busy when we got to the canteen at six-thirty. The noise of chairs scraping over the tiled floor, the clattering of plates, dishes and cutlery on the bare, laminated tables, the dozens of yelling children, running circles in the big hall and adults shouting to be able to understand each other, was terrible. Such a strong contrast to the meals we had in the posh dining room aboard the 'Southern Cross' during the last five weeks.

After a breakfast of cereals and sausages on toast we went for a walk around the hostel grounds. We realised how lucky we were to have such a nice new apartment, when we saw that other immigrants were still living in the 'Nissan huts' that people on the ship had talked about. These large corrugated-iron 'water-tanks, cut in half lengthwise', were built in the 'fifties, when people from all over Europe flocked in droves to this 'land of milk and honey' to build a new future. With their homelands torn apart, afraid of rising communism and another world war, their reasons for emigration were very different from ours...

When Thursday passed without a word from Sam, we became angry and frustrated with the Department of Immigration. Most of the people in the hostel were Greek and Italian, with large families. We had been told in Holland that with more than four children we could not go to Australia without a sponsor, yet some of those people had a dozen children or more and they could stay in the hostel until they had found work and a place to live in. The apartment we were in had ten beds.

Afraid of missing Sam's phone call, we stayed in the hostel all day. The friendly manager of Midland had warned us to be careful of salesmen, especially our own country-folk, who would come to our door. There were people wanting to sell anything from vacuum cleaners to a whole house of furniture. One very persistent Dutchman wanted to sell us his house to enable him to go back to Holland, as nothing in Australia was good enough. The man finally gave up when Fred said that he had not given him any reason for wanting to stay in Australia.

To get the sour taste of the man's depressing talk out of my mouth, I ate one of the unbelievably sweet oranges we bought in the fruit and vegetable stall across the road from the hostel, early that morning. Only one dollar for a ten-kilogram bag, which Fred carried back to the hostel on his shoulder. The meals in the hostel were nothing to look forward to, but they were cheap. Having no idea what lay ahead, we did not want to spend a penny more than we strictly had to.

Sam's phone call came at last on Monday evening. His voice came over the crackling line from an enormous distance.

"Why didn't you come on Wednesday?" he asked. "I waited all afternoon for you at the airport."

The Department of Immigration had informed Sam that we would be coming that day. We would arrive by Fokker Friendship at four o'clock but, because of the terrible dust storms they were having, the plane had come in very late that night.

"It was too bad that John and I wasted a whole afternoon," Sam said in half Dutch, half English. "But I'm *ackcely* glad you didn't come, cause I don't have the bathroom ready yet."

"How far are you with the house then?" I asked hopefully.

"The house?" Sam repeated. "The foundations are in and I have built a couple of arches for the carport but I haven't started on the house yet; I'm talking about the bathroom in the shed where I live."

Where will we sleep?" I asked getting more desperate.

"Oh! You'll be all right. I've got some old caravans from friends you can use," Sam said light-heartedly. "They may leak a bit but it seldom rains here anyway."

I could not tell Sam when we would be arriving, as the customs officer said that it could be a while before there were enough seats available on the plane for the eight of us.

"It's going to be quite an adventure," I said to the children when we came back from the office, feeling drained of all enthusiasm and excitement.

Now that we had spoken to Sam we were free to leave the hostel and go for long walks. When we went past a big timber-mill the following morning, Fred decided to call in to see what it was like. After talking for only a few minutes the manager offered him a job. Horrified by the lethal, out-of-date machinery they were still using, Fred declined.

We missed Henk very much; why did he have to be in Perth while we needed him so much here? He had lived in Melbourne several years and knew the way; he could have taken us around in his big Ford Fairlane, looking for a job for Fred and a place to live here so that we didn't have to go so far away...

When we returned from our walk late that afternoon, there was a message for us: "Please call this number immediately."

It was the Dutch Immigration Officer, saying that we would be taken to the airport the following morning at five-thirty.

"At five-thirty in the morning?" I gasped. "I'd better not go to bed at all." I stared at Fred in disbelief when he said that we were only allowed to take twenty kilograms of luggage with us on the plane.

"What on earth am I going to take?" I asked in desperation. "Twenty kilos will fit into one suitcase, what are we supposed to do with the other three?"

"They'll have to go by train. It'll cost a fortune to take them with us on the plane," Fred said resolutely. "We have to take as much as we can carry in our handbags."

I still see myself sitting in the hostel that night, endlessly sorting through the kids clothes, trying to decide what they would need most, wondering again what we had let ourselves in for. (We did not find out until we were at the airport that Fred had misunderstood the officer. We could have taken twenty kilograms each, eight times as much!)

Late that night, Fred took the three other big suitcases to the office. The manager promised to take them to the railway station the following morning. Afraid of sleeping through the alarm, which was set for four a.m. I hardly dared to close my eyes. Fred did not sleep much either, nervous about the flight and what was ahead of us. I had never flown before and the only flight Fred had been on was when he went to New Guinea in an old Dakota in 1953. A few hours into the flight he had asked the stewardess why the plane was flying in circles around a green light in the distance. He had wanted to sink through the floor with embarrassment when she answered that the light was on the tip of the plane's wing.

At five-thirty on the dot, two taxis arrived at the door of our apartment and within a few minutes we were on our way to Melbourne airport. The drive by taxi from the hostel near Footscray to the airport seemed a long trip, but it was in fact only a few suburbs away. It was still dark and quite chilly when we got there. Overwhelmed by all the activity even at that early hour, I kept the children close to me while Fred took care of checking us in which seemed to take forever. Nervous and bewildered about the fact that we could have taken all four big suitcases instead of one, we aimlessly waited for ages before we boarded the plane. I had never seen an aeroplane other than in the sky and was amazed at its size. When it took off I pretended to be in an enormous bus, climbing a very steep hill, holding my breath, afraid that it would not be able to make it to the top; then the 'huge bus' drove over a smooth, straight road.

The breakfast we were given soon after we were seated was pure luxury for me. It helped me take my mind off the fact that we were high in the sky and could crash any minute. At times I thought that I was dreaming until reality hit me again. We were on our way with six children to the isolation of the remote heart of Australia, to start a new future...

Landing in Adelaide two and a half hours later was so smooth that I could hardly believe we were on the ground again. As soon as we came out of the plane we heard our names being called over the intercom. Inside the building we were whisked from one desk to another, having our papers and bags checked. Then we were hurried out of the building towards a small plane on the tarmac. It had been waiting for half an hour especially for us, the attendant said. With our children around and between us we climbed the stairs as quickly as we could. At the door I looked bewildered into a plane full of black faces...

"Oh my God! Where are we going?" I thought suddenly panicking. The doors closed immediately and the plane taxied to the take-off point. I felt somewhat relieved when I saw a few white faces at the back of the plane while I adjusted my seatbelt. My breathing returned to normal when our hostess, who had the biggest bunch of the brightest red hair I had ever seen, told us that the black men were an Aboriginal football team, returning to Alice Springs from a competition in Adelaide.

Fred explained to our children that the plane, a Fokker Friendship was made in Holland by the firm where our friend Kees worked as an engineer. It was a fifty-four-seater; quite different from the big jet we had just left. The children took turns at looking for the inspection plate near the toilet door, which Kees told us about. They were fascinated with the toilet too. I was glad they were speaking Dutch when they were speculating as to where it all went. After we had eaten our lunches, the children were invited to have a look in the cockpit. I finally managed to relax when they came back very excited.

But my peace of mind did not last for very long. All the blood drained out of my face when a sudden storm rocked the plane. Holding onto the edge of my seat, I looked at the little window that was darkened with red sand. All we could see when the storm subsided was swirling clouds of red dust. Shortly afterwards the plane descended.

"Are we in Alice Springs already?" I asked Fred hopefully.

"I don't think so, it's too early," he replied.

"This is only Leigh Creek", a voice behind us said. "Alice Springs is hours away."

A strong hot wind took our breath away when we got off the plane for a breather while the plane refuelled. Apart from a corrugated iron shed, there was not a house to be seen anywhere. We were glad to get out of the dusty hot wind on the tarmac, only to be attacked in the shade by hundreds of tiny flies we frantically tried to brush away.

"You shouldn't worry about them when you are going to Alice," the man who sat behind us on the plane said. "There are plenty more there. And it is a lot hotter too," he warned.

"It can't be hotter then this!" I said to Fred in Dutch. The expression on my face must have spoken for itself.

"It's only hundred-four," the man answered. "That's nothing; it gets up to over hundred-thirty degrees in Alice." We looked at the thermometer on the outside wall of the tin shed they called an airport. It was forty-one degrees Celsius and it would get over fifty-four In Alice Springs? That could not be true; Sam had never written about that, or had he? Fred recalled how he wrote that one day they had cooked their breakfast of eggs and bacon on the bonnet of their car. It must be terrible if it was already that hot in the morning.

It seemed ages before we could get on the plane again. It was just as well that we had to keep up our spirits for the children, who still saw everything as one big adventure; there was absolutely no way back for us.

Shortly after taking off from Leigh Creek, a small mining town a few hundred kilometres north of the beautiful Flinders Rangers in South Australia, the weather deteriorated quickly. For a while all we could see outside were clouds of red sand. Relieved when the storm had passed and the plane stopped rocking we frantically looked for any sign of a town but, even though the aircraft flew very low, there was not a house to be seen.

After a while, clouds of dust blocked our view again and the plane started to rock violently. The air-conditioner did not seem to work any more. It became very hot and stuffy in the plane. One after the other the children were sick and had to run to the toilet. While ten-year-old Eugene was throwing up, the plane suddenly dropped in altitude and his vomit went all over the place. After the third one threw up, our hostess asked Fred to help her clean up while the other hostess assisted me with the two little ones, Richard and Regine. So far they had been able to use the bags that were provided, but when the hostess was getting a new supply, Regine threw up over her own dress as well as mine and the seats. By that time, I must have looked green as I felt my stomach coming up too. There was no way I could help Fred and the still smiling hostesses with the cleaning. The experience made me realise that being an airhostess was not all glamour like we are made to believe. It's probably also the reason that none of our girls ever wanted to become one.

The storms died down and the sun broke through when we came closer to Alice Springs. We eagerly looked for houses or other signs of life, but even the trees had become scarce. Only occasionally did the sun reflect off a tin roof, which would have been a station building. We were fascinated by the squares we saw now and again on the bare red earth, wondering what they could be. We later learned that they were dams, watering places for cattle.

Both the friendly airhostesses came to talk to me for a while. With the help of a lot of sign language I seemed to get across to them why we were going to Alice Springs.

"What do you do for a living?" the red-headed lady asked.

"My husband is a cabinet-maker," I answered, glad that I had learned that sentence, but that was not what she meant. She wanted to know what I was doing.

"I am a housewife, and I can sew," I said while my hands made the movements of a needle and thread.

"What do you make?" was her next question. As I did not know the word for bridal-dresses I said: "I make *bruids-toiletten*." People behind us grinned. The two girls looked at each other, trying hard not to laugh.

"You know, for wedding," I stammered while a deep red coloured my face. "Long white dress," I added, tugging at my skirt.

"Oh! For a moment I thought you made toilets for brides," one of the men behind me said. Everyone laughed and although I felt terribly embarrassed I laughed shyly too.

It was nearly six o'clock when we came closer to the hills surrounding Alice Springs. They were beautiful, dark-red in the shade and pink where the sun shone on them. There were only a few cars on a narrow road and a couple of buildings with corrugated roofs, but I could see no sign of a town. The biggest of the sheds was the airport, our hostess said. Apart from a few cars parked at the back of the building we could not see anyone. What could we do if Sam was not there to meet us? I held my breath as we touched down, shivering at the thought that we had finally arrived at the place where we would start our new life. I was about to meet my brother again after ten years… invading his single-man's life with six lively children…

There was absolutely no way back... ever!

Settling In

By the time we had gathered our belongings we were the last to leave the plane. Hot air rose up from the tarmac as we came down the stairs.

"Welcome to Alice Springs" said a large sign in front of the big, corrugated iron shed. There were only a few people waiting on the small lawn in front of the building. I did not see Sam standing near an enormous hedge of brightly flowering red geraniums, until I came closer. Although he had warned me that he had lost a lot of hair, it was still a shock to see my thirty-two year old brother nearly bald. And so brown! Surrounded by the children Fred introduced them to him and his friend John, who had come to the airport with him.

"It's just as well that the plane was two hours late," Sam said after we hugged each other. "This way I could go back home again and sweep the sand out of the caravans before you came. It doesn't look so bad now."

John shook his dark curly head and laughed. "I don't know about that!" he said while he shook hands with me. It had been a 'bugger of a day', they said; one of those in which you had to have the lights on all day otherwise you could not see for the dust. John was a handsome looking fellow the same age as I was, thirty-one. He was born in Holland and 'escaped' to Australia when he was only seventeen, he said. His Dutch was terrible but at least he could understand what we were saying.

"Is that really all you have?" he asked when he picked up the only suitcase we had. He looked doubtful when I said that the rest would come by train in a couple of days. The boys recognised Sam's ute immediately when we got to the almost deserted car park.

"Where do we all sit?" I asked. "We can't possibly fit in John's car." John's car was a station wagon, but the back was filled with tools and building materials.

"Well, I figured that if Fred and the girls go with John, you can sit with me in the front of the ute and the boys can go in the back," Sam replied. "I've put an old blanket in it for them," he laughed when he saw the worried look on my face. The three boys were delighted, but I insisted that Richard, who was only six, could not sit in the open tray of the ute.

On the way to our new home, Sam slowed down to show us the first Alice Springs radio station, 8HA that had been operating for a few months. Before that they could only get the ABC, transmitting from Adelaide. Then he pointed out the dry bed of the Todd River, telling me how it became a raging torrent after a bit of decent rain. The drought had already lasted now for over three years; it had been years since it had run a 'banker'. He could not remember when it had rained last.

"It might be six or eight months ago and it wasn't much," he said. "Before that it hadn't rained to speak of for eight successive years. You wouldn't believe it, but there wasn't a blade of grass to be seen anywhere."

I remembered Sam writing about those terrible dust storms. The streetlights had been left on for days so that people could see where the road was going. That terrible drought finally broke in January '66 when the rain pelted down non-stop for four days, flooding the whole town.

While Sam was talking, I wondered how the beautiful white trees along the riverbanks as well as those in the riverbed had survived without water for so long. The lovely flowering bushes on the side of the road were desert roses, Sam said. He went on, talking about the strong resistance of the plants to the dry weather in the centre and about the underground reservoir of water believed to be big enough to support a town of a hundred thousand people. That was, of course, providing water was used as sparingly as it was then. Alice Springs was expected to reach that number of residents by the year two thousand, which fortunately did not happen. Twenty-eight thousand were counted in the census in 2001.

For a while we drove between the dry river and a single railway track that came all the way from Adelaide, fifteen hundred kilometres away. The river, the road and the railway went side-by-side through a gap in the steep hills of magnificent dark-red rocks, opening up to a large stretch of bare red-brown soil in front of us. Not a tree to be seen anywhere. "Connellan Airport used to be here until a few years ago," Sam explained. "In a few years time it'll be full of houses. My place is over there," he said, pointing to some buildings in the distance.

"Only one train a week comes in," he grinned when a moment later he crossed the railway track without stopping or even looking sideways.

One train a week! I quickly pushed the thought away that it would be a whole week before our belongings came in.

The weather was perfect. The sky was still bright blue but the sun was going down quickly in a pink and mauve haze. It bathed the mighty rocky mountain on our left, called Mount Gillen, in a warm red glow.

"It's hard to imagine that the wind swept up the dry red sand so much that it obscured the sun only a few hours ago," I said.

"Don't worry, you'll see for yourself tomorrow," Sam promised. "It has been like that for weeks now and there will be a lot more to come."

We passed a few newly built houses. With their small windows and corrugated iron roofs, they looked like sheds to me.

"They're commission homes," Sam said. "You can rent them cheap from the Government." Some better houses were being built on the next couple of blocks. They were private homes.

"This here is my property," Sam announced proudly when he turned into

40

his driveway, after we had passed a couple of large half-finished houses. Before me were a lot of big arches, a huge slab of concrete and a couple of old caravans around a newly built shed.

"These arches here are going to be another carport," Sam explained when we got out of the car.

I was dumbfounded. The house was going to be a mansion, far too luxurious for us to live in! When Fred joined us Sam pointed out where the lounge, kitchen and bedrooms were going to be. My heart sank even further when he showed us the three old caravans he had hired from friends. They all had broken windows and most of the vinyl seats were ripped. One of the caravans had no lining on the inside at all. Although Sam had swept the dust out of them before he went to the airport, a thin layer of bright red dust was still left everywhere. Then we went into the shed where Sam lived himself, a brick room of four by six metres with two small windows, built onto one of the fancy open carports. It was *ackcely* a granny flat, he said. A narrow sliding door in the middle of the back wall gave access to a three-foot wide bathroom. It had a toilet at one end and a shower in the other, with a narrow hand-basin under the little window in the middle.

"I tiled it yesterday and did the grouting this morning," Sam said. "It would be better if you didn't use it today."

Letting the hot water wash over me was the nicest thing I could think of at that moment, but there was no time for a wash anyway. Sam suggested taking us out for dinner, because he had nothing to eat in the shed. Knowing how tired we would be when we came back from the restaurant, I insisted on preparing the beds for everybody first.

There were no lights in the old caravans Sam had collected with John a week earlier, when we were expected to arrive. Dark came unbelievably quickly. We had to finish wiping the fine red dust from the old vinyl mattresses by the light of a torch. In the meantime Sam managed to find a sheet or a thin blanket to lie on for everyone and Lilian helped him make eight pillows from towels and folded jumpers. Then we all had a bit of a wash at the tiny hand-basin between the toilet and the shower, combed our hair and straightened up our clothes, ready to go out for dinner.

As John had gone home, Sam's ute was now the only form of transport available and I wondered how on earth the nine of us were going fit in. Sam, Fred and I went in the tiny cabin with Regine on my lap, allowing Richard to sit with the other four in the open back of the car.

It was after eight-thirty when we arrived at the Memorial Club where Sam was a member. The kitchen was closed but the proprietors, who were serving at the bar, immediately offered to cook a meal for us when Sam told them that we had just arrived from Holland.

"What would you like?" Sam asked. "Steak and chips with salad?"

"What is steak?" I asked. We all knew what chips were.

"Yes, a bit of beef and chips would be fine," I agreed when Sam explained what it was. "But don't order any meat for Regine," I called after him as he walked to the bar.

Cooking nine meals takes a while. Because they had been up so early, the children soon lost interest in watching some men playing snooker and darts. They hung listlessly and sleepily in their chairs. I was fighting sleep myself, feeling very tired after the long, memorable day, but my eyes opened wide, instantly awake when the meals were being brought to our table; I had never seen such enormous pieces of meat being served in my whole life. The big oval plates were overflowing with meat and beautiful crisp potato chips and a bowl heaped up high with fresh salad was put next to each plate. Sam had ordered eight T-bone steaks; I would make do for two days with one such a piece! Too embarrassed to leave all that food on the plates I struggled with the food on my plate and made the kids eat far more then their stomachs could handle at that hour of the day.

I felt very uncomfortable when we left the table as the dinner must have cost Sam a fortune and some of the plates were barely touched. I wonder now why Sam did not ask for a 'doggy bag'; we could have used the leftovers for several days to come.

It was after ten when we left the restaurant and Sam took us up to the top of Anzac Hill from where we overlooked the lights of Alice Springs. The town was surrounded by hills on all sides. It had only nine and a half thousand people but it seemed quite large in the dark. It was said to be the fastest growing town in the whole of Australia, Sam said. The population was expected to double in the next couple of years. The fact that there was no other town or city for hundreds of kilometres around made me shiver.

Before we left Sam's place he had shown us a map of the area. I had been happy to see other places quite close to Alice Springs.

"Oh, you mean Hermannsburg, Papunya and Yuendumu," Sam laughed when I asked him about them. "They are all black-feller places."

"But Hermannsburg is a German name," I protested hopefully. Sam had explained then that a German missionary of the Lutheran Church had established the settlement in 1877.

With growing apprehension I looked at the gap between the hills, the only way out of town to the south, a dirt track of fifteen-hundred kilometres before any sign of civilisation. There were only two towns, a lot smaller than Alice, on the narrow bitumen road to Darwin, fifteen hundred kilometres to the north; Tennant Creek at five hundred, and Katherine, twelve hundred kilometres away.

"The further north you go, the hotter it gets," Sam warned. "I don't know how people can stand it in summer."

We were fascinated by the stars; we had never seen so many and so clearly. The Milky Way looked like fairyland.

It suddenly got chilly. By the time we got home from the bumpy ride in the ute the children were all complaining about being cold and having sore tummies. Eugene threw up as soon as he got out of the open back of the car. We skipped brushing teeth and let them sleep in their clothes, trying to make them as comfortable as possible on the hard, slippery vinyl beds. We had only just gone to bed ourselves when Richard vomited all over the place. Trying not to breathe in the appalling smell in the stinking-hot caravan, I held the torch while Fred mopped up the mess.

Although I had been up since three o'clock in the morning and I was dog-tired, I slept little that night. Wednesday, the thirteenth of October 1971 had become the longest day in my life. And we had no idea what lay in store for us...

The voices of Sam and the children woke me up early the following morning. I looked through the torn curtains of our caravan and saw that the sun had been up for quite some time. There was not a cloud in the blue sky and it was already quite hot. Fred was still soundly asleep on the bare mattress beside me. I slipped out of the old van and found all six children in the shed watching in amazement how Sam made himself a sandwich for breakfast. On a thick layer of old newspapers, spread before him on the table, he buttered two pieces of brown bread with a large pocket knife, careful not to miss any of the edges. Nearly the entire contents of the old fridge were arranged around the edge of the paper; beef, cheese, a cucumber, an onion, half a cabbage, a tomato and a large can of beetroot as well as butter, milk, mustard, peanut paste and honey.

"Mornin' Sis," he greeted me while he took a big slice of cooked beef from an enormous pile, folded it and put it on one of the pieces of bread. He peeled a leaf from the cabbage and folded it on top of the beef, followed by sliced cucumber, a heap of raw onions and half a tomato. Then he opened the can of beetroot, took a big slice out with his fingers and wiped the excess juice off on the edge of the can. The kids were in stitches when he held it up high and sucked the last drops of juice from the bottom of the beetroot. Because Sam's tongue was tight at the bottom, he could only poke it out a little and the children showed him eagerly what they could do with theirs.

With the beetroot on top, my brother's sandwich was now about ten centimetres high, but Sam was not finished yet. He picked up a hunk of cheese, cut off several slices and laid them carefully on top of the pile. After smearing some mustard on the cheese, he covered it with the second piece of bread.

"How on earth are you going to eat that?" I asked. Sam grinned and grimaced at the children while he wiped his fingers on his skimpy shorts.

"Well, you do it like this," he said, rolling his eyes, enjoying the attention. He put one hand on top of the other on the sandwich and pushed the whole lot down to the great delight of the children. He picked it up using his little fingers to support the back corners, took a big bite out of it and washed it down with a big mug of tea, sweetened with milk and lots of honey. After preparing and eating a second sandwich in the same fashion, Sam announced that he was now going to have his 'dessert'; a thick crust with a layer of butter and peanut paste. The children's eyes widened when he topped it with a tablespoon of creamed honey.

"Yukkie!" they giggled, pulling faces and having great fun.

"How can you still be so skinny?" I asked in astonishment while I handed him another mug of sweet tea.

Sam laughed. "You don't get fat from healthy food, Sis," he grinned.

When he finished eating, my dear brother wiped his knife on the edge of the newspaper and put it in his pocket. He rolled up the dirty top layers of the paper and threw them in the rubbish bin saying, "So, now my table is ready for my next meal and I don't have to do any dishes."

In the meantime Fred got up and Sam showed him the building plans of the house. While I gave the children some plain sandwiches with milk, made from dry powder according to Sam's instructions, I wondered if we would ever change our simple Dutch habit of a couple of slices of bread with cheese or jam, to this elaborate Australian breakfast.

Because there were only three chairs in the shed, only Richard and Regine could sit near me at the table. The four oldest children had to sit on Sam's bed in the corner with strict instructions to be careful not to spill their milk. While I kept an eye on them I had a look around in the shed.

The day before we arrived Sam had bought the brightly patterned plastic tablecloth that covered the solid old table, 'to brighten the place up a bit', he said. The three vinyl covered kitchen chairs were badly worn. Apart from Sam's bed and the fridge out of the year zero, there was an old, single door cupboard for his clothes and household linen as well as a supply of groceries. On top of the cupboard was a small suitcase, which had held all Sam's possessions when he left Holland ten years before. Along the remaining walls were boxes with tools and building materials for the house. A tall fan beside Sam's bed provided the only relief from the stifling heat. There were only a few old plates, a couple of forks, knives and spoons, half a dozen big coffee mugs and some foam things called 'stubby-holders', apparently to keep a bottle of beer cool while you drank it. I could not see anything to cook on, and no pots or pans either. Sam never cooked for himself. He had figured, that I could cook in one of the old caravans which had a built-in gas stove.

While Fred and I ate our sandwiches outside, in the shade of the carport, we planned the days ahead. Sam was taking a few days off; he was sick of working, he said. From where we sat we could see John working on a nearly finished house across the road. Sam sent one of the boys over to invite him to join us for a 'cuppa'.

"How are you getting on with that eccentric brother of yours?" John asked with his boyish grin, when he walked into the carport. We laughed with Sam. We were still talking about the beautiful morning, which would soon turn into another stinking hot day, when a white station wagon turned into the driveway.

"That's Pat, John's missus," Sam announced.

"What are you sitting on your bloody bum for at this hour of the bloody morning instead of working," the blond, sturdy lady said when she came out of the car and walked towards us.

"I've taken the day off," Sam laughed.

"I told that bastard of a brother of yours to hurry up and get the bloody house finished before you came, but this is what he does all day," Pat said when Sam introduced me, ignoring my hand I held out to shake with her. I felt awkward and silly, as I already knew that only men shake hands in Australia. Pat was in her late forties with short, blond hair and a smooth complexion. The dimples beside her mouth gave her face a girlish appearance when she smiled. Because I had never met a couple of which the man was a lot younger than his wife, I understood that Pat was John's mother until Sam said, "You should have been here half a year ago; we had a fantastic party when they got married in April."

Up until meeting Pat Govers on that first day in Alice Springs, Fred was still called by his Dutch name Fre. People could not pronounce that properly and made it 'Fray' or 'Fry'.

What does it stand for?" Pat asked.

"Frederick, peace-maker," Fred said. "My father called me Frederikus at the registry office but when I was baptised later that afternoon, he had a few to many *borreltjes* (small glasses of strong liquor) and called me Franciscus."

"We'll make it Fred," Pat decided. Then she asked me: "What did you say your name was?"

"Mien," I said, "from Wilhelmina, the queen of Holland."

"Mean! That sounds bloody awful; make it Willie," Pat suggested.

"Oh, no, not Willie!" I protested. For some unknown reason I truly hated that name.

"Make it Wilma then," Pat said. "Mean is no name for a bloody girl." Fred and I looked at each other and laughed.

"Oh! Yes, I can see it now," I said in Dutch, "Fred and Wilma and the Flintstones!" We all laughed, as the Flintstones were apparently very popular in Alice Springs too. From then on Fre introduced himself as Fred but I kept my name as it was.

"Even though it sounds mean, I'm not mean by any means," I now say to anyone who can not pronounce it properly. But I often wished I would still be called Mientje or Willemien.

"Ask your sister if there is anything she needs," Pat ordered Sam who translated it for me.

"Oh! Yes, I need everything, but I think it will come tomorrow with the train," I said in my broken English.

"Not bloody likely!" Pat replied. "The trains here are taking their bloody time. I'll see what I can get you."

"What is all that blood for?" I asked Sam when we watched her drive off in the car. Sam laughed. "That's just to sound tough," he chuckled.

"Pat is always ready to help anybody in trouble," Sam had said when she left. Two hours later she came back, her car loaded to the brim with just about everything I needed. There were sheets and blankets, with a warning that it could still get very cold at night, pillows and pillowcases, pots and pans, cutlery, plates and all sorts of dishes. She even brought a folding table and chairs, as Sam's table was too small to fit us all around it.

Pat was very angry with Sam; she really got stuck into him. Using 'bloody' before every second word, she scolded him for the lousy way he had prepared for us. Sam just smiled and let it all wash over him.

"I got them a roof over their heads and a meal; what more do they want?" he laughed.

By the time Pat left, it was lunchtime. The sandwiches Sam had made for breakfast proved to be his staple diet for lunch as well, day in and day out, without any variation. I decided to stick to the usual heap of plain sandwiches for lunch for the time being; a single layer of cheese or cooked beef between two slices of bread and a single piece of bread with jam, peanut paste or brown sugar for dessert would be a lot cheaper.

The temperature had climbed steadily during the morning. By ten o'clock, a hot wind was blowing up huge clouds of dust, but Sam assured us that that was nothing compared to what it had been the last weeks and was expected for that day. He offered to take us out in the afternoon. Keen to see the town by daylight and visit the children's school, we all piled in the ute as soon as we had finished doing the dishes.

The town consisted of only a few streets but it was a relief for me to see some good shops. Woolworths had just expanded their supermarket in the main street and there were two other fairly big grocery shops in town. A brand new one, called 'Ivy's Mini Market', close to Sam's place, was opening the following Saturday. The Catholic Church, a lovely sandstone building which seated four hundred worshippers and had a lot of windows, had only been in use for a year. The doors were wide open, so Sam showed us around. Because Fred had worked with 'glass-in-lead' in Holland, we were particularly interested to see that there was a stained glass window in the middle of Australia.

"I have never been to any church since I left Holland," Sam confessed when we walked out again. I told him that we had not been going every Sunday as we used to either, as things had changed drastically in Holland during the last few years.

The double storey school next to the church was a lot larger than I had expected. Sam and Henk had done the some of the brickwork together the previous year. While they were working on one of the high walls, Sam had a bad accident, which had nearly cost him his life.

The school was built out of huge cement blocks, twenty centimetres high, twenty wide and forty centimetres long. Although they were hollow, they weighed a ton. One of those blocks had fallen off the scaffolding from the second floor on top of Sam's head. While he told us what happened he showed us the dent in his bald scalp where one of the corners of the brick had hit him. He had been taken to hospital with concussion and was unconscious for four days. As he had only mentioned the accident briefly in one of his sporadic letters, long after he recovered from the ordeal, we had no idea about the seriousness of his condition at the time.

At the main entrance of the school we met Mother Ida, the principal, a friendly nun in her late sixties. After she shook hands with us she talked to each of the children. Holding their hands in both of hers, she asked them their names and ages, then she told them in which class they would be and their teachers' names.

"You can come tomorrow if you like or wait until Monday," she said. "The school bus stops very close to where you live. Don't the Harvey children live near you?" she asked Sam. Yes, they did, Sam said. Because our children had only been to school for a fortnight during the last four months, they were all eager to go the following day, Friday.

"As you probably notice, the school is very quiet," Mother Ida said while she walked with us in the schoolyard. "We believe in discipline."

"That suits us fine," Sam translated for us. "Let's go for a drive in the bush," he suggested when we strolled back to the car.

Excited by the prospect of seeing what the bush was like, the kids stumbled over each other, wanting to be the first to get into the back of the ute. The four of us, Sam, Fred, Regine and I, crammed into the cabin again. The temperature had now risen to a hundred degrees Fahrenheit, close to forty Celsius. Even though the windows of the ute were open as far as they could go, it was very stuffy in the small cabin. The drive over the bumpy dirt road out of town through a haze of dust was uncomfortable but I hardly noticed it, as I did not want to miss anything of the countryside. I wanted to take it all in as well as keeping an eye on the rear-view mirror, watching the children bouncing in the open back of the vehicle. With their hair blowing in the wind and their eyes closed to a slit, they pointed enthusiastically to the hills in the distance and the huge cloud of dust trailing behind us.

After a 'short' drive of about twenty-five kilometres, without seeing any houses at all, Sam stopped the car and announced that we were at 'Simpson's Gap'. From where he parked we could only see a big hill. After stumbling through a thick layer of white sand in a dry riverbed for about kilometre and a half, stopping often to admire the majestic white gum trees and incredible rock formations, we came to the most splendid view I had ever seen in my life. Towering high above us, on either side of a deep waterhole of about six or seven metres wide, were steep, dark red rock formations, believed to be millions of years old. The bright white trunk of a gum tree, growing out of one of the many cracks in the huge walls, was reflected in the rippling water. The sun, going down behind the rocks, gave the leaves and branches of the trees a golden glow against the vivid blue sky. Overwhelmed by the height of the rocks and the beauty around me, I felt like a tiny ant when I sat down on the sand. Breathing deeply the cool soothing smell of eucalyptus it seemed that time stood still.

The happy voices of the children, echoing between the ancient walls, brought me back to my senses. The older children were climbing the layers of rocks like monkeys while Regine and Richard threw small stones in the clear, icy-cold water. Sam and Fred counted with them to see how long it took until the stones hit the rocks at the bottom of the waterhole, which was said to be eighteen metres deep at the time. Although it was thirty-nine degrees that day, goosebumps appeared on my bare arms and legs while I sat there, admiring it all.

The sun was going down quickly in a pinkish purple sky, and it was a lot cooler as we drove home. The incredible bright light, during those last minutes of sunshine, turned the hills into a spectrum of beautiful colours, which made me feel like I was on a different planet. It took me a long time to get used to the rapid change from broad daylight to darkness, as soon as the sun went down.

Back at Sam's place, we had to clean a layer of dust out of the stifling hot caravans before we could make the beds. Then, by the light of a torch, I cooked a simple Dutch meal of cauliflower, potatoes and meatballs for the nine of us in the unbelievably hot aluminium caravan. It was the first meal I had cooked since we left my mother's farm in Holland, nearly two months earlier. In the meantime, the girls had a one-minute shower, while Sam hosed down the boys in a forty-four gallon drum in the back yard. After Fred peeled the potatoes he brought tables and chairs into the carport.

Although hundreds of insects were keen to share our meal outside, it was much better than being in the shed where it was still unbearably hot and stuffy. While I dished out the food, Sam provided a bottle of wine to celebrate our first day in the Alice. We happily toasted each other with lemonade and wine, drinking out of Pat's lemonade glasses.

The First Day in 'the Alice'

It was still early when I woke up the following morning, our second day in Alice Springs. Despite my worries about our future, I had fallen asleep immediately the previous night and had slept like a log, probably due to the wine. I would have liked to linger a bit longer in bed, but there was no time for daydreaming. The children were going to school for the first time and I still had to decide what they could wear. Not that I had much choice, with only one suitcase of clothes for the eight of us. I desperately hoped that Pat was wrong and our belongings would arrive that afternoon after all. Mother Ida had asked me to provide the children with school uniforms as soon as possible. I needed my sewing machine to make them; the price I was quoted to buy them in the shop was ridiculous. Lilian was going to the High School after Christmas and as there were only six weeks of the year left, she was allowed to wear her normal clothes. By eight o'clock we were on our way to town in the ute with Sam, leaving Fred behind with Regine.

I was horrified to see that they were selling lollies, cakes, lemonade and other sweets in the tuckshop at school, where Sam showed me how to order lunch for the day. After he introduced me to a solidly built red haired lady who managed the shop, he tried to explain to me what the difference was between a roll, a sausage roll and a meat pie. I was taken aback when I heard the prices, settling for a sausage roll each. They did not look very appetising but at seven cents they were the cheapest items on the menu.

"They will have to take a sandwich to school next week," I said to Sam in Dutch, which he translated. The redhead screwed up her nose.

"It's not that bad!" she said. Feeling humiliated and a terrible scrooge, my face turned red and I became hot and sweaty. Luckily the kids had already gone to their classrooms and we could leave the school quickly.

Sam took me to the Bank of New South Wales, now Westpac, to see if our money had come through. Several people were already lined up, even though we still had to wait twenty minutes for the bank to open at nine. When Sam told the clerk that I had arrived the previous day and explained what we had come for, the teller went away. He soon came back with a document that stated that, after all costs had been deducted, we owned the grand amount of nine hundred dollars and a few cents.

For a moment I felt the ground sway under my feet as I gazed at the figure; the equivalent of ten weeks wages was all we had to replace the car and all the furniture we had had to sell in such a hurry before we left Holland. Fred needed more than that to buy a decent car! The previous afternoon Sam had taken him to several car dealers, but there was nothing worth buying under a thousand dollars.

"I still hoped you would have a little more so that we could go into business together," Sam said disappointedly. He had also hoped that we could buy his house... I felt my heart sink in my shoes, thinking of all the other things we needed to replace. Second hand furniture was worth nothing in Holland, but Jurian had warned us that you paid the earth for it in Alice Springs. Looking at me more sympathetically he added: "Well, you'll still be able to buy a reasonable car with this amount of money."

I came to my senses when the clerk handed me a chequebook and asked me to sign my name on some documents he put in front of me. He looked at my signature, Wilhelmina Johanna Blom-Hooft, then handed it back to me.

"You are Mrs. Fred Blom aren't you?" he asked.

"Fred is my husband," I said. The clerk nodded.

"Is Hooft your maiden name?" he asked.

I looked at Sam. Maiden name?

"Yes," Sam said. "She's my sister." The clerk explained to Sam that I could only use my husband's name in Australia, no hyphenated names were allowed unless they were a family name by birth.

"But I have always signed my name like this," I protested.

"I'm sorry, but it's not acceptable to the bank," the clerk replied.

While the two men were watching, I tried my new signature on a scrap of paper. W.J. Blom. I stood there staring at it for a while; it looked awfully bare. Sam's words seemed to come from a distance:

"From now on you'll be called Missus Fred Blom."

I felt naked when I left the bank, stripped of my identity. After all these years I still like it when I get a letter with my full name on it.

Before we went home, Sam showed me the sandstone fountain he had built at the end of the main street to commemorate the first Alice Springs Centenary 1871-1971. I had commented earlier that there were so many men wearing beards. "A lot of people grew them for the celebrations in April," Sam said. "They must have liked the fact that they didn't have to shave every day."

After a cup of coffee at home, Sam left with Fred to see his German friend Heinz who had promised Sam that he would give Fred a job. They were also planning to look for a car. While they were away, I introduced myself to Stephanie, a tall, slim lady who had moved into one of the brand-new Commission houses at the back of Sam's place, the previous week. She was born in Russia and had come to Australia when she was still a little girl. I told her about my visit to the school and that I hoped that our belongings would arrive that afternoon so that I could make the children's uniforms.

"Oh, no! You can't expect them today. The train takes ages," she exclaimed. "But don't worry about it. You can sew in my house, I'm not home during the day anyway."

Stephanie told me where I could buy the material and we arranged that I would go to her place the following Monday afternoon. While we were talking over the wire fence, the wind had started blowing up lots of loose sand and it was getting very hot and sticky again. Fred looked disheartened and upset when he and Sam came back just before midday.

"You know bloody well that the piece of paper I signed to give your brother-in-law a bloody job, was just a formality," Heinz had said when Sam introduced Fred to him. Even so, he said he would see what he could do. Then, when Sam told him that Fred's tools were still on the train, he had said rudely: "I don't employ no bastard who hasn't got his own bloody tools. Don't bother to come back without them."

The machinery they worked with in the cabinet-making factory was even more old-fashioned and dangerous to work with than what Fred had seen in the sawmill in Footscray, and he doubted that he would ever get used to being scolded like that by any boss. He depended on his tools to be able to work and needed a car to get there, but we needed the money to feed everybody, including Sam who was paying the rent for the old caravans. My heart sank. What if it really took several weeks before the train came in with our goods, as people said it would?

After lunch, Fred borrowed Sam's car for a few hours so that we could do some shopping. Like the previous day, we were amazed to see that there was hardly any dust around as soon as we had left the new suburb being developed, which was only five kilometres out of town. At the bank, we withdrew a hundred dollars to pay for the school fees, materials to make uniforms and to buy food for the next couple of days. The only shop in town that sold material for school-uniforms had no green striped cotton to make the boys shirts. The green checked material for Simone's dress was the only thing I could get. I bought enough for one dress only. Across the arcade, I discovered that making the boys' shorts would not save me any money. We bought one uniform for each of the three boys. We just had to wash them after school. It would be no problem to have them dry by the next morning in this hot weather.

Our next stop was 'Woolies' where I had the biggest shock. The price of groceries was outrageous! We were told that an average wage was eighty dollars a week; with that amount Fred could not even keep us alive, let alone save up for a house or buy fuel for a car.

"You look as if you have seen a ghost," Fred said.

Again I heard my mother's voice saying, 'Soup is never eaten as hot as it is served'. On the way home, I could not keep my mind off the situation, feeling more and more depressed. I don't know how I got through the rest of the day or what I did. I only remember how I cried myself to sleep that night.

My eyes were very swollen when I got up early the next morning, and I felt like a limp dishcloth. Surrounded by the kids, Sam was already eating his elaborate breakfast.

"It can't be that bad Sis!" he said between two bites. "People can make more money here than a basic wage, without working themselves into the grave."

As our washing machine had not arrived, I set out to do the washing by hand. Pat had given me an old baby bath and Sam had a bucket I could use, but he had no clothesline.

"I never needed one," he said. He washed his underpants, shorts and shirts while he had a shower and hung them over the curtain rail to dry. Once in a while, he would give his bed linen and towels to a friend who would put them through her machine for him.

After breakfast that Saturday morning, Sam and Fred went to town to buy a clothesline. They came back a few hours later with a car as well. It was an old station wagon, coloured pink and grey like the beautiful parrots that were flying around in large flocks. A friend of Sam's had sold it to them for only three hundred and fifty dollars. The tyres were bald and the gears weren't working very well, but at least it was a Holden, Australian made, and should last for a while, they said. The upholstery inside was dirty and torn but it looked quite decent from the outside. We decided to call it the 'Galah', after the parrots.

An hour later, the washing was flapping in the hot wind on the Hill's-hoist, a clever construction like an umbrella without a cover. Still talking about why we didn't have them in Holland, Fred and I went across the road to see what John was doing. The house he was building also had several arches, but these were across the full length of the front of the building, providing a long verandah, which made the house cooler inside. The front door opened up directly into the living room, which I later learned was the case in most houses.

"G'day!" John said. "Has Sam turned you into Aussies yet?" He showed us around the house which had four spacious bedrooms, a large lounge, a family room as well as a dining room, a washroom which John called a 'laundry', and a huge kitchen, all with big windows. Two of the bedrooms had 'ensuites', private bathrooms with built-in wardrobes; such luxury! In the past, the houses had small windows to keep the heat out but now that there were air-conditioners the windows could be bigger, John explained. He was fitting beautifully made cupboards in the kitchen, lots of them. He had not much time to talk, he said, as the family wanted to move in as soon as possible.

I was making sandwiches for lunch a little later, when I noticed Sam talking to Pat in the driveway.

"She came to invite us for a barbeque tonight," Sam said.

"What is a barbeque?" I asked.

"Cooking meat outside on a barbeque. You know - a wood fire," he explained.

"Oh! That's nice, but what do we do with the kids?"

"Take 'em," Sam said, matter-of-factly.

"You mean that Pat is going to cook meat for all of us?" I asked, sure that Sam had misunderstood her.

"That's right," Sam replied. "Just bring a plate."

Of course, Pat had given me a lot of plates and she would not have enough left if she invited so many for dinner.

"Is she only one plate short?" I asked a little puzzled.

Sam laughed. It was apparently not what she meant.

"You are expected to make a salad to take with you," he informed me. I had no idea what a 'salad' consisted off. Surely, we could not take lettuce with mayonnaise as we made in Holland? Being no cook to speak of, I had paid no attention to the salad we'd had at the Memorial Club. I only remembered those awful, harsh lettuces that looked like endive, with raw onions, cucumber and tomatoes with some sort of dressing on it.

"Don't worry, we'll take a couple of bottles of wine instead," Sam said. "Pat will have plenty of food anyway."

I had no time to worry about it. We could always eat a sandwich when we came home, if there wasn't enough. Folding the washing and putting the sheets back on the beds after I had cleaned the dust out of the caravans made the afternoon go quickly. Then we all had to take a shower. I was glad there was no need to iron anything in this heat; the wind had done that for me.

We were all looking forward to going out in our 'new' car. Warned continuously not to get their clothes and shoes dirty in the loose sand, the children ran back and forth until we finally told them that they could get into the car. The next minute Regine screamed at the top of her voice. She had her fingers jammed in the door. When I came running Fred was already carrying her around, trying to calm her down.

"Which one is it?" I asked anxiously. Still screaming her little heart out, she let me have a look at her thumb, which was already terribly swollen and turning blue.

"Put it in your mouth and suck it," I ordered. It may not help to stop the swelling, but it always works, since no one can suck a sore finger and scream at the same time. Regine was still bawling when we got to Pat's place where I had my first taste of 'bush-nursing'.

"Come to the kitchen with me," she said. "I'll fix it."

Pat got a needle and lit the gas stove. My stomach turned when it dawned on me what she was going to do.

54

"Look the other bloody way if you're planning to faint," she barked at me. Feeling terribly sorry for Regine, I braced myself, holding her little hand.

"This is not going to hurt much at all," Pat said softly to Regine while she cooled the blue thumb with a wet cloth. When she gently pressed the red-hot tip of the needle into the nail a squirt of blood went up into the air, relieving the pressure immediately. Within minutes Regine was happily playing with the others in the back yard.

Pat took me to the verandah at the front of the house and introduced me to her other guests, who had just arrived. Nick, a Dutchman of around fifty-five, with whom John had come to Australia in 1957, and an Australian fellow, called Jim, who was an architect. Jim lived in Adelaide and rented the house next door to Pat and John, as he often came up to Alice Springs to do some work. Glad to be able to speak Dutch, Fred was already in deep conversation with Nick, who was a builder.

"There is plenty of work around if you're not afraid to rough it a bit," I heard Nick say while I was introduced to Jim.

Pat declined my offer to help with the food.

"John and I are managing fine," she said. "You just enjoy yourself and keep an eye on the kids."

I was already watching the kids like a hawk as the whole place was filled to the brim with expensive antiques. There were masses of fragile knick-knacks on the magnificently carved sideboards and tables in the large entrance hall, as well as in the passage, the lounge and the formal dining room. The walls were covered with paintings and shelves. Every available space was used to display their treasures. Pat's pride and joy were her fantastic collection of beautiful old kerosene lamps and an enormous quantity of old bottles in all shapes and sizes. Our eldest children were very interested in the wall of *sigarenbandjes,* little cigar-bands. They had given away their own collection before we left Holland.

Pat was apparently regarded as quite a character in town. Every Saturday night she played the piano in the Stuart Arms, the most popular pub in town at the time. She regularly took tourists into the bush in her four wheel drive vehicle, and she was well known for her home-style cooking at weddings, private parties and other functions around the town. She had even provided meals for several Royal Visitors. On top of that, she was a good seamstress and a keen photographer. She had her own weekly radio program on the ABC and reported on social events around town in the local newspaper called the 'Centralian Advocate'.

Sam told us how Pat had gone into the Harts Ranges, a hundred and forty kilometres north of Alice Springs, on a camel a few years earlier when she was suffering from a broken heart. When she came back a year later, she had single-handedly built the entrance to the now famous 'Gem Cave' in town, using all the stones she had collected in the ranges.

Our elderly friend, Bob, who was in charge of making roads for the government at the time, told me recently how Pat had stopped one of his bulldozers one day. They were working at the site of the former airport, when a lady had suddenly leaped in front of the dozer, frantically waving her arms.

"Stop! Stop!" she had yelled. "You can't go any further."

"Lady, I can't just stop working. I have a living to make," the fellow on the dozer had said.

"Who's your boss?" Pat had demanded. "Go get him! Tell him that I want to talk to him immediately," she had ordered the stunned driver.

"How much does it cost me to stop your bloody dozer for a day?" Pat had asked Bob, who replied that it cost him fifty pound a day if his machine wasn't working. Pat had given him the money on the spot and told him to 'nick off' for the rest of the day. She had apparently known that there were a lot of old bottles buried at that particular spot, the 'dump' of the old Connellan Airport.

I carefully sipped my wine and relaxed, watching the children play with a couple of orphaned kangaroos, while sitting under the shady 'bush' verandah - a roof made with twigs - surrounded by Pat and John's beautiful garden, with flowering shrubs and plants in all shapes and sizes. Pat had taken the kangaroos home and reared them with a bottle as their mothers had been killed on the road, or shot by hunters.

Nearly every plant in the garden was native to Central Australia. "It's a waste of time and money to grow anything else here," Pat said when she showed me around later that night. It was a splendid evening; the temperature was just perfect. I marvelled at the scarlet bottle-brushes and the majestic, bright, white gumtrees, as I watched the pink and grey galahs screeching among the branches of the tall, old trees. The children were doing handstands on the well-kept lawn, and the mouth watering smell of fried meat came from where Pat and John were cooking on a wire rack above an inbuilt, red-hot wood fire.

I could not believe my eyes when the food was being served. There was a huge variety of meat, salads, sauces and bread on the long trestle table, which was covered with a white tablecloth and a big arrangement of fresh flowers in the middle. There were sausages, pork and lamb chops, mince patties and chicken legs, as well as a stack of those huge steaks we had been served at the Memorial Club on the evening of our arrival.

Was that really only three days ago? I wondered in amazement. It seemed ages ago; so much had happened! Coming from a country where one kilogram of minced meat and an occasional piece of beef had to last us for a whole week, I was stunned by all this luxury. By the time we left Pat and John, very late that Saturday night, I felt a lot more confident that there would be a future for us in Alice Springs too.

It was just as well that it was far too hot in the caravans to sleep in the following morning, as it was Sunday and we had planned to go to Mass at ten o'clock. During the last year we had started to skip going to church on Sundays but, because it always made me feel terribly guilty, I intended to go regularly again when we came to Australia.

Because it was late when we came home from Pat and John's place the previous evening, I had forgotten to wash the children's Sunday clothes they had worn to the barbeque, before I went to bed. The excuse that we should stay home because they didn't have anything good enough to wear, appealed to all of us. I was not prepared to skip Mass on our first Sunday in Alice Springs, but I had great difficulties getting the children dressed. We were all feeling very self-conscious in our second best, when we got out of our old-fashioned pink and grey station wagon and walked to the church.

It was quite cool inside the church, as a lovely breeze came through the wide open doors and windows. We were early and there weren't many people in the church, but it soon filled up to the last seat. Sitting at the back I slowly relaxed, happy to see so many large families filing into the pews in front of us. It became awfully noisy in the church. Everybody seemed to have taken their babies and toddlers with them, and some people behind us talked continuously during the entire Mass. I didn't understand much of what the priest was saying, but the familiar Latin of the Gregorian hymns made me feel at home.

The Catholic Church had changed drastically in Holland during the last years, but time had stood still in Australia, where the holy bread at communion was still put on your tongue instead of in your hand. Simone, who had just taken her first Communion before we left Holland, was horrified when she had had to poke her tongue out to the priest aboard the ship. Having to call a priest 'Father' somehow gave me cold shivers. I had very few memories of my own father and my stepfather, and our local priest had been anything but a loving father to me...

After the Mass ended, people stood talking in small groups at the back of the church, but because we didn't know anyone, we went straight back to the car. At home, the hot wind was blowing a gale again, sweeping up a ton of dust and sand as usual. In the afternoon Sam took us for a drive around the town in the old 'galah'. We all wanted to go up Anzac Hill again, to see what the town was like by day. Fred had not been game enough to drive up the steep road with the car's bald tyres, but Sam saw no problems with it. From the top of the rocky hill we could see the thick clouds of dust swirling above the bare area of the former airport, while in town the sky was perfectly clear.

Sam pointed out the hospital, hotels, schools, police station and other major buildings in town. Apart from the hospital and the hotels, most of them had been recently built. During the ten years that Sam had lived in Alice Springs, the town's population had grown from about three thousand people to eleven and a half thousand.

I held my breath when Sam drove down the steep hill with the nine of us in the old station wagon, worried sick that another car would drive up, as there would be no way we could pass each other on the narrow road. Sam laughed about it, saying that that was nothing compared to places he came across on the way to some of the Aboriginal settlements.

He drove on to the Old Telegraph Station, the town's favourite picnic place, which in those days seemed miles out of town. The children had a wonderful time playing at the edge of the waterhole, fed by springs from an underground reservoir. We strolled between the empty buildings, built in 1871-1872, when the first telegraph wire had been erected between Adelaide and Darwin. Reading the names and dates on the headstones in the overgrown graveyard made me realise what a hard time those early settlers must have had. Later, while we sat in the cool grass near the waterhole, Sam told us a little more about the early history of Alice Springs.

The original settlement, now an impressive museum, was named after the wife of Sir Charles Todd, the Director of Posts & Telegraph in South Australia. He was in charge of building the Overland Telegraph around 1870-1872. The nearby Emily and Jessie Gaps, are named after his daughters. Because the waterhole was surrounded by millions of boulders and rocky hills, a second township was built three kilometres south of the springs around the turn of the century. The town was called Stuart from 1888 until 1932, when the Post Office was moved into Parsons Street.

Back in town, we were amazed to see that the grocery shops were all open on Sundays, as well as all day on Saturday. Sam treated all of us to an ice-cream at Hoppy's store on the way back into town. By the time we got home at five o'clock, the dust had settled again for the day. With Fred's help, I set about the daily routine of sweeping away the red dirt before I could cook a meal again in the sweltering aluminium caravan. It was late when we went to bed, hoping the temperature would drop so that we could have another good night's sleep…

Getting Established

At seven thirty on Monday morning, the children went happily off to school on the bus with the Harvey's, who lived in the street behind us. They were the scruffiest bunch of kids I had ever seen. All sorts of household items and toys lay half buried in the sand around their yard. There were more clothes lying in the dust beneath their clothesline, than hung on it. Eugene and Raymond had been to their house after school the previous Friday afternoon.

"You should see their house Mama!" Eugene had said when they came back. "Their bedroom has lots of old mattresses on the floor where the kids can play, and they sleep with their clothes on. They have no sheets, only some old blankets."

"Your friend's family in Holland was like that," I reminded him.

The parents of those friends were both child psychologists, bringing their ten children up with lots of freedom, believing that children should have as few restrictions as possible. Only time would tell what was best...

Regine cried bitterly when the others left for school. She had been to preschool for two weeks before we left Holland, and had loved it. I promised to take her in the afternoon to the brand new preschool a few streets away to see when she could start. Fred dropped us off on his way to town to get his driver's licence changed, calling in at the railway shed to see if our luggage was expected on the next train that was coming in at the end of the week.

Before we left, Fred asked Sam what he should do about membership with the Workers' Union. The emigration officer in Holland had told him that it was necessary to become a member as soon as possible.

"Like John and Nick told you, the union is a dirty word here," Sam said. "They are regarded as communists, preventing a man from doing an honest day's work, lining their own pockets and only pestering the bosses."

When Fred asked the men at the barbecue on Saturday night, they told him in no uncertain terms, not to bother with any union. Their motives were nothing like they were in Holland, they assured us.

"Don't bother to mention the union to Heinz," John had warned Fred. "He would not give you a job even if he was desperate." Fred decided to let it rest. At the preschool, I was told that there was a long waiting list. Regine had to wait till her fifth birthday, more than six months away. There was little chance of a vacancy becoming available earlier, the teacher said. Regine cried all the way home, but she forgot about it when I put her bathers on, telling her that she could be my 'washing machine'. A little later she danced happily on the dirty clothes in the old baby bath, cool suds flying in all directions.

With the washing dry and in the cupboard, and Regine asleep on Sam's bed, I went to Stephanie's house in the afternoon to make Simone's school uniform. Those uniforms were an absolute blessing. We should have had them in Holland, too. No arguments about what to wear, or crying because other kids had better clothes than they had; I loved it.

Stephanie said that there was no need for me to have a key to get in; she would just leave the front door open when she went to work in the morning. I felt very uncomfortable walking into the neighbours' house while nobody was there, especially going into the master bedroom where the sewing machine was set up. I had not even met the man of the house!

The front door, the only outside door in the house that I could see, opened directly into the family room. A black vinyl lounge suite, and a round table with four simple wooden chairs, stood on the bare vinyl covered floor. Short, floral curtains covered the two tiny windows at the front of the house. An open kitchen, with a small room at the back that had a built-in broom cupboard and a washing machine, joined onto the family room, and an open passage led to the bedrooms and a small bathroom at the back of the house. The main bedroom, which had a small window on either side, was quite large. The sewing machine stood on a long bench beside a double bed. On the left, underneath one of the windows was a chest of drawers. There were two other, very small bedrooms in the house. The whole place, including the cupboards, was painted cream and only one or two pictures were hanging in each room.

With the small windows and bare walls, the house looked like a shed to me; a vast difference from the cosy homes in Holland which always had an entrance hall, a toilet usually next to the front door, and carpeted rooms filled to the brim with furniture, pictures and all sorts of ornamental things. Most houses in Holland had very large windows, which were left open, even at night, by most families. I am not sure if that was to show that the house was kept neat and tidy at all times, or just to show off. Stephanie and her husband had moved in only a few weeks before, which perhaps was the reason their house was so bare, I thought. They only had one child, a seven-year-old boy.

It was as hot and stuffy in the house as it was in Sam's shed, but the tiled floor was lovely and cool to walk on after I kicked off my shoes. Not many Commission homes had an air-conditioner, and like in Sam's shed, the windows had to stay closed to keep the dust out. The little fan, standing on the bench beside me, gave little comfort. It was very still in the house. The only sounds came from the wind blowing up tons of dust again, and a skinny Siamese cat, meowing around my feet. I normally liked cats but for some reason I was not keen on Siamese; I never trusted them. The cat probably felt my resentment. It hissed angrily and scratched my hand when I wanted to pet it. The cat's endless cries, echoing off the bare walls, gave the house a sinister feeling, which soon started to get on my nerves. I had already drawn up the pattern and cut Simone's dress out the previous afternoon, and decided to stitch it together as quickly as I could.

While I sat behind the machine, facing a blank wall, I kept an eye on the cat, feeling that it was stalking me. I felt relieved when, after a while, it went to sleep, but my peace of mind did not last long. Ten minutes later the cat was awake and meowing again. I relaxed when it sat down quietly on the pelmet above the window across from the bed, about four metres away from me. I was concentrating on the last seams of the dress when the rotten cat suddenly and silently jumped from the pelmet straight onto the back of my neck, digging its sharp claws deep into my skin.

For a moment I felt that my heart had stopped beating. I chased the cat out of the room, quickly closing the door. Leaning against it, I waited for my heart to beat normally again, then quickly gathered my belongings. I would finish the dress at home by hand and never come back again!

When the children came home on the school bus, they told me enthusiastically about their second day at school. Being the new kids who didn't speak English, they were the centres of attention in their classes. While I fitted Simone's dress, I told them what had happened at Stephanie's place that afternoon. The girls did not think it funny, but Sam and the boys killed themselves with laughter. Fred, who did not like cats at all, did not seem to think that it was a laughing matter either; "You could have had a heart attack," he said.

"I thought I had," I laughed.

Fred showed the kids his new Australian driver's licence. It was only a bit of paper, a far cry from the elaborate Dutch licence with a stamped passport photo in a plastic, triple folded wallet. When Fred bought the car the previous Saturday, he had been reluctant to drive it without an Australian licence, but Sam had laughed about his concern. Sam's friend, who had sold him the car said, "No worries mate. You've got a licence, haven't you?"

At the motor registration office Fred had to fill in a form with a few questions about the road rules and regulations, pay a dollar and got his licence for three years; as simple as that! There had not been any paperwork about our belongings at the railway office.

"No paperwork, no goods," the attendant had said. "Come back in a few days mate."

Fred could not wait to help Sam to get the house finished, but Sam did not feel like starting at all. He had worked 'bloody hard' before we came, and he preferred to work on his own anyway, he said.

"Let's make a vegie patch; grow our own stuff," he said enthusiastically that afternoon. "I'll finish the house when you get your tools and you can work at Heinz's place."

Sam had already planted a variety of fruit trees: a mulberry, a lemon and two each of oranges, mandarins and grapefruit. Together with the boys, they pegged out an area for the vegetables along the low wire fence at the back of the house. The ground was rock-hard. It needed soaking with a hose for quite a while before they could get a spade in and turn the soil. In the meantime, Sam emptied the back of the ute, and went off with the boys to get some 'decent soil'. They came back with a load of the reddest sand we had ever seen. Then they got several loads of cow manure at the abattoirs.

"We've got to soak it first," Sam said. They rolled a couple of forty-four gallon drums close to the prepared garden and Fred filled them with manure and water. It stank to the high heavens when the muck was spread over the loose soil. "It's *ackcely* much better to let it rot for a couple of weeks," Sam said. "The stench will be far worse then," he laughed.

Sam and Fred worked through the heat of the following day, stopping briefly to drink the warm water from the hose or to wipe the dust that stuck to their sweating faces away with a handkerchief. During the following two days they planted carrots, beans, peas, radishes, onions, silver beet and goodness knows what else, filling the trenches around each patch with water, two or three times a day. By Saturday, there were already lots of green bits showing, to the delight of the children. With Sam's help they had pegged out a garden of their own, separate patches of about eighty centimetre round mounds with a ditch around them to grow cucumbers, rockmelons and watermelons, leaving plenty of space between the patches for the vines to spread.

During the following week, Fred went with Sam to the building suppliers around town each day, preparing for work on the house the following morning, but when morning came, Sam decided to take another day off. He never bothered what day of the week it was, he said, whenever he needed a break he took a day or more off, but he usually kept working until the project he was doing was finished. Fred pleaded with him to let him help while he was waiting for his tools.

"*Ackcely*, you can give me a hand sorting out the bricks next Saturday," Sam promised when he finally agreed.

Sam had used single, twenty centimetre wide bricks, made of cement for the foundation. They were forty centimetres long and ten centimetres high with two holes in the centre. The rest of the house had two, ten centimetre wide walls with a bit of space in between them, just as they did in Holland. Because Sam did not want to plaster or paint any of the walls, the bricks were made with white sand and had to be perfect on all sides. He had ordered them especially from Adelaide. One by one, they were carefully inspected for any faults or damage and divided into several piles: missing right hand corners, left hand corners, two corners or more, scratched and discoloured ones.

The happy sound of the cement mixer woke us up very early on Sunday morning. We were all up and dressed in no time at all to see what Sam was doing. We had breakfast very early that day.

"No wonder Sam could not get the house ready before we came," Fred said, when he came in for a cold drink from the old fridge an hour later. "You should see how he works!"

I had forgotten how fussy Sam always was, taking after my father who was regarded as the fussiest farmer in the whole of Holland.

The children all wanted to stay home from church to watch Uncle Sam laying bricks, but I insisted that they all come to church with us first.

"We have been three times already this week," Raymond and Eugene complained loudly, but I did not want to listen to them.

That week, Fred and I had been to the presbytery, to give the parish priest the stack of papers our local priest in Holland had prepared for him, but, as they were all in Dutch, he did not know what to do with them. He told us to 'hang on' to them, wrote our names down in a book and said he expected to see us at Mass on Sunday. I could not believe the casual way he treated us. We were out of the door within a few minutes. We did not know then that he had only been in Alice Springs a couple of weeks himself, and thought that we had been in town a long time before we came to see him.

After Mass, we called in at Henk Guth's gallery to bring him regards from his brother Jurrian and his wife Cor, who had shown us the slides of their trip to the centre of Australia, before we left Holland.

The famous artist's colourful paintings on every wall overwhelmed me. I think it was the light in them that caught my eye. The daylight in Australia is so vivid and sharp, so completely different from the skies we were used to. Even when the sun is shining on a cloudless day, the sky in Holland is still grey in comparison.

"Please call me Lynne," Mrs. Guth said iñ Dutch, when we introduced ourselves. "People don't bother much with such formalities here." She went on to say that Henk was not home.

"He is on holiday in England," she said while she showed us around the gallery. "I never know when he will be back when he goes away. He had pains in his chest. He went to a specialist in Adelaide, who advised him to take a holiday."

Apart from Henk's oil paintings, there was also a large collection of watercolours, painted by local Aborigines. Lynne told us a bit about the many Aboriginal artefacts on display. Many were sacred, she said, given to them for safekeeping. Then she showed us their enormous collection of coins and paper money from countries all over the world. Glad to be able to speak Dutch again, we stayed for coffee and talked for a long time.

"Did you say that you are a cabinet maker?" Lynne asked Fred when we were about to leave.

"Sort of," Fred replied. "For the last six years I made small furniture in a factory. I'm waiting for my tools to come in on the train so that I can start working here."

Fred was delighted when Lynne asked if he could make a couple of frames for her. Henk had produced a lot of paintings before he left, but she had run out of frames. We could not believe our eyes when we saw the huge number of paintings waiting to be framed, in a room at the back of the gallery.

"Oh, yes! Henk paints lots." Lynne said proudly when she saw the stunned look on Fred's face. "There are times when he paints thirty a day when he is in the right mood."

"Thirty a week?" Fred asked astonished.

"No! Thirty a day!" Lynne replied, obviously enjoying Fred's reaction. "Well, little ones, of course!" she laughed. She told us how Henk painted an eight by ten-inch (twenty by thirty centimetre) painting, in the gallery, while a busload of tourists watched to the end. The whole procedure took about twenty minutes, and at the end of the session, the painting was raffled among the visitors, who had each been given a ticket on arrival.

"After the demonstration, the tourists often buy every single painting we have on the wall," Lynne said. "Because the bus drivers are paid a handsome commission, they are eager to book ahead for their next visit to Alice Springs." For a long time, Henk also made his own frames but he could not keep up with the demand for his paintings and the picture framer they'd employed had left town. Before we left the gallery, arrangements were made for Fred to make some frames for Lynne the following Tuesday.

"No wonder Henk had heart trouble," we said to each other in the car on the way home. "Who would be able to keep up a tempo like that?"

Our children had taken to life in the centre like ducks to water, but Fred and I worried, as nearly two weeks had passed and our luggage had still not arrived. The early mornings were beautiful, but they never lasted long with temperatures soaring to forty degrees each day. The wind was often stormy, still blowing up big clouds of dust every day, from about nine in the morning until four in the afternoon. I later learned that they were known as 'October winds'. The developers had not left a blade of grass or a single tree when they cleared the old airport site for building. Stephanie and another lady, who lived in the street behind us, came around with a petition, lobbying the Town Council to plant trees along the roads and grass in the areas set aside for parks. Sam translated it all to me, as I understood little of what the ladies were talking about.

"How can they allow this to happen?" Stephanie asked in an article in the

Centralian Advocate that week. "When you think there are penalties for collecting wood out bush because of fear of erosion, this denuding of whole areas close to town should be considered a real crime."

Apart from Regine, the children all left early in the morning for school, and did not return until three thirty in the afternoon. Because of the dust, I stayed in the shed all day, bored to tears. Despite the big fan, standing beside Sam's bed going at its highest speed, I was sweating and felt dirty all the time. I was sick to death of having to clean the caravans each night before the kids could go to bed, and cooking a meal for the nine of us each day in the stinking hot caravan was no pleasure either. I still spent most of my time writing letters to family and friends but as it was hard to find anything nice to say, I did not enjoy it at all. I missed the English lessons I had packed in one of the other suitcases, thinking that we would have them back within a week.

Fred was getting more frustrated by the day, too. Talking to Sam about accepting his help to get the house ready quicker, was just impossible. Sam was used to working on his own. He simply refused to be hurried. After Fred had made the first lot of frames for her, Lynne Guth had asked him to come back in a few days time. He was looking forward to going back to the gallery, but he also hoped that his tools would arrive, so that he could start at Heinz's factory, even though the hazardous machinery scared him to death. Nothing had adequate safety standards, and it worried him that he had no experience with cabinet making, building to customer's specifications. The only real cabinetwork Fred had done was fitting out a chemist's shop, several years ago. He was only a hobbyist, not a tradesman at all.

Sometimes I walked with Regine to the new corner store in the morning, a ten minute walk away from Sam's place, but groceries were even more expensive there than in town, and too heavy to carry home in the heat. Because I saw our money disappearing like snow in the sun, and there was no way of knowing how long Fred would be out of work, I worried about the amount of food we needed. Raymond and Eugene could eat just about a whole loaf of bread each per day, but I limited them to four slices per meal. I peeled the potatoes as thinly as I could so that not a scrap was wasted. Because the lettuces were so harsh and bitter, I cooked the outside leaves like endive, covered with white sauce and nutmeg. Funny how our tastes can change, I looked forward to eating the nice soft lettuces when we went back to Holland six years later, but I found that they had absolutely no taste at all.

Fortunately, Sam occasionally brought a big bag of groceries home, as he was used to a big dinner. It was a great relief when, after a few weeks of eating with us every day, he missed his friends and often went to town for his evening meal.

On the last Saturday of October, two weeks after our arrival, Sam took us to the yearly fete at the Youth Centre. A ride on a camel was the highlight of the day for our children. My thirty second birthday a few days later was a far cry from the normal celebrations. Instead of a house full of relatives in the evening, we were on our own. I missed my family terribly that day. There were not even any letters from home to mark the occasion. Because Fred's birthday was three weeks later, our families wrote to both of us in the same letter, somewhere in between the two dates. Sam's birthday is on the third of November. 'Wait until you're my age!' he always says during the four days that we are the same age.

On Friday afternoon, the day after Sam's birthday, I was writing a letter when Fred called me to have a look outside. It was strangely still as there wasn't any wind for a change. The sky was perfectly blue, apart from an enormous dark cloud coming over the hills from the south. While we watched, it formed a huge, pitch-black roll, covering the full width of the sky. A truly spectacular sight!

"We'd better tie down as much as we can," Sam warned. "This can get very nasty." We were only inside a few seconds when all hell broke loose. It got dark almost instantly, as tons of red sand blasted the windows with such force that I was afraid they would shatter any minute. I held my breath when small rocks and other missiles pelted the little window, which normally looked out over Heavitree Gap, the entrance to the town from the south. The light went out as the power failed. It became unbearably hot in the shed. I panicked when I suddenly realised that it was just after three o'clock and our children were on their way home in the school bus. The deafening noise of sand and debris on the iron roof made it impossible to hear each other. I yelled at the top of my voice that the kids were in danger, well aware that there was absolutely nothing we could do about it. After fifteen minutes, or so it seemed, the racket died down a little.

"I'm going to the bus stop to see if the kids are coming," Sam said. He protested when Fred insisted on coming with him. "You'd better stay here, the storm is not over yet," he warned.

My heart was beating in my throat while I waited for Sam to return. As he predicted, the storm came back in full force the minute he came back inside, the door nearly flew off the hinges. There had been no sign of the children; he could not see more than a metre in front of him, he said.

The storm suddenly subsided and it started to rain; the biggest drops I had ever seen! Within seconds they had turned into a frightening downpour, the deafening sound of which reminded me of midnight on new year's eve in Holland, when millions of crackers are set off at the same time.

It was still raining heavily when the children came home, soaked and white from fear, but excited about the adventure. The school bus had stopped on the road close to home when the storm had started. Apart from being hit by rubbish bins and other items flying around, they had been quite safe in the bus. My blood curdled when I realised what could have happened to Sam while he was looking for the children. A freestanding wall he had built that morning had collapsed only seconds after he had briefly sheltered beside it, before he could make the dash back to the shed.

The mess after the storm was incredible. The local paper described it as the worst dust storm in three years, with wind gusts of up to fifty six knots, ninety six kilometres, an hour. Our street had turned into a river. Dunes of sand were left behind, and deep ruts had washed into the ground everywhere. Our vegetable patch was washed away. The area where we lived had been the hardest hit. Across the road, a couple of half-finished Commission homes, wooden structures built in with small bricks, had collapsed and lay flat on the ground. A neighbour's roof had lifted off and landed on top of the house next door and every iron fence and shed in the area had toppled over or vanished. Because the rain had been short and savage, it had washed the top layer of soil onto the roads and gave us no relief from the drought. Within days it was dry and dusty again, but the temperature had dropped considerably and made the weather very pleasant.

"There may still be water in Sixteen-Mile-Creek," Sam said the following Sunday morning. "Let's go there."

Taking a stack of sandwiches with us, we left soon after returning from church. Following Sam in his ute on the road heading north, I held my breath when the narrow, single road went steeply down to cross the Charles River, worried sick that a road train would suddenly come around the corner. Sam had taken us to see those enormous trucks; cattle trucks at the abattoirs, tankers at the Shell depot and freight carriers at the trucking yard and the railway; up to three or four huge trailers behind a big rig with some sixty wheels. The cattle trucks were mostly double deckers, which looked as if they could tip over easily when they went around a corner. Sam said that it made no difference that it was Sunday; they were always on the road, day and night.

About ten kilometres north of town, we stopped on a long flat stretch of road, at a five or six metre high circular monument, built with small clay bricks. It marked the highest point on the Stuart Highway, two thousand four hundred feet, about eight hundred metres above sea level. Alice Springs itself was three hundred and thirty six metres above the sea. While I stood there on the side of that endless, straight road, I suddenly felt that I had seen myself there before, in a dream many years ago, exactly like that!

Sixteen miles north of Alice we turned left into the 'bush', following the sandy track beside the dry creek. After a while, we came to a lovely spot in the creek filled with beautiful, clear water. The kids jumped out of the tray of the ute straight onto a nest of inch long bull ants!

"Get in the water! Drown the ants... Quickly!" Sam shouted to them while Fred and I yelled to be careful, as the waterhole could be very deep.

For a while we all frolicked in the cool water in our under pants, as it was hot and I had left our bathers in the suitcases in Melbourne. We enjoyed the day so much that we decided to go again the following week on our own, as Sam did not want to take more time off. Before we set out after Mass the next Sunday, Fred carefully checked the water, the tyres and the fuel as he had always done before we made the sixty kilometre trip from Oosterbeek to my mother's place in Hooglanderveen. In the meantime, I packed a picnic lunch, towels and a drink for everyone. We were halfway down the dirt track when the old galah started to sputter and steam as the motor overheated. With a shock we realised that we had forgotten the extra water Sam had told us to take.

"Just in case," he had warned...

Closer to the waterhole the car started to boil. Realising how far away from home we were, Fred panicked. He stopped the car, opened the bonnet, grabbed an old cloth and screwed the cap off the radiator... A fountain of boiling hot water squirted high up, barely missing Fred who had jumped back quickly. He scolded me and the kids for forgetting the jerry can with water he had filled earlier, and himself for being so impatient. He knew that he should have given the water time to cool down. Now there was only a little left in the radiator. I felt terribly guilty for putting my family in danger by wanting to go to the waterhole in the first place. The thought that Sam would not worry about us until dark and we might have to spend the night in the bush frightened me.

"Soup is never eaten as hot as it is served," I reminded myself, when I felt a terrible sense of isolation coming up. I tried not to show my fear to the other children while Fred and the two oldest boys were getting water from the waterhole. It seemed hours before they got back. The waterhole had been a lot further than we expected and the water had just about dried up, but fortunately, they had enough to get us back home.

We did not speak much while we drove slowly home, keeping our fingers crossed that we would make it. Sam laughed when we got home late in the evening and told him what had happened.

"Well, you've learned your first lesson in bush driving," he chuckled.

Practising Patience

"It would *ackcely* be good if I made the sink in the carport first," Sam said while we were drinking coffee one morning. He had been building straight walls for three weeks and he wouldn't mind doing something else for a change, he said. Since the day we arrived I wished that there would be a basin in the carport. As it was, we had to do the dishes in the tiny hand basin in the bathroom, in a bucket outside, or on the table in the simmering hot shed. But I had not wanted to ask him, as I would much rather he finished the house first.

During the next hours Sam drew up a picture of an elaborate kitchen sink, one metre twenty long with an archway underneath for some buckets and a garden hose. The connection for hot and cold water was already in the wall, as he planned one day to have a kitchen in the shed, which would turn it into a 'granny-flat'. After lunch he went to town and came back with a trough big enough to bath Regine and to do the washing in. He spent the rest of the day, until late at night, working out how to go about it. Next day, he changed his mind about the design and drew up a proper plan. Another day went by before he had cut the form of the archway out of a piece of plywood and drawn the bricks in place. The bricks were then cut to size, one by one, to fit the curve perfectly. By the end of the week, there was little to show for all the hours Sam had worked on it.

I was stunned. How on earth could he work so calmly on this project of love while we were desperate to get out of the caravans and live a normal life? Fred was fuming. The previous week, he had made the cement and put the bricks ready for Sam, making good progress with the house; now he could do nothing to help, which drove him up the wall.

In the second week after our arrival, realising that we had no hope of buying or even renting Sam's house as we had originally planned, we had put our name on the Housing Commission's list. The lady at the counter told us that there was no hope that we would get a house for at least a year, probably eighteen months. Because Sam had signed a paper saying that he would supply accommodation for us for twelve months, we were as much stuck with him as he was with us. If only Fred had his tools and could earn a living! We had already been in Alice Springs more than a month and our luggage had still not arrived. Apart from the few frames Fred was making for Mrs. Guth, we had no income. As our money was disappearing fast, we were getting quite desperate. Sam was disappointed that we were unable to contribute to the cost of building the house. He was running out of money too. We could not expect him to pay Fred for helping him either. When he finally finished the elaborate sink three weeks later, he had to go out bush for two weeks to earn some money.

During those weeks, Fred became more and more depressed. He had kept himself occupied by making a lawn in the back yard, but he became very quiet and withdrawn. One evening, a few days after Sam left, he lay on top of our bed, crying his heart out like a child in distress. He would have been prepared to crawl back to Holland on his knees if that had been at all possible, just as I had on the second day after our arrival. It broke my heart to see him sobbing like that. I felt paralysed. At that time I still believed that it was me who had pushed for immigration. Filled to the brim with guilt, I sat down on the bed beside him, put my arms around him and cried with him…

The following morning the sun was shining brightly as usual. Fred stayed in bed until it was too hot to stay in the caravan. After a long shower and a cup of coffee, while we talked about our future, he felt much better. I reminded him that there were families with nine and ten young children in church, ordinary people like us, who looked healthy and happy, and they each had two cars. It couldn't be much longer until our luggage arrived and he could work. When I had my sewing machine, I would sew for other people, even if I had to do it in the stinking hot shed.

The windows for the house, most of them floor-to-ceiling, had been delivered just after the big dust storm. Sam was afraid that the sand and debris that was still blowing around every day would damage them, so they had to be put in the shed. There was hardly any space left for us to sit, even though some of the windows had been installed and, when Sam came back from Papunya the following week, the rest would go too.

Fred was making picture frames in the shed behind Gallery Guth that afternoon, when a short gentleman with longish, thinning hair came in.

"And who are you?" he asked, seemingly surprised to see Fred there.

"Lynne asked me to make some frames for her," Fred answered. "You must be Henk." After introducing himself, Henk told him that he could make as many frames as he liked during the following week as there were still a lot of buses expected to come in before Christmas and he could always leave them for next season, if he couldn't fill them now.

When Fred went to the railway later that same afternoon, the paperwork for our luggage was in. The clerk told him that we could expect the three large suitcases which had been put on the train in Melbourne, as well as the two crates we had watched being loaded onto a truck in Holland many moons ago, on the next train. Life was looking up! I was now glad that the remainder of the windows and the door frames of the house were inside the shed so that the crates could be put in the carport, since most of our furniture had to be stored in them until we could get into the house.

We were shopping at Woolworths one Sunday after church, when Lilian, our eldest daughter, wanted to know why I always complained that everything was so expensive.

"A loaf of bread is only eighteen cents and in Holland you had to pay one guilder", she said.

"Everything looks cheap if you look at the price on the shelf," I agreed. I explained that we had to multiply the price by four because we had to pay four guilders and five cents for one dollar, then compare it to the wages Fred could earn when his tools came in. Unless he worked a lot of overtime, we would be very poor.

Shortly after we arrived, there was an uproar in the local paper because the prices of meat and bread had gone up. I could not understand for the life of me why people made such a fuss over a few cents extra on the price of meat, which was less than half of what we had to pay for it in Holland. A loaf of bread was a little cheaper too. People were furious about a one-cent rise while almost everything else in the shops cost two or three times as much! Vegetables were even worse! It wasn't until many years later when we drove down the dirt road to Adelaide, where most of the supplies came from, that we realised the high cost of transporting goods to the Centre.

Fred and I were discussing what kind of vinegar we should buy when a voice behind us said: "You won't find any *azijn* like you're used to here."

Surprised to hear our own language, I turned around as if I had been stung. The woman behind us was short and quite solid, with untidy dark hair and a front tooth missing. While she pointed to a bottle with a leaf of tarragon in it - the closest in taste and four times the price - I noticed two buttons missing off her dress, revealing much of her unrestrained breasts. She invited me to come to her place to see the Dutch 'goodies' she sold from home.

Ann lived only a few streets away from us in a big half-finished house; one of the few houses in town that had a tiled roof. Ann's husband, a tall, skinny man, was a tiler. He was working on a wall in the kitchen when I came in. We had already noticed that tradesmen like plumbers, builders, bricklayers, painters and electricians, owned the best houses around town. Boxes and containers with groceries and other Dutch merchandise were stacked everywhere in the house, barely leaving room to walk. They had moved in nearly two months ago, and were still waiting for the shed they had ordered from Adelaide, Ann explained. I could not believe my eyes when she took me into a room full to the brim with very expensive Dutch goods; there were windmills, clocks and clogs and all sorts of other souvenirs as well as a great variety of foods in tins, jars and packets. When I commented that there were very few Dutch people in town, Ann assured me that other people bought these things as well. Feeling very uncomfortable, I carefully selected a few treats for the kids we could ill afford. Ann noticed my agony. "Don't worry," she said. "We started like that too."

Before we left she gave Regine a little doll in Dutch costume and me a big box of *speculaas*. Before the war, those delicious spiced cookies were only made for Sinterklaas in December, but were now eaten all year round.

It was mid-November when Sam came back from Papunya. Although the wind was not as strong as it had been, the temperature stayed around forty degrees every day. We still burned our fingers if we forgot to take a cloth to open the door of one of the aluminium caravans during the day. The Aboriginals at Papunya had warned Sam that big rain was coming soon. "They always know", he said. Thick clouds had gathered in the sky for several days when it finally pelted down on Thursday afternoon. Such joy to be dancing in the rain with the kids! It kept raining, heavily at times, throughout the night and all day on Friday, a welcome change from the oppressive heat.

"They said on the radio that the Todd is coming down," Sam said late in the afternoon. "Let's go and have a look."

We all piled into the two cars for a drive along the normally dry riverbed. Hundreds of people apparently had the same idea, but the river was still as dry as a bone; the water was not expected till late that night. When we got up on Saturday morning, Sam said that it had come down at eleven the previous evening. Leaving Fred in bed, I went with him and the kids to have a look. Even at that early hour, there were lots of people around, but there was only a brown, muddy trickle coming down like it had done after the big dust storm two weeks earlier. I could not see what all the fuss was about.

That week, we eagerly looked forward to seeing our belongings again, but nothing happened. The train was delayed due to heavy rain down south that had caused several washouts along the railway track, and our cases would not be in until Tuesday. When the train finally arrived on Wednesday afternoon, our goods were still not there.

"They probably ran out of space," we were told at the railway office the following Saturday. "Your things may be on next week's train."

In the meantime, Fred had taken me out on the new roads around Sam's place, teaching me how to drive our car so that I wouldn't be stuck in the house all day. After several lessons, which gave Fred near heart attacks, I still did not understand the basics. I refused to go with him again, crying that I'd rather do without a licence than be scolded all the time. I felt stupid and angry with myself, vowing that one day, when we had enough money, I would have a proper instructor and show Fred that I was not as silly as he said I was.

The crates and suitcases finally arrived on Friday afternoon, in the beginning of December, more than seven weeks after our arrival. With great excitement and anxiety, I watched the crates being lifted from the delivery truck. I held my breath while the crates were swung by the crane, apprehensive that they would be dropped before the young driver could get them into the carport. It had been so long since we had packed them that it seemed all our Christmases (Sinterklazen) had come at once. Everything was there and our fears that it might be wet and mouldy proved unfounded.

Before we had left Holland, we'd bought red folding beds for each of the children to make sure that they at least had a bed to sleep on in Australia. After checking the crates, we wanted put the beds back in, but the children begged us to let them sleep outside on them. They all said that they could not bear the slippery beds in the stinking hot caravans for a single night longer. We set all six of the beds up on the lawn beside the carport. We all went to bed very late that night, as the kids were having a ball. They only slept outside a few nights. As soon as the walls of the two bedrooms at the back of the house were finished we put the beds in there. Raymond, Eugene and Richard shared one of the roofless rooms, Simone and Regine shared the other while Lilian made the spacious bathroom in between, into a cosy little room. For the first time in her life she had a room to herself.

"With the millions of stars above me, it felt as if I was sleeping in heaven," she said the next morning.

Early a few days later an unexpected visitor called in.

"Hey, Sammy! How come you've been hiding from me so long?" a lady shouted to Sam, who was laying bricks at the front of the house. "Didn't you want me to meet your sister?"

"Ai, Willy!" Sam laughed, "I wondered how long you could stay away from me."

"I'd expected you to bring the kids around for an ice cream," Willy replied. She was the manager of Grandad's Ice cream Parlour in town, Sam said, when he introduced me to her. Willy was a little younger than I was, with a difficult French sounding surname. She was born in Holland and came to Australia when she was nine years old. With her long, curly black hair, she looked French or Italian rather then Dutch to me, but she could speak our language quite well. She spoke with a high-pitched voice and laughed a lot. I liked her instantly.

After having to make myself understood in English for weeks, I was glad to speak Dutch again. Talking non-stop, I showed Willy how we lived. Although it was only eight o'clock, it was already very hot in the shed. The sewing machine stood on the table where I was making curtains for the front window of the shed. The big fan, standing in the corner beside Sam's bed, roaring on its highest speed, made little difference to the stuffy atmosphere.

"How can you bear to sit in here all day?" Willy exclaimed sympathetically. "Why don't you come to my place while the kids are at school?" She laughed heartily when I told her about my sewing session with the Siamese cat at Stephany's place.

"I don't have any animals to bother you and my husband is out bush," she laughed, adding that I could do some sewing for her if I wanted to earn some money. Thrilled to bits with the prospect of getting out of the hot shed as well as earning some money, we arranged that Willy would pick me up before she went to work the following morning. She was there at eight; dressed in a sparkling white uniform with bright red buttons, matching red earrings and not a hair out of place. When she stepped out of the small truck she was driving, the high heels of her red shoes sank deep into the loose sand of Sam's driveway.

Willy's house was in the middle of town. It was a large old house with a big verandah at the back as well as the front, hidden from the road by fully-grown shrubs and trees. The house was full of furniture and knick-knacks. The many Dutch ornaments scattered around the place made me feel quite at home. The air-conditioning made a lot of noise, but it kept the place lovely and cool. Before she hurried off to work, Willy showed me briefly where I could find the sewing gear and where I could make myself a cup of coffee. As soon as I had finished the curtains for Sam's shed, I happily set out earning my first couple of dollars by doing some mending for Willy. A week later, when she picked me up again, she informed me that Graham had come home from the bush and was working in town.

"He'll probably come in to take a shower now and again," she said. "He likes his showers when it's so hot."

Here I was again, alone in some stranger's place without having met the man of the house, and this one was coming home to take a shower!

At about ten-thirty it started to rain and, within minutes, sheets of water were coming down, making an incredible racket on the corrugated iron roof of the old house. Suddenly, a male voice shouted at me. I froze instantly. When I dared to look up, I stared with open mouth into the face of Elvis Presley.

Graham was a slim fellow, nearly two metres tall with long sideburns and dark hair, greased and combed in the style of the famous movie star. He wore a sparkling white singlet that showed his arms, which were covered in tattoos. His neatly pressed jeans fitted tightly around his hips and he wore very pointed, high-heeled boots. For a moment I thought that I was dreaming, but his voice soon brought me down to earth.

"Come on! The river is down!" he shouted above the noise of the pouring rain. "Hop in the car. I'll take you there."

Graham grabbed an umbrella and gave it to me, but I was still completely drenched before I climbed beside him into the high ute, parked at the front of the old house in Bath Street.

It was only a short drive to the river, but because the drains could not cope with the incredible volume of water that was coming down, some streets were flooded and we had to make several detours. A lot of people were driving in the direction of the causeway, a concrete road through the normally dry riverbed. When the Todd came down, the only way to the other side of the river was the narrow footbridge that ran beside the causeway and it was closed, as the water was too high for safety. Nobody seemed to take any notice of the rain. Some people were taking pictures without bothering to open their umbrella to protect their camera.

The view of the roaring, wild, swirling, muddy water was truly spectacular. It was unbelievable how a normally dry riverbed could turn into such a dangerous torrent of water within hours, minutes I was told. Sam had once seen a six-foot high wall of water coming down when it had not even rained in town. It only has to rain a lot in the catchment area, a hilly area of about a hundred square kilometres north of Alice, for the Todd to run. This time it was a 'banker' as it filled the entire width of the riverbed and spilled over the edges.

I watched in amazement as a high school student was being rescued from a tree, a few metres away from the edge of the wild river. His rescuers had backed a truck into the water and thrown ropes onto a thick branch of the big, old gum tree. There were a lot of photographs of the rescue in the Centralian Advocate a few days later. The young fellow had apparently been in the water for ages. Before the truck had arrived on the scene, volunteers had been in great danger themselves, trying to get him out in the pouring rain. The truck had sunk deep into the riverbed and had to be pulled out by a bulldozer when the water subsided.

In another incident that day, an elderly couple had lost their lives when their car had been swept away whilst they had tried to cross the river.

When we arrived in Alice Springs, the headlines in the paper talked about the farmer's fear of another drought. There had been no decent rain since 1968 and this was the third time the river had flowed in six weeks. It seemed that we had brought the rain with us. Weather patterns had apparently been broken in Holland too. Until we left it had been a dreadful wet summer. Letters now told us that the sun had been shining there from the day we left...

As we walked away from the rescue on the river's edge, the rain suddenly stopped. When the sun came through, thick clouds of steam came from the bitumen road; another sight I had never seen before. When we came back to the house, Graham handed me a towel and Willy's dressing gown and disappeared into the shower himself. When he came out a little while later he was carefully groomed again wearing another sparkling white singlet and freshly pressed jeans with sharp creases. I found it hard to believe that he was a house painter. The singlet he had taken off had no paint on it at all, only a few marks on his jeans had shown a little colour.

Graham spoke fast with a husky voice and a broad, Queensland accent. I found it very hard to understand what he was saying. I presumed that he wore overalls but he said that he hated the bloody things, as they were far too hot in summer. When I asked him how he kept himself so clean he said that he painted houses, not his bloody clothes! Later in the afternoon, when Willy took me home, she told me that Graham showered and changed at least two or three times a day and refused to wear singlets which were not spotless, or jeans if they were not clean and pressed properly. I could not begin to imagine what it would be like to be married to a man like that!

Willy and Graham had one little boy, Kevin, who was deaf because Willy had had German measles when she was pregnant. I soon learned that they had been quite wild when they were young. Both were hot-tempered and sparks often flew between them.

We lost contact when they moved to Queensland several years later. When we met again in December 1995, I could not believe what a gentle couple they had become, dedicated parents to their three sons. Together they were battling with Graham's cancer. He had been diagnosed with leukaemia just before his fifty-second birthday, two and a half years earlier and, according to the statistics he had less than half a year to live. Determined to 'beat the bastard' they juiced truckloads of carrots and celery for him to drink.

"We use twenty six kilos of carrots every week," Willy laughed. "You should have seen Graham's skin!"

Graham also went to a monk, who taught him to meditate properly. Despite the heavy dosages of chemotherapy, he had he never lost his hair and was looking well when we met up again three years later.

"The monk told me that he could not cure the cancer," Graham said, "but he taught me to look at life in a different way. Meditating twice a day has made me come to terms with it, taking things as they come. And I'm still here, aren't I?" he laughed. Having baffled the doctors obviously gave him a great thrill too. Graham died peacefully at home, surrounded by his family two years later.

When Willy drove me home after my first sewing session at her place that wet afternoon in December 1971, we noticed a straight line across the road. Willy stopped the car so that we could have a better look at it. On one side of the line the road was wet and on the other side it was as dry as a bone. It had not rained a drop in the parched area were we lived, which was only a few kilometres from town.

A few minutes later, I was listening to the roaring noise of the Todd River while I watered the grass and the vegetables in our garden with the hose again...

Summer Holidays

The children had been at school for six weeks when the eight-week summer holidays started at the beginning of December. We expected them to have to repeat the year, but each of them had a good report and went up a grade. In Holland, the end of the school-year is at the beginning of July and the new year starts again in mid August and, as we had left on the first of September, they had only been for two weeks in a higher class before they had another six-week holiday. On arrival, Sister Ida had put them into a class according to their ages, a grade higher again. For instance, Richard was in grade one (in Holland) for two weeks, in grade two for six weeks and he was going to grade three, after the summer holidays. It was amazing how quickly they picked up English, especially the rude words of course! I learned a few new words every day from them in turn, even though we spoke Dutch to them at home, most of the time.

After the rain, a fortnight before Christmas, we had a few beautifully cool days. Then the temperature went up to the high thirties again and, due to the high humidity, it had become very sticky. Although the children always had plenty to occupy themselves with outside, I preferred them to keep out of the sun during the day as most of them had Fred's fair skin and burned easily. The thought of having to be crammed into the shed during the heat of the day for weeks was appalling to everyone.

Two days after school broke up, we had unexpected visitors again.

"Bill Dooley; a true Irishman," Sam laughed when he introduced him to us. "And this is his lovely wife, Pat."

Bill and Pat had three children with them; the eldest was in Richard's class. They had come to see how Sam was getting on with the house and how we were managing on the building site. Until he had a roof on the shed, Sam had rented a room at the back of Bill's place and up to the day we arrived, he had gone back to Pat and Bill's every evening to take a shower before he went to town to have something to eat. They had not seen him since. I made a cup of coffee for the visitors and, after a pleasant hour or so, we waved them goodbye. Later, that same afternoon, Bill came back and talked to Sam, who was still laying bricks.

"Bill came to ask if you would like to live in their house while they are away on holiday," Sam said after Bill left.

"Are you saying that they'll have the eight of us in their house?" I asked, astonished at the offer. "They don't even know us!"

"What do you mean? You've met this afternoon," Sam reminded me.

It was hard for me to understand how anybody could leave their house, with all their belongings, to virtually complete strangers. And for six weeks!

When it sank in that we would be in an air-conditioned house at Christmas, I felt overwhelmed, crying with happiness and relief. By the time they would come back, at the end of January, we could move into Sam's house. Our hardship would be over for good!

A week later, the day before Bill and Pat left for Brisbane in Queensland, we went to visit them. They lived in an old house on the main road, not far from town. A scruffy dog, barking wildly when we tried to open the gate, scared the living daylights out of me, but it stopped barking immediately when Bill shouted at him to be quiet. The house was built on an enormous block of land, hidden by some tall trees and thick bushes. Most of the ground was left bare, with a small lawn at the back of the house shaded by a big gum tree, and surrounded by abundantly flowering bougainvilleas and three-metre-high oleanders. Beside the lawn was a carport overgrown with grapevines. The row of one-room flats at the back of the empty block next door that also belonged to Bill, were nearly all occupied by single men who had run away from their nagging wives, Sam said.

A lovely cool breeze with a musty smell came towards us when we went into the house by the back door; the front door was never used, Bill said. Several old rattan armchairs of different shapes and sizes stood against a whitewashed wall in a narrow room. The dark green paint was worn off the concrete floor of the walkway to the adjoining kitchen. After a cool drink for all of us, Pat showed us around the house.

A three metre wide verandah, right around the house, was made into several rooms. The outside walls had lots of louvre windows; horizontal strips of glass that opened up to let the breeze go through, covered with short floral curtains. A completely square room in the centre of the house, called the lounge, was the only room that was carpeted. It had a comfortable old lounge suite arranged around a small table, and an open fireplace in the corner. There were only a few ornaments around and few pictures on the walls, which made the place quite bare but easy to keep clean. Before we left, Bill gave Fred the key to the house, and said we could move in the following afternoon.

We were ecstatic when we drove back to Sam's place to spend our last night in the hot caravans. A few days later Sam returned one of the vans to the owners, but he decided to keep the other two, just in case the house was not ready when Bill and Pat came back from their holiday...

It was absolute heaven for me to be in a proper house again. I danced from room to room with the kids when we moved in. At lunchtime the following day, the children and I watched curiously as a strange light appeared in a corner of the lounge, slowly illuminating the whole room. I held my breath as the light was growing brighter and brighter, expecting a ghost or the Holy Mary to appear any moment, when I suddenly realised what was happening.

The sun was going straight overhead - being the twenty first of December - and it shone directly into the chimney.

The children immediately made friends with Rex, the protective dog of mixed breed, but I never felt at ease with him. Maybe because my uncle's big black Bouvier had bitten deep into my arm when we came to say goodbye to my mother's favourite brother a few months earlier...

From the Dooley's place it was only about a quarter of an hour's walk into town. Lilian had been to the library with her class and she suggested we get some books to read so we could learn more English. It seems strange to me now, but I had never been inside a library before. My mother, who had been a nun for four years before she married my father, thought that books, like films, were evil. The only time I read without fear of getting caught or feeling guilty was when I was in hospital, awaiting and recovering from surgery. The last time - in April 1970 - I was so engrossed in *The Mantel*, the Dutch translation of 'The Robe', that I had completely forgotten where I was when the orderlies came to take me into the operating theatre.

We soon went to the library every second day, bringing a stack of children's books back, which were the only ones I could read and understand at the time. We also discovered the town's swimming pool. It was old and not very big but it was cool and shady and not too far to walk. It seemed incredible to us that we were often the only people there apart from a few black kids, while it was so hot. In Holland we seldom went to a swimming pool, as we were like sardines in a tin as soon as the weather was warm enough to swim. One day I panicked when our four-year-old daughter Regine went too far away from the edge, towards the deep end of the pool.

"*Kom aan de kant! Kom aan deze kant!*" I kept yelling at her, waving my arms frantically, shouting to her to come back to my side of the pool.

"Mama! Stop!" our children shouted, "people are laughing at you because you are saying a bad swear word."

There were quite a lot of people at the pool that day. By the time I realised what I had said, Regine was safe, while I wanted to sink to the bottom of the pool until everybody had gone home. I should have known! Willy had also warned me not to use that word when I wanted to buy lace, as that had the same meaning in English.

Another time when we were at the pool, a child vomited in the wading pool. It turned my stomach to see that none of the other kids seemed to take any notice and just kept on playing in the muck. We did not go back for a week despite the oppressive heat, and when we went again, I only watched the children playing. After the holidays, the old pool was closed for good as plans for a new Olympic-sized pool were being completed.

On the first of December, a few days after his tools arrived, Fred had started work full time at Heinz's furniture factory. His job was to hang doors in a frame made of two by one inches of raw timber, for the new high school that was being built close to Sam's place. A thousand students were expected to move in halfway through the following year. Lilian would be one of them.

It was very hard for Fred to use inches as he was used to the metric system, which was much more accurate to read. It seemed ridiculous to talk about 'one-sixteenth' or 'one-thirty-second of an inch' to us. It was also extremely frustrating for him that he did not know the necessary technical terms. At his former job in Holland he had been known as a fast worker but here the other men were much quicker than he was. Because of the heat, the raw timber he worked with twisted, making it impossible for him to get the doors to fit properly. After letting him struggle for a couple of days, one of his work mates had shown Fred how to go about it. He simply nailed the two by one to the wall, so that it could not move!

Because Fred did not understand the jokes the other workers were telling, he often had the feeling that they were laughing at him. But the hardest of all to take was the language his boss was using, scolding him for a 'f'n bloody bastard' time and again. Although it was just Heinz's way of talking to everybody and he was 'fair enough' as a boss, Fred detested working for him from the start.

As Fred had not earned any money since the middle of August, apart from the frames he made for Henk Guth's gallery, I eagerly waited for him to come home with his first pay on Friday afternoon. The shed was spick and span and his favourite meal ready to be served on the stove. Getting more and more worked up as time went by, I waited for him until late at night. He had been drinking with 'the boys' after work.

"I hope you're not starting that on a regular basis," I said, trying to keep my voice as calm as I could, when he handed me the money. The Australian habit of drinking with your 'mates' after work scared me to death. Fred assured me he knew his limits; three beers, then he could still drive home safely…

The following Friday Fred came home at four in the afternoon to get changed for the Christmas party that was being put on at the back of the workshop. Because I was afraid of him acquiring a bad habit, he promised not to stay long. About two hours later, he came back.

"The party hasn't even started," he said disgustedly. "They are all just standing around, drinking beer. When I asked how long that was going on for, they said that it would take all night."

Fred had understood that the party was for the staff only, but half the town had been there. He had felt extremely uncomfortable, as he was unable to laugh and joke with the others. Knowing that he would get drunk if he had another beer on an empty stomach, Fred had left them to it. The following morning when he went back to work as usual on Saturday morning, he found an incredible mess. There had been a pig-on-the-spit and the tables were still laden with leftover food, inundated by millions of flies. Some men were still drinking, others were still asleep in the creek beside the factory and nobody wanted to work, nor were they capable of doing any.

Fred no longer felt rude for leaving. He was glad that he had gone home. And so was I...

The job of hanging doors continued week after week. Although he detested the job, Fred was keen to work overtime on Saturdays when the cupboards that had been made during the week were installed at the new school, which was only a five-minute walk from Sam's place.

It did not feel like Christmas at all when we drove to church for the midnight Mass, dressed in light summer clothes instead of being rugged up to keep warm. With the windows of the car wide open, we could hear the familiar sounds of the church bells filling the warm night-air with a cheerful thrill. They could be heard from quite a distance, just as they had done in Holland when we walked to church at midnight, often in the snow. Christmas carols coming through the wide open windows and doors of the church gave me goosebumps all over. People flocked to the church from all sides, and in all states. Most were dressed up in their very best, but some came in their work clothes. Several obviously came from a Christmas party or straight from the pub, as they seemed quite drunk. At the back of the church, people stepped over a well-dressed young man who seemed unconscious. A whiff of alcohol nearly choked me when I passed by. With a shock I recognised the young fellow who had delivered our crates with the crane a few weeks earlier. Later, in his welcome address, Father M said how good it was that even a bloke in such a state had made the effort to get to the midnight Mass.

Although we had left home early, the church was already quite full. We stayed at the back, wondering if there was still a place for all of us at the front, but in no time at all the church filled to the brim. With the congregation packed tightly in the pews, I thought several times that I would faint in the stuffy heat. There were a lot more Aboriginal people than on Sundays, when no more than half a dozen attended Mass. They were usually very shy, their eyes cast firmly down to the pavement and keeping as much distance as possible when they passed us in the street. But they seemed happy and at home in the church.

When the singing of the carols stopped and the Mass began, the priest invited people to come forward. Just like in Holland, there was plenty of space at the front, but most people preferred to stay at the back. Several seats had been placed around the altar from where we could see what was going on in the church. The breeze wafting through the open windows, and the big fan standing nearby, made it a lot more comfortable.

I didn't understand much of what was being said, but the service was quite entertaining. Crying babies were continuously being plugged with dummies. Toddlers wandered away, sucking on bottles with milk or cordial and dogs walked in from the street, looking for their owners. Some of the townsfolk, men as well as women, were snoring their heads off, sleeping right through the service, while others were talking as if they had not seen each other for years. I later learned that that was probably the case for many of them. Some people answered back to the priest or commented aloud on what he said. Most of the time Father M didn't take any notice, but occasionally he stopped speaking until it was quiet before he continued his sermon. When the Mass ended people stayed to talk but as we still felt like strangers, we went home as usual. Sam had come to church too and joined us for the traditional Dutch midnight breakfast. We were extremely grateful to Pat and Bill, as it was heaven to spend our first Christmas in Alice Springs in a house instead of the caravans.

Before we left, we had put the kitchen table in the lounge where the Christmas tree was set up with some of the decorations we had brought from Holland. The breakfast consisted of a variety of bread rolls, *krentenbrood* (fruit-loaf) with almond filling we found in the local bakery, bush biscuits and knacker-bread (rye biscuits) instead of *beschuit* (Dutch rusks) and a large choice of toppings, mainly sweets. A burning candle beside each plate on a nicely decorated table always made midnight breakfast at Christmas a happy affair.

Sam rubbed his hands when he came into the lounge.

"Ahaah! Just like home!" he laughed gleefully. With tears in his eyes he picked Regine up and swung her around above his head.

Because our money was dwindling fast, we had 'forgotten' Sinterklaas on the sixth of December. I had wrapped up a few accessories I had bought for school along with other necessities, but I had no idea how Santa operated. As they had not been expecting to get anything, the three eldest children had saved the little pocket money I had given them, as well as the money they had earned by doing jobs for Sam, to buy something for everyone, including Sam. They had wrapped every little thing in large individual parcels so that there were a lot of presents. When the youngest children were asleep, we put all the gifts in front of the chimney, to be opened in the morning as Sinterklaas always did in Holland. It wasn't until fairly recently that we learned that Santa Claus was adopted from our Saint Nicolas and not the other way around as we had always believed.

Everybody was happy when we unwrapped the presents early the following morning. Most popular were the little soldiers the boys had bought: one hundred for only eighty cents! At first they played all sorts of games with them inside. Later they built big forts outside in the dirt, from where they made believe that the soldiers shot at each other.

New Year's Eve was celebrated with a lively party at Willy and Graham's place. They would look after the food, they said, we just had to bring 'a carton'. "Filled with beer, they meant," Sam explained.

The party started after nine, when the children had gone to bed. As soon as we arrived, Willy introduced me to Barbara, the quickest dressmaker in town. While I was sewing at Willy's place the previous week, I had started to make a new dress for her. She had been amazed how many measurements I took of her and watched me draw up the pattern.

"Barbara just lays out the material, draws a few lines on it and cuts it out," she said. It only took her a couple of hours to make a whole dress. When I had put the dress on for a fitting, she told me that Barbara always fitted the dress inside out so that she could pin it where it needed to be taken in. I had been stunned. The first thing Sister Adriana-Marie had taught us in sewing classes was that every person has two different sides to their figure. A dress, made like that, could never fit properly. Willy, who was very fussy what she wore, assured me that the dresses Barbara made looked good and always fitted very well. As I was only an amateur, I felt very uncomfortable talking to Barbara, seeing my future as a dressmaker go up in smoke.

It was extremely tiring for both of us to speak English all the time. Listening to a group of people, all talking at the same time, made my head spin. As Fred had soon run out of conversation with the men too, we were glad when the food was served shortly after our arrival. Like at Pat and John's, there was an enormous smorgasbord of salads and snacks, beautifully arranged on a decorated table. By eleven o'clock the chairs were pushed aside and the table was taken into another room to make space for dancing. After a few tame records played on the gramophone, Willy put on rock-and-roll music. Within seconds Graham grabbed her and they were swinging away, soon followed by their closest friends, Kay and Jeffrey. Before she had put the music on, Willy had changed into a short white dress with black, velvet roses, complemented by red high-heeled shoes and a red rose in her black curly hair. The dress had a full circle skirt with multiple petticoats underneath. I could not keep my eyes off them. It was as if I was back in Holland, watching Elvis Presley dancing with a pretty girl on a glamorous television show.

Fred loved rock-and-rolling but I could not jive at all. He pulled me onto the floor, but I felt so embarrassed by my wooden performance that we soon sat down, itching to get back on while watching. While the dancers recuperated, Fred and I happily swirled around to the tunes of a foxtrot or a waltz on the almost empty floor. At midnight the music was stopped briefly to listen to what must have been a recording of Big Ben on the radio, announcing the New

Year, 1972. Tightly embracing each other we wondered what would be in store for us...

It was strange to think that in Holland the New Year did not start till eight hours later. Afraid to break up the party, we did not want to be the first ones to leave, so we stayed until past two o'clock when I could no longer keep my eyes open. By that time most of the guests slumped in their chairs. Some were fast asleep. Graham and Willy, and their friends Jeffrey and Kay, were still dancing, hardly being able to stand on their feet.

The following morning the children were angry with us for having left them at home alone on that special evening. Although the eldest three were allowed to stay up, they got bored playing games on their own with no television to watch, and so they had gone to bed before midnight. Because there were no fireworks, it did not seem to them that a new year had started. I had not even fried oliebollen, the traditional Dutch treat, because the ingredients were too expensive.

In Holland, oliebollen were fried on the last day of the year and eaten throughout the evening and New Year's Day. Spoonfuls of batter, made with flour, sultanas, currents and chopped apple, were fried in very hot oil. They were covered with icing sugar, representing the snow at that time of year. A plate-full of freshly fried oliebollen was taken to close neighbours and friends with best wishes for the New Year.

We spent most of New Year's Day making a tape recording on Sam's reel-to-reel for our families back home, as we had promised. Even though we had been in Australia for such a short time, the children often had to search for the right Dutch word, as they were thinking and speaking English most of the time.

Unfortunately, we had taped over old music that came through when the tape was played. Because of the difference in voltage between the two countries, the tape also went a lot faster in Holland, which had made it very difficult for our family to listen to it. However, from the letters they wrote, we knew that they had enjoyed our stories as much as we had enjoyed recording them.

A Taste of the Wild West

During the first week of the New Year (1972), we wondered time and again why on earth we had left the safety of our own country.

On New Year's Eve the grave of the well-known Reverend, John Flynn, had been vandalised. The vandals had painted intricate designs in yellow, green, red and white paint all over the monument, from the natural rock foundation to the big boulder on top, which had been brought down from the Devils Marbles four hundred kilometres north of Alice Springs. People were appalled. Who in his right mind would do a thing like that, to the monument that held the ashes of this great and much loved pastor who had brought medical treatment to people of every creed and colour in the inland of Australia?

The following night, a gang of about thirty Aboriginal men bashed the leader of a band in front of the Overlander Steakhouse where they had been playing. They claimed that the musician had sacked the drummer of his band, because he was black. Fighting amongst the gang had blown up into a full brawl. Several people were in hospital, badly injured.

A few days later two men, Americans who worked at the Joint Defence Facility, commonly referred to as the 'Space Base' at Pine Gap, were beaten up by a group of six Aborigines in the main street. Later on that night, a young girl was punched in the stomach on her way home from work by the same group, and ended up in hospital.

On Friday evening, our children's school bus driver went with his wife and two small children to see how the restoration of John Flynn's grave was progressing. As they approached the monument they noticed someone with a rifle hiding behind the big rock. The couple became scared and returned to the car, followed by the gunman. They had been able to get into the car but, while the bus-driver's wife closed the door, her husband was shot in the back of his head through the back window. He had died instantly and fell off the seat onto the dirt beside the car. The killer had dragged the driver's body away and ordered his wife to get into the driver's seat. While he pulled her out of the car, the lady told him that she could not drive, begging him not to harm her children. When a car approached on the road, the man had disappeared into the bushes. The following day aboriginal 'trackers' followed the man's footprints which came through Sam's property and disappeared into the town.

A shock of horror went through the town at the time. People rallied to collect money for the bus-driver's widow and her little children. Our three eldest children went with the school to the funeral service a few days later; the first funeral they had ever been to.

On Saturday night, a week after the murder, we were invited to Pat and John's Govers' place to raise money for the unfortunate widow. It was a beautiful evening. Pat had arranged tables in small settings around the garden, complete with checked tablecloths and fresh flowers in small vases. There were a large number of people, perhaps sixty or seventy. In return for a donation, Pat and John provided all the food which they cooked and served with the help of a few volunteers. Everyone had brought their own beer but an unrestricted quantity of wine was also supplied with the meal.

John took us to our table saying that they had put us with some other Dutchies so that we could talk our own 'lingo'. He introduced us to Henk, the baker, and his wife Ria, who had moved into Pat's house next door during the previous week. Henk was happy to hear that it had been such a surprise for us to find *krentenbrood* and *gevulde koeken* (fruit loaf and almond filled cakes) available at Christmas, which we had enjoyed so much. We soon felt at home, talking and laughing about the things that happen to newcomers to Australia.

Later, when the meal was served, a tall, balding man with spectacles and a small square moustache joined our table. Pat presented him as 'Ted, the local newspaper baron,' and left us to introduce ourselves. By that time, the men had drunk several beers and started on the red wine, which was served with the dinner. One glass of it was enough to make my nose bright red and to get me talking non-stop. Sam, Henk and Ria, who had also been in Australia for many years, did a lot of translating for us.

As the evening wore on, we were all doubling up with laughter. The funny way Ted was holding his belly, throwing his head back and laughing with a deep 'how-how-how-how', as Santa Claus did, left Ria and I in stitches, holding onto our bellies too. After dinner, when most of the other guests had left, John joined us. He kept filling our glasses, even before they were empty. I started to worry about going home to the kids as the killer of the bus driver had still not been found, but my arguments were waved aside.

"The kids are all right. They've got the dog to take care of them," Fred reassured me. He had already had far too much to drink and insisted that I could drive the car home, which petrified me.

"Have another glass of wine," John said, while he filled up my glass. "She'll be right; you'll see!"

It was close to three o'clock in the morning when we finally got to the car. Our hosts assured me that there was no one on the road at that time; not even a cop. Sam drove off in the ute while I started the car, cheered on and encouraged by the people who were still at the party.

After I finally got the old Galah into the right gear, I managed somehow to turn it at the end of the cul-de-sac where Pat and John lived. I bunny-hopped past our waving and cheering friends and drove onto the main road.

"It's not far; only a few kilometres," I reminded myself again when I swung the old car onto the back track, a dark dirt-road along the railway line, now the main road into town, holding firmly onto the steering wheel.

As always when he had too much to drink, Fred was extremely happy. Saying what a good driver I was he wanted to tickle and cuddle me. As I needed all my attention to keep the car on the road, I pushed his hands away with my elbows time and again, begging him to stop his foolish behaviour. When the blinding lights of a car came from the opposite direction, I suddenly realised that I was driving on the right side of the road, as we were used to in Holland. Luckily, Fred had seen it too and pulled the steering wheel to the left; just in time! Glad to get into the Dooley's driveway, I made a wide circle in their back yard before I stopped the old Galah in front of the carport, sighing deeply.

"You've done that very well," Fred complimented me. "But you can't leave the car here. You have to drive it neatly into the carport."

I protested strongly, but he kept saying that I could easily do it. Knowing that he would not take 'no' for an answer when he had too much to drink, I decided to show him that it would indeed be easy after driving the car all the way from Pat and John's place in town. I started the engine, pulled the car into gear and drove slowly into the narrow carport, straight into the last pole.

I was furious: "See what you made me do!" I yelled.

"Shhh! You'll wake the kids," Fred warned. When he staggered out of the car and saw the bent-over pole, he burst out laughing saying that everybody would think that it was a great joke.

The cool night air must have hit him when he got out of the car as he suddenly felt sick and his legs gave way. On all fours he crawled into the house where I helped him into the bathroom. Unable to get up, he hugged the toilet bowl and emptied his stomach in violent heaves, swearing that he never, ever would touch red wine again.

Over five thousand dollars, a year's wages, was raised for the widow of the school bus driver. The killer was never found. A lot of rumours went around, saying that it might have been a set-up job, but Mr Andy McNeil, the police inspector who led the case at the time, assured me that that was all a 'load of rubbish'. It was pure speculation.

"I am convinced that the man was shot for no apparent reason at all," he said firmly when I asked him about it. They knew who it was, but there wasn't enough evidence to prosecute him.

"The Aboriginal man with the rifle was tracked down by an Aboriginal tracker," Mr Dick Kimber, our local historian said when he checked my story. "The late Salley Mahomed (one of the first cameleers) saw him hiding in the hills and called the police. Unfortunately he eluded them again."

I wrote the first draft of this story on the 12th of September 1995. Three days later, I was stunned to see that the murder case had been re-opened. The story covered the entire front page of the 'Advocate'.

When I had my hair cut a few weeks later, I talked about it with my hairdresser. She told me that the widow of the murdered bus driver had been coming to her for years to have her hair done. My hairdresser had not known who she was until the last time she had been. They had talked about a lady who had been murdered by a demented Aboriginal man the previous week.

"They were lucky to get the killer," she had said bitterly. "It's twenty-three years ago since my husband was killed and people still think that I did it myself."

My hairdresser had been too shocked to ask any questions. When she told me that she was going to have her hair done again on Melbourne Cup day, I asked her to tell the widow about my writing and gave her my phone number in case she wanted to have a chat with me.

I was very excited when the widow phoned me early in the morning, after Melbourne Cup day. She came with her daughter for a cup of coffee the next day. Tracy was three and had been sitting in the back of the car when her father was shot. She was now in her mid-twenties and 'slow'. She hardly said a word. Marie a soft-spoken woman with a motherly figure, told me about her difficult life. She lived only for her children and could not possibly harm a fly.

When the rumours after the murder had become too much for her to cope with, Marie had gone to live with her parents in Queensland. Because her children were missing their friends, she had returned to Alice Springs after a while. During the following years she had gone back and forth to Queensland, suffering two nervous breakdowns and a couple of major operations. She had married again but the marriage did not last, due to her recurring depression. Eight years ago she had settled in Alice again, hoping there would be a better future for her children and grandchildren.

After the recent murder, the police had contacted Marie again. Hoping that someone would come forward with new leads to find the killer of her husband, Marie had been happy at the chance for the truth to come out. She had been horrified to see her ordeal splashed all over the front page of the paper as well as seeing it on television.

"How can they possibly blame me?" she asked while tears filled her eyes when we said goodbye. "As if I would have taken my children, if I had planned to kill my husband."

Fearing another nervous breakdown as the same rumours were now going around again, Marie left Alice Springs shortly after I met her, hoping to return when her name was cleared.

In the meantime I had talked about it with some people who had lived in

Alice Springs for a long time. A friend of many years was convinced that it was foul play.

"Of course she did it herself!" she shouted. "It's ridiculous to bring it all up again." Goosebumps crept over my skin.

"How can you be so sure?" I asked. "Have you ever met her?"

No, she had not, but it was obvious, she said. It was stupid to think otherwise. She had read enough detective stories to know how a criminal's mind worked. The town was too small for the police not to know who had a rifle and for the murderer to escape as he had.

"We were asked at Mass on Sunday morning to pray for this woman who was sitting in the front row with her three children, and give generously to the collection to be given to her," she said. "None of my friends in town had ever heard of her and we never saw her in church again." My friend had seen every detective movie she could lay her hands on, she said. There was absolutely no doubt in her mind that the woman had a boyfriend and wanted to be rid of her husband. When I told my friend, who was so convinced that the accusations were true, about my meeting with the bus driver's widow, she went very quiet. "I'd no idea," she said softly. "It all seemed so unbelievable at the time..."

Our six weeks' stay at the Dooley's place went quickly. The children never ran out of things to do. The little ones held tea parties with Pat and Jim's daughter's dolls and teddy bears and, together with the boys, they made dinosaurs, motorbikes, cars, trains and houses with the Lego set we had brought from Holland. They also took a new interest in their stamp collection. Apart from the yearly series of fundraising *kinder-zegels,* the Dutch stamps always had the Queen's face on them. But they eagerly collected those boring stamps to swap them for the fantastic variety of Australian stamps for when they were going back to school again.

One day, early in the new year, Eugene walked to the post office in town twice in the same afternoon, to select stamps to decorate his letters to his friends. Because of the intense heat, he got a touch of sunstroke and spent the following four days in bed, sick with headache and a high fever. Another lesson learned the hard way...

The boys often walked to Sam's place, bringing him a bag of grapes from the Dooley's vines, and often staying there for the rest of the day. They loved being with Sam on the building site, doing jobs for him and playing with their friends in the neighbourhood.

During the school holidays, I took the children to the dentist. The three eldest ones needed braces at once as their treatment had already started before we left Holland. At the clinic we were met by the orthodontist, a cheerful man who introduced himself as Dr. Krantz. He counted the children one by one, shook their hands and asked them their names.

"Are all those beautiful kids yours?" he asked. "You lucky thing!"

While he examined each of the children's mouths, he joked about the kids all having the same buckteeth problems. "Made in Holland" he called it. After he studied the reports the dentist in Arnhem had given me he said: "Now Mother, tell me, why has it taken you so long to get here? You were told to come immediately after your arrival, weren't you?" he asked, looking at me over his glasses.

A bright red colour crept up from my neck while I told him that I was scared of the cost. We would never have been able to afford the treatment until someone had told us that it was free in Australia.

"Aha! I see!" Dr Krantz laughed. "You've come to the lucky country, haven't you?" He then explained that the braces were only free in Alice Springs because the orthodontist, Dr Moe, who had invented them, lived here and they were still experimenting with them.

A few months before we left Holland we saw an article in a popular weekly magazine about a new way of bracing children's teeth in Australia. The photo showed a Chinese looking man with a broadly grinning girl showing steel rings around every single tooth. A thin wire, fastened on every ring would pull them back in the right position. We felt sorry for the girl and were worried that ours might have to have such a mouth full of metal. I had since seen several youngsters around town wearing them and they did not seem to be bothered about it at all.

Dr. Krantz was very interested to see the two thin retaining wires that were attached to the plates Lilian and Eugene were wearing. During the five-month lapse of adjusting the wires, the room that was created by pulling some of the kid's teeth out had allowed the back teeth to come forward instead of pulling the front ones back. He decided to start treatment with them immediately. Because one of Raymond's front teeth had never come through, an X-ray had been made shortly before we left Holland. It showed that we could have waited forever as the root was missing too. All six children would need braces, Dr. Krantz said. When he finished making a list of appointments, he asked about my teeth. I felt embarrassed, as I knew that they were badly in need of attention. I had been secretly glad that we could not afford the expense because I was terrified of sitting in a dentist's chair. I would rather give birth than go to the dentist; until I was in labour again and then I would swear I would willingly go to the dentist instead!

I had good reason to be scared. When I was sixteen, the old dentist in our village had sent me through the roof when he pulled out two wisdom teeth without proper anaesthetic. We were astonished when I heard that people had an injection here when they only had to have a filling!

Before we left the clinic, I also made an appointment for Fred who had complained about toothache. As soon as Dr. Krantz looked in his mouth the following day, he shouted triumphantly:

"Aha! Here is the troublemaker in the family!"

When Fred was a young boy, he was nicknamed 'horse-mouth' because of his big, forward standing teeth. His sister Bep, who was eight years older than Fred, had taken him to the dentist, insisting that he do something to straighten them up. Because Fred's family was unable to pay the high cost of the treatment, there was nothing that could be done about it, the dentist had said, no matter how much Bep had pleaded with him. Later, when Fred was in the Royal Dutch Navy, he had gone from one dentist to another to have them pulled out and replaced with 'falsies'. But, as his teeth were strong and healthy, nobody wanted to touch them. He did not give up however, and an eighty-year-old doctor finally agreed to do the job. When he came home on leave a few days after the operation, his mouth was still sore and swollen, but his new teeth were already in place, something unheard of at the time. Everybody said that he looked much better, but it had taken away the friendly look on his face.

I never had any trouble getting the children to their friendly dentist. Even though the treatment was often very unpleasant, they always went by themselves. I seldom had to remind them of their appointments, nor did I have to make sure that they cleaned their teeth properly.

Dr. Krantz had told them how his parents had been unable to afford straightening up his own teeth. That was why he was very happy to be able to do theirs, instead. The job was obviously very satisfying for him.

By the time our three youngest children needed to start the straightening process in 1978, it was no longer free. At the time, Fred had lost his job and I was waiting to go into hospital to have major surgery again. We were paying for Richard and Simone's treatment and could not pay for Regine's at the same time. As time went on and her teeth were nearly fully grown, Dr. Krantz sent her home with a note for me to come and see him. "Something has to be done soon," he said. He had offered Regine a new method they were experimenting with, which was free of charge. It was called 'The Cat's Whiskers', an awful looking contraption of wires that went around the head. He had already talked the matter over with Regine, who was prepared to go ahead with it. Everyone in the family felt sorry for her. After months of waiting for the materials and equipment, Dr. Krantz called me in again.

"I'm sick of waiting," he said. "I want to get on with the job. I've decided to give Regine the same system as the others had. You can pay it off later when things are better again." Like the others, Regine complained at times when the wires had been tightened, but they are all grateful for their beautiful, straight teeth, thanks to Dr. Krantz who now lives in Queensland, enjoying the favourite pastime he could not indulge in Alice Springs: Fishing! It's people like Pat and John Govers, the Dooley's, Mother Ida, Willy Prolongeau and Dr. Krantz, who made us feel at home in the Alice so quickly.

With growing apprehension, I watched the work on the house progressing agonisingly slowly. It soon became clear that there was no way we could move in when Bill and Pat returned from their holiday. With temperatures still around forty degrees every day, I dreaded having to go back into the stinking heat of the shed again. Fortunately, there was not as much wind to blow up the dust as there had been in October and November.

For weeks, dark clouds had built up every afternoon, but the rain they promised never came. The clouds just disappeared in the evening and we woke up to a perfectly clear blue sky the following morning. The dry heat made us feel as if we were in a hot oven. When there were clouds in the sky, the humidity was unbearable.

Back in the shed, I had my first real taste of homesickness - an awful feeling of loneliness and regret that made a knot in my stomach and took the smile off my face. Fortunately, it did not last long as things started to look up again. At last I was able to save some money, as Fred was bringing a pay packet home every week and he also made lots of frames for Gallery Guth in the evenings and on Sunday afternoon. Most of the windows and doorframes had been taken out of the shed and I did some sewing for other people, adding a little to our income.

When I wrote to Fred's sister Bep, who was so concerned for her little brother, about the change for the better, she wrote back that if he had worked like that in Holland, he would have made it there too.

"Is he planning to work himself into an early grave in that God-forsaken country?" she asked.

As Bep had blamed me for taking her beloved brother away, I told her in my reply that it was Fred who had wanted to get away in the first place. I reminded her how sick he had been of working in the factory, unable to cope with mentally handicapped youngsters, and the fact that nearly all the money he earned in overtime was taken out of his pay packet in taxes at the end of the week. I assured her that life was quite different here. Fred was happy to make frames in the evenings and on Sunday afternoon. Most people worked on Sundays anyway. He was his own boss, working as fast or as slow as he felt like, always starting with a cup of coffee and sharing a beer or a glass of wine with Henk before he came home.

Bep replied that she was happy I had refreshed her memory, and she assured me that she did not blame me for taking Fred away. I still wonder why I'd had that idea and why it had bothered me so much.

Driving Lessons

In the first week of February, the children were all glad to get back to school to be with their classmates again. Before we left Holland, we had been worried about taking Raymond, who was always so quiet and shy, into a strange, unknown country, but he was very happy in his new environment, making lots of friends. Soon after our arrival, Richard and Jennifer Harvey, a very quiet girl with black curly hair and dark brown eyes, became friends. During the following two years they were inseparable. Simone was quite happy to play with Regine and did not seem to need other friends. Simone was petite and had a pretty face. From the moment they met, she was Sam's favourite. Perhaps the fact that they were both named after Simon, my mother's father, also had something to do with it. Regine had been a solid little girl from birth and according to my mother I had spoiled her rotten.

After the holidays, Lilian, our eldest, was going to Alice Springs High School, now Anzac Hill High School, on the bank of the Todd River in town. At nearly thirteen, she was already quite grown up. We always treated her as our 'big girl', so it was no wonder she had such strong feelings of responsibility and a weight problem that might last her entire life. Children from well-to-do parents were sent away to boarding schools to get a better education. Although we wanted the best education for all our children, I was secretly happy that we could not afford it so that we did not have to part with her at such a tender age. The new Alice Springs High School near Sam's place was expected to be opened the following June. It catered for a thousand children and would create a lot more opportunities for them in Alice Springs.

We told our children from the start that it was up to them to make the best of whatever was available at school. Because I had not been allowed to go to school after I turned fifteen and I did not speak the language, I could not help them much with their homework. Fred could not help them either. His English was poor and he worked such long days in the heat, that he was glad to have a beer with Sam when he came home, and have some time to himself to read the paper after dinner.

During the last week of February, all six children became violently ill with high fever, vomiting, and dreadful diarrhoea. At that time, they were still sleeping under the stars in the bedrooms at the back of the house, without a roof. With a bare light globe at the end of a long lead from the shed, Fred and I spent all night cleaning up their mess. We had no sooner finished with one, and another would start again. None of them could possibly make it to the toilet in the shed. We were lucky if someone made it to the bucket we had provided in each room.

As the night wore on they became delirious and started to talk nonsense.

While we wiped their faces and bodies with cold water to get their temperatures down, one of them got up and walked over the bed, dripping the revolting muck everywhere. Cursing the fact that we did not have proper facilities, we started cleaning up all over again.

By early morning one after another went to sleep. Fred had gone to bed too, hoping to get a couple of hours of sleep before he had to go to work. When Sam got up, early as usual, he went to a friend in the neighbourhood to use his telephone to call a doctor. After asking how long we had been in Alice Springs, the doctor told him to bring the children into the clinic. He agreed to come to the house when Sam told him that the kids would mess up his clinic before he had a chance to examine them.

By the time the doctor finally came in the afternoon, the children were all quite dehydrated. They could not keep anything down and most of them were too weak to stand up.

"An acute case of dysentery," the doctor said, surprised they had become ill so late, as that usually happened shortly after arrival. He explained that it was caused by the drinking water, which should be boiled until the body was used to it. He prescribed a white medicine that contained opium. It worked wonders! Although they were looking very pale they were all up and about in a few days. It seemed nothing short of a miracle that Fred and I had not been affected, since it was highly contagious.

After another two months of making cupboards and hanging endless doors at the new high school, Fred detested his job. At the end of February, Sam asked Heinz if Fred could have a few weeks off, to give him a hand, putting the roof on the house. It felt like a holiday having him home, being able to drink coffee and have lunch together. Sam had also hired a German fellow called Horst to help, but progress on the roof was agonisingly slow while he and Sam talked for hours on end. Horst seemed to know everybody and everything that was going on, in and around town, and he seemed happy to have found someone who was eager to listen to his stories. By the time the roof was finally on, more than three weeks had passed and Sam had run out of money. The house again had to stay as it was for the time being while Sam went to Yuendumu, an Aboriginal settlement about two hundred and fifty kilometres west of Alice Springs, to build the foundations for several government houses. This time he stayed away for three weeks. He came back for supplies and left again for another three weeks.

In the meantime Fred developed haemorrhoids. He could hardly walk because of the debilitating pain. Because Bep's husband, Bert, had been in hospital to have his 'scraped', a very painful procedure, he refused to go to the doctor, hoping that they would disappear by themselves. In the end he could not sit any more and had to spend the weekend in bed. When he finally went to the doctor the following Monday morning, he was given a few suppositories, which took the pain away immediately. The medication made the piles shrivel up in a matter of days.

On the weekend before Sam left, Pat and John had a party on a large block of rural land they had bought in the farm area. We were again the first to arrive.

"You should have known by now that a seven o'clock invitation means to arrive at eight," John laughed as he greeted us.

I watched, probably with open mouth, how Pat prepared a meal for about a hundred people. On a long table in the big open shed were several big bowls with different salads that she and John had already made at home. Pat was making damper with flour, water, beer and a bit of salt. After she kneaded it thoroughly for a while she put a ball of it in a Dutch oven, a cast-iron pan black with soot, and put the lid on.

"No, you just enjoy yourselves," she said when I offered to help again.

Earlier that afternoon, John had made fires in several holes in the ground. He had filled them with a heap of coal, which was red-hot when we arrived. After filling several pans with dough, John made holes in the glowing coal. Pat put the pots in and covered them with hot coals, which cooked the bread perfectly. While they were working, I told them that in Holland, until the turn of the century, the pans they called Dutch ovens were used above a fire by poor people who could not afford a wood burning stove. I had only ever seen one in the open-air museum in Arnhem, shortly before we left Holland.

Next came the chickens. Together they took two dozen plucked and cleaned chickens out of a big ice-box, wrapped them in aluminium foil and placed them in the hot coals too, followed by potatoes in their 'jackets', also individually wrapped in foil.

Apart from an open corrugated iron shelter, there were no facilities on the block. "If you have to go to the toilet, you go behind the bushes," Sam had said, when I asked what we should do if the need arose. "You'll find some paper on the table in the shed and a shovel to bury it."

It would be fun seeing people, dressed up in their Sunday clothes, going bush with a shovel...

It was a splendid evening. The stars were out in full force, the meal was superb and beer and wine were consumed in enormous quantities. Sam got stone drunk. He spent the night in the open air, oblivious as to where he was. He paid for it the next day with a splitting headache. Fred had learned his lesson and only drank Coke after he had reached his limit of three bottles. I was happy that he could drive the car home himself, as I still did not have a driver's licence. I had just started to learn, from a professional this time!

Driving home from church one beautiful Sunday morning in February, we saw a sign on a Commission home, advertising 'Student Driver Education'. We drove on, apprehensive about the cost of the lessons. In Holland, getting a driver's licence could cost as much as a new car if you were a slow learner, like me. However, realising that it was essential for me to be able to drive as soon as possible, we turned back a little later. The man answering the door was very pleasant, and the lessons were surprisingly cheap. We arranged for him to pick me up the following Tuesday afternoon. Needless to say, I was very nervous when the friendly instructor, who was a little older than I was, called that afternoon.

"I'll take you on the road to Simpson's Gap," he said as we drove off. "There is no traffic to distract you there."

The road to Simpson's Gap was a dirt road, little more than a track at the time. I relaxed a bit when the instructor asked where we came from and how long we had been in Alice after. A few kilometres out of town, he stopped on the side of the road. He explained some details about the handling of the car and we swapped places. When I sat behind the steering wheel the instructor bent over me and adjusted my seat, fussing over it to make sure it was comfortable. Leaning back in the passenger seat beside me, he said: "Before we go on I have to tell you a few things. There is just you and me on the road now, no other cars will come here at this time of the day."

A cold chill ran down my spine and made me shiver.

"There's no need to be nervous," the instructor smiled, and went on telling me about the car.

"Normally an instruction car has double foot pedals so that the instructor can stop the car when things go wrong, but this is a normal car. When I have to stop you, my hand may go like this," he said, bending forward, putting his hand on my bare knee.

Somehow I kept calm, hearing my mother's voice cursing the mini skirts when they came into fashion, shortly before we left for Australia. "It's asking for trouble!" she had said.

"You don't have to be afraid of me; I'm a gentleman," the instructor said, taking his hand away, after giving my knee a little squeeze.

During the following half an hour I tried to concentrate on all those new words I had to learn rapidly. I had just become used to the Dutch words for clutch, accelerator and brakes when Fred was teaching me, and I now mixed up orders to push and pull, making the car bunny-hop along the road while I kept a wary eye on the hands of my instructor.

To my great relief the next lessons were in the built-up area of town. After only the fifth lesson the instructor suddenly said: "I'm going to take you up for the test next Tuesday."

I was horrified. People needed at least twenty lessons before they could drive a car properly! I had not even learned how to do a hill start, or to park the car between two drums.

"You'll be all right," the instructor said impatiently. "At the registration office you answer a few questions on paper, then Bob will come with us for the practical test on the road."

During the week that followed, I heard some terrifying stories about the local car inspector, who was extremely fussy and strict. With trembling knees and sweat dripping down my face, I stood at the counter in the stuffy old office a week later, trying to make sense of the dozen or so questions on the paper in front of me. A line of people had formed behind me, patiently waiting their turn.

"The answer is six feet," a very tall man behind me whispered over my shoulder. "Put 'yes' for the next question," he said.

After I had answered the last of the questions in the same fashion, I handed the paper in and dared to look at the man behind me. I recognised him as Sam's friend, who had sold Fred the old Galah.

A little while later, I sat shivering behind the steering wheel in the instructor's car, waiting for the inspector. My legs had turned to pudding. The instructor beside me had a worried look on his face. Bob, a tall, heavily built man, folded himself in the back seat of the small sedan without saying a word. My knees trembled when I drove off in the direction he told me to go in his soft, mumbling voice. I had trouble hearing him, and asked if he could please speak clearly, as I could not understand English very well.

"Lady! If you want to drive a car here, you have to speak the language," he said firmly. My legs were now shaking violently. Luckily I had to stop soon after, to give way at an intersection. I then pretended that it did not matter if I failed the test the first time, and followed the instructions slowly, as if I had plenty of time. I was sure that the route had been cut short and that I had failed the test when we pulled up at the office again. No hill start, no parking between the drums.

The two men walked away while I locked the car.

"How did she do?" the instructor asked. I held my breath. At first Bob did not answer. Then, just before they reached the door of the office, I heard him say: "She can handle a car. The rest will come with practice."

My instructor seemed as relieved as I was. I later learned that he also owned a flower-shop and another business and that he had left town that same day because people were after him for money.

Fred and the children looked at me with their mouths open when I proudly showed them my licence; just a slip of paper without even a photograph. "Only six lessons!" I boasted.

A few days later I had my first accident. Full of newly found confidence and freedom, I set out to go shopping with the children. The old Galah was very hard to get into gear and I had just started to back out, when there was a big bang, followed by a roaring noise. The car rocked violently.

"Quickly! Get out! The car is exploding!" Lilian yelled.

For a moment the kids looked at me in horror as I hurried them along, then they ran in all directions. From a safe distance we saw what had happened. Even though there was a large open space to back the car out, I had managed to hit the fire hydrant on the next door neighbours' block! The back axle of the 'Galah' sat on top of the red hydrant, which was broken in half. The force of the water was rocking the car.

Fred and Sam came running out of the house, followed by the other children. Sam laughed while Fred scolded me, shaking his head at so much stupidity. Together they lifted the car off the hydrant, releasing a ten metre high fountain into the evening sky we could later see from the new supermarket, several blocks away. Since it was a Saturday night, Sam could not find anybody to turn the water supply off until Sunday morning. For months I was worried sick about getting a hefty water bill, but that never came.

Soon after that incident, I took the kids into town to do the weekly shopping, forgetting that it was the Thursday before Easter and very busy on the roads. I was so relieved to get to the Woolworths car park on the bank of the Todd River, that I pushed the accelerator in instead of the clutch, and went straight through the wire fence, stopping just at the edge of the dry riverbed.

"Gee Mum! You sure need a lot of practice," came from one of the stunned children in the back of the car, making me feel very small.

I have had a lot of practice during the thirty years since and made only a few dents in the successive cars we have had. I still haven't learned how to park between the drums. I really should learn now that parking spaces are not readily available in Alice any more.

Being able to drive the car gave me a great feeling of freedom. With Sam being away in the bush earning money (after all these years in Australia 'making money' still sounds strange to me) and Regine at school, I had the place to myself during the day and I became more involved with the community. With the mother of twin boys who lived nearby, I took turns in driving to pre-school and became a 'fruit' mother a couple of times a week, cutting up fruit for recess. I also helped regularly at the tuckshop at OLSH (Our Lady of the Sacred Heart) primary school where I met several other mothers. Although they were friendly enough, it took me a long time to feel at ease with them. Serving the horde of children at recess and at lunchtime was a nightmare for me. They made an awful racket and I could not understand a word of what they were saying.

In the meantime, Fred had fitted the outside doors and Sam's house was now at lock-up stage. Lilian had to give up her little bedroom under the stars when the roof was being put on, shortly after the children had recovered from dysentery. For the time being, she had to share with her two much younger sisters again. A toilet had since been installed in the bathroom, but we still had to take a shower in the shed and there were no cupboards in the house. The last caravan had been taken back to its owner when Fred and I moved our double mattress in the smallest bedroom of the house, where it was much cooler.

When I finished making the curtains for the girls' bedroom, from mauve material with a pattern of big white flowers and bright green leaves on it, we bought plain purple and green chenille bedspreads, which matched beautifully. A few small pillows made with the left over curtain material made the room look very cosy. The boys chose checked curtains for their room, big red, green and blue blocks, with three red bedspreads for their bright red folding beds. As Sam had made the concrete floors with yellow ochre, I only needed a couple of small rugs so that they didn't have to wake up in shock when they stepped out of bed. Soon after Sam had left for Yuendumu, I had made the remaining bedroom, the future master bedroom, into a sewing-room. Word spread quickly. After the first alterations for a dress-shop, I soon had several regular ladies trying out my sewing skills.

When Henk, the Dutch baker, told us that another Dutch couple had come to town, we went to visit them the following Sunday afternoon. Kees and Tilly and their fourteen-year-old son lived in the oldest part of town in an old caravan at the back of someone's property. When we heard what they had to pay for the hire of the old van, I was speechless. They could hardly move and they had to share the bathroom, at the back of the scruffy old house, with the owners. Talking with them about hardships and difficulties they had to put up with, we soon realised how lucky we had been.

Kees and Tilly had left Holland in the late fifties as a young, married couple. They had worked on different stations for years; Kees as a gardener and Tilly in the household, cooking for the family as well as large numbers of station-hands and seasonal workers. They had to work long hours for little money and had often been dismissed after the season had finished. Later on, they had found a station where they could stay all year round, with only a few hours off on Sunday afternoons. The little bit of money they had been able to save always went on a trip to Holland, as Tilly was very homesick at times. Before they came to Alice Springs, they had been in Holland for eight months but Kees had been unable to fit in with the Dutch way of life. There had been a two-year waiting list for a council home and he found it impossible to find work. Unable to stand the cold, rainy climate any longer, they had decided to go back to Australia and try their luck in the Centre. Kees had found work as a labourer soon after their arrival and Tilly worked in the milk bar at Egar Beavers, which had been the largest supermarket in town until Woolworths came in 1970. While an average wage for a man was eighty dollars a week, Tilly's earnings had just gone up from ninety nine cents per hour to a dollar ten, eight dollars and eighty cents per day, thirty five dollars and twenty cents for a forty-hour week.

Because none of the women in our families had worked outside the family, I had no idea what women were earning compared to men in Holland. The only other dressmaker I knew was Willy's friend, Barbara, who could make a dress in a couple of hours.

I cringe to think how I always worked against the clock to finish a dress in a reasonable time. Because I always made my own clothes apart from buying an occasional bargain in a sale, I had the idea that homemade clothes had to be cheaper than bought ones. That meant that I had to make a dress in eight hours to compete with the local dress shops.

As it happened, one of my first clients was the owner of 'Threads-A-Go-Go', one of the two main dress shops in town. Joan had moved into the beautiful house John was building across the road from Sam's place, shortly after our arrival. Her little daughter often played with our children. Joan was always happy with what I made for her. She could seldom find anything in her own shop that fitted properly and she also provided me regularly with alterations for her customers. After the first year, I concentrated more on wedding and evening dresses. Because I found it near to impossible to say 'no', I had often more work then I could cope with. The way I was sewing against the clock, trying to keeping up with the demands of the children as well as the two men in the house, was asking for trouble...

Going Camping

In the first week of March, Fred quit his job of making cupboards and fitting doors for the new high school since he had a full-time job making frames for Gallery Guth, building up a supply before the tourist season started in April. Things had changed drastically at the gallery now that Mrs Guth was no longer there.

Shortly before Christmas Lynne called in unexpectedly one morning, asking me if her eleven-year-old daughter, Carolyn, who had stayed with us several times before to play with Simone, could be with me that day, as the atmosphere in their house was not very pleasant for a young child. When I asked what the matter was, Lynne burst into tears. I had never seen a smart business lady like her crying. I always thought that only weak people like me did that. I had no idea how to handle the situation, so I made her a cup of tea and let her talk. I was glad that she spoke Dutch so that I could understand her without having to ask what she was saying all the time. When we first met Lynne, her husband had been in Adelaide having a check-up for his heart problems and the doctor had ordered a holiday. Henk's heart trouble had apparently been of a very different nature from what she thought. He had gone to England with a young blonde, whom he had met at the restaurant across the road.

I felt deeply sorry for Lynne, powerless to help her in any way when she told me how difficult life had been for her for years, starting with nothing, slowly building up the gallery to the successful business it now was. Lynne had left town with her daughter Carolyn shortly after Henk returned from England, because he could not paint without his new love. She moved to Melbourne and later settled in England.

It may seem strange but Lynne was the first deserted wife I had ever met. Sure, I had heard about people who had split up, but I could not think of anyone I knew personally in Holland, ever deserting his family.

At the end of the school holidays, I met Elizabeth for the first time. She was a petite, softly spoken lady in her late twenties, with nearly white, shoulder length hair. She asked if I could do some sewing for her and Henk invited us to go out bush with them one day, when the kids had gone back to school. Because we could not trust the old Galah, we had so far only made short trips around Alice Springs and I was looking forward to the outing very much. It was a splendid morning when Henk and Elizabeth picked us up at nine. Starting at Simpson's Gap where Sam had taken us on our first day in Alice, they took us to several other beautiful spots we recognised from photographs and Henk's paintings; Standley Chasm, Ellery Gorge, Ormiston Gorge and Glen Helen Gorge; each one even more spectacular than the one before. We were short of eyes and time trying to absorb it all. At one of the fantastic lookouts on the way, we drank coffee from a flask. Elizabeth had packed a picnic basket for lunch, which we ate sitting on the ground in the shade of the magnificent Ormiston Gorge.

On the way home, Henk stopped at the Ochre Pits where he told us how Aboriginal people made their paints by grinding the many different colours of the striped sandstone rocks. When we got back to Henk's old station wagon, he could not get it started. The men fiddled with the engine for ages while Elizabeth and I sat talking under a tree.

When we finally got home, the children had been back from school for a long time. They were starving as usual. We had travelled over more than two hundred and fifty kilometres of dirt road and longed for a shower, but I had to cook dinner first. It had been a magnificent day for both of us, being out without the kids for a change. We enthusiastically told them about all the wonderful places we'd seen, promising to show them one day.

Fred loved his job at the gallery where he was free to come and go as he pleased and earned a lot more than at Heinz' factory. Because he was employed as a sub-contractor, no tax was taken out and he was not entitled to any holiday pay, sick leave or worker's compensation.

Large bundles of moulding, in several different profiles, which came from Melbourne over three thousand kilometres away, were delivered every couple of months. The raw timber had to be sanded, stained and varnished then finished off with white and gold lines, painted by hand. Fred also put the pictures in the frames, papered the backs, packed them and took them to the post office to be sent all over the country as well as overseas. When the tourist season started properly in April, Henk gave demonstrations to busloads of people again. Fred was stunned at the incredible number of paintings Henk produced each week. Nearly every painting was sold before it was dry. As Lynne had said, sometimes he had to close the gallery because he had nothing left on the walls to sell.

In the beginning, Henk had made his own frames as well as the huge quantities of paint he used, which was now Fred's job too. While mixing the fine powder, he was often covered from head to toe in the colours he had been making that day, looking like a clown when he came home. He also rolled the cut to size masonite boards with an undercoat before Henk painted the pictures on them. Because Fred was paid per frame, he bought a second-hand compressor to nail the corners, which just about halved the time it normally took to put them together. He also used it to staple the paintings into the frames and later to spray paint the undercoats on the boards. Apart from Fred, Henk employed two young ladies in the gallery, which opened every day from nine in the morning till nine at night. The girls were both married. They also painted gold and white lines on the hundreds of frames, during the quiet hours of the day.

"From now on, we won't speak Dutch any more," Henk told Fred on the day he started full-time. Unfortunately, after the first couple of days, he seemed to have forgotten his decision, speaking Dutch with Fred all the time. Because he worked nearly always by himself, and we spoke mostly Dutch at home so that the children would keep it up, Fred's English did not improve much at all those first six years.

In the beginning of March, Regine was able to go to preschool. When I took her for the first time, I was pleasantly surprised to see that her teacher was Dutch. Jose was delighted to have a little Dutch girl in her class, but she was in for a big disappointment, as our little darling refused to speak a word of Dutch. In fact she refused to talk at all. For the first couple of weeks she went around the classroom on all fours, barking like a dog. We were flabbergasted. Whenever I tried to talk about it with her she just pretended to be a dog at home too.

Up to then, it had been fascinating to hear Regine talk to her dolls and toy animals; asking questions in Dutch and answering in broken English. Jose had hoped to be able to sing Dutch songs with Regine, but that never happened either. When she finally decided to be normal again, she spoke only English at school, pretending that she did not know any Dutch.

When Regine had been at kindy for a few weeks, Jose asked me to make a Dutch costume for her and one of the boys in her class, for the Bangtail Muster, an annual parade that was always held on May Day, the first Monday in May. I bought some material and made Regine's outfit right away, a striped skirt with a blue apron, a black top and a white, lacy bonnet. Then I made a necklace with several strings of red beads, closing around her neck with two big, ornamental golden buttons. After I dressed her, I plaited her ash-blond hair, put red bows at the end of the plaits and pinned her bonnet in place; she looked like a postcard. When I set her up near the full-length mirror to take a picture, Regine studied herself in the mirror. Then she said with a puzzled look on her face, "But Mama, I have never seen a girl like that in Holland."

I explained to her that there were lots of different costumes, as she had seen in Bunschoten and Spakenburg, close to my mother's place. They were not worn as much as they had been and we had never taken her to Volendam, where this particular costume was worn. Regine was quite happy to wear the outfit in the parade, but she refused to wear those stupid yellow clogs, real wooden ones, which looked so nice with it.

May Day or 'Labour Day' was one of about a dozen public holidays, spread throughout the year in Australia. The whole town seemed to be watching the Bangtail Muster Parade, named after the mustering, the yearly counting of cattle on the stations. To make sure that every animal was only counted once, the end of each animal's tail was cut off and collected. The many entries of schools, workplaces, sporting clubs and organisations that participated showed a great sense of humour in the town. It was amazing what people had made! The children of Regine's school were dressed in costumes of many different countries and they looked great. Amongst the many entries was a replica of the big new hospital that was going to be built the following year. The whole parade showed great optimism in the future of the town, which added to our growing sense of security.

From where we watched the parade, I noticed a lady I knew from the tuckshop, sitting in a wheelchair in the garden of the hospital. Joan had been hugely pregnant when I met her at school the previous week, and I wondered if she had had her baby.

"Yes!" she smiled, "I had him last night." I was stunned.

"You had your baby last night and sit here now?" I asked.

I told Joan that women in Holland still stayed in bed for eight days after giving birth and how the bossy nurse had barked at me for getting out of bed for a moment, nine days after Regine was born, four years earlier. Unless there were complications, babies were always born at home, supported by a large organisation of maternity home-care. A trained nurse looked after mother and child for ten days. With my last two children, I had also had a full-time trainee; two when Regine was born. So far, I had been very lucky with the nurses, but the last one was terribly overpowering. Normally by the time the nurse left on the tenth day, the mother had been up and about, but she kept me in my bedroom upstairs until the very last day, even though I was perfectly all right. On the ninth day, I had got out of bed and shown our new baby from the window to our neighbouring children, playing in the park in front of our house. The bossy old nurse was furious. She stormed upstairs, grabbed the baby from me and ordered me into bed as if I was a naughty little girl. Unable to stand up for myself, I had burst into tears as I always did when I was angry or upset.

While Sam was building foundations in Yuendumu, the weather turned a lot cooler. Fred started work at the gallery earlier in the morning, staying until ten, then went back for a few hours after dinner at night. During the day, he painted the overhanging facias and gutters of Sam's house, stained and varnished the outside doors and planted more kikuyu grass, which was grown from roots instead of from seeds.

The vegetables, replanted after the storm in November had washed the first lot away, had grown very well, but the swarms of insects that invaded the place time and again now ate a lot of them. Only the cucumbers and melons thrived. We had never seen watermelons grow before and had no idea when they were ready to eat. They were enormous. We expected them to burst any time. When Sam came home he knocked on each of them and listened to the sound. "Maybe next week," he kept on saying. When he finally decided to open up the biggest one we all stood closely around, watching him as if we were expecting a young dinosaur to appear. Disappointed that it was still half-raw inside, we bought another large piece in the supermarket.

One day when I was helping in the tuck-shop at school, the girls were talking about preparations for Saint Patrick's ball, which would be held in the new assembly area at the school the following Saturday night. As the proceeds were for a new library for the school, I decided to buy tickets for Fred and myself. Heaven knew we could do with an outing! Sam said that he would come later in the evening, if he still felt like it.

"Long formal dress," it said on the ticket, "B.Y.O."

"Bring your own drinks," Sam explained, but he was not sure about the long dress, it could mean long trousers for men too, which he never wore. I asked Maree, one of the organisers who lived close by. It meant long for both sexes. "Everybody wears a long dress to a ball these days," she said. At home, I searched Sam's single door cupboard and found that his only pair of trousers, which he had brought from Holland ten years earlier, still fitted him perfectly. I made a royal blue dress for myself with a white sailor collar, which was the latest rage in Holland when we left.

"You are much too early," Sam warned when we were ready to leave at a quarter to eight. The party started at eight and, as we didn't want to be late, we went anyway. Sam was right; the organisers were still preparing the tables when we got there. "No, thank you," Maree said when we offered to help. We sat around for half an hour before a few other people arrived. A while later, an elderly lady came over and asked if we belonged to a group. She was Scottish and very hard to understand. Her name was Minnie, a bit like mine. It took us a while to realise what she meant when she explained that people made up a party, to make up a table. Minnie had come with her son and his wife and she invited us to join their table as they had spare seats. Because we had to ask them continuously to repeat what they were saying, we soon ran out of conversation.

It was close to nine-thirty when the hall slowly filled with people. The ladies were all in long dresses and most of the men were wearing their jackets, despite the warm night. Some four hundred long dresses were a feast for an aspiring dressmaker's eyes! Some of the dresses had obviously been stored in mothballs for many, many years. Others were super modern, risqué or extravagant. I felt very self-conscious in my simple cotton dress, but decided not to let it spoil the evening. Happy not having to make conversation, we danced all night and had a great time. By the time Sam arrived, close to midnight, Fred was ready to go home, but he had to wait until I had had a few dances with my brother. Throughout the first years it was always confusing for us to know if the time you were invited was also the time you were expected, but with Fred drilled in the Navy, we are still seldom late anywhere.

When Sam had finished in Yuendumu, he made a patio in front of the big double sliding doors of the dining room, surrounded by flowerboxes for which he used fancy bricks. Then he spent weeks laying large, chocolate coloured tiles, in the living areas of the house. Although he said that he valued my opinion, I had been unable to stop him buying those dark tiles. They would never look clean as they showed up every speck of dust. One day, when I was helping in the tuck-shop, one of the women asked: "How is Sammy's house coming on?" They all laughed when I answered that Sam was still laying tails. I felt very uncomfortable, wondering what I had said wrong this time when the same lady asked with a straight face: "Where is he laying tails?" I told them as well as I could that he was laying them on the concrete floors in the dining room and the lounge as well as in the kitchen and the laundry, and he would start on the walls in the kitchen when he finished the floors. More laughter. Trying hard to keep a straight face the lady asked: "What kind of tails is he using? Dogs or cats? Or did he go to the abattoirs to get a heap of cows tails?" The other women now roared with laughter. Although I felt stupid I laughed with them as I could see it all before me: Sam sticking 'tails' all over the place. Tails, tiles, tales, tyres, were all very confusing words for me for years. I still have trouble writing them correctly. Lay, lie and lying are even worse.

Sam was doing the brickwork on a house across the road when the cupboards for the kitchen and bedrooms were being delivered, at the end of April. Lots of them! I was worried. Sam planned to live in the shed and rent the house out for a good price as soon as it was finished. He had always only worked the first half of the financial year and spent the other half playing on his thirty-acre block in Queensland. That way he did not have to pay too much tax, he figured. We could forget our dream of buying a block of land at the auction in August, if we did not find another cheap place to live soon. I had been to the Housing Commission to inquire when we could expect a government home, which would be at least another year, I was told. Fred was earning good money now and I earned a bit too, but he was not insured. What if he got sick or he had an accident?

"God always looks after you," Mum would say. She always put her trust in Him, and look where it got her. Her prayers had certainly helped her to cope with the disasters in her life, but they had not prevented them happening. My father had died at the age of forty-two when I was six, just as Mum's father had done when she was six.

"Your husband will be next. You mark my words!" Mum had warned me with trembling lips, a couple of times.

"That's being superstitious!" I had replied angrily and put it out of my head, but the thought kept haunting me now. Fred's forty-second birthday was only a few months away. What if that happened to me too?

There was still a lot of work Fred could do for Sam in lieu of paying him rent. He was busy for weeks, fitting the cupboards in the bedrooms and the kitchen, then staining and varnishing them. Lucky for me, Fred realised that it was most important that we build our own house as soon as possible too, saving every penny we could spare. Sam had bought a block of land for eight hundred dollars two years earlier, but prices had gone up considerably since then. We would probably have to pay double the amount at the next auction, he reckoned. Fred had been to the land sale in March. We could not afford to buy any that time and it seemed impossible to save against those fast-rising prices. To have a chance of getting a piece of land when the next lot of building blocks became available in August, we had to decrease our spending even more. Fred had already cut down on smoking, which had cost as much as the rent we paid for the house in Holland. During the last stressful years, I had started to smoke an occasional cigarette too, to steady my nerves. The last one I smoked was on the ship on our way to Perth. When I inhaled the beautiful pure Australian air for the first time I vowed never to pollute it with another cigarette, which was a waste of money anyway. Sam had been a heavy smoker in his teens when it was said that you were not a man if you didn't smoke. He never liked it much anyway, so he had given it up long ago, but there wasn't much chance of Fred ever giving it up completely.

Feeling at Home

We had been in Alice Springs only a few months when I already knew that I never wanted to go back to Holland, except for a holiday. The children were happy and I liked the easy-going lifestyle. From March onwards the weather had been very pleasant; beautiful clear skies with temperatures of around thirty degrees, going down to about ten or fifteen at night. In May we had the first few nights with temperatures around zero. Winter started on the first of June but there was little change in the weather pattern apart from a few frosty nights and cold days when the temperature did not get higher then twelve degrees. Winter in Alice Springs was far better than any summer in Holland.

The fact that there was no television was absolute heaven for me. We both saw how much better off we were without it. The children were never bored, inventing one game after another. The box no longer dictated the hours after school; the dramas I had when I dared to switch it off! Then, when our deprived children came home from school the next day, they made me feel guilty with their accusations that they had missed out on yet another of the best programmes their friends had ever seen. They now completed their homework as soon as they came home from school so that they could play outside with their friends.

I had hoped that television would stay out of Alice Springs forever but of course progress would catch up with the isolated town sooner or later. One day in March, the local paper published the exciting news that TV was expected to be in Alice by the end of the year. I just hoped that we had learned a lesson and knew how to handle it, when the time came. In the meantime, we enjoyed the social life that was surely going to be a thing of the past when the addictive media came to town.

During the last years my relationship with Fred had suffered badly because of my attitude to the telly. In Holland, we not only had two Dutch channels, but we could also get three German stations. There had always been something that was too good for him to miss. I did not blame Fred for wanting peace and quiet when he came home from work, but I became angry and frustrated, trying to cope with crying children while cooking the evening meal. Bedtime had always been such a happy time. By the time our youngest needed their father, Fred had little time for them; a fact he now regrets. Slowly, everything had come to revolve around the monster. We seldom went for a long walk on Sunday afternoon like we used to, as we had to be home for the sports reviews. When we were visiting, most people would leave the TV on until it was time for us to go home. Then they would say: "You want to go already? We haven't had time to talk yet."

Because there had been so much violence at home when I grew up, I wanted to keep the peace in my own home at all costs. Instead of speaking up, I often cried myself to sleep about our lost happiness, until the bomb exploded and a violent argument cleared the air for a while.

Apart from his favourite soccer matches, Fred did not miss the television at all in Alice. Our family life was as pleasant as it used to be when our oldest three children were small. We regularly took the children to the family movies, shown every Friday night at their school. A lot of parents dropped their children off, but we always stayed and enjoyed the evenings with them, watching a cartoon or a western in the open air, under the stars.

There was a walk-in theatre, called the Pioneer Open-air Theatre, where films were shown regularly. The world premiere of 'A Town like Alice' from the famous book by Neville Shute was held there in 1954. The drive-in had been there for five years too, but for some reason, financial probably, we never went to either of them during our first year in Alice.

At the beginning of May, some of the children had awful eye infections, apparently caused by flies. Raymond's and Richard's eyes were especially affected. Their eyelids were so badly swollen that their eyes looked like the eyes of reptiles. It took several days of treatment with ointment and drops before they could open them properly again.

At that time, the lights for Sam's house had arrived; thirty-two lights, each packed in a separate box. The children had a ball building castles, cars and trains with the empty boxes. Later, they made robots, putting the two nearly-blind boys inside and walking them around the yard.

Sam seldom went out at night. He had had his fill of parties when he first came to Australia, he said. He usually worked from early morning until the sun went down, then after dinner, he went back with a torch to do the 'pointing up', filling the lines between the bricks with cement, taking his time to make them perfectly straight.

Shortly after our arrival, Sam had taken us to see a row of six or seven flats he had built for a friend. Sam had made a bet with him that the bricks had been laid so straight that he could fire his rifle along the joints of the bricks without the bullet causing any damage. The friend had organised a party with plenty of drinks before the bet took place. Evidence along the seventy-metre long wall shows that Sam won the bet.

It was forty-two degrees the day we visited Bryce and Faye Burrows. Their refrigerated air-conditioner, on full blast, chilled me to the bone in no time. After visiting for an hour the heat hit me hard when I came outside. I could not understand how people could stand such a change in temperature. I often wondered if that was the reason why so many children, and adults, in town suffered from colds.

With Sam being home to keep an eye on the children, we went at least once a month to one of the many social evenings and balls in town, where we danced to our hearts' content. We usually went with Kees and Tilly, Henk, the Dutch baker, and his wife Ria. The first time the six of us went out, we went to Papa Luigi's, the most popular Italian restaurant in town. Because I love fish but Fred can't stand even the smell of it being cooked, I always look forward to eating fish when we go out. Everyone, except Fred, had ordered lobster, as Henk said that it was the most delicious of all the fish in the sea. I nearly had a fit when I saw the big, red crab being put in front of me, complete with legs and claws.

"How on earth am I supposed to eat this?" I asked.

Our friends told me to just copy what they were doing. Fascinated with the funny ten-footed red creature on my plate, I kept watching it. By the time I had my first taste of the delicious meat, Kees said disappointedly: "Mine is empty already. There was hardly anything in it."

"I've got heaps," I said while I scooped some out and put it on Kees' plate. When I concentrated on my own lobster again, I stared in horror at the empty belly of the big crab; there was nothing left! Kees had already put the spoonful in his mouth and swallowed it.

"You're too late mate. It was terrific," he grinned. We all cracked up with laughter, doubling up time and again with tears running down our faces as more jokes kept being told about the big fish. My belly was aching when we came home that night, but it was definitely not from eating the lobster!

As it was always a relief to be able to speak our own language, we were usually roaring with laughter when we were together. Another night of fun that sticks in my mind was when the six of us went out for dinner to the Oasis, another favourite restaurant in town. By the time we had finished the main course that night, the restaurant was nearly empty. A short, heavily built, jolly looking man was sitting at a table nearby. His lady companion hung slumped in her chair beside him. She had kicked off her shoes and a button of her blouse had come undone. She had obviously had too much to drink. After smiling at us for a while, Bob came over and introduced himself.

"You're having a good time," he said with a drawling, Scottish accent. "Would you care to join me for dessert? I'll shout," he added, when we looked at each other. "My partner has just about gone off to sleep, but you don't need to take any notice of her."

With his lady friend sound asleep with her head on the table, Bob moved to our table instead. We talked and laughed with him for another hour, then Bob invited us to come to his place for a nightcap.

Henk and Bob dragged the lady to Bob's car and drove off. When we got to his house, Bob had already put her to bed. While we settled, he told us that his wife had died of cancer the previous year. His friends had set him up with a blind date because they could not stand seeing him with a long face any longer. Apologising time and again, he said how happy he was to have met us, hoping that he had not intruded on our privacy. We assured him that he hadn't. We had enjoyed the evening very much.

"Thanks to you, I've come back to life again," he said with tears in his eyes, firmly shaking our hands when we finally left at two o'clock in the morning.

Some day in March, Fred had been stopped for speeding and given a ticket. In Holland you could expect a hefty fine of up to two weeks wages, so I was terrified of the bill. I was reading a book about psychology by Norman Vince Peele when Fred was picked up for speeding in Holland one day. The previous evening I had read out to him how the well-known American author would react in such circumstances. So, Fred had gotten out of the car, and handing his wallet to the policeman, he had said: "I'm sorry officer. I went a bit too fast. You probably have to book me. I'll keep a better eye on the speedometer in future." Seeing that Fred obviously knew that he had been wrong, the officer had let him go.

"You can keep buying those kind of books," Fred laughed when he came home that night.

Weeks went by before the case was due to come up in court. The policeman who had issued the speeding ticket had made the summons out for driving without a seatbelt. Wearing them had become compulsory in January and a blitz had been organised, since few people were taking notice. Not wearing a seatbelt was attracting a hundred-dollar penalty, more than a week's wages. At the time, cars over three years old were not required to comply with the new regulations, so Fred decided to ask about the mistake a couple of days before the case came up. The same policeman was in the office.

"You charged me for not wearing a seatbelt," Fred said, "but there are no seatbelts in my car."

"You must have taken them out," the officer said impatiently.

After inspecting the old Galah carefully, the policeman had no choice but to tear up the court order and tell his superior about the mistake.

"I must have got you for something," he said.

"Not for not wearing a seatbelt," Fred smiled.

"No need to laugh about it mate," the policeman warned. "I'll watch you and I'll get you one day. Don't you worry about that."

The policeman never got Fred. On the contrary, years later, at an auction for charity, we were happy to see how he bought one of Fred's paintings, at double the price we would have sold it in our shop.

Shortly after the incident with the policeman, Fred had another notice to appear in court, this time because we did not have a radio licence. Again we expected a hefty penalty.

On the morning of the hearing, Fred was amazed to see people of every race in town there. The Italians especially seemed upset, shouting that they had no intention of paying the fine, as this was a free country. They could have stayed at home if they were to be charged for every fart they let off they said.

Apparently, a group of inspectors had been to every household in town, asking people to show them their licence to listen to their radio. More then a hundred got caught, as they had not been able to hide their radio in time. The old judge, affectionately called 'Scrubby Hall' for obvious reasons, asked one offender after another:

"Guilty or not guilty?" When the answer was "guilty" the hammer went down and, if it was "guilty, but..." the hammer went down anyway, after a stern "No 'buts' allowed!"

When it was Fred's turn, he said that he did not feel guilty because he didn't know that you had to have a licence.

"You have been here long enough to know," the judge said, then he asked, "Do you have to have a radio licence in Holland?"

"Yes, but..."

"No buts! Next!" the judge shouted while he slammed the hammer down. Fred had wanted to say that you only paid your membership of a particular broadcasting organisation for which you received their weekly magazine. The fine was the same for everyone: ten dollars. I wonder now what happened to the radio licences, as I don't remember having to pay for listening ever again.

A few weeks before the mid-year holidays in June, I was asked to see Simone's teacher. Although I thought that Simone was doing fine at school, I expected to be told that she had to go back to grade four. She had been in that class for only six weeks before she had gone to grade five, after the Christmas holidays.

"Simone is very good in most of her subjects," the teacher, a young Asian lady, said. "I want to put her in the higher group of the class, but she cannot do the spelling tests. I don't understand. Why?"

Relieved that Simone could stay where she was, I laughed.

"Half a year ago, this little girl did not even speak a word of English," I smiled. I then told the teacher, whom I later learned was new to the school herself, about our immigration. She had noticed that Simone had a slight accent but she found it hard to believe that our daughter had learned the language so quickly.

The children all loved school, but after a while Eugene, who was in grade six, became bored with the lessons. He could easily do Raymond's homework and begged me to ask his teacher if he could go into grade seven, too. I went to see Mother Ida and told her about the situation. The head mistress agreed that Eugene had a quick mind and she could see his trouble. "Come with me to his teacher and we'll talk it over," she said.

Eugene's teacher protested strongly.

"It's cruel to take a child out of the classroom halfway through the year and put him with total strangers," she argued hotly. She said that it would not be so bad in the first couple of years at school, but grade six and seven were the most important years of primary education, as the pupils were being prepared for high school. Mother Ida pointed out patiently that every year in school was of great importance to a child, and that during the first grades the foundations for a good education were laid.

"Every teacher likes to think that their class is the most important one in the school, and that is good," she said. "These people are hard-working immigrants. We cannot allow their children to be bored at school."

Quite unnecessarily, I pointed out that our two eldest boys were always together and their friends were mutual, at school as well as around home. Mother Ida had already made up her mind and said that Eugene could go to grade seven after the next holidays.

The children felt comfortable at school, but church was a different matter for them. Things in the Catholic Church had changed rapidly in Holland. A baby no longer had to be baptised on the same day as it was born, and confession was not required unless you wanted to go. Holy Communion was now placed in the hand by lay men or women instead of by the priest, and it had been no a secret that one of our local priests had a girlfriend. The church had become divided and was in continuous trouble with the Pope. The tradition of celibacy and the problem of priests wanting to be married had brought a lot of hardship to people who wanted to hang onto the old ways. Some people travelled long distances to go to Mass where Latin was still used and the priest stuck to old traditions and values.

Going to church three times a week at school was more than enough for our children. I felt ill at ease in church too, having to take a step back in time and I had soon grown tired of trying to get the children to go again on Sunday mornings. Fred was no help since he would much rather stay at home to do some work than be bored in church and we didn't get any encouragement from the local priest either. He never came to see how we managed and was only interested in business. Gallery Guth's business, that was. Father M always stood in front of the church on Sunday mornings to meet his flock, asking the same question every time: "How is business Fred?" It became a standing joke between us, preparing for the question.

"How was business this week Fred?" I would ask when we walked to church.

One day Simone came home from school crying. Because she didn't know what the Gospel reading had been about the previous Sunday, her teacher had hit her over the knuckles with a ruler. I was furious! No teacher had been allowed to hit a child in Holland for decades and, although I did not entirely agree with that, she had no right to punish a child for a 'sin' that was our fault, as we had not taken her to church the previous Sunday. I knew the teacher would still be at school, so I hopped in the car, ready to give her a piece of my mind. When I charged into the classroom and stood before her, however, I suddenly seemed to have forgotten how to speak English. Rattling on in Dutch I aired my frustration. When the look on the teacher's face told me that she had got the message, I burst into tears. On the way home I felt terribly guilty about not going to church regularly. Humiliated by my tears, I vowed to better my life.

Another test to my faith came when Simone was required to take her Confirmation, swearing that she would obey the rules of the Catholic Church until her death. How can a child of twelve possibly know what she is promising for the rest of her life, I wanted to know.

Not to be different from the other children in her class, Simone wanted to go ahead with it, even though I was not prepared to make a white dress for her that she would never be able to wear afterwards. I felt sad to see her stand out like a sore thumb in her long, flowery dress among all the other girls in their elaborate white dresses, which, in some cases, had obviously been handed down from one generation to the next or had cost a small fortune. A year after Simone's Confirmation, I helped the parish mothers make a hundred white robes to be worn by both boys and girls for their first Communion as well as their Confirmation in future. That way they were all equal.

When the time came to go to the land sale auction in August, I was very nervous. Sam would do the bidding on our behalf. We had a map of the building area and selected our choices. Our first choice was a corner block, the first of the thirty-five blocks on sale. I held my breath while the bidding went on. The price went up by a hundred dollars, then fifty dollars per bid. When it got up to sixteen hundred, twenty-five dollar bids were accepted. My heart was thumping loudly when Sam kept bidding. At nineteen hundred, it went up by ten dollars. There was only a young couple and us left. The couple seemed determined to get the piece of land and I whispered to Fred to tell Sam to stop bidding. They had already decided not to go over two thousand dollars, and Sam left it to the couple at nineteen hundred and eighty dollars.

People were appalled at the high price it had fetched. If the first went as high as that, the others would not be any cheaper. Sam liked our second choice better as it was between private blocks without any Commission homes. He pointed out that, even if we had to pay more for it, it was a better buy in the long run as a corner block was a lot more expensive on council rates.

The next couple of blocks went quickly. They all went up to around two thousand dollars. While our choice was auctioned next, I felt all my blood drain from my face and my head spin, as if our life depended on it. While I closed my eyes and said a silent prayer, I heard the hammer fall. The block was ours for eighteen hundred and fifty dollars. My relief was overwhelming. Later that afternoon, we took our excited children to look at the block. While we were searching for the boundary pegs in the totally bare area, an elderly lady came toward me saying: "I'm sure I heard the children speak Dutch. Is that true?" She introduced me to her son-in-law, Les, who had bought the block behind us.

During the following years Riny told me about the hardships they had encountered when her husband decided to go to Australia, shortly after the war. She had been devastated to leave her comfortable existence in Holland because of her husband's wish for adventure. Soon after they arrived, her husband got a job on the railways, often leaving her on her own to cope with their three little children in an old shack.

"I never learned the language properly," she said regretfully. "At first I was too angry to learn, and later I was too old."

"You've got to learn it while you're still young," Riny had warned me when we first met, and I had every intention of doing so. I had not realised that I was already writing English at that time. In her reply to my letter at the end of April, my mother asked: "Oh, Mien! What kind of things are 'elite' and 'ladies'? And what are 'snobs'?"

Mum had not been sad at all for me to leave for Australia. "Why should I?" she had asked. "I knew that you would go sooner or later, and you are going into the sunshine. Why should I feel bad about that?"

At the big farewell party in the attic, Mum had told our guests that she was, in fact, quite happy about it.

"When Mien is there, I can go and visit Henk and Sam one day too. That's better then visiting those two single blokes."

In her first letter after we left, she wrote that she had already put her name down for 'We Are Coming', an organisation which helps parents to visit their children overseas. In my reply I advised her that she should start to learn some English so that she could talk to people when she got here.

While our letters crossed in the mail, Mum saw the paperwork she had to fill in and heard about the injections, money exchange etc. She wrote back that I could forget about it. There was no way she would ever come to Australia.

An Unexpected Week in Melbourne

Two weeks after Mum's letter arrived saying that she would never come to Australia there was another letter from her with a stunning message. My brother Henk was getting married and she would be in Melbourne in two weeks! Mum's letter bubbled over with excitement. I cried reading it all. When Henk wrote to her that he was getting married, Mum had asked him what he wanted for a wedding present. Henk had answered, jokingly, to come herself instead of sending a present. When my younger brother Wim came home from work that night, Mum had given him the letter.

"What's stopping you?" Wim had asked. "Let's go!" Mum had protested that she did not have enough money but Wim had swept her argument aside, saying that he had enough for both of them.

For several years Wim had been saving up to get married, but his girlfriend could not make up her mind. She wanted a career and to try different boyfriends before she made up her mind to settle for life. A few weeks earlier, when she had left for yet another course in nursing, Wim had had enough, and told her not to come crying on his shoulder again. He had been heartbroken and jumped at the opportunity to get away from it all, when Henk's invitation came.

"Henk is expecting you and Sam to come to the wedding too," Mum wrote enthusiastically. "So, we'll see you soon!"

As another week had passed since she sent the letter, there was no time to reply. Henk's letter telling us the happy news came a few days later. Sam had no intention of going to the wedding. He was now working on the new house across the road and had to finish it as soon as possible, and he had no money anyway. Money was tight for us too, but the price of the block of land we bought was two hundred dollars less than we were prepared to pay for it, nearly enough to pay for one airfare and, lucky for me, Fred agreed that I should go. He and Sam would look after the children. "No problems!" they said.

Before I realised what was happening, I was sitting in the plane on my way to Melbourne. I was terribly excited. During the last fourteen years I had not been out on my own for more than a day. Who would have guessed that within a year of our arrival I would be flying around Australia in a big jet, on my very own!

Henk met me at Melbourne Airport. On the way to his home, he told me how he had met Robin, an Australian girl, at a church meeting. He could hardly believe that he was soon going to be a married man. I reminded him of our meeting in Fremantle, when we had just arrived and I had said to him that he could be married within a year.

"Not much hope there!" Henk had laughed sceptically.

Sitting beside him in his luxurious Ford Fairlane, I thought how different the week would have been in the hostel in Footscray, if Henk had been home in Melbourne instead of meeting us in Perth. It was late in the evening when we got to Springvale where Henk was boarding with a middle-aged couple. Piet, a balding Dutchman, greeted me at the door. Bev, his wife, was not coming home that night. She was a senior in nursing and was lecturing somewhere in the country. After a cup of tea, Piet went to bed, but Henk and I had a lot of catching up to do. We only had a few hours of sleep that night. Mum and Wim were arriving at six the following morning and the airport was an hour's drive away.

Even though I had only been away from my family for a year, it was very emotional for me to see Mum and Wim again. I could only guess what it was like for Mum to see Henk, after ten years! He was a man of thirty now, instead of a boy of twenty who had left home as if he were going to see a friend in the country for a couple of days. She was very disappointed that Sam wasn't there and, even though I had written that we lived nearly three thousand kilometres away from Henk, she had still expected to see Fred and the children there too.

Mum was very tired, and her feet were terribly swollen from the long, thirty six hour flight, but we had so much to talk about that we kept going until midday, when she could not keep her eyes open any longer.

When Mum and Wim had gone to bed, Henk and I did some shopping. Mum had been fast asleep when the telephone had woken her up. She had suddenly realised that she was on the other side of the world when the person on the other end of the line spoke to her in a strange language. "Ich nicht ferstain," Mum had said, throwing the phone back on the hook as if a bee had stung her.

"That was German, Mum, not English," we laughed when she told us about it. Bev, a stocky, matron-like woman, had come home shortly afterwards. She was glad to see Henk and I, so that we could translate what Mum was trying to tell her.

By the time dinner was over it was nine-thirty. We were all very tired and went to bed early. Henk worked for a market gardener a few suburbs away and he had to start work at five o'clock in the morning. When we got up at seven the following morning, Bev and Piet had already gone to work too. While we had breakfast, I told Mum and Wim about Kees and Jolanda, the couple we had met on the Southern Cross. We had not heard from them until recently. Before I left Alice Springs, I had written a short letter to tell them that I was going to Melbourne and hoped to see them there. When I showed Henk the address on the way from the airport, he said that the hostel was only a bit up the road from where he lived. Later that beautiful morning we went for a walk to see if we could find the place. I was a little sceptical, as I had learned that 'a bit up the road' usually meant a few miles away, but the hostel was actually just around the corner. There was no answer when we knocked on their door. After I pushed a note under the door, we walked around the neighbourhood aimlessly, admiring the gumtrees and bottlebrushes, which did not grow in Holland.

Mum and Wim could not understand why Henk had not taken the week off from work to be with them. I explained that two weeks holiday a year was all people had in Australia, not three like in Holland. Henk had already booked his honeymoon to coincide with the church conference, which was held in New Zealand that year, three weeks after the wedding.

Bev was cooking dinner when Henk came home from work in the evening. As soon as he came in, he squatted on the floor beside Mum's armchair, but Bev ordered him to have a shower before he sat down. When he came back and sat on the floor near Mum's chair, talking again, she told him to set the table.

After dinner, I was helping Bev with the dishes while Henk was looking at photos with Mum and Wim, when she called him away again.

"Henk! I've told you to put the rubbish out and it's still standing near the shed," she said, as if she was talking to a naughty ten-year-old. "Go and set it on the road immediately!"

We looked at each other in bewilderment.

"I'd better do as I'm told," Henk laughed uneasily as he stood up and went to do the job.

A knock on the door broke the uncomfortable silence. It was Jolanda, who had found my note. Our enthusiasm about seeing each other again soon took the bitter taste out of my mouth. Jolanda could only stay for a few minutes, as Kees had to go to work at nine but I was glad that we could spend the following day with her. I felt uneasy in Piet and Bev's house, probably because I had no defence against bossy people myself at the time. The couple had not been married long. Henk, who was part owner of the house, had lived with Piet since he joined the American-based church which had saved his life when he was down in the dumps and suicidal some years earlier. Piet was like an older brother to him. Their religion was strongly opposed to inter-racial marriage, homosexuality, smoking, long hair, celebrating birthdays and a whole range of other things that we take for granted. Pork meat, along with other animals with split hoofs and fish without scales, such as the delicious smoked *paling* (eel) we ate in Holland, were strictly forbidden. They did not believe in Christmas, the world was sure to end in the not too distant future, and they held 'Sabbath' on Saturdays. Sunday was the first day of the week for them. The thundering sermons of the leader of the church, which were regularly broadcasted on the radio in Alice Springs, always made me shudder. I could not bear listening to him, but I admire people making such big sacrifices for their honest beliefs.

As arranged, we spent the next day at Jolanda and Kees' flat in the hostel which was very similar to the one in Footscray where we had been. It had two bedrooms, a good size lounge and a kitchenette. They were supposed to have their meals in the common dining room but as they detested the food that was served there, Kees had bought a little stove so that Jolanda could cook a simple meal at home now and then. Because cooking was not allowed in the apartment, they often had a barbeque somewhere in a park.

The first months in Australia had been very difficult for Jolanda and Kees. They had lived in a hostel in Geelong, in one of those dreaded Nissan Huts, ex-army sheds, for six weeks.

"It was filthy, infested with insects, and stinking hot," Jolanda said. One day, shortly after their arrival, she saw a rat running in the bedroom and she had been petrified of rats ever since. A 'cardboard' wall divided the hut lengthwise. An unemployed couple on the other side had fought continuously like cats and dogs, using the filthiest language and making it impossible for our friends to go to sleep at night.

"I often sat with the boys on either side, pressing them against my chest, closing their ears with my hands until the noise died down," Jolanda said, shuddering at the memory. They had asked to be moved to another hostel since the day after they arrived, only to be told that there were no vacancies anywhere in Victoria. Their eldest son, Paul, was going to school but there had been no place for Frankie at the local preschool.

"When Frankie went to school too, the loneliness was killing me," Jolanda said. The difference in the boys' school hours had made it difficult for her to find a job. Kees had found work in a factory within a week and he had taken on a second job soon afterwards. During the long days, when he was at work, she had walked around the streets of Geelong day after day to stay away from the awful hostel. "I know them all now," she laughed.

After a month they had bought an old Torana. One Sunday, when they were driving around looking for better accommodation as usual, they called in at the hostel in Springvale, which had several vacancies and they had moved shortly afterwards. Jolanda's face dropped again when she told us how she had cried buckets of tears during the last year. But life was looking up now. She had found a few hours work as a waitress at the local golf club and they had bought a block of land in Lilydale, somewhere in the bush some fifty kilometres away. Compared to her, I had had it easy.

Piet and Bev had another boarder staying with them, Eddy, a young American fellow with a shaven head, like a monk's. Henk loaned Eddy his car to take us to friends of Mum's in Numurkah, a small farming community near Shepparton, the following day. The weather was beautiful again and the drive through the countryside in Henk's luxurious car was fascinating as the landscape changed continuously. We came through forests with huge trees, bare rolling hills with thousands of sheep trying to get fat on the dry, yellow grass, and lush green pastures where lots of dairy cows were happily grazing. We were amazed to see so many paddocks with black and white Fresians again; a heart warming sight for us Dutchies.

Being called 'Dutch' was very confusing for us.

"No. I'm not Duits (German)," Sam had said when he first arrived in Australia, "I'm from Holland."

After several hours we came to the fruit growing country where Marie and Wuf lived. It took ages to find their farm, on a sandy road in a maze of fruit trees, growing in all shapes and sizes for miles on end.

When Mum's two young sisters had left for Canada with their husbands in 1948, Marie came to our place occasionally to do some sewing. Her husband Wuf was a brother of Mum's sister Cor's husband and he had been a close friend of Mum's brother, Uncle Hannes.

Marie and Wuf enjoyed their unexpected visitors and made us feel very welcome. As was the custom in Holland, they invited us to share their hot midday meal, which Marie was preparing when we arrived. We watched in amazement how she set the table with her finest china and silver cutlery, saying that they often had important people coming for lunch or dinner. A little later, Wuf, her down-to-earth husband pushed his highly polished cutlery aside in one sweep, scolding her for her showing-off nature. Mum was delighted when he picked up a fork and made a mixture of the different vegetables on his plate, as she would do at home. While we helped her with the dishes, Marie, who was the oldest girl of a very poor family of eleven children, told us about the origins of the many expensive ornaments around the house. In the afternoon Wuf drove us around their impressive mixed dairy and fruit farm, which left Mum speechless.

On the drive back to Melbourne, Eddy became very talkative. We teased him about his shaven head, which looked like the bare hills we were passing and we had great fun trying to translate what he was saying, imitating his American accent. He was a great fan of Johnny Cash and played his cassette tapes non-stop. Even though none of us understood much of the words, we sang the country and western songs with him, as most of them were familiar to us.

When we got back to Piet and Bev's place, I was relieved to see that dinner was ready to be served and Henk had had a shower. It was Friday evening. Sabbath, a solemn day of prayer, meditation and Bible studies that

120

started at sundown and lasted until sundown on Saturday night. Mum and Wim were happy to go with me to Jolanda's place after dinner, leaving the family reading the Scriptures with their friends, grateful for the excuse that they could not understand English.

Henk seemed relieved when I told him that we could also spend the following day, Saturday with Kees and Jolanda, as he had to be with the congregation and would be away all day. Packed tightly in the Torana, they took us out for a drive to their block in Lilydale. The thousand square metre piece of land on a sandy bush road, surrounded by tall gum trees, was beautiful. Glad to get away from the hostel, they had been camping on the block every weekend, clearing away the huge blackberry bushes. In Holland we had picked buckets full along the nearby paddocks to make jam every summer, but the bushes there were very small compared to these giants. Kees and Jolanda enthusiastically showed us the plans for their three-bedroom house. The builder would start on the foundations in a few weeks time, they hoped.

"You can never be sure with those Australians," Kees grumbled. "They never seem to be in any hurry."

After a picnic lunch on the block, we visited another Dutch family who had been on the Southern Cross, and more memories were recalled. This couple had come to join a brother in his camping supply business. Although a job and a house had been waiting for them on their arrival, and they had enough money to buy what they needed, they still reckoned that immigrating was very difficult. They would not recommend it to anybody.

When we came back from the trip, Henk reminded us that we were going to a social held by his church that evening. We could hardly wait to meet Robin, the young lady Henk was marrying the following Thursday.

"She is no beauty," he warned us, "but she is a lovely girl to be with."

By the time dinner was over and we had all had a shower, it was well past eight o'clock. The party started at eight and we still had to drive to Melbourne where my new sister-in-law lived in a government apartment.

"Don't worry about it," Henk said. "Robin won't be ready. She's always late when we go out." It was after nine when he parked his car in front of the high block of flats. Robin lived in an apartment, which she shared with another girl on the fourth floor of the complex. Henk asked us to wait in the car while he went upstairs to get her. Tired from the long day in the country all three of us would have preferred to go home to bed instead of going to any party.

It took ages before Henk finally returned, without Robin. Henk did not seem to be worried at all. Women always take their time to get ready and Robin wanted to look her best to meet us, he said. But we were fed up with waiting. A party at eight started at eight and not at ten in Holland!

After a while, Henk became annoyed too, and went upstairs again. As more time went by, Wim and I left Mum in the car and went for a walk to keep awake. She was fast asleep when we returned and Henk finally came back and introduced us to Robin, his wife-to-be. Talking rapidly, Robin had to stop frequently to catch her breath. She explained that she had trouble getting her hair to sit properly and parties never started until well after ten o'clock anyway. The hall where the ball was held was not far away and it didn't matter if we came late.

Close by meant a half-hour's drive through the city. Nearly every member of Robin's family was there to meet her in-laws to be, who had come from so far away to be at her wedding. Henk introduced us to Robin's parents, her two sisters and two brothers, the minister of their church and some fifty other guests, who all belonged to the congregation.

In the bright hall I had a good look at my new sister-in-law. Henk was right. Robin was no beauty, but the dimples in her cheeks when she laughed, made up for it. She had just turned twenty and looked rather fragile, completely different from her younger sister who was quite solid, and a very attractive girl with thick black hair, put in a loose bun on top of her head. Robin's face was pale and badly scarred by acne, while her sister had a beautiful smooth complexion. It must be very difficult for Robin to live in her sister's shadow, I thought, but they proved to be, and still are, the best of friends.

Robin's parents had a small farm. Because it was not big enough to provide a living, her father had an outside job to supplement the family's income. Robin's mother, a tiny woman in her late fifties, looked after the cattle and worked in their extensive vegetable garden. Her father's health had suffered badly during the years he had spent in the army in the Second World War. He talked of little else than his experiences during the war. We later learned that he suffered from Alzheimer's disease.

Robin was the third child in her family. She had left home when she was seventeen. After two years at university, she got a job in an office of the Australian Army, but she was going to quit her job after the wedding, to become a housewife. Like a good Dutchman, Henk did not want his wife in the workforce. It was his duty to provide for her.

Supper had already been served, and dancing started soon after we arrived at the party. It was great to dance with my two brothers, Wim and Henk and, as always at a party, Mum got up too. She had never been allowed to learn to dance but she loved to be on the floor. Like me, she simply could not sit still when there was happy music playing. After a few glasses of wine, I was having great fun joking and dancing with American Eddy, when it was suddenly time to go home. Two o'clock and we still had to drive home to Springvale.

The following day, Sunday, Henk took us to Sale, where Robin's parents lived. The flat, lush-green pastures with hundreds of black and white Frisians in Gippsland made us feel very much at home. Most Dutch farmers had settled there in the fifties, making a good living on their dairy farms. Henk said that there were even more Dutch farmers in Tasmania.

"I don't know why they bother to speak English there," he laughed.

Robin had gone home to Sale with her parents after the party. They greeted us at the gate of their property when we arrived. A number of brown Australian cows were roaming freely in the long grass surrounding the house that was hidden by trees and covered by climbing vines. A great variety of flowers and vegetables were growing side by side at the front as well as at the back of the old house. While Henk showed us around the farm, Robin and her mother prepared a true Australian lunch for us in the kitchen: shepherd's pie, cold chicken, cheese, bread, lots of raw, cut-up vegetables and several different salads, enough food to feed an army!

Henk's Dutch had improved a lot during the time we had spent with him and everybody commented that I spoke English very well. Between the two of us, Mum was able to have a good conversation with Robin and her parents, but there was nothing private about it.

Robin's mother proved to be a good seamstress. Apart from Robin's wedding dress, which we were not allowed to see as that would bring bad luck to the couple, she had made her own dress as well as dresses for the flowergirl and Robin's two sisters. With a shock I realised that they were all long dresses. Mum had brought the silver-grey suit I had made for her when my younger brother Bart married in April, the previous year. It was a nice suit but her short outfit would look terribly out of place next to Henk's mother-in-law's luxurious gown of cream brocade. On the way home we decided to ask Jolanda to take us to the city to buy a long dress for Mum.

Shortly after the Saint Patrick's ball in March I had cut my long cotton sailor's dress off and made it smaller for Lilian. I had since made another long dress I planned to wear at the wedding. Seeing that every one of the dresses Robin's mother had made had a high neckline, I became worried that mine would be too sexy. Although the neckline was not that low, on the two remaining nights before the event, I dreamt that my boobs fell out of my dress at the wedding!

An Australian Wedding

Jolanda happily took us into the city the following morning. She had already had a driver's licence in Holland and was used to driving in busy traffic. Kees was on night duty and he would pick the boys up from school in the afternoon. The enormous buildings in the city, the endless towers and arcades with hundreds of shops, astonished me. Amsterdam and Arnhem seemed only large towns compared to Melbourne!

In and out of the shops we went, but we could not find a suitable dress for Mum anywhere. They either did not fit, or they were far too expensive. Sitting on a bench in the sun, Jolanda and I decided we make one for her ourselves. Mum had had enough of shopping but she insisted that Wim went with us to buy the material. There was no need to worry about her; she would be perfectly all right, watching the endless stream of people and the busy traffic going by.

After more than an hour, we still had not found any material we liked. When Jolanda suggested we go to the famous Melbourne market the next day, I suddenly realised that I had completely forgotten about Mum. If she had gone for a walk, she would have become lost in no time at all. As I was hopeless myself at tracing my steps back to where I had been, I found it hard to trust Jolanda, who had not been to the city often either. At every street corner, I expected to see the bench, but every time we had to go further still. I had no idea that we had gone that far. We had been away for nearly two hours when we finally came to where we had left Mum. All three of us spotted her at the same time. We stopped dead in our tracks and burst out laughing.

There was Mum, a typical countrywoman, forlorn in the big city. She was still sitting in the same place as we had left her. Screwing up her face as she tried to hold on to the cigarette in a corner of her mouth - she only smoked about five cigarettes a week - she rummaged for something in her handbag.

"Oh! There you are at last!" she exclaimed when we came close. "I thought that you got lost in this madhouse." She looked insulted when I said that we had been very worried about her.

"Your mother is not as silly as you think she is," she berated me. "I was just looking for Henk's address, I would have taken a taxi home if you had stayed away any longer."

We all laughed, as the only taxi Mum had ever used was that of a neighbour in the village.

Kees was free the following day and took us to the markets. We could not believe the incredible variety of stuff that was there. You could buy 'the devil and his old mother' there, as we would say in Holland.

After a few hours we decided to split up. Wim went off with Kees to look at cars and camping equipment while Jolanda, Mum and I went to the household section. There were lots of different stalls with tons of fabric and most of it was dirt cheap. I would have liked to have bought a suitcase full to take back to Alice with me but, as I had very little spending money, I had to settle for only a couple of pieces. We fell in love with beautiful rich velvet that would make a million-dollar looking dress for Mum, for the grand total of eight dollars. It had the colour of mature red wine with a pattern of small roses in a slightly darker red.

"I'll look like the Queen herself!" Mum exclaimed, when we held it in front of her. As there was no time to lose, I took Mum's measurements and drew up the pattern as soon as we got back to the hostel. As usual, I had bought only just enough material, not noticing that the pile had to go one way. Berating myself for being so stingy, I had terrible trouble cutting the dress out. Velvet is very difficult to sew, but, with the help of Jolanda, we still had it ready for the first fitting by the time Kees walked me to Henk's place, close to midnight. Mum was still up, eager to see what we had made of it. The long sleeved dress with the pointed neckline fitted nicely and looked stunning on her.

Jolanda and I worked on it most of the following day chatting non-stop with Wim and Mum. In the afternoon Kees showed us slides of our voyage on the Southern Cross and the trip to Zululand, the horrible tin shed in Geelong and working on their block of land in the bush. In turn we gave lively descriptions of the funny things that had happened on our trip, killing ourselves laughing. Mum and Wim went back to Piet's place at dinnertime but I stayed behind to iron out some of the seams of Mum's dress. Because I was in a hurry, I did not check the temperature. I nearly died of shock when I saw the long, brightly shining mark right at the front of Mum's beautiful dress.

"Oh my God! I've ruined it!" I cried.

"Soup is never eaten as hot as it's served, Mum always says when things go wrong," I told Jolanda, while my stomach knotted. "How can I possibly tell her this?"

Reluctantly, I left the dress with Jolanda to try to steam the ugly shiny spot out when I left the hostel. Mum would become suspicious if I stayed away any longer.

I did not sleep much that night, cursing myself. How could I have been so stupid? You should never touch velvet with an iron in the first place. I managed to get away to Jolanda's place early the following morning. As I expected, she had been unable to make the mark any less noticeable. We decided to hang the dress in the shower in the hope that the steam would bring the flattened pile up again. There were some problems though. We needed to leave the dress in the steam for quite a while and the other residents of the hostel also used the showers. As we did not fancy staying there for hours, we had to find a way to lock the door on the inside so that nobody could disappear with the dress.

I went back to Piet's place to get Wim, who lifted Frankie over the high wall between two showers. Hanging upside down, Frankie could just reach the lock. After half an hour, we followed the whole process again to have a look how things were going, but it needed a lot more time.

"Where's my dress?" Mum asked suspiciously when I did not bring it with me. I told her that Jolanda was altering it a bit, silently praying that she would succeed. By lunchtime it had still not improved much at all. Jolanda offered to take it into the dry-cleaners while Mum took a nap, only to find that they were all closed on Wednesday afternoons. The wedding was the following day but we did not have to be ready until five o'clock in the afternoon, which meant that we still had time. Henk had the day off and planned to take us out, so Jolanda offered take the dress into the dry-cleaners early in the morning.

Bev did not get home for the night and, as Mum went to bed early that evening, I was left alone with five men: Henk, Piet, Wim, Eddy and another Dutch fellow who was loud and had a rather foul mouth. As the evening wore on they talked freely about the problems of married life. Seeing as I had been married for nearly fourteen years, they wanted me to tell them what a woman liked in bed from a man. Although I was not as prudish as I used to be, the talk became too rough for me. When I announced that I was going to bed, everyone protested loudly. Already quite drunk, Henk urged me to stay up now that they were having such a great time. His friends kept on filling his glass and he told me, over and over again, how happy he was that he would finally be allowed to do 'it' tomorrow, without feeling like an animal. "Tomorrow! Tomorrow is the day!" he kept on saying, which had everybody in stitches.

As the jokes became cruel, I tried again to get away, but the foul-mouthed Dutch fellow held me back. I was the only woman who had ever been at a 'buck's party', he said. By that time Henk, who had been made to drink a metre long glass of beer in one go, was dead to the world, but Wim helped me escape to the safety of my bedroom.

While we were drinking coffee the following morning, I asked Henk what a 'buck's party' was. My face turned bright red when I realised that I should not have stayed up at all, but then, how could I have known what was going to happen? I wondered how it was possible that such religious men could tell such dirty jokes and laugh themselves silly, while they drank themselves into a stupor.

While we were making plans the following morning to make the most of Henk's last day with us, a member of the church called. She and her family had been invited to the wedding but her little daughter had no shoes to wear. Could Henk take her to town to buy them? We were perplexed when Henk said: "Sorry folks! I have to go. You can come with us if you like."

We could not work out how Henk could be expected to change his plans and go shopping with the lady, just because she was a member of the church. Henk explained that they had to show how they loved one another, as the early Christians had done.

"But you haven't seen Mum for ten years!" I protested. "What about her? We're leaving tomorrow."

"She doesn't belong to the church," was Henk's answer. "Church members always come first."

As there wasn't anything else for us to do, we strolled behind Henk and his fellow Christian from shop to shop, looking for suitable shoes for her as well as for her daughter. As he was suffering from a bad hangover and having to translate what was being said, it became a very tiring day for him as well as for us.

In the meantime, the thought of the ugly mark on Mum's beautiful dress was never far from my mind. When it came back from the dry-cleaners at midday, the shiny marks were not quite as bad, but they still stood out like a sore thumb. Mum just had to hold her handbag in front of them at all times.

In the afternoon Jolanda offered to do our hair. Mine was short and easy to get into shape but Mum's hair was quite long and extremely thin. She always pinned it on top of her head to cover a large, balding spot. Jolanda wanted to put hot rollers in but Mum refused, worried that it would burn her hair and she would be left with nothing at all but, after promising to be extremely careful, she allowed Jolanda to do what she liked with it.

With a pounding heart, I slipped the dress over my mother's head, hoping that she would not see what had happened. Jolanda covered her up immediately with a big sheet and fussed with her hair until she looked like a model. Fortunately, there was no full-length mirror in the house and Eddy was waiting for us in the car, by the time we were ready.

Mum looked absolutely stunning in her rich velvet dress that matched beautifully with the rest of the family's outfits. Her silver-grey hair looked thick and healthy and the diamond clip Jolanda had pinned among the soft curls on the top of her head glowed like a tiara in the dim lights of the hall. A large corsage of red-edged, pink orchids pinned on the top of her dress after our arrival was just perfect. I was thrilled when I saw her there, indeed looking like the Queen herself.

I did not tell Mum - or Henk and Robin - about our trouble until after the wedding. I doubt if anybody had noticed the mark at all as Mum had held her handbag in front of her all the time even without me asking her to do so.

Ninety-nine percent of our worries are unnecessary. I wonder how often I still worry unnecessarily, as I did then.

Time went by quickly at the wedding. The only thing I remember of the service was the emphasis on the obedience of the wife, reminding her time and again, that the man was the head of the household, and his wife's duty was to follow him wherever he went. It had made me think about a Dutch saying: "The man may be the head but the woman is the neck that makes the head turn."

After dinner we danced for a while but, because it was a weekday and most people had to go to work the following morning, the party finished early. Henk looked very young and handsome in his black tuxedo and I was happy for him that he had found such a nice partner. They have two lovely sons now and proved to suit each other very well. Although Henk is still an active member of his church, he has become a lot more relaxed about the church's stern rules and regulations.

It was well after midnight before we got back to Springvale, but we couldn't sleep in for long, as Henk and Robin, who had spent the night in a hotel in Melbourne, would pick us up at ten. They would show us their little house at the market gardens where Henk worked, and later in the afternoon, take us to the airport. Mum had still expected them to come with us to Alice Springs before they went to New Zealand for the church convention and their honeymoon, three weeks later.

I was very excited to be going home and bringing Mum and Wim with me to Central Australia. Sam had no telephone, and the time was too short to write letters, so I was anxious to see how Fred and the children coped without me.

Shortly before we arrived at the Alice Springs airport, I suddenly realised that it was the first of September 1972. We would arrive at eleven o'clock at night, exactly the same hour we had left Holland the previous year.

It had been eleven at night when we stood on the railing of the ferry at Hoek van Holland bound for England, waving goodbye to our family and friends in the chill night air. I was still recalling the awful, unnecessary hurry in which we had said our good-byes, when the plane landed. Only Sam was there with our three eldest children.

"Where is Fred?" I asked anxiously the minute I came close. All at the same time they told me that Fred had been as sick as a dog for the last two days. Sam was very worried about him. He had such a high fever that he had not been out of bed all day, and he had not wanted to eat or drink anything at all. It took ages to get our suitcases, and the drive home seemed to take twice as long as normal. I jumped out of the car as soon as we got home and ran to the bedroom where Fred was bathed in sweat. Wiping his body with a cloth drenched in icy-cold water I managed to get his temperature down and with great difficulty, he swallowed some aspirin and drank a whole glass of water. When Mum and Wim came into the bedroom to say hello, he did not even recognise them.

The following morning we asked the doctor to come as there was no way we could get Fred to the clinic. A severe case of tonsillitis was his diagnosis. The injection of penicillin the doctor gave Fred in his behind made him feel a lot better in a surprisingly short time. By the end of the day he was sitting at the table again, rather uncomfortably from the injection. He looked dreadful with a beard of several days' growth and even skinnier than he was when we left Holland. He had lost a couple of kilograms since our arrival and another four during his brief illness. He only weighed fifty-five kilograms when we got him on the scales.

A few days after their arrival, Wim wanted to buy a present for the kids and we decided to go halves in an aboveground swimming pool. The big pool in town had been closed in April, and a new Olympic size one was being built, but would not open till after the summer holidays.

There were plenty of helpers to set up the five-metre round, blue corrugated iron pool in the backyard at Sam's place, since just about all the neighbourhood children were watching. Fred only filled it halfway, so that Regine and her friends could go safely into the pool too.

After I watched them splashing in the icy cold water for a while, I went inside to make a pot of tea. The noise of the excited kids was suddenly interrupted with terrible screams. Richard had hooked his heel on a sharp corner of the ladder used to get in and out of the pool. I shuddered when I saw the blood oozing out of a big, square lump of torn skin.

Fred and I took him to the hospital while Wim fixed the poor workmanship on the ladder. The tear in Richard's heel required nine stitches, which he showed off proudly to his friends when we came back. Putting the stitches in did not cause Richard as many tears as the fact that he was unable to go into the new pool for a fortnight.

It was as hot as it had been when we arrived the previous year and the pool was an absolute blessing.

"It is going to be forty-one this afternoon," I announced to our visitors one morning at the beginning of October. Mum sank instantly onto the nearest chair.

"Oh God! I won't be able to survive that!" she groaned wiping her forehead with her hankie.

Shortly after lunch that day, I walked with Mum and Wim to see how the new Commission houses in the area were progressing. On our way back I suddenly remembered what the temperature was going to be.

"Not too bad for forty-one degrees, is it Mum?" I asked. She agreed with Wim and me that it felt the same as about twenty-eight degrees in Holland. The dry, clear blue sky made all the difference. A week later, when it was overcast, forty degrees was as uncomfortable as thirty-two degrees on an unusually hot summer day in Holland.

Mum and Wim loved their stay in Alice Springs so much that they soon talked about staying longer. They added another six weeks to their visit, leaving on the twenty-second of November, instead of the fifth of October as planned. That way they were here for my birthday as well as for Fred and Sam's. While she was here Mum had no problems with her arthritis whatsoever, probably because of the dry heat.

Because the old Galah gave us endless problems, we decided to buy a new car. Fred had fallen in love with a brand-new red and white Nissan Patrol, a four-wheel-drive of 'only' four thousand and two hundred dollars. We had saved up half of that amount for the foundation of the house but, because we had a letter from the Government saying that we could expect a Commission home in the next couple of weeks, we decided to buy the car first. Fred bought the Galah for three hundred and fifty dollars and got two hundred back for it. We would pay off the rest of the amount over a year. It would take three weeks for our new car, the first brand-new car we ever owned, to arrive.

In the meantime, we took Mum and Wim to all the interesting places around town. Wim spent a lot of time with Sam building a house across the road and Mum helped me, sewing on buttons, and a hem on a dress or mending the boys' school socks. That way I could play cards with her and the children when they came home from school.

Playing cards had always been my mother's favourite pastime; she never grew tired of it. While she was staying with us, I often watched in amazement how she played cards on her own for hours. No, not a game of 'Patience', or any other card game which could be played alone; she would simply pretend that there were several other players around the table and play each hand as if it were her own.

"But you know exactly what those players have in their hands," I protested when I saw her play that way for the first time.

"No, I don't! I only remember what they have thrown out, otherwise I could not play fair," Mum answered, rather annoyed with me.

At the end of September, I was told that it would take at least another eight or ten months before we could expect a house from the Housing commission. It was a great surprise for us to get another letter a few weeks later, saying that we could pick up the key to one of the new houses in Forrest

Crescent on the 13th of October, the day we had arrived in Alice Springs the previous year. Sam had signed a paper agreeing to provide accommodation for us for twelve months and the contract ran out on that day. Although we were very happy to get such a surprise, it would have made life a lot easier for all of us if we had known all along that we would get a house in October.

The day we moved into the Commission house was a very happy one for me. I was always terrified that something would happen to Sam's shiny dark-brown floors, which were a pain to keep clean, as well as to the white, unpainted walls or the brand new kitchen cupboards, made from very soft timber that scratched easily.

Because we now owned a block of land, we were not given a choice of three houses as was the norm, and we could only stay in it for a maximum of two years. Regulations have relaxed a lot since then, but at the time they were very strict, or so we thought. When you owned a block for a year, you had to have a fence around it and after the second year you were expected to live in the house built on it. We later learned that nobody took much notice of those rules.

We had applied for a four-bedroom house, but had to accept a three-bedroom one instead. Two of the bedrooms were very small. When I had placed the beds for the three girls in one room, and the three boys in the other, there was not even one foot of space between each bed. We had to replace the doors of the old cupboards we bought at one of those popular lawn-sales in town with a curtain, and stand on the end of the bed to get to the clothes. The master bedroom was a metre longer and had a window at each end. It had to be our bedroom as well as my sewing room.

The house was only a few streets away from Sam's place on a block that was nearly a thousand square metres and completely bare. Mum moved in with us but Wim stayed at Sam's place. During the following week he helped us plant a lawn, something that was not done in Holland. As we did at Sam's place, we bought a few truckloads of very fertile, deep red sand, which we all helped to spread out before we started planting. Forming a line of people, just like we did when we turned hay when I was young, we put in hundreds of metres of kikuyu runners we got from Sam's place as well as from neighbours and friends. It was amazing how quickly we had a lovely green lawn. The vegetable patch we made along the wire fence at the back, grew very well in the red soil too.

There were several American houses in our street; houses where the Americans who worked at the Space Base lived. An American family across the road from us had nine children; the two eldest were girls, the rest boys. On the Sunday morning after we moved in, we watched with open mouth how Bill, who was a big man, folded himself behind the steering wheel of his Mini

Morris. The rest of the Kennedy family followed one by one. Eleven people in a Mini! They waited eight weeks for their 'Yank Tank', a big four-wheel-drive vehicle, to come from the States. Until it arrived in December, they had to make do with the Mini. When they drove off to church, Kevin their eldest son, waved to us, curled up in front of the back window.

To be in a finished house again, after eighteen months of having to make do, was heaven for me. And, as our swimming pool attracted the new neighbourhood children as well as those near Sam's place, we often had a large crowd of very happy kids around during the hot summer days.

Summer Again

Two weeks after our arrival in the Centre, in October 1971, a three-year drought had broken, and we had some heavy rains afterwards in November, December and March. The NT Government had ploughed huge stretches of arid land and sown grass seeds to combat the dust problems, which blew millions of tons of valuable topsoil away into the Pacific Ocean. After the rain in March, the area around Alice Springs was green. Wildflowers bloomed in profusion and it looked as if the big dust storms were a thing of the past.

While Mum and Wim were with us, the strong October winds blew a gale too, but fortunately, there were few of the terrible, dusty days we had endured when we first arrived in the Centre. The evenings were always pleasant, no matter how hot it was during the day. Now that we had settled in the Commission home, life in Alice Springs had become ideal for us. Fred loved his job, but we were both glad when the tourist season slowed down at the end of October so that he had more time to spend with the family. Because Mum and Wim were still with us in November, I had not taken on much sewing so that I could do some for Mum. She wanted to take a fashionable pantsuit home, to impress her friends. Like most women her age in Holland, she had never worn long pants in her life. Dawn the proprietress of Polkadot, was kind enough to search through the boxed-up winter stock to find some suitable material for me. Sewing a thick woollen outfit in forty-degree heat was as bad as having to fit it, but Mum paraded happily in her new suit for visitors, time and again.

We decided to celebrate our birthdays with a house-warming party at Sam's place, even though heret was still a lot of work to be done before his house was finished. The big open chimney, which separated the lounge from the kitchen, had to be built in with an arch made from the colourful local sandstone. Another sandstone arch was to cover the entrance from the lounge to the bedrooms at the back of the house. There was an enormous high bench, like a public bar in a pub in the open kitchen, but Sam had only had time and money to do the tiling above the stove and the sink. He planned to do a few more of the basics, then rent it out and go to Queensland for three months, leaving the finishing until he came back.

At first we planned to make it a big party but, as it was the first party we had organized in Australia, we decided to invite only a few friends and neighbours. Because everybody was bringing their own food and drinks, the party proved to be very cheap. We only supplied nuts and crackers, made a few salads and bought some meat and sausages for the barbeque, lemonade for the kids and a carton of beer for the adults.

"That's plenty," Sam reckoned, waving away my concern about running out. "Too much!"

With the help of the kids, we decorated the lounge with crepe-paper streamers and we made more seating with bricks and planks, covered by a blanket. I also put a blanket on the narrow concrete platform in front of the big open fireplace for people to sit on.

Lilian had made a long, pink dress for herself with royal blue trimmings. At thirteen, she looked very grown-up with her hair in a bun on top of her head. Compared to Mum, wearing the beautiful red velvet dress she had worn at Henk's wedding, my long mustard-coloured flowered cotton dress looked as cheap as it had been. Sam set his old 'reel-to-reel' up on a trestle table in a corner and put some popular music on. We were ready way ahead of time and the kids waited impatiently for our visitors to arrive. We should have known, but apart from a few Dutchies, they all came late. Our three youngest children who had been dancing since the music had started were ready for bed by the time the first of our guests arrived.

After the barbeque, everybody had a great time, swirling around the shiny tiled floor in the lounge. As the evening wore on, some of the men had had more than enough to drink. I was amazed how they could swallow one bottle of the icy-cold beer after another, without stopping for a moment. Henk, the baker, was a diabetic and stuck to his limit of two bottles. "The consequences aren't worth it," he said. Wim and Sam did not need any beer to become talkative, but a couple of beers never failed to loosen Fred up and made him feel as though he was 'one of the boys' in the navy again. Our friend Kees got quite drunk. He became sombre and sorry for himself, as he usually did when he had had too much to drink.

By midnight, the kids had all taken themselves to bed, and our Australian neighbours and friends left soon afterwards. By one o'clock only the Dutchies were left. As Sam predicted, there was enough food left to feed us all the following day. While Tilly, Ria and I cleared the table and washed the dishes in the open kitchen, we laughed with the men sitting around the lounge room table, exchanging jokes in our own language. Only Kees was not in the mood for jokes. Sitting side by side with Mum on the thick blanket in front of the chimney, he poured his heart out to her. When we were finished in the kitchen Mum stood up, pulling at the back of her dress. "Yuk!" she said. "I'm soaking wet!"

"Oh, no!" I gasped when she turned around, revealing the big dark circle at the back of her dress. Kees' can of beer had fallen over on the blanket beside him and Mum had sat down on it.

"Sorry mate! Sorry mate!" Kees kept apologising time and again, shaking his drunken head. Because she was hot, Mum did not mind having a wet backside. She stayed up happily until the last person was ready to 'hit the sack'. The next morning, when I picked up her foul smelling dress to put it in soapy water, I realised with a shock that Mum's beautiful dress was ruined permanently. The delicate pattern of dark red roses had mixed with the lighter colour of the fabric. There was absolutely nothing that could be done about the ugly dark stain. Mum was very disappointed and upset about it but, because her suitcase was overflowing and she could never wear the dress to impress her friends anyway, she left the ruined dress behind. She went home, quite happy to show the photographs instead of having to drag it out of the cupboard and put it on every time. A few days after she left, I made Mum's treasure into a dress with a long train for the girls to play in. With a crown made of Christmas tinsel, they pretended to be queens in it so often that the dress literally fell apart.

A week before Wim and Mum were due to go back to Holland we finally got our long-awaited red and white four-wheel-drive Nissan Patrol, a real work-horse. Apart from the radio it had no other luxuries. The metal benches in the back were very hard for the children to sit on. I was a bit apprehensive about driving it at first, but realising that if I didn't drive it I would be stuck in the house again, I soon got the hang of it.

We planned to go camping the following weekend but because Mum found it too hot, I had to stay home with her. Fred took Wim and the children out to Trephina Gorge and John Hayes Rockhole, about eighty kilometres along a dirt road east of Alice, where they stayed the night. They came back dirty and happy, telling us enthusiastically about the unbelievable beauty of the place. It was sad to see the shiny new car covered in dust, scratched by the thick bushes along the rough track. The first scratch on a brand-new car would make a grown man cry in Holland. Here it didn't matter at all Sam said. It gave it character.

After having been here for three months, Mum was eager to get back to the fresh, lush green countryside in Holland. She looked forward to playing a decent game of cards with her friends again, but Wim would have loved to stay. Mum's face had dropped every time she heard him talking about coming back again. After my stepfather died in March 1969, Wim and Ties were the last two of her children living at home. I shared her concern. If Wim left for Australia, she would lose Ties, my youngest brother, too.

Except for the three months that Mum and Wim were with us, we have very few pictures of our first years in Alice Springs. Developing a film of twelve pictures cost twenty five dollars, while a man's wages were eighty or ninety dollars a week. When Mum and Wim went home they each had an album full. It had cost them a small fortune at the time, but they always said that it was the best souvenir they could have taken back with them, as every picture had a story that otherwise might have been lost.

Although I was sad to see them go, I was also glad that we could get on with our lives again. Christmas was fast approaching and parties were being organized everywhere. As most women wanted something new to wear at Christmas, it was a great opportunity for me to help save for our own home. Before the month was over I had plenty of work again.

Christmas 1972 was hot; the hottest I remember. In the week before Christmas, the temperature went up to thirty-nine and forty-one degrees. On Christmas Day it was forty-three degrees. There was a cool change on Boxing Day, but it was still thirty-nine degrees, followed by forty-five the next day. While we 'Dreamed of a White Christmas' with Bing Crosby on the record player, we thanked God for the second hand evaporative air conditioner and the pool.

During those hot days we licked cheap ice creams and tried to keep cool in the lukewarm water of the children's pool, sure that we would never, ever, get used to Christmas in the heat of summer. We seemed far removed from the Christmases of short, dark days and long, cold nights, lots of candle light and a lovely hot meal at lunchtime.

Our children never missed the Dutch Christmas much. We still had our traditional breakfast after the midnight Mass, and they now had Santa Claus to look forward to because Sinterklaas could not come to Australia. Christmas was the only time that I missed television, which had come to Alice Springs on the sixteenth of December that year.

Even though a lot of households already had a TV set, often brought with them from the big cities, more than a thousand sets had been sold to a population of less than twelve thousand, prior to the big event. The first night of transmission was one of the quietest evenings in town, the Centralian Advocate reported. Even the usual Saturday night drinkers had stayed away in droves from the pubs. It was a great disappointment for our children that we did not get a TV for Christmas, but I was determined to keep the monster out of the house as long as I could. Our peace was disturbed as soon as the television arrived anyway, as they forever wanted to go to their friends' places to watch it.

We still occasionally went to the pictures in the open air at OLSH, the convent school on Friday nights, watching cartoons and other movies on a fair-sized screen that was tied to the rails of the balcony of the second floor of the school. The children lay on blankets and cushions, each usually with their own group of friends. Fred enjoyed the evenings too, as he loved cartoons and Westerns, especially John Wayne movies, which were often shown. I didn't care much for that kind of film and I often fell asleep on the blanket with Regine. Before they started and at interval, the tuck-shop was open for ice creams, drinks and lollies. They were cheap evenings and I got to know several of the other mothers, but, after we bought the four-wheel-drive, we went to the drive-in more often instead.

Because the Nissan Patrol was a high vehicle, we always parked in the back row with about a hundred sedans and station wagons in front of us. It was great to watch a good movie on the huge screen, sitting on folding chairs under the stars on a summer evening, or watching from our seats in the car with the speaker hanging from the window inside the car in winter.

After advertisements of local businesses and products came a cartoon or film for the kids, who usually sat on blankets close to the screen with their friends, booing and cheering along with the characters on the big screen. By the time the main movie started it was always close to ten o'clock, bedtime for me. Most movies were alright, but I would inwardly be seething when the film was scary or rude. I detested violent movies. I had seen enough violence in our household while I was growing up to last me a lifetime! Sitting with my hands over the girls' ears I'd get more and more worked up, unable to say anything, as that would make even more trouble.

As predicted, the television proved to be tough competition for the drive-in, which had been the most popular spot in town on Friday and Saturday nights for many years. The active social life of balls, musicals, plays, parades and other events soon suffered badly too.

Occasionally Sam came with us to the drive-in. Late one Saturday night, when we dropped him off afterwards, we stared in disbelief at a huge coffin, standing under the light against the front door of Sam's house.

"What in hell is that?" Fred exclaimed.

The kids, hanging over the back of our seats, had the wildest fantasies about it, but Fred soon set their minds at ease. Because work at Gallery Guth had slowed down when summer started and it was closed from November until February, Fred had been taking in furniture repairs, hoping to start his own business in the future. The lid of the highly polished, deep red mahogany coffin had been badly damaged in transport from Adelaide or Melbourne and it was needed for a funeral on Monday morning. The deceased man had been over two metres tall.

Ever since our dreams of buying a block of land became a possibility, we had been drawing up plans for our own home. Because both Fred and I came from large families, having to share our bedroom with two or more siblings, we wanted each of our children to have a room to themselves. Seven bedrooms proved impossible, but we managed six reasonably sized rooms. The two youngest children would have to share until one of the eldest left home. We did not like the Australian way of the front door opening directly into the lounge. Ours had to have a roomy entrance hall with large windows on either side of the front door for Fred to put stained glass in when we got rich. We wanted a good-sized, open lounge and dining room, a separate, four by four metre kitchen and a toilet in the laundry as well as in the bathroom. Before we left we had collected several pamphlets, with lots of new ideas about kitchen and cabinetwork from Holland and Germany, in case Fred would ever work for himself. We adapted a German design of a high, L-shaped breakfast bench with lots of drawers and cupboard space underneath. It had a lower bench with seating space for the eight of us.

I could hardly wait to see our dream come true. Here we were, designing our own home, less than a year after our arrival! Owning your own house was near to impossible for an average family in Holland at the time. We were amazed to learn that Fred could draw the plans up himself, which would be a big saving. For months we tried to work out a balance between what we wanted and what we could afford, until we were both happy with the result. With Sam's help and several trips to the local building inspector asking him about the local regulations, Fred handed in the drawings of what would later affectionately be called 'The Dutch Embassy', for approval in June 1973. They were very simple; a far cry from the complicated structural plans which are required these days.

At the beginning of the school holidays, early in December, we bought an old piano. From a very early age I had envied families who made music and sang together. My father had played the accordion and harmonica but, as I was still a little girl when he died, I hardly remember him playing. Perhaps that's why I love these instruments so much. Fred had played a harmonica in the nav,y and he had a go at playing the guitar when our oldest children were little, but unfortunately he had lost interest.

Simone wanted to learn to play piano ever since she had a tinkle on the old piano aboard the Southern Cross. When I saw one advertised in the classifieds, I urged Fred to have a look at it. The owner of the only music shop in town was selling out, wanting to retire. He had only one piano left. I fell in love with the big up-right, teak coloured instrument immediately. The price seemed very reasonable and it did not take me long to convince Fred that we could always sell it for more if Simone lost interest. We arranged to pick it up the following day, Saturday afternoon.

"You have to bring at least four strong men," Peter, the retiring shop owner warned us after we paid him. "The bloody thing weighs a ton!"

Thinking that three would be plenty, the fellows set out to pick it up in a borrowed trailer. They were unable to move it, however, so Peter called on his neighbour to help. The steel-framed piano had to be lifted out of his house on the banks of the Todd River, onto a trailer, which nearly collapsed under its heavy weight. Half our neighbourhoods' children were waiting for the men when they finally arrived.

138

"Hey! That's my piano!" Teresa, one of the Kennedy girls shouted.

While Sam, Fred and our Dutch friends Kees and Henk sweated to unload the piano and drag it into our house, Teresa told us how they had rented the piano for eight months from the music store. Her teacher had left town and because there was no other teacher available, the piano had been picked up only two weeks earlier and taken to Peter's place. All this hard work, while it could have come straight across the road!

While the men drank their well-deserved beer, the girls happily hammered away on their new toy. It was interesting to learn from Teresa, that her parents had paid a lot more to rent the piano for those eight months than it had cost us to buy it. Although it drove us up the wall at times, the old piano gave us a lot of pleasure through the years. I had a few lessons myself at one stage, but I soon had to admit that I had absolutely no talent at all.

It was a sad day for me when we had to sell the old 1929 Autotone piano when we moved into another new house - our retirement home – in 1993. It was advertised in the paper a couple of times. Hoping until the last our eldest son Ray's place, where it was temporarily being kept while we finished building our new home, but he was adamant that the piano had to go. He was right though. Since Simone had left home and moved interstate in 1984, it was seldom played and there wasn't much room in our new lounge room. The Dutch Embassy, where we had lived for eighteen years, was already empty and to be handed over to its new owners, when I watched my beloved piano being taken away by the piano tuner. It broke my heart to see it in a scruffy second-hand shop a few weeks later, advertised far below its real value.

Our new house was only half finished when all our children came home for Christmas in 1993. It was the first time for several years that we were all together. We were planning carols by candlelight on Christmas Eve when Simone said; "Pity you don't have the piano anymore."

"It hasn't been sold yet. It's still in that awful second hand shop," I said. Visualizing us all singing happily while Simone was playing was too much for me and, on the spur of the moment, I decided to get it back. That same afternoon I went to see Steve, the tuner, and arranged to have it brought back. Then I worried all night how he would get it up the hill on the sandy track, and how on earth I was going to break the news to Fred.

The following day there wasn't a suitable opportunity all day to tell Fred what I had done. I finally told him about it only a few minutes before the piano was being delivered. I had asked Ray, Eugene and Richard to be there to lend a hand, and I made sure that most of the grandchildren were there, to avoid a scene.

Fred had rolled his eyes, said nothing, and supervised the difficult task of bringing the incredibly heavy instrument up the hill over the rough, un-paved road. I held my breath when they lifted it over the highly polished doorstep into the lounge where I had cleared the space designed for Fred's aquarium. When I paid Steve for the job after he had tuned it, the whole house echoed with the happy music from my beloved piano.

"We'll soon get rid of it after Christmas," I heard Fred say while he was having a drink with the boys. That's nine years ago now and the piano is still there, being played regularly by our grandchildren. Occasionally, the subject of getting rid of it comes up but lately I suspect that Fred is actually happy that it's there. Now that he is building Dutch street-organs he is often using it to get the tune or pitch for the flutes right.

Floods, Loneliness and Dogs

After the heat wave at Christmas, which lasted over three weeks, the heavy rains at the end of January 1973 were a welcome relief. When the rain stopped, we drove to the Finke River, a hundred and thirty kilometres south of Alice. The normally bone-dry ancient river was at that point nearly two kilometres wide. It looked like a big lake. The strong current had washed away large sections of the dirt road and the railway line. More than a hundred people coming up from the south on the Ghan or by car were stranded for days before they were airlifted into Alice Springs by a small aircraft. The grocery shops in town soon ran out of fresh vegetables and we were back to powdered milk, the only milk that had been available in town when we came to the Alice, apart from a few cartons of goat and cow's milk from local farmers.

Heavy rains continued in South Australia, which kept the road closed indefinitely due to flooding. Because people were panic-buying, the town ran short of all food supplies - our first taste of real isolation. The RAAF's Hercules aircraft brought in tons of groceries, but by the time we got to the shops, most of it was already sold out. When the first trucks could get through again, they cut deep ruts into the muddy road. Most of the perishables were badly deteriorated by the time they reached the town; fifteen hundred gallons (six thousand litres) of milk was sour on arrival.

Fortunately the shortage only lasted a week, but then the road workers went on strike. To everybody's relief, the dispute this time ended after two weeks. Strikes were virtually unheard of in Holland but here they disrupted life, time after time. The previous year, our two eldest boys were among a group of scouts who volunteered to help in the hospital when the staff was on strike, sorting towels, bed linen and napkins. Throwaway pads and napkins had not reached Alice at that time.

In June we had the heaviest rainfall for that month in more than fifty years. Again we were cut off from the rest of the world for a week. Then on the eighth of November, the beginning of the wet season, all hell seemed to have broken loose when a terrifying hailstorm hit our area. Some of the giant hailstones were bigger than golf balls! The storm, with gale force winds of up to a hundred and sixty kilometres per hour, spectacular lightning and some nerve shattering thunder, lasted about fifteen minutes, leaving a path of destruction half a kilometre wide. It had brought down power lines, uprooted trees and ripped roofs off a dozen houses. Several people had been bombarded with the missiles as they hurried home. I could imagine what their backs looked like when I saw Pat and John's lovely vintage Ford, which had been standing in their driveway when the storm hit. There were deep dents all over the bonnet and the newly upholstered canvas roof had holes in it everywhere.

'One person's loss is the other's gain' or, as the saying is in Holland "one man's death is the other man's bread". The plumbers did a roaring trade, since the thick glass panels of every single solar hot-water system in the area had been shattered. So did the glaziers, as a lot of windows had been blown out, including one of ours in the living room. A frightening experience! It's a very humbling feeling when the elements are playing havoc like that. It made us all feel very small and vulnerable.

Two weeks after the hailstorm we had another downpour that made the rivers burst their banks. It was a Sunday morning, so we all climbed into the Nissan and went to have a look at the Old Telegraph Station, picking Sam up on our way. While we drove through some twenty centimetres of water in the Charles River, we could hear the deafening noise of the Todd. The enormous volume of water roaring around the boulders in the normally dry riverbed provided a truly spectacular sight.

We wondered where Raymond and Eugene would be. They had gone camping with the scouts somewhere at the Telegraph Station the previous afternoon scouting. They had joined as soon as we had settled in Alice Springs. Unlike Holland, where the scouts only went out once a year, they had been camping every couple of weeks, and loved it.

"They'll be alright," Sam assured us. "Their leaders know where to go." After watching the turbulent river for a while we went home, but when we got back to the Charles the water was much higher. Sam got out of the car, took his thongs off and walked to the middle of the strong flowing river where the water reached above his knees.

"It's still rising," he said thoughtfully. "It would be safe to cross but we have to do it now." Sitting behind the steering wheel, Fred looked doubtful.

"Move over," Sam ordered. "I'll drive."

The water spilled over the running board as soon as the car went into the water. We all held our breath, watching the water leaping past the open door on Sam's side, expecting to disappear into a deep hole any minute. Sam laughed when we let out a sigh when we safely reached higher ground on the other side of the creek. A few hours later, Fred and I went back to the Telegraph Station to see if we could find our sons. The Charles had dropped to a safe level to cross but the Todd River was still pretty wild. We followed the track into the bush behind the buildings until we came to the Todd again where several cars were parked on the edge of the river. A group of boys was standing on the opposite side of the fast flowing water.

"That's them!" Fred said, pointing to another lot of scruffy looking kids across the river. At first I could not recognise any of them. Then I spotted Eugene, wearing a big beige shirt that reached far below his knees.

142

"What would he wear that stupid shirt for?" I asked. "He took plenty of clothes of his own."

The men on either side of the river shouted back and forth, but I could not make out what they were saying because of the noise of the roaring river. Another four-wheel drive arrived. The parents of one of the other scouts came out with big thermos flasks.

"The kids have lost everything," they said when we asked them what was going on. "They're lucky to be alive."

Max and Colleen were both scout leaders. They had gone home to get soup and sandwiches for the kids, because they hadn't had anything to eat since the previous night. It didn't dawn on us how serious the situation was until the men were setting up a contraption, made with ropes, called 'a flying fox' to bring the boys across the river.

"Can't you leave them there until the river has dropped?" I asked anxiously. They couldn't as more rain had fallen up north and the river was expected to rise again in a couple of hours. Colleen told us that they had been there early in the morning to see if the boys were all right. When they discovered that the scouts were camping on an island in the middle of the river, they had raised the alarm. The ranger at the Old Telegraph Station had set out with a tractor, but by the time they came back to the river it had been too high for the scouts to cross. As the water level was still rising rapidly, Bob, the boys' scoutmaster, had asked them to fetch the flying fox from the scout hall, but when they returned, the river had been too high to set it up. Bob then suggested a helicopter to rescue the boys, but there was none available at the airport.

By the time we arrived on the scene, it was well past midday. It seemed ages before the equipment was finally set up about thirty metres downstream, where the river was narrower. A safety line was put across the river about ten metres further on, for the boys to grab if anything went wrong. A strong swimmer, tied to a tree by a long rope stood by to get them out of the wild stream. A big cheer went up when the first young fellow was across. Even though every boy came across safely, my heart was racing madly when our two sons were swaying above the torrent on the flimsy device.

By four-thirty in the afternoon the last of the thirteen boys, aged between nine and fourteen, was safe. By that time we had already taken Raymond and Eugene home and heard what had happened that night.

It had rained off and on for a couple of days before they left that Saturday afternoon. While they were collecting wood for their campfire, Bob's four-wheel drive had become stuck in the soft sand on the bank of the Todd River. They tried to get it out until well after dark when Bob decided to leave it there until the morning. Although more rain was expected it was highly unlikely that the river would flow more than a trickle. Along with the other boys, Raymond and Eugene had pitched their tent on a flat piece of grass, not far from Bob's vehicle.

At about four o'clock in the morning, Eugene rolled over in his sleep, awake instantly as his hand fell into water. He had grabbed his torch from underneath his pillow and switched it on, just in time to see their metal pannikins bobbing out of the open door of the tent into the dark night.

Eugene woke Raymond and another boy, who were still asleep in the tent. Then they woke Bob, who slept on top of his vehicle. Within minutes everyone had gone to higher ground from where they watched the water rise steadily, sweeping away the boys' tents and later Bob's four-wheel-drive, with all their food supplies and camping gear. All they had left was a wet blanket. Eugene was wearing Bob's shirt as his own had disappeared with the rest of his clothes. When it started raining the scouts had been soaked to the skin in no time. Cold to the bone, they had to wait for another three hours before Max came looking for them at daybreak.

Ironically, the town's Emergency Services had been at Emily Gap, ten kilometres on the other side of town, for an exercise weekend. They too had become trapped by the unexpected mass of water, which had come down from the catchment area in the northern hills. They had to be rescued themselves by the police.

When we had a look at the scene the following afternoon, one of our thick, Dutch sleeping bags was hanging high up in a tree, badly torn and covered with mud. Their tent was nowhere to be seen. Bob's car had been washed away for miles and was a complete write-off. Because a scout leader was a volunteer, taking the kids out at his own risk, Bob was never compensated for his loss. He never gave up on scouting though. He was recently honoured for his fifty years active service.

At the beginning of the New Year, in January 1973, I started enthusiastically on my sewing again. Happy that I could contribute to getting our own house, I could hardly wait for the children to return to school at the end of the month. I soon found that word of mouth was the most effective form of advertising in town. The first wedding dress I made before Christmas, brought me orders from people who attended the wedding and, with the different balls and a charity play coming up in March and April, I was having more work than I could cope with.

At first, I loved being on my own but, after the first couple of weeks, I started to feel very lonely. Most of the women who had their dresses made were working. They usually called in at lunch or dinnertime, always in a hurry and, as I was struggling to get through the orders, there was no time for a long conversation with the occasional person who came for a fitting during the day. When Fred wasn't at Gallery Guth he was working at Sam's place, often until

144

late at night. When I complained to him that I had nobody to talk to all day, he suggested that I get a dog again.

While we were living at Sam's place, our Dutch-born friend Willy gave us a puppy, a cute, fat little black labrador with white feet and a white spot on his nose. After a few months Bobby started to have twitches and lose control over his movements. A few days later he was foaming from his mouth and started to fall over.

"Looks like he's got distemper," Sam said. "We'll have to shoot 'm if it gets worse." It was a very sad day for all of us when Sam and Fred took the lovely little dog into the bush and came back without him. We promised the children that we would get another dog as soon as we had a Housing Commission house.

All six children came with us to the pet shop one Saturday morning in March. We came home with six-month-old King, a mixed breed: a bit of Doberman, German Shepherd and goodness knows what else. His name was a bit much for a mongrel we thought, but King proved to be a very noble dog, good company for me as well as the kids. Fred was most impressed with the fact that King always stayed close to his side when we took him for a walk. He obviously had been well trained by his former owner. We grew very fond of him in no time at all but our happiness was short lived. King had a bad habit that cost him his life. He was crazy about chasing cars and biting their tyres.

We only had him six weeks, when he was run over by a car in the front of our house, one Sunday afternoon. There was absolutely nothing we could do for him but watch him die, whimpering softly while the children were gently stroking him. We buried him with an appropriate ceremony in the back yard.

After I wrote this last sentence I sat staring at the words, wondering why I could not remember where we buried him. Our son Eugene soon refreshed my memory when he read the story.

"What a load of bull!" he scoffed. "Sam and I shoved his body in a couple of cement bags, put him on the back of the ute and took him to the dump." Of course! The only animals buried in the backyard in Forrest Crescent with appropriate ceremony were the two guinea-pigs which had been killed when we dropped a heavy cupboard on them, while we were moving into the house.

The children were devastated and I felt lonelier than ever in the weeks that followed King's death. I desperately wanted another dog but Fred did not want to hear about it. One day, I drove him to work in the morning so that I could have the car. I just had to look for another dog. I went to the Council pound where stray dogs were taken and didn't cost anything, but there were only a few sick-looking creek-dogs in the cage. The pet shop had some lovely puppies, but they were far too expensive. When I tried the pound again a few days later my heart skipped a beat seeing a replica of King; perhaps a bit older but I wanted it, desperately.

The pound was closed when I picked Fred up from work, but we could still see the dog through the fence.

"That's an old dog," Fred said disappointedly. "He's nothing like King at all." I pleaded with him to let me have it anyway; I was going crazy at home on my own. Fred shrugged his shoulders and, after warning me that I might be sorry, he gave in.

The following morning I set out happily to pick up our new dog. The attendant told me to keep him indoors for a week to get him used to the new premises. He didn't know what his name was. I decided to call him 'Bingo' but now I can't think for the life of me why I chose that name.

"The bloody thing is covered with ticks," Fred said when he came home that afternoon and patted Bingo on his back.

"What ticks?" I asked.

"Look here; these horrible things!" he said while he lifted one of Bingo's ears. I shuddered when I saw a couple of those revolting fat creatures stuck in the poor dog's skin. Fred asked for a pair of tweezers and a jar of water. Half an hour later, he had taken out at least a hundred ticks, little red ones and fat grey ones. Fred explained that the little red ticks became fat and grey when they had sucked themselves full of the dog's blood. The only ticks I had ever seen were the little black deer ticks I had to pluck from Fred and his father after they had been picking blueberries in the forest in Holland. And later the 'royal' tick Regine had gotten during our visit to Zululand when she sat on the Zulu king's lap.

Our younger children were quite happy with our new dog but Raymond and Eugene were disappointed.

"You should've waited until we could afford a puppy," they sulked. "Now we won't get a proper dog for a long time."

I kept Bingo inside for two days, but he disappeared as soon as I left the gate open. I was quite surprised to see him back in the yard after several days. He had obviously been in a fight. He was bleeding from his side and had some deep scratches on his nose. He smelled of perfume, a strong scent of lily of the valley. I cleaned him up and fed him but he was not very hungry.

During the next week Bingo stayed at home even though the gate was often left open. Just as I thought that he had settled in, he disappeared again. This time he stayed away for a week and when he came back he was a very sorry sight. He was covered in blood and mud, and he had big cuts on his hind paws. Again he smelled like the same perfume. Bingo licked his wounds and stayed at home for another week or so, then he went off again. We had not expected to see him anymore but he turned up three weeks later, dirty and hungry, and yes, again smelling like the sweet lilies of the valley.

When he had recuperated, Bingo went away once more but this time he did not return. Perhaps he had finally realised that I had lost interest in him and stayed with the person who made him smell so nice.

Half a year had gone by when Fred suggested we get another dog to keep me company during the long, lonely hours of the day. We all piled into the Nissan and went to the new, privately owned kennels for unwanted dogs. We all fell in love with Josie, a small, golden-brown coloured labrador mix, when we saw her sitting alone in a cage sadly looking at us and licking our hands. Josie turned out to be fantastic fun for everyone, but she could not cure my sense of loneliness for long.

Through my sewing, I met most of the influential people in town, as they could afford a dressmaker. Because I was self-taught, I was always nervous about cutting into a piece of expensive material. It made me think of the time I had gone out sewing at peoples' homes as a sixteen-year-old, pretending that I knew it all. I still shudder, thinking back to the awful mistakes I made and my desperate attempts to cover them up.

Because I always made my own patterns, most people just gave me a picture or described what they wanted. I spent hours figuring out how it was done with old newspapers or bed sheets, which had to be cut up for dust-cloths anyway. I did not trust any of the bought patterns but some people insisted on supplying them with the material, then complained that I charged a dollar to alter them. At times it was much quicker to draw up a whole new pattern, but I did not dare ask the full amount for making it. At that time I thought that a homemade dress had to cost less than a bought one, so I was forever working against the clock.

Most of my clients paid what I asked, others said it was not enough and gave me another dollar or two, but one lady always complained that it was too much. Dorothy, a tall, soft-speaken English lady in her early fifties came in regularly with alterations. She always brought me the most out-dated clothes, expecting me to make them wearable again for a few dollars. When I explained one day how much time it took to unpick the necessary seams, she took the garment home to do it herself. When she brought it back a few days later she had opened the wrong seams and cut into the material in several places. Suggesting that I could do it in the evening so that I did not have to charge full price, she grudgingly left the unpicking up to me again.

Dorothy always had plenty of time to talk while I kept an eye on the clock, hoping she would go. It would be rude to keep working. I was amazed at the old clothes she kept bringing until she told me that she was getting them at the 'op-shop', the second-hand clothing shop for the poor, where she worked as a volunteer. Although it was always interesting to hear about her experiences, by the end of the year, I could not bear to listen to her complaints about charging too much any longer, and told her that I had no time for alterations anymore. I was upset when I later learned that she and her husband were among the richest people in town. They owned three cattle stations as well as a big hotel in Melbourne.

Many years later I met another of those thrifty and conservative persons, a beautiful looking American blonde, who was getting married to the son of one of the big business people in town. I had made her wedding-dress for half the price I should have asked but, when she picked it up she did not bring enough money to pay me for the extras, such as the zipper, buttons, cotton and lining I had bought out of my own purse. Because she could not find any shoes in town at the time, our eldest daughter Lilian sold her leather wedding shoes to her for twenty dollars, less than half what she had paid for them. The girl never came back to pay me. I went to the shop where she worked several times but she never had the money. I finally caught up with her several months after the wedding. After she told me about her extended holiday, she paid me grudgingly for the accessories but she insisted on giving Lilian's shoes back, saying that she had no use for them anymore.

"What about paying my daughter the twenty dollars for loaning them?" I asked. I left after waiting another twenty minutes for her to get the twenty dollars as she decided to keep the shoes after all.

Poor rich women! Why would they make life so difficult for themselves and others? I could not help feeling sorry for them.

Dreams Come True

The simple drawing Fred had made of our house was sent to Darwin the capital of the Northern Territory, for approval in June 1973. During the six weeks we waited for it to return, we were afraid of having to go to an approved architect to have a new set drawn up, as much stricter building regulations had been put into place. With trembling fingers I opened the big yellow envelope from the Government's Building Department in Darwin. The plans had been approved without a single alteration!

In the meantime Henk Guth's dream of building a castle to house a sixty metre panoramic painting started to take shape. It was going to be something like 'Panorama Mesdag' in The Hague but with the beautiful mountains, gaps and gorges around Alice Springs instead of the famous seascape. I had never seen this huge circular painting but Fred, who had been to art-school when he was young, knew about it and shared Henk's enthusiasm. It would attract thousands of tourists to Alice Springs he reckoned. The plans were drawn up at the beginning of 1973 but work did not start until June 1974.

We were very happy when Henk gave Fred the big three by nine metre shed that stood at the back of the gallery where the Panorama was going to be built, instead of trying to sell it. Pulling it apart, transporting it to our empty block and setting it up with the help of our two Dutch friends turned out to be a heavy job that took many weekends and several cartons of beer. Henk also gave us his three-year-old fruit trees, a lemon, a grapefruit, a mandarin and two orange trees, which provided us with tons of beautiful sweet fruit throughout the coming years.

In September, Fred went to work at the gallery earlier in the morning so that he had more time to dig out the foundations of the house in the afternoon, while I had the car to get quotes for the foundations, bricks, windows, electricity and plumbing. As the soil was rock-hard in the area, Fred hacked out a shallow trench first, and then filled it with water so that it was thoroughly soaked before he could get the spade in further. He worked fast, hoping that the rain would hold off. It was such a thrill to see room after room of our own home laid out on the bare block! To our great relief the concrete was dry before the heavens opened.

Another two months passed before Sam had time to build up the foundations and the plumbing was in so that the floor could finally be poured. In the meantime, Fred made cupboards for the house starting with my sewing room, which was to have a tall cupboard for wedding dresses and a long desk along the inside wall. In November, Sam suggested that we go to Adelaide to buy building materials, as they would be much cheaper there.

So here I was, flying away from Alice Springs for the second time since our arrival two years earlier! It was the first time our children had been left on their own longer than a couple of hours. I often wonder now how we could have left the six of them aged six to fourteen, home alone for a whole week. How could I? Of course, the neighbours and Sam would keep an eye on them, and Lilian was a very capable girl for her age. When I was fourteen I had often been left to run our household of ten but Mum had almost always been home at night. Adelaide was fifteen hundred kilometres away and there was no means of being contacted other than by mail. I must have been out of my mind!

But then, times were quite different in Alice in 1973. Or were they?

After my first awful flight in the Fokker Friendship that had brought us to Alice Springs, it was a pleasant surprise to fly to Adelaide in a big jet within two and a half hours. Dirk and Joyce, our former neighbours who had left Holland three months after us, met us at the airport. They arrived in Australia with four children aged between six and one, scant furniture and little money. Shortly after their arrival, Dirk got a job at the Holden car factory and supplemented his income by working at a service station several nights a week. On top of that he had picked up painting landscapes again, selling them at vantage points along the highway on the weekends. After living in a hostel for six weeks, they had moved into a Government Housing Trust Home in Elizabeth, some forty kilometres north of Adelaide with an option to buy.

While we were there Dirk was deeply depressed. His paintings were selling so well that he had considered giving up his job at the car factory to paint full time. But in the previous week, his hopes that Joyce would take on a part-time job when their youngest child could go to kindergarten, had gone up in smoke when the doctor confirmed their suspicion that Joyce was pregnant with their fifth child. Unable to face having to go into the workforce, she had forgotten to take the pill. I felt terribly sorry for both of them. They hadn't had an easy life.

Joyce, who was adopted as a child, was sixteen and Dirk was seventeen, when she first got pregnant. When Dirk's father found out about the pregnancy, he had kicked his son out of the house for the shame he had brought on the family. As Joyce's elderly parents could not bear to see their only child in such a condition either, the young couple had stayed away from home and eloped to be married in Scotland. However, shortly before the birth of their baby Joyce had been reconciled with her adoptive parents. They had given them the house across the road from us in Holland.

Soon after the baby was born, the young couple was told that their little girl was retarded and would not grow very much. By the time we met them they had three children; the eldest was six and the fourth on the way. During the four years we had known them they had been struggling with Joyce's inability to cope with her responsibilities and Dirk's bouts of depression. At times, when his fatherhood had become a too heavy burden for him, he would turn to alcohol for support.

In 1982 Dirk and Joyce returned to Holland, after ten years in Australia. Joyce had become homesick after an earlier visit to her elderly parents. Everybody had been so nice to them. At that time Dirk had become very disheartened with Australia when an art dealer, a fellow countryman, had taken advantage of his work. Promising to promote him as one of Australia's best artists, the dealer had sold Dirk's beautiful landscapes for triple the contracted price he had paid him for them, while he never kept his promise of a better car and a new house.

When we paid them a surprise visit in Holland some years ago, Dirk and Joyce lived in a brand new house in a very nice area near Arnhem. Although neither of them, nor three of their grown up children had worked since they had been back in Holland, they owned a good car and a big boat they took out regularly, sailing the lakes and rivers in Holland as well as in Germany. Joyce was glad she had decided to go back home, where the much praised welfare system looked after them, but neither were happy. Dirk's heart was still in Australia. He was painting another Australian bush scene to add to his collection, when we called in unexpectedly.

Things changed dramatically for them when a few years ago the Dutch government cracked down on unemployed people who owned a boat while on welfare. Dirk and Joyce were very apprehensive of having to accept jobs that later proved an absolute blessing for them. Dirk taught painting at a local college and Joyce demonstrated new products in a large supermarket. Dirk loved his job, and meeting people had opened a whole new world for her, Joyce said when she called me recently. All their children had jobs too, and even their eldest Downs-syndrome daughter was happily working in the office of a sheltered workshop.

The week in Adelaide, a well-planned spacious city surrounded by beautiful clean parks and gardens, went quickly. Dirk and Joyce had taken us to several huge places which sold building materials, but in the end we had only ordered the roofing timber there. To forget their troubles for a while, they had taken us to a very funny vaudeville show we thoroughly enjoyed. As it was still too early for our friends to go home, they took us to a nightclub afterwards where I watched a strip-show for the first time in my life. I had heard about them and seen pictures in a magazine but I was not at all prepared for the incredible way people behaved when they were being encouraged to let their hair down; not my idea of having a good time at all! Half the time I was too embarrassed to look but our companions seemed to feel quite at home. Several women went hysterical when a nearly naked man came dancing on the stage. A little later an excited man in the audience pulled his pants down when the girls took off their last bit of skimpy clothing.

On the way home I could not stop thinking about all those people, hyped up by the show. The whole show had been rather vulgar and revolting, but it was fun to re-enact some of the dancing later in the privacy of our own bedroom.

We had seen lots of places around Adelaide and Victor Harbour where we would like to live if we grew tired of Alice Springs, but although it was nearly summer, it was very cold at times, we were both eager to get back to Alice again at the end of the week.

The children were all at school when we got home. There was a 'Welcome Home' sign waiting for us on the door. The house was tidy and everything seemed to have gone all right. Nobody could explain the pink stain on the ceiling in the living room, which later proved to be from a spoonful of spaghetti that had somehow got out of hand. It wasn't until many years later that we heard from one of the neighbours that there had been a terrible fight between Lilian and the boys, as she could not get them to do their share of the housework. Well, I had not expected them to behave like angels, at least not all the time.

Among the mail waiting for us when we got home, was the approval of our bank loan to finish the house. We had been knocked back the first time we applied and advised to ask for a lesser amount.

Memories of the application for that first loan came flooding back to me when I sat in the bank managers' office in 1993 to apply for what was called a 'bridging loan'. We had to sell the 'Dutch Embassy' to be able to build the a house that was going to be more suitable for our needs now that we were retired and there were only the two of us left in the house.

When the manager asked what our assets were, I laughed.

"That reminds me of my answer to that question in 1973, when we applied for a loan to build the house we now want to sell," I said.

Apart from the block of land with a shed and the foundations of the new house, we only had the Nissan Patrol, the old piano and some household goods we had brought with us, or bought at a lawn sale. When the manager shook his head, I had looked at him for a moment, sat up straight in my chair and said with all the confidence in the world: "We have six beautiful children who are worth at least a million dollars each."

"They are liabilities, not assets," the manager had replied, but he told me later that my answer had made a big difference in his decision to grant us the loan. It had made him confident that we would make it.

"It would not make any difference these days," the manager laughed.

"Now that Alice Springs is on a par with the rest of the world, only hard figures count."

Now that the loan was granted we could order the bricks, which were made locally, but Sam was not ready to work on our house for a long time. When he had finished the big house across the road he had started another big one in the neighbourhood and this one was built with very small white bricks. Sam had been sick of working for a long time, and he became more depressed as time went on. Life was passing him by. Too much work and not enough play, he said. His talking about going to Queensland for a couple of months to play on his property in Nambour worried us sick too. We wanted our house built so that we didn't have to pay rent as well as the interest on the loan. When my younger brother Wim wrote in his letter for my birthday, at the end of October, that he was getting married the following Spring, it hit Sam hard that he was now the only one of my siblings who was still single, apart from young Ties.

"I should stop working altogether and look for a wife," he said. "But I haven't even got the time to finish my own house."

I felt very sorry for him. Nearly a year had gone by since we had moved out of Sam's place and he could not rent it out because there was still so much to be done to it. A picture the Advocate of the wedding of a well-known young woman a few weeks later, was the drop that made the bucket overflow, and Sam broke down.

"She promised to wait for me and I haven't even had the time to keep in touch with her," he sobbed when he saw the photograph.

Fred and I looked at each other curiously. We did not understand what he was talking about. Of course a pretty young girl in her early twenties wasn't going to wait for a guy of thirty-five with a bald head. But that was not the point. Sam had stood still for the last ten years, and he suddenly realized that his young days were over, wasted away by working long days, having no time to enjoy himself and meet some eligible girls. He stayed in bed for a day. Then he decided to finish the house he was working on and go to Queensland for a long holiday. The plans for our house just had to wait again.

Sam was his old self again when he came back from Queensland in the middle of January. While he was away, the cupboards for his house were delivered. Fred had stained and varnished them and made his shed into a one-bedroom flat. Sam was delighted with the flat, the first finished place of his own since he had come to Australia. Although his house still needed a lot of work done to it, he rented it out to a nice young couple and started on our house immediately. He was keen to finish it, do whatever needed to be done to his own place, then move to Queensland permanently to build a bit of a house and play with his old bulldozer on his block of lush, green bush land.

Progress on our house was agonisingly slow. Building up and moving Sam's scaffolding, consisting of several forty-four-gallon drums and long, narrow planks, took ages. By the time he got to the chimney, he had two of those big drums on top of each other, a very primitive and dangerous set up in our eyes. Working at his own slow pace, being incredibly precise and stopped time and again by the persistent rain and people who came for a chat, it took another six months before the brickwork was finally finished at the end of June. Fred had hoped to be able to put the roof on before the tourist season started again, but the roofing material he had ordered had been lost in transport. After weeks of inquiring, it turned up in Tennant Creek, five-hundred kilometres further north with half of the timber missing.

Work at the gallery had slowed down as usual at the end of November but the building for Henk's dream 'Panorama' was taking shape rapidly. Henk had gone to Holland early in December to look for two or three artists who would help him paint the huge, three-hundred-and-sixty square-metre painting. While he was away, Fred made tons of different colours of oil-paints in a contraption of big coffee grinders Henk had invented himself for the purpose. He often came home covered with the fine dust that got into the pores of his skin, looking like a clown in ochre, red, blue, yellow or green, or whatever colour he had been making that particular day. An incredible amount of paint was used in the panoramic painting, which was to be the largest in Australia.

Joining the forty-eight panels of canvas into a continuous circle created endless problems. Even if they could find a way to get it under a machine to stitch it together, the canvas would stretch too much. In the end Henk adopted the idea of folding the edges to the back, held in place between two strips of aluminium, pop-riveted together. Fred stained and varnished the western-red panel boards of the big high ceiling before the huge canvas was hung in place. Later he helped Henk with filling the vertical joins in the canvas until they were hardly visible and painted the whole canvas with a thick layer of undercoat. Raymond and Eugene had great fun going bush with Fred to collect sand, grasses, sticks and rocks to place in the foreground between the viewing platform and the painting.

In the meantime Sam had finished laying bricks out on our house. He had just started building the fountain at the Panorama when the roof of our house finally arrived. Together with Raymond and Eugene, our two eldest sons, who had turned fourteen and thirteen in July, Fred put the timber on at the weekend. The boys were just as eager to get the house finished as I was. They could hardly wait until the following weekend when the sheets of corrugated iron could be put on.

People said to us that only a third of the house is ready when the roof is on. I did not believe them until we were doing the endless jobs of plastering, electricity, ceilings, tiling, painting, etc. Although Fred had already made the cupboards for the kitchen and the bedrooms while Sam was laying the bricks, progress still seemed painfully slow while Fred was kept busy at the gallery, and most of the work had to be done at weekends and in the evenings.

We loved visitors, but as work was being put on hold sometimes for hours, there were times I wished they would stay away, Kees, in particular. He came around every weekend and always brought half a dozen cans of beer with him. Bored with his own way of life, he was never in a hurry to leave and kept on talking while Fred went back to work. Time and again Fred would realize that he had made a mistake because of lack of concentration. The entrance at the front and the cupboard dividing the kitchen from lounge, which were put in the wrong places, were a permanent reminder of our friend's visits. On the other hand of course, we could always count on a pair of strong hands to help lift the heavy furniture. And, seeing us build inspired Kees and Tilly to build their own place. They were amazed to see the progress we had made during the three years since our arrival.

"We have been in Australia for eighteen years and still have nothing to show for it," Tilly often said. They had 'worked their guts out" at different stations in Victoria and New South Wales before they came to Alice Springs, half a year after we did. They were still living in the old, hired caravan at the back of someone's house with their fifteen-year-old son. They were also paying off their car. They both had a good income but somehow the money always disappeared, mainly on drinks, smokes and clothing, before the week was gone. The money they saved was used every couple of years on a trip to Holland as they often felt miserable and missed their families. While they watched us building, they soon learned that they could live from one wage, when they put their mind to it, without Kees having to give up smoking or his drinks. Within a year they were able to pay cash for the dearest block of land on sale at an auction, for more than double the amount we'd paid for ours.

At the beginning of October, we received a letter from the Housing Commission to advise us that the rent was going up by a massive twenty-five per cent the following month; from twenty-eight to thirty-three dollars twenty a week. It seems a pittance now, but most men only received ninety to a hundred dollars per week. We decided to move into our new house as soon as possible. Work was slowing down for Fred at the gallery, so he took a week off to put the kitchen sink in, tile the bathroom, and fit the outside doors. It was no wonder I got violently ill at the end of October. I was completely worn out trying to get as much done as possible after I came home from my job at the 'Emporium' where I worked at the time. My brother Henk, who came up from Melbourne for a two-week holiday with Robin and their baby son Ben, ended up helping Fred, while I slept off my second attack of tonsillitis.

On Sam's birthday, the third of November 1974, we moved into the house our friends referred to as 'The Dutch Embassy', exactly two years after we had moved from Sam's place into the government home. Although our house did not have any inside doors and we would have to make do with the bare concrete floors for quite a while, it was wonderful to move into the very first home we had ever owned.

A beautiful dream had become true.

Breaking Out

For the Alice, 1973 was a very wet year, but records were broken again during the first weeks of January 1974. By the end of that month, thirty centimetres of rain, more than twelve inches, had fallen in Alice Springs, the highest since recording began in 1877. Monsoonal deluges not only flooded huge areas of the Northern Territory and South Australia, but flooding was even worse in Queensland. Our next-door neighbours blamed the unusual wet weather on the nuclear tests that had been carried out at Maralinga in South Australia in the early sixties. Max, Rose and her brother Peter who had lived there at the time, all died of cancer in the early eighties.

Nearly every time the Todd River floods, there is an accident, due to carelessness and under estimating the suddenly changing force of the water. This time, a young boy who lived only a few doors up from us was drowned in the normally-dry Chinaman's Creek in front of our house. When our youngest son, Richard, got to the creek to join his playmates, his friend, Colin, had just disappeared downstream. The little fellow's body was later found about five hundred metres further downstream, stuck under a bridge. His younger brother by two years had been pulled out by two of his friends.

The fifteen hundred kilometre long railway line from Adelaide, where our main supplies came from, was again washed away at several places, making it impossible for any trains to get through to the Centre. The dirt road, still the only road to the south, had soon been covered by an inland sea. The force of the water altered the course of the rivers, washed away bridges and large sections of the road on its way to the lakes in the southern part of this enormous continent.

No supplies were able to get through. People were soon panic-buying again. Within two weeks the shops in town were looking rather bare. With a sigh of relief we read in the local paper that the end of the rain was in sight within a week. But we soon learned that it would take weeks for the water, which was in some places two or three metres deep, to subside and the damage to the road and the railway to be repaired. In the meantime, more rain ruined the repairs as soon as they were carried out, and supplies were running out fast. Very little meat was available, since cattle could not be moved to the abattoirs. We were lucky that we had bought half a cow just before Christmas, which would last us for six months if I kept using the meat as sparingly as we were used to in Holland. The big bag of potatoes, still our staple diet, would last a few weeks and, although limited, the vegies in the garden were thriving with the persistent rain. Our main problem was bread, still our main meal for breakfast as well as for lunch and we hated having to use powdered milk again, as there was no fresh milk available in town.

Two weeks after the town was isolated from the world on the twelfth of January, the first RAAF Hercules aircraft flew in with the most necessary goods. Because of the high cost of the airlifts, which were heavily subsidised by the Government, the goods had to be first approved by a specially formed Emergency Committee. Working out which goods were the most urgent and distributing them among the many food stores in town was a very difficult task for the people who organised the airlifts to town. To then have several items cut off their lists by red tape was making tensions run high at times. And of course, the fact that there was no beer left in this thirsty town did not help matters either.

The supply of beer had only lasted a couple of weeks. A Territorian could not possibly survive without beer. They prided themselves on being bloody good drinkers. Songs like 'The pub with no beer' and 'Alice cried and cried all night' became very popular during the weeks that followed. Perhaps the fact that people could not spend money in dry pubs and empty shops was part of the reason they gave so generously to the appeals for the victims of floods in Queensland. Many people had lost all their possessions when walls of water had swept through their towns.

As the weeks went by, goods that had been sitting on the shelves for years were all being sold. 'Use-by-dates' had not been heard of at the time. Because there was nothing else to replace it with anyway, it was no use complaining if something tasted a bit old or mouldy. Glad that I could get a few kilograms of flour, I happily sifted the weevils out of it, something the early settlers always had to do. With some sultanas and dried apples (fresh fruit was not available) mixed into the batter, the stack of pancakes I baked with it disappeared in no time.

The local bakery had soon run out of flour and restrictions were brought in stating that you could only get one loaf per family. Debbie, our American neighbour felt so embarrassed to ask for more, that she took the majority of her nine children with her to the supermarket to show them that she was genuine when she said that she needed more. Another way around the restriction was to go to different supermarkets in turn, just like the panic-buyers did from the beginning.

At one stage, mushrooms were growing in profusion on the banks of the Todd River. Jimmy, an Italian cook who lived across the road from Sam was picking a bucketful for his restaurant.

"How do you know which ones are not poisonous?" I asked him.

"Thas easy!" Jimmy said in his strong Italian accent. "You feed 'm to the Fred. If the Fred dies they're no good."

As time wore on, the shelves in Woolworths were as bare as in any of the small stores even though their supplies were brought in with their own

158

planes. Apart from household goods, there were only packets of sweets left on the racks. The amount of supplies that came in was inadequate to feed the thirty thousand people in Central Australia, including Tennant Creek and in the numerous Aboriginal settlements in the area. Whatever was brought in by plane twice a day, disappeared in no time. As in wartime, we all waited for the shops to open when another consignment was expected. By the middle of March the power was cut off for four hours every day throughout the town because of the shortage of fuel.

Thinking back on those twelve weeks of deprivation, the biggest problem for me seemed to have been the lack of dog food and toilet paper. Cutting up old newspapers for the toilet reminded me how I used to be yelled at for making the pieces too big when I was a child; even newspapers were scarce in our family when I grew up. I'm wondering now what we were using when Mum was a widow and we had no newspapers either. Were cabbage leaves really used before newspapers were available, as it says in that old nursery rhyme?

As I was barely able to cook enough to feed our family of eight, there were no scraps left for Josie, our new dog of undefined origin. She was never left hungry as the kids gladly gave her some of the food from their own plates. At the end of March the ordeal was finally over and life was slowly getting back to normal. A few weeks later we met a childless middle-aged Dutch couple in a caravan park. We both felt sick in the stomach with disgust when they proudly showed us their cupboards full of tinned and dried dog food, saying that their two German Shepherds would not have gone without their favourite food even if the roads were closed for a whole year. The fact that they were Dutch made us feel ashamed of our own country-folk.

The wet weather conditions brought mosquitoes in by the millions. Although they were a lot smaller than the ones we were used to in Holland, these mosquitoes were dangerous. Warnings of encephalitis made us stay indoors, because there were no repellents available in the shops. We also had a taste again of the terrible mice plagues people on the land often had to cope with. Brought in from Europe with the ocean steamers, they had multiplied to enormous proportions and thrived in the Centre where the grass had grown to previously unknown heights. The fat, furry creatures were everywhere. One evening, when we drove into town after dark, they were running across the street, occasionally 'plopping' under the heavy wheels of the Nissan. After a few weeks, they disappeared as swiftly as they had come.

The mice, the huge colourful moths as big as the sparrows in Holland, swarms of big grasshoppers, curtains of tiny insects and the tons of flies appearing one after another had made me think that we had landed in Egypt instead of Australia, when we first came to the Centre.

The tall grass, which dried out quickly by the hot sun, kept the local fire brigade on their toes for months. Older people still remembered the terrifying fires after the floods of the early twenties, which burned for weeks.

Because it was difficult for me to reach my sewing clients and vice versa, we had a telephone connected at the beginning of April 1973. My mother's birthday was on the seventh and we decided to call her. Not many households had a telephone in Alice Springs at that time and an overseas call had to be connected by an operator. We waited for two hours before we got through. The echo in the line and the lump in my throat, speaking to my mother for the first time in two and a half years, made the conversation very difficult.

"But Mien is on the other side of the world," Mum said a couple of times before it sank in to her that it was really me she was talking to. Unable to speak, I gave the phone to Fred.

"*Jong toch! Jong toch!*" she kept repeating to him; "Is it really you?"

We had both been so overcome with emotion that we were hardly able to talk at all. Mum later wrote that she had been terribly confused when the call came through. Just before she had thrown the phone back onto the hook for the third time, she had heard the word *bemiddelaar,* the Dutch word for mediator. Because my brother Wim's girlfriend's name was Gerda Middelaar, Mum had been glad when the phone rang again a few minutes later. Expecting Gerda, she could not understand how she could possibly be talking to me.

That first three-minute call had been the talk of the day for her as well as for me for a long time, which was just as well; at nine dollars per minute, I had to sew for a whole week to pay for it.

Through my sewing I met some very nice and interesting people. One of the many good memories I have is of Lynne, a tall Australian-born lady. In church on Sundays with her children, four or five of them, they would always be dressed immaculately; Lynne and the girls in frilly frocks, her Italian husband and the boys wearing expensive suits. Lynne loved nice clothes and so, apparently, did her husband.

"I'm forever running to the dry-cleaners," she said one day. "He has thirty-five suits in his wardrobe and he never wears the same suit for more than one day."

Lynne was one of the few women who said that I wasn't asking enough for my sewing and always gave me a little extra. She knew what it was like to start with nothing, she said. In those early days, back in the sixties, they had lived in a tin shed in remote areas of the Territory, building houses for the Government on Aboriginal settlements. She told me about those hard and often funny times they had in the bush. She knew both my brothers Henk and Sam, who had lived with them, along with several other labourers. There had not been a moment of privacy in those sheds as every word echoed through the thin walls, and into the bush.

Lynne and her husband had been newly-weds at the time. Their bedroom in the big corrugated iron shed was only divided by another corrugated iron wall from where the boys were sleeping. As they could hear every word, even those that were whispered, the couple had to wait until the fellows were asleep before they could make love. Being an impatient man, Lynne's husband had told my brothers and their work mates, time and again, to put their heads under the blankets, and their fingers in their ears. Poor Lynne! She had nearly died of embarrassment when her husband was making love to her in true Italian fashion, with much moaning and groaning.

Lynne remembered very well the night of the shoot-out in Papunya, two hundred and forty kilometres west of Alice Springs, when Henk and Sam first arrived.

"Yes, we had some terrible, hair-raising moments there," she said when I asked her about it. That night Henk and Sam had camped in a dry creek bed, very close to the scene of a 'pay-back'. Henk had been scared out of his wits, thinking that the natives were after them instead of fighting amongst themselves.

The first dress I made for Lynne was a beautiful ball gown made out of pure, bone coloured silk, in an old-fashioned style. The long dress had a high neck and big puffy sleeves with tight-fitting cuffs reaching to the elbows. It closed at the back with a long row of self-covered, plastic buttons and there were another dozen of those on each of the long cuffs. The end result gave me great satisfaction; with her slim figure and her dark curly hair pinned on top of her head, she looked stunning.

About a year later, Lynne rang me. The mice had taken a liking to the buttons and they had eaten heaps of them. I was amazed to see that they had only attacked the buttons. The dress had not been damaged at all.

Another great lady to sew for was Denise. Her husband Paul was a lawyer and would later become the Chief Minister of the Northern Territory. Our eldest daughter Lilian did a lot of baby-sitting for them. I felt terribly sad for them when I heard many years later that their marriage had broken up.

The most difficult jobs I did were two wedding dresses I made from velvet that winter. My machine did not like the spongy material. After sweating - and crying - over it for days I ended up doing a lot of the seams by hand. I hated making bridesmaids' dresses; three or four identical dresses, which often took ages to make. Women in Holland could not bear seeing someone else in the same dress as theirs, so I felt awful asking a decent price for making them. The only bridesmaids in Holland were little ones, and they usually wore white dresses like the bride.

Despite the progress on our own house during that year, my sense of isolation deepened, and at times I was quite homesick. At the beginning of

1973 Fred had bought an old orange coloured Morris Minor for me so that I could go to town whenever I needed, but, although I was thrilled to bits with it, I still felt very lonely and isolated. Being home on my own from eight in the morning until three-thirty in the afternoon, I felt as if the walls were coming down on me. I was under constant pressure to keep the house clean and tidy at all times; not an easy task with six lively and creative children.

When the school holidays started early in December, I worked until late at night to get through the orders for Christmas. Lilian, then fourteen, had been a great help to me, but she had taken on a job at the hospital for the holidays. I was dying to be with Fred at the block helping him make cupboards or planting a garden. But he expected me to be content at home cooking and cleaning, doing endless loads of washing and writing letters to his as well as my family while trying to get through my sewing orders.

I became cranky and yelled at the kids; at times they yelled back at me and I could not get them to do anything for me. I would send them all out of the house shouting at them to leave me alone; I'd rather do it all myself. One day Eugene, who would have been thirteen at the time, said to me: "It doesn't make any difference if we do a job for you or not. You never sit down and read a book anyway because you always find other things to do."

"He's right!" I've often thought since. It's no fun for them to do things for me at all. Work is just never ending.

I wanted to quit sewing and get a job somewhere but whenever I brought up the subject, Fred pointed out that I could make my own hours and I was always home when the children were sick or there was no school, or he needed me himself. I just had to be more selective, put my hourly rates up and learn to say no, so that I had more time to myself.

When school started again at the end of January, I no longer made bridesmaids' dresses and frocks from cheap cotton and the only alterations I took on were those for Mrs. Holden, the proprietress of a local dress shop. I always enjoyed her company and most of it was sewing hems by hand, which I could do in the evenings.

"A woman's hand and a horse's teeth should never be still," my mother always said.

Mrs. Holden was a petite lady, always perfectly dressed and groomed. I had the greatest admiration for her and looked forward to her usually brief visits. Her life's stories kept me sane during the ensuing months. "Please call me Pat", she'd asked when I met up with her later in life.

Pat was a young girl when she came to Alice Springs for a holiday in 1932. She got a job with a distant relative in a merchant enterprise for a couple of months. She was married and had two small children when the war ended in 1945. Her husband came back from active service a mentally and physically

162

very sick man, and Pat still had to provide for the family. Expecting to have a better chance of making a living in Alice Springs, she returned in 1950 with her husband and two young children.

Pat's relatives who were managing the Riverside Hotel at the time, gave her a job in the 'sample' room, where travelling salesmen showed their wares. The room was later made into an elite dress shop where only the best names were sold. Because Pat had a corsetry diploma, corsets, which were still very much in use at that time, together with glamorous underwear, were added to the shop. Pat had also made prostheses for breast mastectomies and fitted men with medically prescribed corsets.

When Pat's husband died in 1957, life became somewhat easier for her. She opened her first dress and bra shop in town in 1962, and branched out to Tennant Creek in later years. When her son took over the running of the shops in 1985, Pat continued to help him out until a few years ago. In her eighties she still drove around town, visiting lonely people and working for charity organisations, until cancer got the better of her. She was a truly beautiful lady and a great inspiration to me.

To get out of the house and involved with the community, I joined the cast of the Matthews Passion in March 1974; the first and last time I was ever in a play. I was Veronica, the woman who dried Jesus' face when he fell under the cross. With a group of other women I had to wail and cry which proved to be no problem for me. I was feeling so miserable at the time that during the first rehearsal my tears had soon became real. Unable to stop the flow, I was still crying my heart out when I came home that night.

The following morning, one of my regular customers Mrs. R. who owned a material shop in town, came in for a fitting. Embarrassed about my swollen eyes, I told her that I was fed up with being at home all day.

"Come and see me if you want to give it away," she said. "I'll give you a job!"

I again tried to talk to Fred about letting me have a job outside the house, but he didn't want to hear about it, saying that he would be too ashamed if I did. None of the women of our families in Holland needed to go out to work. If that was the case here, we might as well go back to Holland.

During the following weeks our relationship deteriorated to an all time low. I became suspicious of the good life Fred had at work in the gallery laughing with Frits Pieters and Thys Mauve, the two well-known Dutch artists Henk had bought out from Holland to help him paint the Panorama. Fred was forever talking about the jokes he shared with them and the girls. To see the Panorama grow was very exciting. After taking the artists out bush for a couple of weeks to get a feel of the bright Australian landscape, Henk had sketched the scenes on the huge canvas and they had now started painting

163

them. I envied the drinks they had with Henk after work, and got angry when Fred came home late in a happy mood, wanting to hug and cuddle me.

As time went on, time-consuming mistakes made my fingers tremble while I was sewing. Unable to express my anger any other way than to cry about the unfairness of life, I became more and more frustrated. My inability to stop crying, knowing that it was no fun for Fred to come home to a wife who was always in a bad mood, made me sink deeper and deeper into depression. It was my own fault that he stayed away longer after work.

One particularly bad day in May, I burst into tears when I burned the potatoes while waiting for Fred to come home. I had already given the children their dinner when he finally arrived home, in a very happy mood. He wiped my tears away, saying that it didn't matter that I had burned the potatoes, he would just eat a sandwich.

We went early to bed that night. Fred was soon snoring his head off but I could not sleep. Sometime during the night Fred got up and found me in tears again.

"What's up with you now?" he asked. I sobbed that I could not go on like this any longer. I felt like I was going crazy. He was having such a good life while I was feeling miserable all the time. He took me in his arms saying that life for him would be a lot better if I could pull myself together and accept life as it was; be happy instead of feeling sorry for myself. I pulled myself out of his embracing arms and got into a fury.

"Keep your voice down. You'll wake the kids and the neighbours", Fred hissed. Something inside me snapped and in the flood of accusations that I yelled at him, I made one big mistake. I called him a selfish bastard.

For some reason, something that happened in the navy, calling him a bastard worked like a red flag on a mad bull. He had taken it as an insult to his mother, whom he loved dearly. Fred turned as white as a sheet. He grabbed me, demanding an apology. But I was beside myself, adding oil to the fire by saying that that was exactly what he was. Like a cat driven into a corner, I clawed at him until he let me go.

When we had calmed down somewhat, Fred went to bed, saying that we would talk things out in the morning. I could not believe my ears when he was snoring only a few minutes later. I thought of packing my bags and leaving the lot of them. But where would I go? There was nobody I could turn to. Why couldn't Fred understand that I felt so unhappy, alone all day while he had such fun at work? Eventually, I fell asleep on the couch in the living room. When I saw the deep scratches I had made in Fred's arms the following morning, I felt terribly guilty.

"What's going to happen to the special cupboards I made for the sewing room, if you don't want to sew anymore?" he asked.

164

"It can be Lilian's room," I said timidly. "If you make some shelves in the tall cupboard. It will be perfect for her."

Before he left for work, Fred admitted that he could see I was going crazy. He took a very deep breath and grudgingly allowed me to look for a job. Afraid that I would become like Tante Jans, my mother's older sister who had gone mad at the age of sixteen when her mother had forbidden her to go out with a young man from a poor family, my mother had let me get married at the age of eighteen. Mum's lips were trembling when she said that I had pestered her into letting me go because she was sick to death of my selfish whining. After I wrote *Father Forgive Us, Coming to terms with my tears*, I have now broken with that pattern, I think...

Writing about my family made me realise that the suffering of my unfortunate aunt might have saved me from a similar disaster more than once. By putting the things that happened into perspective, I have truly come to terms with my tears. As we now talk freely about our feelings instead of bottling things up, a good cry now and again clears the air and prevents me from being depressed for weeks on end. I wonder though, why it has taken me another twenty years to accept my limitations and stand up for myself.

Work Experience

A week after my disastrous outburst, Mrs. R came for another fitting. True to her word, she said that I could start in the material section of the 'Emporium' as soon as I wanted. Two weeks later, on the first of May 1974, I drove off in my Mini Minor to my first real job in the work force, feeling quite nervous and excited. It felt as if I was sixteen again when, after a long struggle with my parents, I was on my way to Amersfoort, on my pushbike, to my first sewing job at a stranger's house.

The Emporium was an enormous shed, divided into a large grocery shop and haberdashery. The two shops were connected via a doorway in the middle and an office at the back of the building. Because the shop was on the opposite side of town I had only been there a few times.

On arrival, I was met by a shop assistant who took me to the supervisor, Laurel, a tiny lady with curly shoulder-length grey-blond hair. In her soft voice and quiet manner she introduced herself and showed me what my job was going to be, then she introduced me to the other two girls; Julie in ladies and children's wear, and Kerry who worked in the babies' section. They were both quite young and had not been there longer than a few months.

Surrounded by a hundred or more rolls of material, I felt immediately at home in my corner, and full of confidence, I served my first customer. A lady with an olive complexion and raven black hair wanted a zipper and a reel of cotton to be put on account.

"I have to ask Laurel," I started.

"Oh gawd! Here we go again!" the lady complained loudly in her harsh voice. "There's no need for that. The book is there, under the counter." Impatiently she bent over the counter and grabbed the book herself. Uncomfortably I looked at Julie for help. With a big grin on her face she indicated that it was all right.

"What name?" I asked still a little nervous.

"Dick," the lady said while she pulled one of her two boisterous children into line with a look that could kill.

I looked up as if a bee had stung me.

"Yes! You heard! Just Dick: D.I.C.K.!" my customer shouted so that it could be heard at the back of the shop.

"I'm Greg's wife," she added while she looked around for the other girls. I had no idea who Greg was, but I was soon informed by his Italian wife that he was the manager of the whole complex.

I wiped the sweat off my face when she went through the door. Killing themselves with laughter, Julie and Kerry told me what a character Mary, the manager's wife, was.

The rest of that first day went fine. I was happy to have company at coffee breaks and lunchtime and liked my two colleagues from the moment I met them. Julie was a few years younger than I was. She had short dark hair and an infectious laugh. She was married to a Canadian aircraft mechanic and had one little boy. Kerry's hair was long, very straight and almost white. She had a low voice and a very dry sense of humour, and she had only been married for a few months. Wearing the smart mauve uniform of the household section gave me a sense of belonging to the team. I was still serving a customer that afternoon when the other girls left at five-thirty.

Coming home was lovely that first evening. Tired from the long day on my feet, I was happy to see that the house was tidy and Lilian was already cooking the evening meal I had prepared before I had gone to work that morning. Fred had been home early and told me to put my feet up. While he made a cup of coffee for each of us, I chatted happily about my first day at work, saying that I might stay there forever. The following morning I was met at the shop by Greg, the manager, a big man in his early forties, I thought, but he was in fact several years younger than I was.

"You must be Miny," he said before I had a chance to say 'hello'. "You're pretty slack, aren't you?"

I felt as if he had hit me in my face. "What do you mean?" I asked.

"Well! Last night you were the last to leave, weren't you? And you didn't bother to lock the door behind you. People could have just walked in and taken off with whatever they wanted."

'But Laurel was still here," I stammered. "I told her that I was going."

"Don't take too much notice of Greg," Laurel advised me with her sweet smile a little later. "He's a big bully but quite a softy underneath."

But my day was spoiled. I had no idea what 'slack' meant and I did not dare ask the other girls for fear that I would burst into tears.

When I came home that night I told Fred what had happened. We then looked the word up in the dictionary. I was horrified; careless, lax, slapdash, thoughtless, irresponsible... I could not see the rest for my tears of anger, hurt and frustration.

"You are not going back there any more," Fred said furiously. "I'll tell them myself if you won't!"

As I had no intention of staying at home again I dried my tears, saying that I wasn't going to give up that easily. The next morning I went back with lead in my shoes, trying not to take any notice of my aching throat, which later developed into tonsillitis.

My first job in the morning was sweeping, dusting and mopping the floor in my department before the shop opened at nine. The material section proved to be busy and I had to learn a lot. Between serving customers I labelled and priced the new items that were delivered daily and kept the area tidy, and I was relieved not to see Greg all day. At 'smoko' I learned that I was not the only one who had been intimidated by his bullying. His wife was a niece of Mrs. R.'s; that's why he had become the manager, they said. Joy, an older lady who worked in the supermarket, also assured me that he wasn't a bad bloke when you got to know him better. Like Laurel, Joy had been working at the Emporium for many years, taking no notice of the young manager's terrible manners.

After a few days I felt happy again and looked forward to going to work in the morning. The metric system had come in earlier that year, 1974, and people were very confused about the new measurements. As I had been used to centimetres and metres in Holland and had to convert to yards and inches when I started dressmaking, it was a piece of cake for me. It was hard to keep a straight face if people asked for three kilometres of material to make a dress or three millimetres of elastic. I would tell them that kilometres were mainly used to measure road distances and that a metre of material was ten percent more than a yard. When someone asked for three millimetres of ribbon or elastic, I would cut an eighth of an inch off, which got the message across quickly.

About a week after I started at the Emporium someone had dropped a twenty-dollar note on the floor behind the counter. I picked it up and automatically handed it in. Weeks later during a coffee break I heard that dropping money to test the honesty of a new employee was common practice in a lot of places.

During the following months my workload increased steadily. I learned about invoicing, mark-up and pricing, and the re-ordering of goods we had run out of in my department was soon left up to me. I liked working with Mrs. R, a big motherly woman with a friendly nature. Apart from the Emporium she and her Italian husband, a short stockily-built man with a grey moustache and a balding head, also owned the restaurant where I had tasted my first lobster, as well as an ice-cream parlour, a bakery and goodness knows what else. Mrs. R worked long hours in their shop, as well as helping her husband in the restaurant and the milk-bar during the day and in the evenings.

After a few months Mrs. R asked me if I would take care of the bra section of the shop. There was quite a lot of work involved keeping up the supply of the many different styles and sizes as the garments were invariably put back in the wrong places. Bras were very popular with Aboriginal women of all ages. They would come in large groups, laughing and giggling while they chatted in their rapid language. I was stunned the first time I saw one of the elderly women taking out a roll of notes from her abundant bosom to pay for the many bras and dresses the group had taken at random off the racks. Because most of them were living in the creek, they could not fit the items for health reasons, but that did not seem to bother them at all. They always seemed happy and contented with their new clothes.

I learned a lot of things at 'smoko', especially how the average Australian husband treated his wife and children. Some of the women virtually brought their children up on their own as their husbands were out bush for weeks or months at a time. Others spent their evenings and most of their wages with their friends in the pub, only coming home to eat and sleep. Several couples had lived in a caravan all their married lives, waiting for their restless husbands to move on again. The contrast between people working in Government jobs and ordinary folks working elsewhere was appalling to me.

At that time my Dutch friend Jose, Regine's preschool teacher, was about to have her first baby. She had planned it so that she would have her two-months holiday at Christmas, then six weeks paid leave before the baby was due, followed by another six weeks on full pay after the baby was born. She could then stay at home another six months on half pay.

Because it was difficult to get teachers and other public servants to the Northern Territory, the government offered them cheap housing and a six week holiday. Teachers had twelve weeks a year and free airfares every second year for them and their families.

I told Jose about Diane, who worked in the supermarket and lived in a caravan. When she was expecting her sixth baby a few years earlier she had been worried sick that she would lose her job if she could no longer do the heavy work that included stacking shelves with groceries. She needed her meagre wages to survive on.

Jose's wages were a lot higher than the fifty dollars a week we were paid, the going rate for shop assistants. Her husband had a good income too. She had worked out that she would be paid over eight thousand dollars, while she would be at home, while Diane would get nothing at all, having to go back to work as soon as possible after her baby was born.

Having been in business myself since, I know very well that it is out of the question for small businesses to pay those kinds of benefits. While teachers are on holiday, the school is closed. In a shop, you have to employ someone else, or do the work yourself. I also understand now why so many people got the sack before their boss had to pay them three months' long service leave, after ten years.

Apart from being very informative, the coffee breaks at the Emporium were often a lot of fun. For weeks on end, one of the girls kept us informed on how she planned to become pregnant. She had been married for some time and desperately wanted to have a baby. She worked out when she was ovulating, and until then her husband was not allowed to touch her so that he could store his sperm. One day she announced that she was having the following week off. During that week she was going to lock her 'hubby' in the bedroom and they would make love as often as they could. This time she was going to conceive for sure!

"I may be totally exhausted when I come back," she warned us, "but it will be worth it." However, the poor girl did not conceive after all. Some of her colleagues generously offered her their husbands to try. She left a few months later and I never saw her again.

When I first started at the Emporium, things went well at home, but the novelty of me going out to work soon wore off. Fred wanted to work on the block as soon as he came home from the gallery, instead of having to keep an eye on the children who were often watching TV at the neighbour's place instead of making their homework and doing the household tasks they were supposed to do. Because we were also trying to finish the house so that we could move in when my brother Henk came for a visit at the end of October, I became over-tired. I asked Mrs. R. if I could start an hour later so that I could do some of the never-ending loads of washing before I set off to work in the morning. Although she did not like it, she agreed. It was very disheartening for me to see that the floors still had not been done when I came in at nine-thirty the following Monday morning. On the second day Mrs. R. happened to come in while I was having smoko at ten-thirty, my usual time.

"You come in at nine-thirty and sit down to have coffee an hour later?" she fumed. "How dare you!"

I protested that I had to race to get the work done at home, but she said that was my problem. I had to make sure I had a break, so that I was fit for work when I came in. She was right of course, but at that time I did not understand how she could be so harsh. Fred was treated quite differently at Henk's place. He got coffee before he even started work!

"I told you before; quit the bloomin' job!" he said angrily when I told him what had happened. He would have been very happy if I had stayed at home again.

The following weekend I was in bed with high fever and a badly swollen throat. "Inability to speak up for ones-self; swallowed anger," Louis Hay says in her book on alternative healing.

Henk would arrive from Melbourne with his wife Robin and little Benjamin on the last Sunday of October. I had not seen them since their wedding day and asked Mrs. R. if I could have the week off. She refused. It was a very busy time and I had not even been there for half a year. I shouldn't have asked, she said. Although I was disappointed I also realised that she was right. She would be forever short of staff if people could take time off whenever they felt like it.

On Friday afternoon, the day before Henk and Robin were to arrive, I suddenly got the cold shivers at work.

"What's up with you?" Laurel asked. "You look as if you've seen a ghost!"

"I think I've got a fever again," I stuttered, barely able to stop my teeth from chattering.

After asking me if I thought I could still drive the car, Laurel sent me home. Glad to be able to slide between the cool sheets, I fell immediately into a deep sleep. I had not heard Fred and the children come home that afternoon. The following morning, Saturday, I was too sick to get out of bed. At lunchtime Fred had to go to the airport without me, to meet Henk and Robin and their little son Ben. Glad that Robin took care of the household, I slept all day Sunday. On Monday morning Fred took me to the doctor.

"Acute tonsillitis again," he said. "You should seriously consider getting your tonsils taken out." He gave me an injection, told me to come back for the second shot in two days time, and to stay in bed for a week.

When I returned to work a few days after Henk and Robin had gone back to Melbourne, I had lost several kilos. My uniform was hanging on me like a bag. By the third week of November, when we finally moved into our only half-finished house after working hours, it became obvious to me that I could not cope with my workload. Mrs. R seemed happy to give me a part-time job as from the first of December.

By Christmas in 1974 we had been in our new house for six weeks. At that time in Holland, every room of a house even the toilet, was wall-papered and I was determined to have it like that in Alice Springs too, no matter how many people warned me that I would be sorry. Most houses in town had plain plastered walls, painted with the same cream or off-white colour, which was of course very practical but also very boring. I could not brighten up the living room in the Housing Commission home since wallpapering was forbidden, but in our own home we could do as we pleased. I had seen only a few papered walls in Alice Springs, so I was pleasantly surprised to find a good supply of wallpaper in town.

I had learned the art of wallpapering at a very early age. Because of the smoke from the wood-stove in the old farmhouse where I grew up, the living room needed new wallpaper every year after the long winter months. Fred had done wallpapering for a living in Holland for a while and hated it. As usual, our tempers were flying when we tried to do the job together and he gladly left me to it after a while. I did not mind as long as he did not interfere with the way I went about it. Standing on top of a ladder afraid of heights, trying to avoid air-bubbles in the long strips of paper while juggling them to get the pattern straight, was a nerve-wracking affair. It was made worse with half a dozen children at home on school holidays, watching every move.

It took me weeks to do the entrance hall, the lounge-dining room and the kitchen, then each of the six bedrooms and eventually the bathroom and the laundry, since I was working at the Emporium every afternoon. The result was worth every moment of my time and effort, including my sweating in forty-degree heat without an air-conditioner and cursing when my patience was stretched to the limit.

During the eighteen years we lived in 'the Embassy' I changed only a few of the feature walls when we replaced the old furniture, carpet and curtains. The original walls were still looking quite good when we sold the house in 1993. People and their habits change. In Holland nearly every house now has plain white wallpaper, embossed with relief patterns that can be freshly painted every year. In our new retirement home, I only papered one feature wall in each room with a soft pattern of flower arrangements. The rest of the house has plain brick walls painted in an off-white colour, very practical and no longer boring to me. Maybe Australia was not way behind, but twenty years ahead in fashions after all!

Because we could not afford to put carpet in the house and I could not stand the bare concrete floors, we bought sea-grass matting; thirty centimetre plaited squares, sewn together to cover the full width of the rooms. They were cheap but looked quite attractive and they matched perfectly with the old rattan lounge-suite Henk Guth had given us when we moved into the Commission house two years earlier.

Before we left Holland, we were told that there were no lace curtains in Australia. I could not imagine such bare windows and we had brought a big roll of patterned netting with us only to see that there was plenty of it available, even in Alice Springs, and very reasonably priced as well. I had also brought the heavy, gold-brown, ceiling to floor living room curtains I loved so much. Because there was not enough to cover the three large windows in the lounge-room I hung one length of fabric on either side of the lace curtains for appearance until we could afford to replace them. Being summer nearly all year round, heavy curtains were seldom needed in Alice Springs to keep the cold out during the six weeks of winter.

With the cheap Chinese matting, the old rattan lounge-suite freshly covered with moss-green corduroy, and some nice pictures on the wall, our lounge looked great. I finally allowed the kids to set up the Christmas tree two days before Christmas, our fourth in Australia and the first in our own home. It was also the first time our family was not complete at Christmas, as Raymond and Eugene had gone with Sam to Queensland for the summer holidays. They would have a marvellous, adventurous time with the three-wheeler motorbike Sam bought before he left, but I missed them very much, especially at the traditional coffee table after the midnight Mass.

172

As had become the custom, sharing the candle-lit meal with other people always added to the excitement. This time our Dutch friends Kees and Tilly joined us. The Christmas carols playing softly on the radio, the lights on the tree and the little, decorated candles burning beside each person's plate created a very happy atmosphere during the fancy-bread meal. Afterwards, while we put away the left over food, Simone and Lilian played the piano. Tilly and Kees stayed long after the children had gone to bed. During all the years they had been in Australia, they had never become used to celebrating Christmas and New Year in the middle of summer, probably because they could not share it with their own family.

"It's as if we are back home," Tilly said time and again. "It's the happiest Christmas I've had since we left Holland, twenty years ago."

Christmas 1974

No matter how late we went to bed on Christmas Eve, everybody except Fred would be up bright and early the following morning. Our Christmas presents for the children during those first years in Australia consisted only of clothing with a book or a game, but the number of parcels under the tree was increasing every year. Lilian was working in the hospital during the holidays again and, as in the previous years, the others had saved their pocket money and bought gifts or made something for each other. Sinterklaas' (Saint Nicolas) birthday on the sixth of December was almost forgotten. Although they would have preferred to have both, they had happily exchanged him for Father Christmas, when I gave them the choice in our second year in our new country. Later on that Christmas morning in 1974, they were all happily playing with their new games while Fred and I were drinking coffee, when the music on the radio was suddenly interrupted for a news bulletin.

"Be quiet! I can't hear what they're saying," Fred shouted at the children while he turned the sound of the radio up. An eerie chill crept over my skin while we listened to the devastating news that Cyclone Tracey had flattened Darwin during the night. All communications were badly disrupted... full details would not be known for some time.

Unable to move, we stayed glued to the radio all day forgetting to cook the usual Christmas dinner. We would be unable to enjoy it anyway. Some people from Alice Springs who had been with friends in Darwin flew into town in the afternoon. In an interview on the radio they described the horrific scenes in the destroyed city. Roofs had been torn off, whole houses had disappeared, the electricity supply and telephone lines had been cut. They believed that hundreds of people had been killed by flying debris or been buried under tons of rubble. The children's Christmas presents had all been blown away. People were frantically looking for family and friends. Some children had been blown away, beds and all, they said.

With the extreme humidity at that time of the year, the drinking water would be contaminated within the next couple of days and people were fleeing the city of twenty-four thousand in droves. About three thousand were expected to arrive in Alice Springs the following day, Boxing Day, which was a Thursday.

By that time we had learned that the cyclone had blown most of Darwin away from the top of Australia. Because we still had no television, we waited eagerly for the 'Advocate' to come out with the pictures the following week. As Christmas day was on a Wednesday that year, there was no paper until Thursday the second of January 1975. In the meantime we watched hundreds of badly battered and overloaded cars coming through Alice Springs. In no time roadblocks had been set up everywhere along the Stuart Highway, still a single lane bitumen road, where the road-worthiness of the vehicles was checked. Necessary repairs, changing tyres and re-fuelling were all carried out free of charge. Because people had left in a hurry, many had been stranded along the way. Hundreds of badly damaged cars, from people who could not be expected to make the fifteen-hundred-kilometre drive to Adelaide, still a dirt road at the time, or wherever else they wanted to go, were put on the train in Alice Springs.

We had seen how generous people had been in Holland when there was a fund-raising appeal for some worthwhile project, but the way people in the Centre rallied was absolutely fantastic. It was heart-warming to see and hear how young and old pulled together to raise money through barbecues, auctions, walkathons, lotteries etc. for the unfortunate people who had lost everything and had been through such a traumatic ordeal, while we were happily celebrating Christmas Eve. Tons of food, clothing and furniture were collected in no time. Money kept pouring in for the appeals and an army of volunteers worked around the clock to keep the ever-increasing stream of refugees fed and moving.

On Friday afternoon, the day after Boxing Day, when I was involved in the relief work at the old Anzac Hill High school, I became aware of the deep shock most people were in, huddling together in little groups, looking lost and forlorn. Some of them barely noticed the sandwiches, cups of soup or coffee I offered them, until I spoke to them or touched their arms.

With more than five and a half thousand people travelling through during the first three days after the cyclone hit, accommodation became a big problem in town. Schools, hotels and caravan parks were soon overflowing. On Sunday afternoon I took a young family home with me. Uncertain what Fred would say, I became more apprehensive when I noticed the two bull terriers in the back of their battered and overloaded station wagon. Fred hated them. On the way home I reminded myself that I did not need to worry. They were only puppies, the owners had said.

Fred and the children came out of the house as soon as we drove into our driveway. He introduced himself to Ian, a tall, balding man in his early thirties who worked for Telecom. Their house in Darwin was still standing but it had lost the roof and all its windows. The rain, which had been pouring down since the cyclone hit, had ruined every piece of furniture they owned. They told us later how they had spent the terrifying night in the bathroom while the storm ripped their house apart. Their car had a huge dent in the roof as a big branch had fallen on it. The front window was held together with tape. When Ian opened the back of the car to let the dogs out, a gush of water poured onto the ground. Ian's wife, Joan was a tiny woman in her late twenties with long, dark curly hair. Her face was pale and covered with freckles, which made her look very young. She hardly spoke a word during the first days of their stay. Their little girl, Kerry, was six and very small for her age. She soon felt at home playing with Regine, Richard and Simone.

The two ugly looking puppies were another matter though. One of them, a mix of swirling brown stripes with a bit of white on the snout, was called Brutus, which suited him perfectly. With his bare little tail sticking up from his fat body, he growled angrily, the minute he was let out of the car. The other one was white, a dirty white, with her pink skin shining through the thin hair. Her name was Lady, but her looks as well as her behaviour were anything but ladylike. Although they were only three months old, they already fought like grown up bullterriers. With the best will in the world, I could not see how anybody could possibly love those horrible looking pig-dogs. There was absolutely nothing cuddly about them. A couple of days after their arrival the two little darlings got stuck into one another properly. They got hold of each other's ears and were not prepared to let go, no matter how hard the owners tried to separate them. By the time they were finally parted each ear had been ripped open by long cuts and bits were missing from the edges. Both covered in blood they were sound asleep a few minutes later, cuddled up against each other as if nothing happened. The next day Fred and Ian made a cage for them which fitted into the back of their car, divided by chicken wire so that they could not rip each other further apart, at least while they were travelling.

Looking at the pictures in the newspaper, showing that whole suburbs of Darwin had turned to rubble, it seemed incredible, an absolute miracle that only sixty-four people had been killed in such unbelievable chaos. As the majority of houses were built on stilts with timber frames, clad with iron or fibro-boards, corrugated iron roofs and louvre windows, we had expected a lot more people to be injured by the sharp materials flying around at such high speed. People had managed to hide under mattresses and in safe places such as bathrooms built underneath the houses.

When it became clear that they could not return to Darwin, Ian and Joan decided to travel on to West Australia where they had lived before Ian was transferred by Telecom. During their stay, Ian had dried, sorted and cleaned the household items the couple had packed while they were still in shock. Most of it belonged to their neighbours who had gone to Perth on holiday a week before the cyclone hit.

"They seemed the only things worth taking for them," Ian said looking sadly at the assortment of wet, smelly pieces of furniture on the lawn. A lot of water had been sloshing around in the TV for the three days it had taken them to travel the long distance from Darwin to Alice Springs. Fred did not see any point in dragging the useless items halfway around the continent, but they decided to take it all anyway. Five days after their arrival in our household we waved Ian, Joan and Kerry goodbye feeling sad for the couple having to rebuild their lives. They would finally arrive in Perth after a gruelling drive of almost four thousand kilometres, most of it dirt roads, but at least they still owned a house there.

"After all the trouble we had with the dogs, we had to give them both away shortly after our arrival," Joan wrote a few months later. Their house had been rented out for another two years and they had hired a flat, so they were unable to keep the boisterous dogs in such a small place. Although they realised that they had been luckier than most refugees, who had to start from scratch, life was very difficult for them and Joan's letters showed that their hearts remained in Darwin for a long time after they left.

There is something unique about that hot and sticky place in the far north of Australia. It had not taken long to rebuild the town after the Japanese bombed it in February 1942, and the same happened after Cyclone Tracy. Forty-seven thousand people were living in Darwin in 1974. It has since grown into a large, modern city with some eighty-five thousand citizens. We love to go there in winter when the temperature drops to around zero and it gets too cold for us in Alice Springs.

When Sam came home from Queensland with the boys at the end of January, they were sorry to have missed out on the excitement of seeing all those smashed up cars. Sam had not bothered to listen to the news at all. The boys looked tanned, skinnier and several centimetres taller. They had spent most of their time in the bush helping Sam clearing away the tall weeds on his over-grown block. They had planted banana trees and two long lines of poplars to make a lane for bow and arrow shooting. During the day Sam had kept the boys' enthusiasm up by anticipating take-away meals and playing at night with his three-wheeler on the beach at Maroochydore, a few kilometres away from his block.

Among all sorts of 'useful' items in Sam's overloaded ute, was a huge bunch of green bananas. Somewhere on the three and a half thousand kilometre long road they had picked up a thorny devil lizard, which Eugene had nursed on his lap all the way home. We put the beautiful creature in the birdcage where it entertained us for months with its funny backward and forward way of walking. When we found it dead one morning with a feather stuck in its throat, we realised that it would have been better if we had set it free in the bush.

After I started to work part-time at the Emporium on the first of December, a fifteen-year-old girl was taken on to sweep and mop the floors, which took her all morning. The bulk of the work was still waiting for me when I came in at noon and the young girl was little help to me in the afternoon. Some of the girls in the supermarket were upset with me from the start, because I never stayed a minute longer than the allocated fifteen minutes for morning and afternoon breaks. Most of them were forever stretching it, sometimes to half an hour, until they were told, usually by Greg, to stick to the rules or they could leave. After Christmas Mrs. R. asked me to check the old stock of knitting wool and help her with the ordering of the new winter supply, which was an interesting job. As I now only had five hours to do the allocated work I often forgot about smoko, or I was back in the shop within a few minutes. It seemed grossly unfair to me that I had such a big workload while Kerry and Julie were often bored in their sections.

"Give me some of that stuff; I'll price it for you," Kerry said one day in March. She had done little jobs for me before but this time she took a huge box into her baby department.

"What do you think you're doing?" Mrs R asked her when she came into the shop a little later. "You each have your own jobs to do. If you want extra work, you ask me or Laurel."

I felt terribly hurt and decided to quit the job as soon as I found something else. I had always wanted to become a nurse or a social worker, but studying was out of the question for me when I was growing up.

"You want to help others out of the *stront* (shit) and push us in," my mother had said in her usual, colourful language, whenever I mentioned that I wanted to go on to high school after I turned fifteen.

Because I liked elderly people I went to the 'Old Timers', the local nursing home one morning, to see if there was a vacancy. I was a little nervous, since I did not have the slightest idea what to expect. The long corrugated iron roof of the complex, on the road to the airport, gave the impression of a huge shed. Trees hid most of it and nobody I knew had ever been there. The place seemed somewhat mysterious to me. I parked the Mini at the front of the building and looked for the entrance that was somewhere in the middle. A big, child-like man and an Aboriginal woman with long, white hair on her chin were sitting near the front door. The little woman beside him rolled her lips while chewing something in her toothless mouth. She looked at me curiously through a slit of her one good eye; the other was closed permanently.

"Good-day!" the man stuttered. "How-a-ye-goin?"

"Hello! I came to see the manager," I said, thinking that he had asked me where I wanted to go.

The man, who called himself Reg, stood up. Unsteadily swaying on his feet, he pointed to a house near the end of the complex, saying that the manager lived there.

"George is not home but Sister Perry is inside," he said, stumbling over his words. "She's the matron."

With his one good hand he opened the door for me.

178

"Here you are," he grinned. "My mother always told me to open the door for a lady."

The double doors opened into a large, bare room where a small, elderly lady in a dirty grey-white uniform was mopping the vinyl floor. With her back towards me, she kept mopping. Her short grey hair was thick and badly cut and her bare feet were stuck into brown, worn-out shoes. She turned around when I greeted her.

I still see her standing there; one foot on the pedal of the mop-bucket, a cigarette dangling from the corner of her mouth; her hair cut in a straight line above her eyes. The wrinkled, parchment-like skin of her face folded into a big welcoming smile when she took the cigarette out of her mouth.

"Ohoo! Good-day! We have a visitor!" she exclaimed in a slow, drawn-out voice. "What can I do for you?"

I told her that I had come to see if there was a job for me, as I liked working with old people.

"Ohoo! You wanna work here, do you?" she asked. I wasn't so sure anymore but answered that I would love to.

After I introduced myself and told her a bit about my family, Sister Perry explained that the only lady employed from town was Hazel, who came in every weekday to do the washing. Everybody else was sent from head-quarters in Sydney, volunteers who agreed to working long hours for little pay, as the Old Timers Home was part of the Australian Inland Mission.

Thinking that Fred did not mind how much I earned, I said that that did not matter. All that counted for him was that I was doing a worthwhile job instead of the shame of me working in a supermarket, he had said many times. When I reminded Sister Perry that I had no nursing qualifications and it did not matter to me what kind of a job I would be doing, she looked me up and down for a moment. Then she asked slowly:

"If you have six children, you would know how to wash a dirty bum, won't you?" While I laughed, she promised to ask permission from Sydney to employ me. I left a few minutes later with very mixed feelings. The place was a far cry from the luxurious hostels people in Holland lived in during the last years of their lives.

A week later I got a letter from the A.I.M. welcoming me to their staff. I could start on the first of May, six weeks away. The following day, on Friday afternoon, I told Mrs R that I was going to work at the Old Timers, giving her plenty of time to look for a replacement. She said that she was sorry to be losing me and appreciated that I had told her so early. Then, before she left the shop on Monday afternoon Mrs R came over to talk to me. After asking, as usual, if everything was all right in my department, she said casually: "I've found a lady to replace you. She's starting next Monday. You can work her in for a week and if she proves to be the right person for the job, you can go."

I looked at her in utter disbelief.

"You mean you are giving me the sack?" I asked.

"No, not really. But fair is fair! You're telling me that you don't want to work here any more, so I'm telling you that you can go when I've found someone else."

Although that must have made perfect sense to her, I could not believe my ears. I just stood there after she left, unable to move. Julie and Kerry came over.

"What's the matter?" they asked. "You look as white as a sheet."

"I've just been told to leave," I said, bursting into tears.

"They have no right to do that," they said in unison, when I told them what had happened. "Go and ask Laurel."

Laurel was, as usual, working in the storeroom at the back of the shop.

"No," she said, "Mrs R has no right to send you away like that. I'll have a word with her tomorrow, if you like."

"Don't bother!" I sobbed, mortified by my tears. "I don't want to stay a minute longer than I have to. How much notice do I have to give?"

"Being a part-timer I don't think you need more than twenty-four hours. Wait a minute; I'll find out for you," she said sympathetically.

When she came back from the office a few minutes later and told me that I did not have to give any notice at all, I asked her to get my pay ready so that I didn't have to come back for it later.

"I would do the same thing, if I were in your position," Laurel said, shaking her head. "I'll miss you Minny. You were a damn good worker."

Laurel's parting words softened the pain a little, but I felt terribly disillusioned for a very long time. Driving home I suddenly realised with a shock that I would still have to face Mrs R again, as Simone and her daughter had become good friends. After managing to avoid her for about a year, I had sufficiently recuperated from the ordeal to face her again. I had come to realise that it would not be easy to be fair to everybody when you employed such a large number of people on an ever-changing staff. But that did not stop the wild pumping of my heart when I picked Simone up one day from her friend's birthday party and Mrs. R. opened the door.

There had been no need to worry. Mrs R did not seem to remember any disagreement we ever had, chatting like the best of friends for quite a while, as we had done when I was sewing for her.

When I left the Emporium, I had six weeks to myself before I would start my new job at the Old Timers Home. Although there was plenty for me to do in our new home, the feeling of being alone, locked up in a cage, immediately came back to haunt me. When, at the end of the first week I saw an ad in the paper asking for 'Home Help' I enquired about it. Mrs Rose, the manager of the organisation, was happy to have an extra pair of hands, even though it was only for a few weeks.

The first lady I was sent to looked vaguely familiar to me. We recognised each other at the same time; June was the lady who had prepared the meals for our family at the Memorial Club on our first night in Alice Springs.

"What a waste of time and good food!" June laughed, holding her painful belly, when we recalled how the kids had all picked at their enormous meals and thrown up later.

"At least you got paid for it," I chuckled.

After four and a half years I suddenly realised that the meal would have cost Sam a small fortune, which he could ill afford at the time.

The next day I was sent to Judith who had also had a hysterectomy.

"The operation must be in fashion here," I joked.

Judith told me then that a specialist came up from Adelaide every six weeks to do the major surgery. That same afternoon there was a letter in the mail from Fred's sister Bep telling us that she too had to go into hospital to have her womb removed. I had never been in contact with anyone who had to have this operation and here were three cases in one week from both sides of the world. And mine had started to play up too.

Both June and Judith had only one child each and their homes were spotlessly clean. I went to each of them two mornings a week, and loved it. The work was easy and I trust that our conversations were as beneficial to them as they had been to me.

I was due to start my new job at the Old Timers Home on the first of May 1975, the day after Princess Anne's visit to Alice Springs. I was on duty from eleven in the morning until eight o'clock at night. I liked the light blue uniform I made according to the instructions from headquarters in Sydney. I had pinned the royal blue epaulettes that were included in the letter onto the shoulder seams, with 'A.I.M' in shiny silver letters on the edge of the short sleeves, and a silver button on the pointed end near the collar of the open neck. A small, colourful medal with the emblem of the mission was pinned onto the collar and a navy blue cardigan completed the smart looking outfit. There was no difference between the uniforms of a trained nurse and a nurse's aide. The qualified sisters' uniforms were white with red epaulettes and a red cardigan. After seeing photographs of past years I was glad that the big, funny looking nurse's hats were no longer worn.

Our house was spick & span, the hot evening meal was prepared and a couple of loads of washing were hanging on the line, when I was ready to leave at twenty to eleven that morning. Looking at myself in the mirror, taking a deep breath, I hoped that things would turn out all right, as I had no experience in nursing whatsoever. Although I felt great in my new uniform, I kept wondering what I had let myself in for, when I walked with pounding heart into the front door of the mysterious establishment.

There was nobody to be seen in the bare lounge, but a lot of noise and laughter came from the direction of the kitchen. There was nobody there either. The laughter came from the storeroom, behind the kitchen. I called out a couple of times but there was no answer.

Suddenly, the door flew open and with great merriment an elderly lady, looking like an old-fashioned movie star with a tight bunch of blond curls on top of her head, came marching into the kitchen. Dressed in a frilly pantsuit with a long, pink scarf trailing behind her, she was holding onto a long French bread-stick, pointed at me from between her legs.

The woman nearly died from embarrassment when she saw me standing in the kitchen, no doubt with my mouth wide open.

"Oh my gawd! Oh my gawd!" she kept crying out with her hands in front of her face. The French stick, which had fallen to the ground, was picked up by one of the two young nurses, who had followed her into the kitchen. Unable to look at me, the stockily-built woman went around and around in circles crying out her shame, while the others were doubled up with laughter.

"You must be the new girl," an older woman, who later introduced herself as Chris, said. "Welcome to the circus! There is never a dull moment when our Lill is around."

Lill was normally a quiet lady, the nurses assured me. She lived in one of the new cottages that had officially been opened by Princess Anne the previous day. When Lill and I had both recovered from the shock, she told me that she was still excited from Princess Anne's visit. When I wanted to shake hands with her, she put out her left hand. The Princess had held her right hand and she was not going to wash it for weeks, she said.

"Why didn't you come yesterday?" she asked. "The Princess was marvellous!"

"I would have loved to" I assured her, "but I did not know anybody here. I would have felt terribly out of place."

Lill kept apologising for her 'dreadful' behaviour.

"Don't worry about it. I'm glad to see that the place is not as dead as I expected it to be after my first visit," I laughed.

I soon learned that Lill came from Sydney and that she had been a comedienne from the time she could barely walk. She had played in all sorts of cabarets and shows and had brought life to the Old Timers Home with her happy nature.

I was still talking to Lill when Sister Perry, who was in charge until a new matron was found, came in.

"You can be Ann's off-sider on the south wing today," she said after she greeted me, welcoming me to the staff and hoping that I would be happy there.

Ann, a qualified nurse, was Scottish. I had to listen very carefully to be able to understand what she was saying, since half her words were getting lost in her strong accent. Ann told me that she had just turned sixty. She had been a grandmother at thirty-six and was already a great-grandmother of four 'littlies'. I soon found that she had a heart of gold, and a temper to match her flaming red hair. Chris, who was on the north wing that day, seemed a typical English lady to me. With her motherly figure and her dark hair, combed back smoothly into a bun at the nape of her neck, I felt instantly at home with her. She was a trained nurse and in her early sixties, like Sister Perry and Hazel, a rather old-fashioned looking lady who came in from town to do the washing from Monday to Friday.

Within the next hour I was introduced to nearly every member of the staff as well as to the 'oldies' while I helped serve their midday meal. The two young nurses both came from Sydney, on contract for one year. Rhonda was blond, nearly six foot tall and very skinny, while Kathy was short and stocky. Kathy's straight, dark hair was tied at the back in an untidy ponytail. Frances the cook, a pleasant, down to earth lady was a few years older than I was. There were two other members on the staff: Margaret, the kitchen hand who was on her day off and Liz, the night nurse, who was on duty from nine at night until seven in the morning, four nights a week. Every one of the staff, except Hazel and Liz, lived in a flat on the premises. I would soon find that Liz seldom did any work during the night, but in the eyes of Sister Perry, she was an 'absolute God-send'.

"What would I have done without her?" she asked me when I compiled this story. "I was the only qualified sister there at the time, on call twenty-four hours a day, seven days a week."

Apart from being in charge of the staff and responsible for the administration, Sister Perry also shared the cooking with Chris on weekends. On top of that, she worked normal shifts as well as the other three night duties, and filled in for anyone who was sick. At sixty-two she was working anything from eighty to a hundred hours a week!

Thrown in the Deep End

Before I started work at Old Timers, I had heard about the Reverend John Flynn, the founder of the Australian Inland Mission, who had worked tirelessly to make his dreams come true. He had truly opened up the inland of Australia, by building hospitals and children's hostels in the most isolated communities of this enormous continent.

Adelaide House, the first medical centre in Alice Springs, with its unique cooling system, was designed by Dr Flynn, and opened in 1926. It had a men's and a women's ward of three by four metres, just enough for three beds each. Patients were brought in from miles away, often inundating the little hospital. They were cared for by two Australian Inland Mission nurses, and an occasional visiting doctor.

It wasn't until 1939 that the government built a thirty eight-bed hospital, in town. At that time, the railway line into Alice Springs had been completed for ten years. The narrow, single lane, dirt road to Darwin was sealed by civilians, in conjunction with the Allied Work Council, during the war. They new hospital still had only one doctor and two registered nurses. Army nurses assisted them at the end of 1941, when some four thousand men were based in town to transport supplies from the railway station to the troops that were sent to the top end of Australia, to fend off a possible invasion from Japan.

Together with Alfred Traeger, who had invented the pedal wireless radio, Dr Flynn also established the Royal Flying Doctor Service, which has since become world-famous for providing medical services to remote areas via aeroplane, by transporting doctors and nurses to isolated patients. The wireless communications also made the School of the Air possible a short time later.

Dr Flynn was a young man when he visited the Northern Territory for the first time in 1912. He had been given two commissions; one was to report on the needs of the white settlers for the Federal Home Mission Committee, the other to report on the Aborigines for the Foreign Mission Committee. In an article in the Inlander 1914, Dr. Flynn pointed out the great challenge of confronting authorities to try to change the white man's attitude, especially within the church. In his reports, he stressed that "the Aboriginal people were treated rotten". I read in one of the books about possibly the greatest pioneer of his time, that nothing resulted from his reports for a while, after which Doctor Flynn was given the task, on behalf of the Home Mission Commission, to start a mission for the white settlers in the bush. Building the Old Timers Home, a 'resting place', initially meant for white bushmen who could no longer look after themselves, was one of John Flynn's many dreams. Because hospitals and other medical projects were more urgent at the time, it was not until 1949 that the first cottage was built on the twenty-five acre block on the banks of the Todd River, in Alice Springs.

An orchard of two hundred citrus trees was planted and three bores were sunk but the bores salted up and, because of financial and other difficulties, the original plans for the garden settlement, which would accommodate twenty to twenty five men, had been put on hold for quite some time. A fresh start was made in the fifties, when another seven cottages were built. The new irrigation system that was put in made the endless job of watering the fruit trees, of which half had survived, a lot easier. It also made it possible for the residents to grow their own vegetables. When, in 1959, women were allowed to live at the community of old bushmen, a married couple moved into one of the cottages. The two-hundred-and-forty foot, seventy-two-metre long hostel, where I worked, was built in 1960. Another eight cottages had been added in 1964, followed by a six-bed hospital a few years later. As the original tenants became frail and around the clock nursing care was needed, the number of nursing staff was slowly increased and another fifteen cottages and seven self-contained flats for the nursing staff were built between 1972 and 1974. When I joined the staff in May 1975, there were twelve people in the hostel, nine men and three women, and six in the hospital, two men and four women. Five of them were Aboriginal. Another thirty-five elderly people, all white, lived in the cottages, dotted among flowering shrubs and beautiful white gum trees around the property. The citrus trees were laden with nearly ripe fruit. I had never seen so many birds anywhere in town.

After lunch, on my first day, Scottish Ann showed me around. She told me about the daily routine and a bit about each of the residents. There were six rooms on the right wing of the Rosetta Flynn Hostel, named after John Flynn's mother, another six to the left, and there were two additional rooms next to the front door, which opened up into a large lounge and dining room. With the help of Kathy, who would be back in the afternoon, Ann had already finished the cleaning when I came in at eleven o'clock. Most of the rooms were very bare. There was a single iron bed, a built-in cupboard with a mirror and some deep drawers, next to a narrow wardrobe and one or two old kitchen chairs. Cheap, ill-fitting curtains were hanging limply in front of the louvre windows. None of the rooms had any carpet.

"They (the 'inmates') don't need much and it's easy for us to clean this way," Ann said while we walked from room to room. "You only have to make the bed, tidy up a bit, dust the cupboard and the louvres and sweep and mop the floors."

Swedish Bob's room was the last on the right wing. His room was filthy and full of junk.

"He seldom allows anybody in to clean it," Ann apologised when we walked back to the dining room to serve the hot midday meal. "We don't interfere with peoples' privacy. We just have to do the best we can."

After lunch we took the dry washing off the line together, folded it and sorted it into big piles, and took it around to the hostel rooms and into the little hospital. Although Ann finished duty at three o'clock she stayed on to help me do everything that had to be done until I could go home at eight that night. I protested that that was making it a very long day for her, but Ann just smiled.

"This is home for me and I haven't anything else in mind for the evening anyway," she said in her singing Scottish accent, which I tried to copy for Fred and the children when I got home later in the evening.

At five o'clock we served the evening meal, which had been prepared by Frances the cook, before she had gone off duty at four. When we had done the dishes, mopped the floor in the dining room and given the residents their last cup of tea for the day, we set the tables for breakfast and covered each with a fly net. Most people were already in bed when I left a little after eight o'clock. I drove home in the dark feeling happy and excited, but the thought that it would probably still be dark at six-thirty the following morning when I was expected back, dampened my enthusiasm. I liked to get up early in the morning but I wasn't sure how Fred and the children were going to cope without me.

Everybody was still asleep when I slipped out of the house at a quarter past six the following morning, the second of May. I had hardly seen the children the previous evening. Fred had allowed the youngest to stay up until I came home and they had gone to bed with the others, shortly after. I felt guilty, as Fred and the children had to get ready for work and school without me hurrying them along, for the first time. But the next minute I drove off happily with a great sense of relief: it was Friday and I would be home all weekend. It was a beautiful morning. The sun had just come up over the horizon when I drove through the Gap. It was still cool, promising to be another glorious day. I sucked the fresh air coming through the open windows of my little car deep into my lungs, feeling more alive than I had done for a very long time.

Chris was already preparing breakfast in the kitchen when I arrived. She introduced me to Margaret, a big slow moving girl, about my age with a friendly round face. She was taking the fly nets off the tables in the dining room. I stuck my hand out automatically to shake hers, but she had obviously not expected this as she awkwardly touched my fingers.

Scottish Ann was already there too. After saying 'Hello' briefly, we left the kitchen to get the residents ready for breakfast. Most of them came to the dining room, but a few were served in their rooms. Ann went to the right wing and I went to the left. When I got to Little Joe's room a dreadful smell overwhelmed me. Joe was a small, very fragile eighty-two year old man. Ann had told me the previous day that he was not expected to live much longer. He barely opened his eyes when I lifted the blankets gently off his skinny torso, appalled by what I saw. I found Ann talking to Chris in the kitchen. They exchanged a curious glance at each other when I told them what I had found in Joe's room.

"The poor man must have pooped himself early last night," I said indignantly. "It's all caked on his body, up to his neck."

Chris screwed her mouth up in a peculiar way I would come to know so well. "Hear nothing, see nothing and say nothing in this place," she advised, as she turned back to the stove.

"If you take this tray to Tom in the first room, I'll go and clean Little Joe up," Ann offered.

"No, Joe is on my wing, I'll wash him," I protested. "Just tell me where I can find the things I need."

I had never seen a grown-up person in such a revolting state before and wondered how I would go about the task of cleaning him up. Joe was unable to get out of bed, let alone get into the bath. I broke out into a cold sweat when a sudden thought hit me. The old man could die while I was working on him.

It was very chilly in the room. The strip-heater on the wall I had switched on when I came in earlier had made little difference. I kept the little man's body, a bag of skin and bones, covered as much as possible while I soaked the muck off him bit by bit with warm water and plenty of soap, talking to him as if he were my favourite uncle. When he finally lay between the clean white sheets he rewarded me with a beautiful smile.

Little Joe became very special to me and he responded accordingly. I took great care feeding him as much as his stomach tolerated. His will to live soon started to come back again. By the end of the following week, he could sit on a chair while I changed his bed.

"It won't be long and you'll be sitting in the dining room again," I promised him. Every time I made his bed, I set the chair a bit closer to the door, then around the corner in the passage. Joe enjoyed the attention of his fellow residents so much that I dressed him in his normal clothes again.

After several weeks, the day came when he was able to walk to the dining room on my arm and eat his meal at the table, as I had promised. I was extremely happy seeing how his old buddy Tom, the whip-maker, greeted him, but the look on the faces of some of my colleagues showed that they did not share my happiness. When I asked what was the matter, they looked at each other uncomfortably. After I pressed them to tell me what they were thinking, Chris screwed up her mouth and said: "Why didn't you let the man die in peace? You're only making more work for all of us." I was stunned.

"What if he was your father?" I asked. Chris pulled up her shoulders. "It won't last," she said reluctantly. "Then the poor fellow will have to go through it all again."

Four months later, at the beginning of October, I went to Ayers Rock, camping with Fred and the kids for a couple of days. While I was away, Little Joe died peacefully in his sleep. I felt very sad that I had not been there for his funeral. It had been a very lonely affair as George, the manager of Old Timers, had been the only person there. But I do have a lot of happy memories of him.

I don't know much about Joe's life, except that he grew up in the bush and had been in one of the first weather-board cottages at Old Timers for many years. His mind had slowly deteriorated and one day, he had apparently gone 'off his rocker'. Stark naked he had chased his cat around the property one evening and hacked it to bits with an axe, because it had piddled in one of his pot plants. He had been living in the hostel ever since the incident, which happened several years before I met him.

Little Joe was vague and confused, but once a month or so he would fast for a day, refusing to eat or drink anything but water. For a few days afterwards his eyes and his mind were very clear and he was able to tell me stories about his life in the bush. Perhaps that's what I should do to clear the cobwebs out of my mind too...

In the afternoon of that first Friday at Old Timers I witnessed what it took to entice Blanche, the Aboriginal lady who was sitting beside Reg at the front of the building when I applied for the job, to have a bath. She always started yelling as soon as the word 'bath' was mentioned to her.

Every morning and every afternoon Blanche shuffled to the kitchen on her skinny legs to get her ration of chewing tobacco and a bottle of stout. Once a week, twice in summer if we could manage it, those treats were withheld until she'd had a bath.

"I don't need a bath; I'm a clean woman!" she would say angrily, wailing loudly for hours. Time and again she was reminded of the bath when she came to the counter and there would be another outburst of yelling and screaming at the top of her lungs, shaking her fists.

"Have a bath yourself, you bitches!" she would yell, looking furiously at us with her one eye: "I'm not dirty. I'm not going to bed with men. I'm a clean woman."

The weekly drama was watched with amusement by the other oldies. Some of them encouraged her to stand up for herself, and not to let us boss her around. Time and time again Blanche would plead for her beer and tobacco in her sweetest manner. As a newcomer, I was her usual target. She would tell me how she had nearly drowned when she had been a young girl of about twelve. Her so-called friends had thrown her into the Todd River when it was

188

in full flood. I had seen the violence of the masses of water when the otherwise dry Todd came down, and felt very sorry for her. When it was my turn to bath Blanche, I would tell her that I would put only a little bit of water in the tub and make it nice and warm, but it hardly made any difference. Sometimes I was successful when I promised to put curlers in her usually shoulder-length hair, which was bright white and beautifully soft when it was washed. One day when I was putting rollers in, I offered to cut the big clusters of long, white hairs off her protruding chin but she did not want to have a bar of it.

"That might bring bad luck," she said.

The struggle to get Blanche into the bath often continued for days. By-passers on the main road to and from Adelaide or the airport must have thought that we were about to kill her, the way she carried on. She would walk up and down beside the road wailing and cursing, telling people who happened to stop their car what a dreadful bunch of hypocrites we were. Although she screamed a lot, she seldom used bad language. She had lived in the convent for a while and threatened to go back there, whenever we were pestering her to have a bath, but afterwards, Blanche would immediately be her sweet self again, apologising profusely for the trouble she had given us.

"Come! Let me give you a kiss darlin'," she would say, and in the same breath; "You gimme another beer?"

One day Blanche told me that she had been the first black woman who had married a white man at the Overland Telegraph Station, which is now an important tourist attraction. She had felt terribly shy in the white, lacy dress, made by Mrs Gillen, the first postmaster's wife. Blanche's husband was a Scotsman, but she refused to mention his name.

"He was very tall," she said, staring in front of her. "He was a good man, but he died many years ago."

Blanche and George, a tall Chinese looking Aboriginal man who had a room on the right wing, had both grown up at the Telegraph Station at the turn of the century. They often sat together, talking in their own language, spiced with English. One day, they told me what had happened when they saw a 'motor-car' for the first time.

"We was only kids and very shy," Blanche said. "We only knew horses an' camels pulling carts. This one made a lot of noise an' it was smokin'. We was very scared an' all run away. Old people too. We was watchin' from a safe distance."

George's eyes were shining and he smiled a little, something he seldom did, his inseparable pipe dangling from the corner of his mouth.

The kids had slowly moved closer when the strange buggy stopped. They all stood in a circle around it, laughing and joking about the funny cart that moved without being pulled by a horse or a camel.

"It was still makin' noise and it was puffin' smoke," Blanche went on. "While we was watchin' a stream of hot water came from underneath the cart. It made a big puddle in the sand," she chuckled.

George cracked up laughing, when Blanche recalled how one of the big, cheeky Aboriginal boys had yelled out: "It hasn't got a horse, but it sure can piss!"

The first car that came through the Centre was a Talbot, called the 'Angelina' driven by Harry Dutton and Murray Aungar in December 1907. Because Blanche often talked about Mister Gillen, the first postmaster at the Telegraph Station, who had left in 1899, she must have been a lot older than was thought. I checked the story with local historians. One of them, an expert on vintage cars, told me that the radiators of the first motor cars produced a lot of steam and the cooling of the engine released a stream of hot water, which made the puddle underneath the car. Later, I read a lovely story about the exciting event that had sent the Aborigines scurrying into the trees, in Doris Blackwell's well-known autobiography 'Alice on the Line'.

When Chinese George died, not long after Blanch told me this story, she blocked her window and the keyholes of her room and she wailed for weeks. When I asked her why she had stuffed paper in the keyholes and barricaded herself in her room at night, she looked around suspiciously to see if anyone else could hear her.

"Come here, I'll tell you," she chuckled secretively, instantly forgetting that she had been crying only a few seconds before. She put her arms around my neck, pulled my head down and whispered with her toothless mouth close to my ear:

"He may peep at me through the hole, or come in my room when I wanna get undressed an' go to bed."

"Who?" I asked.

"You know. Him!" Blanche answered impatiently. She shuffled back to her room, wailing again. According to Aboriginal law, she could not mention George's name after he died, but I did not know that at the time.

During the first couple of days at Old Timers, I was assigned to the left wing and got to know the routine. Only Little Joe needed assistance in the morning; the others had to be woken up in time for breakfast, which was ready at seven. Being May, it was getting very cold in the morning but some of the oldies were already up, saying that they had been dressed for ages, I later learned that most of them often slept in their clothes, but others were still sound asleep, snug under their blankets. I felt awful having to wake them up. It seemed such a pity, as there was nothing for them to do all day anyway. But I soon realised that it would be impossible if everybody came to the kitchen for breakfast at different times and some people would probably stay in bed all day. Although they grumbled about having to get up at such a dreadful hour, nobody skipped breakfast unless they felt unwell, usually because they had been drunk the previous night.

The people in the left wing were very quiet. Only Blanche walked up and down a lot from her room to the kitchen, mainly to ask if it were time for her beer or tobacco. The only other Aboriginal woman in the hostel was Blanche's sister Marjory, a shy but friendly little thing, as quiet as a mouse. She was only there temporarily to get her strength back after an operation. She returned to her family in town a few months later.

Then there was Edna, a short stocky woman in her late fifties. She walked on tiptoes and said little but her mind, and often her legs, seemed to be working overtime. For many years she had been a live-in barmaid and a housemaid at the Stuart Arms, one of the favourite watering places in town, until the drink got the better of her and ruined her brain. Just like a three-year-old toddler, she would be off in a flash. She was often out of the gate before anyone realised that she had gone. A big billboard on the road near the entrance of the home, asked motorists to give an Old Timer a lift into town and Edna never had to wait long. Although she was often found before she got a lift, she managed to escape regularly. George the manager knew exactly where to find her since she always took the same route, first to the employment office, then to Woolies to ask for a job, and across the road to The Stuart Arms where there would always be someone to buy her a drink. Sister Perry was never in a great hurry to get Edna back.

"Let the woman have a bit of fun," she would say in her slow manner. "Nobody will do her any harm."

One day, when I went to the road to get Edna back, Betty, one of the new nurses, was talking to her, pulling her skirt up and pointing her thumb in the direction of the town.

"What on earth are you doing?" I asked her when I got close to them. The new nurse laughed.

"I'm showing Edna what she should do to get a lift quickly," she said in her singing, Yorkshire accent.

I could not believe my ears. Here was Betty, who continuously talked about Jesus and the Bible to anyone who would listen, showing Edna this sexy way to attract a car driver's attention.

"You could get her into real trouble," I said patronisingly. "You'd better come back with me Edna. It's too late to go to town today anyway. The shops are all closed," I lied.

Betty came from England, volunteering as a missionary. Although she had been at Old Timers for some time, she was quite shocked when I told her that Edna was going to the pub in town.

"I had no idea Mien, truly I didn't," she would say whenever I met her for weeks afterwards. Of course she hadn't. Betty's mind was always pre-occupied with matters of heaven, rather than earth.

Edna escaped regularly, no matter what we did. At one stage, when she had managed to get away several times in one week, Sister Perry was sick and tired of having to ask George to pick her up in town. She told us to dress her in a nightie so that nobody would give her a lift. But the 'bushies' who came past the home could obviously not see the difference between a nightie and a dress, and took her anyway. Sister Perry then pinned a note onto the back of her nightie with safety pins, but Edna was not stupid. When the first couple of cars had stopped and the drivers had told her that they could not take her after reading the note, she came back to me, asking me to take it off. When I said that I couldn't do that, she went around asking the old boys in the hostel and she ended up in town anyway. After a few months I was occasionally asked to retrieve her, a task I rather enjoyed. Edna's outings stopped when a new matron increased her sedatives. It was a sorry sight to see her sitting in a chair like a zombie and we all missed the excitement she had brought to the place.

The only other person on the left wing was Big Joe, a very independent, well-groomed gentleman who had lived at Old Timers for a long time. He was not a big man at all. It was only because the other Joe was so small that he was referred to like that. Joe looked very much out of place in his bare room. He often went to town, walking or catching a lift with anyone who went that way. I was surprised to see him in the kitchen, drying the dishes for Chris one day. He told me then that he used to help out a lot with the household chores before additional staff had been put on.

"The place was more like a home then" he said sadly, "and now they're talking about making the place double the size."

I remembered the note of despair in Joe's voice again two years later, when the work on the new place was in progress and he literally starved himself to death by refusing to eat.

192

1. Fred: What have I started?

2. Mien: Happy the decision is finally made

3. Boarding the Southern Cross

4. Regine between the future King of Zululand and his elderly father

5. Meeting my brother Henk in Fremantle, Western Australia

1. Arrival at Alice Springs airport

2. My brother Sam aged 33: What have I let myself in for?

3. The house won't be ready, but you love camping don't you?

4/5. Our sole possessions

1. Mum playing cards on her own

2. Fred between my brothers Wim & Sam

3. School uniforms - what a blessing!

4. Our first visit to Ayers Rock

1. Thrown in the deep end: nursing at last at the Old Timers Home

2. The six of them, at home alone in 1977

3. Taking part in the yearly May Day parade, "The Bangtail Muster"

4. The "Dutch Embassy"

A Dangerous Job

During the weekend I looked eagerly forward to returning to my new job on Monday morning, this time assigned to work with the residents in the right wing. They were all men, two of whom could become violent if they were rubbed up the wrong way, I was told. One of them was Reg, the big man who had so gallantly opened the front door for me on my first visit to Old Timers. Some years earlier he had a stroke that had made his right hand useless and his speech slurred. He quickly became frustrated when he could not say what he wanted to, gnashing his teeth in a frightening way. I was the best of mates with him right from the beginning, mainly because I was a Catholic. He always talked about his mother but I could never be sure if he meant the Holy Mary or his own mother.

Reg needed to be showered and shaved two or three times a week. After I had watched Chris and Ann shave him a couple of times, I had a go at it myself one day. As I did not like being watched when I was doing something, I had not told anybody that I was going to shave him. My hands were shaking a little and Reg gnashed his teeth a couple of times when the razor was pulling a bit. I would stop and say 'Sorry', and ask if he was all right. Reg would grimace, take a deep breath, grin broadly and say: "Yes; go on!"

I took a deep breath myself when I cleaned the shaving gear in the bathroom, glad that it was all over. Reg was happy with the result and I felt mighty proud when he walked into the dining room and showed off his clean face to Chris.

"You shouldn't have done that without supervision," Chris berated me later. "He could have hurt you badly. I told you that he had broken the matron's arm last year while she was shaving him."

Chris wasn't the only one who had told me about the incident. I felt very foolish, even more so when Chris told me, yet again, how Reg had grabbed the matron's arm with his abnormally strong left hand and twisted it, when she cut him while she shaved him.

When I wanted to shower Reg for the first time a few days later I asked Chris about it. She exchanged a glance with Ann.

"I think she'll be all right," Chris said.

"Reg likes her," Ann agreed cautiously. "Leave the door open so that we can check on you," she warned as I walked away.

There was only one bathroom in the middle of each wing, which was shared with the other men as well as the women. The rooms, which were no bigger than three by three metres, had a narrow bath and two hand-basins each. The only toilet in the wing was separate, next to the bathroom. Everything went all right that first time. Although I did not particularly like showering or

193

shaving Reg, it soon became a normal part of my job, but one day, things went terribly wrong. Come to think about it, I consider myself lucky that I am sitting here, writing the story.

That afternoon I helped Reg get undressed, talking to him as usual. The only thing he was still wearing was his singlet, which was badly frayed on the edges and had some holes in it.

"You know what we do when Fred has a singlet with holes in it like this?" I asked.

"No. What do you do?" Reg stuttered, grinning in his childish way. Without giving it another thought, I put my finger in one of the holes saying: "I let the children put their fingers in the holes and rip it off like this..."

His reaction made my blood curdle instantly. Baring his big, yellow teeth to the gums, his twisted face turned blue. His arms were tightly pressed to his sides, the knuckles of his clenched fists white. I felt the blood drain from my face when I realised the dangerous situation I was in, but somehow -God only knows how- I managed to stay calm.

The bathroom door was slightly open but, as I was standing with my back against it, there was no hope of getting out. While my mind raced ahead, I kept on talking to Reg without losing eye contact.

"Don't worry Reg. I'll buy you a brand new one. I should have known that it was still all right for you to wear. I'll get you another one as soon as I go home at three o'clock and I'll bring it to you right away."

With a great sense of relief I watched Reg's face slowly relax and his clenched fists return to their normal colour.

"You shouldn't have done that," he stuttered.

"No Reg, I shouldn't have. I'm really sorry," I agreed.

A few minutes later, I guided him under the lovely warm shower and left him to enjoy it. Leaning against the wall, outside the bathroom, I tried to stop my knees from trembling and my heart pounding.

I now think that because Reg stiffened up instantly while his arms were hanging down at his side made it impossible for him to hit me or grab me by my throat, while he was angry. He could surely have choked me to death before anyone could have raised the alarm. The fact that I had kept eye contact with Reg, must have been an instinctive reaction, as I had had no training whatsoever at that time.

Writing about the incident made me aware that there is no need to worry unnecessarily about events that may never happen. I now feel that we can safely put more trust into our instinctive reactions in times of sudden, dangerous situations.

The other fellow who could be violent was Arthur. With his charming smile, that reminded me of a three-year-old child, he seemed a gentleman who would not hurt a fly. As long as someone filled his simple needs for food and regular smokes, Arthur was quite content in his own little world and, because it was so easy to make him happy, every body liked him and talked to him.

Arthur had been an electrician. A metal plate had been inserted into his head after a bad accident at work that left him brain damaged. He had lived in a cottage for several years until he got out of control one day. He too had attacked his cat in a moment of utter frustration.

There must be something about cats, which brings out the worst in a man. My stepfather had killed four beautiful six-week-old kittens in a gruesome scene when we were children. The more we cried and begged him to save the poor creatures, the madder he became. I can still hear his awful, madman's laugh while he killed our beloved pets, one by one.

My sister-in-law had a similar experience. She and her siblings had been at school when her father killed their five much-loved cats. They had searched for their pets everywhere, unable to find them until she noticed the big, fluffy tail of one of the cats waving above the soil in the garden. When they dug up the badly mutilated bodies they found that that one was still alive. For many years afterward the badly handicapped cat at my brother's place was a constant reminder of that dreadful incident.

There were two Toms in the hostel; one was called 'the gardener' and the other 'the whip-maker'. Tom, the gardener was a cantankerous little man, but for some reason or other, I got on his good side. He was seldom angry with me and after I one day fixed his funny fingernail I could do no wrong by him.

Many years before, Tom had had an accident with a chainsaw. The nail from his right index finger had since grown over the top of his finger, like a bird's beak. Because he was always working in the garden, the nail was dirty and gave him a lot of trouble. When I commented on the strange looking nail, he told me that a friend in Sydney filed it off every now and then, but he had not found anyone in Alice he could trust to touch it.

"I'll give it a go if you like," I said without thinking.

Tom took me up on the offer immediately and went into town that same day to buy the right file. The following afternoon, I started filing away shortly before it was time to knock off. It seemed to take forever, but I finally got through the hard top layer an hour or so later. I was amazed to see the two holes in the piece that came off, exactly as those of a parrot's beak. I still had a lot of filing to do before it looked like a normal nail. When I got home late that afternoon Fred was angry with me, which dampened my happiness considerably, but it had been worth it since I had made a friend for life.

Tom had come to Alice Springs from Sydney to be near his only son. He came to Old Timers a year later when his son left town and there had been nowhere else for him to go. Tom was a little man, just skin and bones, without a tooth in his mouth. Shortly after his arrival, he had been given a small piece of land in front of the manager's house beside the hostel, in which to grow some vegetables. He had extended his plot to a substantial garden during the following year. He now grew a variety of soft fruits and vegetables. Unfortunately, they were often useless because the insects had free range in his garden. He grew the most beautiful, big cauliflowers but they were forever infested with tiny insects and caterpillars. Tom would be in the foulest of tempers if his vegetables were not served with the midday meal and we spent ages helping the cook to try to wash the grubs out. Knowing how much time and effort it took to grow a few vegetables in this harsh climate, I understood Tom's frustrations very well.

That first year when I met Tom, the insects were particularly bad. There was no way they could be washed out from between the stalks of the cauliflowers. In the end, the cook we had at the time just pretended that they weren't there.

"A bit of fresh meat won't do anybody any harm," she said, covering the dish with white sauce and a lot of finely chopped parsley. My stomach turned when I saw the old folk eagerly digging into the delicacy.

Tom, the whip-maker, was the complete opposite of his cranky namesake. He was blessed with a lovely nature, loved by everyone who came in contact with him. It seemed to me that he had been at Old Timers for ages when I first met him. It wasn't until I compiled this story that I realised he had actually been there for only a few months.

Tom came from Hamilton Downs station, now a popular youth camp, eighty kilometres north-west of Alice Springs. While I was collecting information about him, I spent a lovely afternoon with Mrs Prior, the station manager's wife, who visited him at Old Timers regularly. Dawn filled the gaps in some of the stories Tom had told me.

Tom grew up in the bush around Birdsville in Queensland. He had never been to school and could not read or write. By the time he was ten years old, he had become the best stone-thrower for miles around. One day, Tom had hit another boy with a stone from a great distance, which had caused a deep cut under the young fellow's eye. Tom's mother, who had to bring up her two children on her own, was furious. Knowing that he was going to get a hiding, Tom ran away and stayed out all night in the bush. When he came home the following afternoon his mother seemed to have forgotten all about the incident and acted as if nothing had happened. She made something to eat for her hungry son and, while he was eating, she asked him to run to the police station to give the policeman a message. Relieved to see that she was not angry anymore Tom happily obliged. As soon as he had handed the policeman the letter, Tom turned to leave, but the policeman called him back, asking him to wait a minute in case the letter needed an answer. After reading the note, the officer put it on the table.

"Close the door boy," he said. When Tommy came back, the policeman had taken his belt off and given Tom a good thrashing as his mother had asked him to do in the letter. Tom needed to be taught a lesson but she would never be able to catch him, since he was much too quick for her. I shuddered involuntarily, remembering how my stepfather had done the same to my brother Wim when he was eight years old.

"Tom learned more than one lesson from the incident," Dawn laughed. "He never delivered any messages for his mother again, and vowed to learn to read and write. He left home when he was twelve years old to go on his first cattle drive and never went back home again. Around the camp fires at night, one of the men taught Tommy to read and write, using the inside of empty cigarette boxes and a stump of a pencil."

Tom, who was a top saddle maker as well as an all-round handyman, had been at Hamilton Downs for many years before Dawn and her husband Bill came to live there in 1957. He had been married, but his wife had left him, taking their two little children with her. He had not seen any member of his family for many years until some years ago, Dawn received a letter from his only sister, who was a lot older than Tom and lived in Sydney. She was coming to Alice Springs, hoping to see her brother with whom she had lost contact thirty-eight years earlier. Dawn had asked Tom if he wanted to go to town to meet his sister or if preferred her to come out to the station.

"You know what I'm like when I go to town," Tom had said. "I may never see her at all."

"When Tom went to town, he would go straight to the pub and that would be the end of him for at least a fortnight. He was very naughty at that time," Dawn laughed. Then she added thoughtfully: "It was lovely to see Tom and his sister meeting after all those years. 'Good to see you copper-top!' his sister said. They just stood there hugging each other for a long time." We were silent for a while, then Dawn continued.

"A few years later, Tom's daughter came to see her father. She brought her four-year-old son with her. He was the spitting image of his grandfather with his chubby cheeks and his red hair. The two were inseparable while he was here. It was heart warming to see the old boy so happy when they were together."

Again we sat in silence, each with our own thoughts.

"You should have seen Tommy's dog!" Dawn said, laughing again. "He had this bull-terrier crossed with a blue heeler, the funniest dog you have ever seen. The whole dog was white except for one small black patch on one eye.

197

'Wee-eye', it was called. Tom was extremely fond of that dog. Where ever he went, the dog was with him," she continued. "One day the dog had been badly injured. He nursed it day and night but it was never the same again. Ever after the accident, the dog growled at everybody that came near him. One morning, Tom came into the main kitchen of the station, where I was making breakfast and told me that he had to shoot his dog. 'I have no choice,' he said. 'I'd never forgive myself if he attacked any of the children.' I knew how much that dog meant to him. I took the children into the lounge and waited. I heard a few shots soon afterwards. When he had buried the body, Tom came back into the kitchen. I felt really sorry for him."

Silently, Dawn had handed Tom a brandy. By the time she and her husband had gone to bed, late that night, Tom had still been sitting there, quite drunk singing softly, then crying, laughing, singing, and crying again, not wanting to go to bed. Unable to go to sleep, Dawn had gotten up after a while and taken him gently to his room, next to the saddle shed. By that time Tom did not object when Dawn put him to bed. She was taking off his shoes when Tom suddenly asked: "Will you sleep with me tonight?"

When Dawn had told him the following morning what he had asked her the previous night, Tom had been most upset.

"Never!" he had shouted. "Never! I swear to God!"

"I believe you," I laughed. "He asked me to cuddle up with him and warm his bed, one night too, when he came home drunk."

During his last years on the station, Tom had several blackouts. He needed to be close to the Alice Springs hospital and therefore had been taken to Old Timers where he was very unhappy. Whenever Dawn visited him he kept begging her to take him home to the station.

"Six weeks after Tom left I saw a taxi driving up to the homestead," Dawn recalled. "I was wondering who it could be as I was not expecting any visitors, and certainly not in a taxi. Tom had packed lock, stock and barrel, disgusted with 'that place'. He could not stand it a day longer, he said. When I asked him what was so bad about it, he said: 'I've been there six weeks and not once have they given me cabbage for me dinner!' Tom was back at the station for a few weeks when he had another blackout. When he was discharged from the hospital, he was taken back to Old Timers. From then on he settled and became everybody's favourite."

"Tom was getting plenty of cabbage when I met him, which was apparently only a few weeks later," I laughed. "It was on the menu at least twice a week."

As soon as Tom heard that I had three sons, he wanted me to bring them over so that he could teach them the art of plaiting stockwhips. Time and again the sounds of Tom cracking his whips on the lawn behind his room, were

198

ringing between the buildings, echoing from wall to wall. At eighty-six, Tom still had all his teeth but, as he used them to bite off and stretch the leather strips for his whips, they were worn off to the gums. He had to bring the strands close to his eyes to see them properly, but he never wanted any glasses.

Tom's whips were plaited coarsely with uneven strips of leather of up to a centimetre in width. Shortly after I met him, he asked Paddy, an eccentric lady who had a room in the extension next to the front door, to show me her father's whip. While she shuffled to her room to get the priceless item, Tom told me that Paddy's father had been the champion stockwhip-maker of Australia for many years.

The beautiful whip Paddy handed to me a little later was plaited with the finest leather strips, no more then two millimetres wide. The handle, which was about two centimetres thick and half a metre long, was also covered with the same, delicate pattern. It had a big, decorated knob on the end and was joined by an intricate knot onto the two and a half metre long whip, which tapered off smoothly into a single strip of leather. Tom's fingers caressed the perfectly crafted whip.

"Paddy's father was truly a champ," he repeated admiringly. "The best whip-maker who ever lived."

One afternoon, when Fred came to pick me up, he had a go at cracking the whip too, but he could not get a sound out of it.

"That's a Chinaman," Tom said. "Let me show you how it's done." He took a long whip in each hand, cracking them non-stop, like fire-works.

Tom called everybody who did not know what he was doing a 'Chinaman'. He told Fred and the boys how he had sold two stock whips, made from raw hide to a 'Chinaman' on a fencing contract somewhere in the bush. They wanted to go to town for the weekend but Tom's mate did not know what to do with his new whips. Afraid that they would be stolen if he left them in the camp, the fellow decided to bury them deep in the sand beside the fence.

"I warned him," Tom said. "But he didn't want to listen. When we came back after a fortnight, the dingoes had dug them out and chewed them to bits," he laughed. "They can smell rawhide a mile away. It doesn't matter how deep you bury it, they'll find it all right."

Tom was always busy in the corner behind his room, under the veranda. He repaired anything that needed mending in the old bushman's fashion, using big rusty nails, pieces of wire and string or strips of leather.

"Nothing was ever wasted in the bush," he would say. His pride and joy was the most comfortable chair he had ever had, an old camping chair he had fixed up by tying an old hessian potato bag to the metal frame with a few metres of thin wire.

Tom's liver had been badly damaged by his drinking and his stomach was giving him a lot of trouble, but he had lots of interesting remedies for his ailing health. Apart from his daily drink of stout or brandy, or both, he would make a mixture of port, red wine and brandy, set it alight and drink it as quickly as possible when the flame had died down, to cure his gastric trouble. Drinking a mixture of apple cider and vinegar would fix his arthritis. When his back was aching, he was often hanging by his arms from the doorframe of his room. Being no more than one metre sixty, he needed a footstool to reach the top of the frame. How he could hang there for so long, I'll never know, but it seemed to work all right.

Like most of the other old fellows, Tom was keen on Senega of Ammonia, a cough medicine that had a percentage of alcohol. A one-litre bottle, which was meant to last for at least a fortnight, was often empty in a couple of days.

Tom always had a couple of stouts each day in summer, and when it was cold he drank brandy. About once a month he would cadge a ride with George, the manager, or with one of us into town to 'do a bit of shoppin', which meant that he would disappear into the pub. George would go looking for him later in the afternoon but he was usually having a good time and not yet ready to leave. He would come home late at night or early in the morning by taxi, waking everybody up with his happy singing.

Tom was not the only one who liked the bottle. Most of the men were under the weather when they came back from a day in town, but not one of them was a happy drunk like Tommy.

Such is Life

It did not take me long to feel at home and love my job at Old Timers, but the long, odd hours were a strain on my family life, especially because Fred still resented me going out to work. He felt that I was taking more interest in the old people than in my own family, which made it difficult for me to share my experiences with him. Whenever I came home exhausted or mentioned problems at work, he instantly reminded me that he would be much happier if I stayed at home, pointing out that I could make more money in less hours, if I took up sewing again.

My pay had dropped considerably. I was getting less than two-thirds of what I earned at the Emporium and I was doing shift-work, which would later also include working on weekends. I had looked forward to getting an airfare to Adelaide at the end of the year like the other girls, but I was told that that was not applicable to me, because my home was in town.

I liked the variety of the shifts and the different areas I worked in. An early shift in the hostel was from six-thirty in the morning until three-thirty in the afternoon, and a late from eleven in the morning till eight o'clock at night. A broken shift went from six-thirty until eleven in the morning, then back again from four till eight at night. In the little hospital, a day shift was from seven until four, and a broken shift from seven till eleven, then from four till nine at night. The hardest for my family was a broken shift in the hospital, followed by an early morning start in the hostel. On those days I would not see the younger children at all.

Although the oldies could be very difficult at times, I enjoyed the contact with them very much. The work was relatively easy and never boring, but the days were long. When, after six months of working full-time, forty hours became too much for me, my shifts were reduced to thirty-two hours, or four days a week.

In the beginning, I could not clean the bathrooms with the old-people's smell and their revolting sputum mugs without feeling nauseated, but I got used to it eventually. Disposable gloves were not heard of. The men would occasionally urinate in the hand-basin, because it was much easier for them than sitting on the toilet. Some of them would get drunk every fortnight after pension day. They would usually clean up after themselves, but the dreadful stench of vomit could hang around for days if it wasn't cleaned up properly, especially in summer when it was often extremely hot.

After a few weeks I took my turn to be the breakfast cook on the early shifts in the hostel. I was pretty nervous that first morning, having half a dozen pairs of critical eyes watching me from the dining room. Cooking is no hobby for me and I had never made scrambled eggs in my life. I loved the smell of freshly fried bacon, but I could not understand for the life of me how people could possibly stand fried sausages on an empty stomach.

I had soon found out how hard it was to please Tom, the gardener. His porridge was never cooked to his satisfaction and his toast was always too light, too dark or stone cold. But as I was one of the few in Tom's good books, he never complained when he knew that I was cooking.

When Marjory had regained her strength and returned to her family, her room was taken by Alice, a very heavy, friendly lady with a smooth complexion and a very sharp tongue. She was no more than five feet tall, as round as a keg of beer, and she walked with the help of a walking frame. I was shocked by the enormous size of her legs when she came in. Her condition was appropriately called 'elephantiasis'.

Alice came from New Zealand. She had come as far away from her family as she could she said, as that was the easiest way to keep the peace. I'm not sure how many children she had, two or three, I think. There were few pictures of her children and grandchildren in her room. She received an occasional letter but I never saw any of her family in Alice Springs. When I told Alice that I had six children, she looked stunned.

"You have six children?" she exclaimed in her high pitched voice; "You are only a spring chicken yourself!"

Alice settled in well and soon became part of the furniture, her sharp eyes not missing a beat. She always laughed the loudest when I called out to everyone to 'get on the table' when dinner was ready to be served. Nobody wanted to tell me what was so funny. Had I said something wrong? They would just laugh and say; 'Oh, no!' or 'Nothing!'

Once or twice a week, Alice took a bath, but she never wanted any assistance. I often wondered how she could possibly manage to get her heavy torso in and out of the deep, slippery bath without any help. Whenever I offered to wash her back for her she would say: "Thank you, but I prefer to be left on my own. I'm not a pretty sight in the bath, you know."

Alice had to pay a painful price for her unnecessary modesty. One afternoon she asked me to come into the bathroom and have a look, as she was hurting under her breasts. She was sitting in a few centimetres of water, washing herself with a facecloth. No wonder she still reeked even when she had just had a bath. When I lifted her enormous breasts, I was horrified. Much of the skin was rotted away, leaving angry red sores. It was not the only place she was hurting either, and it took ages to heal.

Alice's mouth and hands were seldom still. She was always knitting, crocheting or embroidering something. Her unsolicited advice was not always appreciated, but I always remembered old Alice when things went wrong. One day I talked to her about the problems we had with one of our teenagers.

"Yeah! You can't wait for them to grow up, only to find that things get a lot harder as time gets on," she said. "Why do you think you are pregnant for nine months?"

"I'll tell you," she said, when I shrugged my shoulders. "It takes that long so that you can get slowly used to the fact that the little screamer is going to turn your whole life up-side down. By the time they are crawling, you can't wait for them to walk, only to find that you have to keep running after them every waking moment."

As I laughed, Alice continued. "You think that life gets better when they grow up and they can think for themselves, but that's only the beginning of your troubles."

"So I've noticed!" I smiled ruefully.

"You're learning as you go," Alice sympathised. "It's just a preparation for the next step. You think that you have won when they get married and leave home, but that's when real trouble starts!"

Alice's remark would echo in my head time and again several years later, when our estranged son-in-law had left our daughter for her best friend and had later kidnapped our eldest grandson...

When I wrote to my family in Holland about my new job at Old Timers, they at first thought that I was looking after vintage cars instead of old people. Mum wrote that she was happy that I finally had my wish and I was now a nurse after all.

On the whole, Fred and the children were coping quite well at home without me. Lilian, our eldest daughter, was fifteen when I started work at Old Timers. She was a very capable girl. She liked cooking and took care of Regine, the youngest, who was eight. The others were old enough to get themselves ready for school in the mornings. At times, some of them left without having a wash or their hair combed, they would be late, or forget to take their lunch. Although I worried about it, I told them that it was not my problem. I made sure that everything they needed was there, and I woke them up early enough. Homework was their own responsibility and they each had some small tasks to do after school. But of course, at times they were in no mood to do anything at all as far as household chores were concerned and between the six of them, they could get the place in an awful mess. For some reason or other, their bad moods always seemed to coincide with mine. Those were the days I was dragging my feet at work in the afternoons, longing to go home. Then, when I finally came home, I wondered what on earth I wanted to go home for.

I often took our children to visit my old friends on the weekends. The girls especially loved chatting to Tom, the whip-maker, Lill, the lively cabaret lady from Sydney, and Alice, who gave them all her discarded tubes of Hobbytex paints. As I had made some dresses for Alice soon after her arrival, we became the best of friends.

When I started work at Old Timers in May, everybody there was already working for the fete, a yearly fund-raising event held in August, which was becoming more and more popular with the townsfolk. There were tons of citrus fruit from their own orchard for sale, as well as a great variety of homemade preserves and locally made arts and crafts. There were second-hand stalls with hundreds of books, clothing, furniture and other household items. Numerous boxes of beautifully handcrafted goods had been donated to the Inland Mission by various churches, Australia wide. Our three girls and two of their friends had great fun helping Lill sell hundreds of lovely, embroidered hankies at that first fete, in August 1975. Dressed in long period costumes I had made from light blue, yellow and mauve crepe-paper, they went around with their baskets, adding another interest to the happy event which raised fifteen thousand dollars on the day. The beautiful weather as well as the entertainment, which was provided free of charge by many talented artists in town, made it a happy family day.

The Old Timers Fete, held in the middle of the tourist season, is still going as strong as ever, and attracts thousands of people. During all these years it has never rained on the day of the event. For many years our whole family has been involved with the fete, frying and selling 'oliebollen', the Dutch New-Years-Eve treat, a mixture of sultanas, currants, apples, self-raising flour and skim milk, deep-fried in hot oil and served with icing sugar. We were frying and selling some three and a half thousand oliebollen each year.

I enjoyed being part of the fun very much and it satisfied my need to be involved in the community and do some social work. Our grandchildren loved to help on the stall, getting dressed up in their 'Dutchies'. As it was also important for them to be part of the community spirit, we expected to be there for a few more years yet. But, due to the stringent health regulations that were imposed in 1999, having to wear gloves, covering the food and forbidding our young grandchildren to help in the stall, our family lost interest. They were no longer prepared to spend the many hours that were required for preparation as well as on the day.

Swedish Bob, a tall, blond man who lived in the last room in the right wing, took a liking to me from the start. Because I came from Holland, a country not far from his own homeland, it felt as if I was his neighbour, he said. He loved talking to me but the only time I had to listen to him was while I cleaned his room. As I mentioned before, Bob's room was an absolute pigsty. At first he was reluctant to let me do anything while we talked, but later I could do as much cleaning as I wanted, so that even his curtains and bedspread were being washed regularly.

Bob had arrived in Australia as a sixteen-year-old stow-away aboard an ocean liner. He had never been back to Sweden. He couldn't, he said. The police would lock him up immediately. A few years after his arrival in Australia, Bob had killed a man in a fight, or so he thought, since he had not hung around long enough to see if the man got up. Bob had spent most of his life hiding from the police, on stations around the Northern Territory where he lived in a shed or a caravan. Although he had been deeply in love with at least one particular girl, he had never married because he was an illegal immigrant and he had no papers.

"The girls always dropped me after the first night I went out with them anyway," he said one day with a twinkle in his eyes. He chuckled when he saw the knowing look on my face. He then told me about a stunningly beautiful girl he had fallen for when he was a young man.

"She could have had any feller she wanted to," he said, "but one day she agreed to go out with me. When I picked her up in my old car, she wore this long blue dress, one of those dresses with a high neck and hundreds of buttons at the back as well as on the long sleeves, up to her elbows. Because I'd said nothing about the dress on the way to the ball, she asked me if I didn't like it. I told her that I liked the colour of the dress all right, but I hated all those little buttons. 'I'll never get it off,' I said. The girl made me take her straight back home again" he giggled. "She didn't even want to go to the ball with me anymore."

Bob often played his mouth organ or his accordion while I did his room. I still have his accordion, which he sold to me when he went back to Pine Hill station, two hundred and forty kilometres north-west of town.

Bob had cancer of the stomach. He had been at Old Timers several years before I started working there. His food had to be strained as he fed himself via a tube he had to put in his throat. He often talked to me about 'Dutchie', a nursing sister who was in charge of the medical ward in the Alice Springs Hospital. She visited him regularly, but for months I was never on duty when she came. Then, one afternoon, Bob came excitedly looking for me in the opposite wing. He impatiently pulled me to his room to meet his beloved Dutchie. That was the first time I met Margot who would later become our next-door neighbour and a very good friend.

In November 1979, a year after Bob went back to Pine Hill station, Virlie, the station owner's wife called to tell me that Bob had died on his eighty-fourth birthday. According to his wishes, he was going to be buried at the station and she asked if Margot and I could attend his funeral. Bob had died in his caravan but his body had been taken to the morgue in Alice Springs until they could get permission to bury him at the station.

It had rained cats and dogs the previous day and all night, but the sun was shining in a bright-blue sky when Margot and I left for Bob's funeral at nine in the morning. We went through some deep creek crossings on the main road, north of Alice, before we turned into a dirt road full of puddles and potholes, for the last forty kilometres to the station. I had visited Bob at Pine Hill once before with Fred but the road seemed to be twice as long this time. Margot's little sedan was slipping and sliding from one side of the road to the other. I was glad that she was driving.

"The old bugger will be laughing his head off if he can see me struggling to keep the car on the road," she laughed.

At the station we were greeted by Virlie and her husband Gill, the station owner, who introduced us to Bill, a station hand. We were late, but the hearse carrying Bob had not arrived either. After an hour, Gill and Bill went looking for them. Virlie laughed when they said that the hearse, a station wagon, had got stuck up to the axles in the mud.

"Trust the old bugger to be late for his own funeral," she chuckled. "The last laugh is still on him!"

I felt privileged to be part of the small gathering at the short service, led by our local undertaker. It was so peaceful under the beautiful white gum tree on a rise not far from the homestead, such a lovely spot to be put to rest.

Bob had begged Virlie to take him back to the station every time she visited him at Old Timers, promising never to bother her. He had kept his promise all right! He had allowed Virlie to cook his meals for him but he had not permitted her ever to set foot in his caravan to clean it. The van was so filthy and infested with cockroaches and other insects that they had put a match to it, burning it down to the ground with everything in it.

While he was at Old Timers, Bob and Paddy, a skinny woman who continuously chewed her gums if she wasn't smoking, were good mates. Well, they were good friends most of the time, that is.

Paddy was confused and very restless. She loved Sister Perry who took care of the place, time and again, between the different matrons. Nobody else could make Paddy's bed properly, and she could knock on Sister Perry's door at any time, day or night, for a sympathetic ear.

Because of her chronic backaches, Paddy got up at all hours during the night. In winter she often slept on the bare floor beside her bed in a strange looking sleeping bag. The thick padded bag looked more like a flyer's suit. It had a hood, which was usually drawn close around her face and thick mittens attached to the sleeves. Paddy used to own a dress shop in town. She had been the first woman to drive up by car from Adelaide. When I called her for breakfast on one of my first mornings at Old Timers, she was fast asleep on the floor beside her bed.

"Where's my car?" she asked anxiously with a frightened look on her face, when I woke her up. Later that day she showed me her car, an old Hillman Minx, which stood in the back yard at Old Timers, where it was rusting away, overgrown with weeds.

While I was writing Paddy's story, I rang her friend Reg Harris, a well-known identity in Alice Springs.

"I have always had the greatest admiration for Paddy," he said when I visited him and his wife Marjory. "She was a terrific business woman."

Reg had met Paddy for the first time in 1949, when she was in her forties and she came up on her own from Adelaide with a car-load of frocks, which she sold from her room in the Alice Springs Hotel, one of the oldest hotels in town. She had divorced her husband, who had run off to Japan where he later married a Japanese girl.

Paddy had made a living for herself and her young son by buying and selling dresses and writing knitting patterns. She had shown me two of those books. Being a knitter myself, I had admired the intricate designs of baby and children's wear, but I had no idea at the time that she had written so many. There were ten different books she had written under the name of 'Eve-Lynn'. Forty to sixty thousand copies had been sold of each of those!

Paddy's well-kept diaries show that she had made the long trip from Adelaide to the Centre, during the fifties and the sixties, thirteen times.

"By that time she had set up a large shop in town which she ran very efficiently," Reg said. "She was very particular about the dresses she brought up with her. There was never more than one of any design or colour. If a supplier sent up a red and a blue frock of the same style, she would send one of them back immediately."

Paddy was very proud of her only son who was a pilot for the RAAF. Had she conveniently forgotten that she had deserted him as a child, as people said, or had she dumped him on her close friend during the war to give him a chance of a better homelife? I wondered.

I always thought that Paddy had received the flying suit from her son, but I now know that she had been an accomplished glider pilot herself. From Reg and other people who knew her well, I heard that Paddy was always the life of a party, smoked like a chimney, drank like a fish and swore like a trooper. Paddy was said to be 'one of those tough business women in town'. She would have had to be tough! In the fifties and sixties, the fifteen hundred kilometre road to Alice Springs was only a track from bore to bore, with hundreds of kilometres of nothingness before she would get to the next shabby roadhouse. She had usually travelled alone and slept on the bare ground beside her car in her flyer's suit.

"Somewhere along the line something went terribly wrong," Reg continued. "To be able to cope with her personal problems in the sixties, Paddy went to a doctor who prescribed valium. During the following months she had been to two more doctors in Adelaide, who also gave her valium to calm her nerves. She said that one of them had even told her to take the pills with a nip of whisky!"

Paddy had steadily gone down hill, drinking heavily at times. Her business had suffered badly and Reg had got her out of trouble time and again. At one stage Paddy had ended up in hospital to dry out. While she was away Marjory, Reg's wife had cleaned out Paddy's house. She had collected half a bucket of pills, hidden in and around the house.

"Paddy told me that she had a fight with you and broke your nose. Is that true?" I asked, breaking the silence.

Reg laughed heartily and told me what had happened.

That day, Reg had broken his nose while he was playing footy. As the match had been broadcast on the radio, Reg thought that everybody would know about it as news spread rapidly through the small town. When he and Marjory left the hospital, where Reg's nose had been set, they decided to visit Paddy. As usual, he had parked his car on the lawn in front of Paddy's two-storey house, even though Paddy had asked him several times to park it in the driveway.

"Get your bloody car off the lawn or I'll punch you on the nose," Paddy had yelled when she came out of the house.

Thinking that she was joking about his broken nose, Reg had put his head through the open window of the car and said: "Well! Here's your chance!"

Paddy had not hesitated for a moment and, even though she had hardly touched it, Reg's nose was broken, again.

By the time I left Old Timers in December 1979, Paddy had just about given up her endless fights with the different matrons, and stopped begging the visiting doctor for drugs to relieve her agony. Her mind was occupied day and night with her bowel movements, about which she wrote in her diary. The excessive saliva in her mouth, from chewing her gums, drove her insane, trying to get to sleep with cotton wool in her ears and a hankie in her mouth.

It had been very hard for Reg and Marjory to see a strong, independent woman like Paddy deteriorate over the ensuing years, becoming a mindless bag of bones, unable to do anything for herself until she finally died in 1984. But I know how much Paddy always looked forward to their visits during the five years that I worked at the home, giving her a couple of hours of happiness in her miserable existence.

Like Bob, Paddy had been late at her own funeral too.

"We were waiting for her at the church for half an hour," Reg recalled.

"I went to the funeral parlour in George Crescent to find out what had happened and I was told that the hearse had a flat tyre."

According to her wishes, which she had written years earlier on a scrap of paper, Paddy had been cremated and Reg had arranged for a small plane to scatter her ashes over the old South Road. When he got the box, which contained her ashes, it rattled.

"I thought that ashes were not suppose to rattle and I decided to have a look," Reg said. "It was hard to get the lid off and, when it finally flew off, her ashes spilled all over me and the table. Even after her death the old bitch was still giving me a lot of trouble," he laughed.

Shortly after George, the Chinese-looking Aboriginal man died, a Canadian man named Frank took his place. We had made his room ready the previous day, but he did not arrive at the expected time. Sister Perry did not seem to be in the least bit concerned.

"He'll turn up in his own sweet time," she smiled in her usual, relaxed way. "When he's ready. The poor man is probably scared to death of coming here."

Late the following afternoon, I was on duty in the hostel on my own when Frank, a small solidly built man arrived by taxi. He shuffled more than he walked through the front door, supported by his walking stick. He stood there in the empty lounge, reminding me of a frightened little bird, which had fallen out of its nest. The taxi-driver set a small suitcase on the lounge room floor and left him to it.

Sister Perry had been right. Frank had been scared to death of entering the home. He had been so scared that he had drunk himself into oblivion the previous day. Late that afternoon, he had finally found enough courage to take the big step. By the time I said good-night to him later that evening, Frank was more relaxed, happy that I would be back at six-thirty the following morning to introduce him to the other residents.

"It wasn't half as bad as I expected," he said before I left at eight.

Frank was a cranky man, keeping the staff as well as the other residents at a distance with his grumpy manners, but I soon realised that he was just a very lonely fellow and quite a softy underneath. As with many others in the home, the drink had got the better of him; an easy way to kill the pain of being homesick and feeling utterly alone in the world.

Frank came from Nova Scotia, a beautiful island somewhere off the coast of Canada. When I saw the small tattoos on his arms, I asked if he had been a seaman.

"That's how I got here," he said impatiently. "I came on a cargo ship and should have gone back with it." As he had been stone-drunk, the boat had left the following day without him. Scared of the consequences of jumping ship, and without any identification papers, he too had gone into hiding from the police for years.

Frank had already been in the home for more than a year when it suddenly occurred to me to write to his old home address, to see if anyone was still living there. Unable to write other then sign his name, Frank took me up on the offer immediately. I still have the letters that came back from his excited family, saying that they could never express their appreciation of finding their long lost brother and uncle. One letter was from his eldest brother's son, an art teacher in Cape Cod, who was making a family tree.

"You can only imagine what a wonderful thing you have done for us," he wrote. "We were all crying when we heard that Uncle Frank was still alive, and even our children are excited to learn about an uncle they never knew existed."

Frank was never able to make a trip back to his homeland and he died before his family had saved up enough money for the long trip to Australia. But there was a noticeable change in Frank's attitude to the people around him, and I had added another friend for the duration of his life.

Albert was another fellow who came to Old Timers during the first year I was there. He was an American who had also jumped ship when he came to Australia on an ocean steamer. He was very skinny and of medium height. He spoke softly and wore very thick glasses. Although Albert hit the bottle regularly, he was always a gentleman and never seemed to get angry.

It was wonderful to see how our friend Graham Prolongeau's father, Les, took care of Albert, visiting him, taking him out and nursing him when he was sick. In turn, our friends Graham and Willy took care of Les in a marvellous way for years after he had a stroke, which had left him incontinent and unable to speak. Then, in the mid-nineties when Graham struggled with cancer, their three sons were a great support to him and Willy.

Life is grossly unfair at times. You never know what is in store for you, which is just as well. It also has the tendency to bounce back on you. The old proverbs 'You reap what you sow' and 'A little kindness goes a long way' are getting a deeper meaning for me now that I'm writing all these little stories.

So Much To Learn

I had been at Old Timers for several months when I had my first experience of working in the little hospital. As I had been sent over several times to help with feeding at lunchtime, it was not entirely new to me and I knew most of the patients. I could not help but feel deeply for Mrs Moore, a big, pale looking woman who was a diabetic. One of her legs had been amputated at the knee and the toes of her other foot had started to get black too. She had been taken to Old Timers when her family could no longer care for her at home. She always looked extremely sad, nervously crumpling her wet hankie.

Together with her late husband, Mrs Moore had built up the first bakery in town, which meant many years of hardships and long days of hard work with little time left for socialising and outings. Time and again she told me about her son's struggle to keep the family bakery going because he had to pay the high cost for her being at Old Timers.

"I am a terrible burden on my family," she would cry. "Every day that I stay alive I'm bringing him closer to bankruptcy."

Before we left Holland, I had been warned about the big difference between the old age pension system there compared to Australia, but until I worked in the hospital at Old Timers, I had not realised the impact it had on people. In Holland everybody automatically received a pension at sixty-five, women at sixty, regardless of other income or whether they had been paying into a fund. It was understood that rich people provided for their pensions through the high taxes they paid. The additional income of the pension and 'super' would be added to the income and paid back in taxes at the end of the year. But here in Australia, people had to use most of their own money first. It surely did not pay to be thrifty.

Mrs Heenan, a petite lady with a lovely gentle nature, was another hardworking, pioneer woman in the home. Together with her husband, she had set up the first milkbar and grocery shop in town. Luckily for her and for us, Mrs Heenan was blissfully unaware of what it cost her family for her to be there. She pottered around happily in the little kitchenette where we would put the clean cups back in the sink, time and again, to keep her occupied, preventing her from wanting to go home.

It seemed grossly unfair to me that people who had spent all their money on grog and smokes were better off in the end than people who had been thrifty in the hope of providing a better future for their children. Most of these old folk who had never saved a penny, complained bitterly about the fact that their pension cheque went to the home and they were paid a pittance in pocket money every fortnight. They had absolutely no idea how much it cost for them to be cared for. I didn't know either until I worked in the office in 1979. Of

211

course, with the money devaluating at an alarming rate, it would be very difficult for them to comprehend the cost involved in running the place, even if their minds had not been affected by alcohol or dementia. Although I agreed with them that the home was shabby and very basic, I knew that most of them had never had it so good in their lives.

Seeing the way things were done at Old Timers sometimes made me cringe. It made me think about my grandmother, who had been taken in by the nuns in 1953, when her family could no longer care for her. But this was the mid-seventies! Even though sanitary pads had been on the emergency goods list during the floods the previous year, we were still using rags instead of pads for incontinent people. To see Hazel do the washing made my stomach turn. I never expected to get used to that, but I did. There was only one washing machine, which stood in a narrow open shed at the back of the pantry. It was a normal large household machine into which everything went in as it came to hand: clothing, towels, bed-sheets and urine-soaked rags, as well as tablecloths and even the tea towels. To be able to get through the workload, the machine was always filled to the brim. Hazel was employed from seven until three, Monday to Friday, and did what she could during that time. It was just as well that the sun was almost always shining, thereby to kill the germs. Perhaps it was due to our daily exposure to germs, that we became immune to them.

When I first came to Old Timers, it was winter and freezing cold in the open shed, as the wind blew in one end and out the other. Hazel always had trouble finding enough space on the two big clotheslines to hang out all the washing, but in summertime she could take off one load before hanging the next. When the work on our wing in the hostel was finished, we took turns helping her taking it off the line and folding it. I loved being alone with Hazel, especially when things were upsetting me. Over sixty and with a lot of life experience, she provided an excellent shoulder to cry on in her private laundry. With her soft-spoken voice and laid back down-to-earth manner, she soon had me back on track again when I was down.

Hazel's life had been far from easy. Left by her first husband, she had made a living for herself and her three young children by managing a boarding house, mainly for young men, and later on a caravan park. Our friend Willy's husband Graham had lived with her for many years. The boarders thought the world of her. She always managed to calm them down when they got themselves into trouble. Graham and Willy still called her 'Mum'.

Hazel's second husband was a big man, a lot younger than she was. He had turned out to be an alcoholic. "I'm paying for my mistake," she said, when I first met her. Work had become a happy relief for her. Everybody loved her as she gave freely of her time to everyone.

Work in the tiny hospital started at seven in the morning when breakfast was brought in from the main kitchen. With the two of us, we fed, showered and dressed the six patients, made the beds, dusted and tidied the rooms and mopped the floors. Then, at eleven o'clock, one of us went home while the other was on duty until four in the afternoon. It was hard work to get everything done during those first four hours. Some of the patients needed both of us to get them under the shower, and we had to keep an eye on the others constantly, as a couple of them would run away, or get themselves into all sorts of trouble.

Apart from Mrs Moore and Mrs Heenan, there were two other ladies, Tessa and Alice. They were both of Aboriginal descent and each had had a stroke. Poor Tessa had been in the hospital for quite a while. She was completely paralysed and suffered badly from arthritis. Unable to do anything for herself, she depended on us for every move. She spoke slowly and with great difficulty, but her mind was very clear. Although she was always in pain from arthritis and bedsores, Tessa seldom complained. She was probably the saddest person in the home during the three and a half years I was involved with nursing at Old Timers.

We fed her breakfast in bed, and then we had to put her on a commode beside it. Later, when we had showered her, she had to be put back on what they called the 'potty-chair' for another couple of hours, to prevent her from getting bedsores. Because it was usually colder inside than out in winter, we usually sat her outside in the sun. By the time she had been fed her midday meal, she was begging to be put back into bed. Getting her twisted body in and out of bed, was a real art. Lifting people properly is one of the first things taught in training, but because I hadn't had any training, I never felt comfortable; especially when I helped with Tessa, terrified that I would hurt her and break her frail bones.

Tessa's husband Tim, a small white man, in his early fifties, came every day without fail to feed Tessa at lunchtime and he often came back in the evenings again. Her face always lit up as soon as she spotted him. Tim would straighten her up in the chair and talk to her continuously, while he fed her or massaged her aching limbs.

Tessa died about a year after I met her. I had not seen Tim for years, when I met him at the post office one morning, some years ago. He recognised me immediately when I said 'Hello' to him.

"Give's a kiss to wish me luck love. I'm getting married this afternoon," he said when I asked him how he was.

"The lucky girl!" I exclaimed, taken aback by the information and his demand for a kiss. Tim was at least seventy.

"I'm seventy-five," he said, as if he had read my mind. "My wife is only thirty-two. I hope she'll not regret marrying me," he added apologetically.

"I'm sure she won't Tim," I reassured him. "I'll never forget the way you cared for Tessa. If you treat your new wife the same way, you won't have anything to worry about." Tim told me then that his new wife was a Filipino bride. He was marrying her so that she could stay with her sister in Australia.

"It's purely a platonic relationship," he said. "She'll do some of my housework in return for a roof over her head."

Before we parted, I told Tim that he deserved the very best and I sincerely hoped that his young wife would never let him down in any way. I felt awkward when I gave him the kiss he had asked for. It was no more then a peck on his cheek, but it was a kiss he said he was not likely to ever get from his new wife.

Alice, the other part-Aboriginal woman in the little hospital had 'blown in' from Darwin with Cyclone Tracy. She was a heavy woman, paralysed on one side and bound to a wheelchair. She could not speak and only made guttural noises, but one word was clear enough; 'Smoke'. After weeks of patiently teaching her, she could eventually say, "A smoke please". Because it was too dangerous for Alice to have her own matches, and she would smoke one cigarette after another all day long, we had to light them for her. She was often in a foul mood, having to wait for one of us to light another cigarette. Peace was usually short-lived, as she finished it in no time. How much easier would our lives have been if we had had access to anti-smoking tablets or patches in those days?

The other two patients in the nursing home were two Aboriginal men, Jack and George. I had heard from Jock, an old postman-drover, that Aboriginal people could be very cruel to the sick and weak members of their families. Jock had delivered mail by camels or horse teams for the best part of his life, to the most isolated places of Northern Australia. He lived in one of the cottages and came to the dining room in the hostel for his meals.

Jock, a very skinny man, over six-foot tall, made it no secret that he hated Aborigines. He seemed rather proud of the fact that he had killed several of them during his younger years, when he had been working up north. They behaved worse than animals he said, leaving their old and injured behind without food or water, spearing other tribal members in never ending paybacks. He told me one day that he had been disgusted to see how a woman fed only one baby of a set of twins, leaving the other to die. They had no respect whatsoever for each other, he said. I was horrified when I realised that there was absolutely no doubt in Jock's mind that he had done the world a favour by getting rid of some of those 'dogs', as he called them.

Seeing old Jack and his dedicated family showed me the opposite side of the callous picture Jock had painted me. Jack was well into his eighties, blind and crippled with arthritis, unable to walk.

214

'Poor bugger me!" he would say to anyone who came near him. Although he cried a lot, and yelled out continuously to get the attention of the staff, everybody loved old Jack, who always had scores of family and friends visiting him.

Old George was another kettle of fish though. Nobody knew who he was or where he came from. One evening, he was simply dropped off at the gate by someone who had found him, completely naked, in the bush somewhere on the West Australian border. George, named after the man who found him, was a bearded old warrior, with many large scars on his bony chest. It was believed that he might never have seen a white person in his life, and that he had been left on the side of the road to die, as he could not keep up with the rest of the tribe. He was almost blind, filthy dirty and covered with sores and lice when he arrived at the home. From the stories I heard later about the eventful task of cleaning him up, I considered myself lucky that I was not on duty at the time.

In the beginning I was quite scared of old George. He kicked like a mule and forever tried to pinch my nipples when I finally got him under the shower. Of course, George could feel that I was afraid of him, and kept me on my toes. I eventually learned to talk to him in a reassuring way, but I was wary of him at all times. The cheeky grin on his face when he saw that I was scared always reminded me of a camel. Although George was nearly blind, he still walked around the gardens at an amazing speed on his wobbly legs, which looked like knotted sticks. He climbed over any obstacles he came across, no matter what they were. It was rather funny to watch him climb over the garden chairs while people were still sitting on them. Even Jock, the old postman, just moved to the front of his chair and let him go his way behind him.

We were happy to let old George sleep under the shade of a fruit tree during the day and bring him back to the hospital, whenever he strolled away too far. Following Sister Perry's example, we would turn a blind eye whenever George took his pyjama pants off and wandered around in his natural state, until someone complained about it. Scooping up behind him was a lot easier then cleaning him up which was often quite a nasty job.

George normally slept on a mattress on the bare floor in the room he shared with old Jack, until inspection time was coming up. One day I wondered what all the fuss was about, when I helped Sister Perry set up a proper bed for George. She hardly spoke a word while we made it up with white sheets and clean blankets. She later apologised, saying that she could not bear the interference of city people who had no way of knowing what it was like to care for people from the bush.

George did not like his new bed much either. He insisted on lying on the vinyl floor underneath it. As soon as the inspectors turned their backs to leave the property, George's bed was taken away again. The old bushman would snore happily on the bare mattress on the floor, while Sister Perry slowly returned to her normal easy-going ways again.

Although I found a lot of things that happened at Old Timers appalling, I had great respect for Sister Perry who had been nursing in the bush all her life. Until she died suddenly in August 1997, she lived in a flat at Old Timers where I visited her occasionally. I found it difficult to call her Grace, even though she asked me to and my colleagues had done so for years. It seemed disrespectful; not at all what she deserved.

"When do you think you will write your memoirs?" I asked her one day. "Your story would be fantastic, I'm sure."

"Whatever would I do that for?" she replied rather indignantly, in her slow, lisping way of speaking. "I'm quite content to stay in the shadows."

Sister Perry never liked to be the centre of attention. She hated it with a passion, she assured me.

"I just want to be left to myself, pottering along," she said. "Head-quarters in Sydney wanted me to be the matron, but I always refused. I never had any ambition to meet with high society like some of the others." A little later we talked about her age.

"My age is nobody's business," she said. "They know here that my birthday is on the twenty-fifth of September, but they're always fishing to see how old I am. It's private, and it hasn't got anything to do with anybody else."

"They might just want to give you a big party when you turn eighty, eighty five or ninety," I said innocently. Sister Perry laughed.

"You are fishing too," she smiled in her laid back way. "But I'm not going to tell you either."

"It would be easy to find out from the records in the office," I laughed, but Sister Perry thought that there weren't any records there. I respected her wishes by not asking.

It was always a pleasure to see Sister Perry enjoying life. Every afternoon she would have a glass of wine with Bernie, one of her male friends who lived in one of the cottages. She was a great support to him as his wife Dhal, who was a sister at Old Timers when I was there, had been in the nursing home for years, completely paralysed by a series of strokes.

It was a great shock to me to learn that Sister Perry had died of a heart attack and I had not even been to her funeral. I had read the death notice in the Advocate about a lady called Grace Perry, who had died aged eighty-two, but I dismissed it, thinking that it could not possibly be 'our Grace'; she was still so fit and well.

Bernie was devastated. Sister Perry had complained about a bit of pain in her chest when they shared a glass of wine just before she had set out to do her twice a week paper round, he said. A member of the staff had found her, sitting motionless on a bench under one of the beautiful gum trees.

"She could not have wished for a better way to go," he said through his tears.

Sister Perry had worked as a bush nurse all over Australia, but mostly for the A.I.M. in Aboriginal communities in Northern Queensland. She came to Alice Springs early in 1971, only three months before I started. At the time, the matron of Old Timers had left and she had been asked to hold the fort until another matron had been found. The new matron had not stayed for very long, and Sister Perry had been at the helm again for another twelve months before another matron took over. Another three matrons would follow in quick succession, leaving of their own accord or being sent on vacation for a variety of reasons. Although Sister Perry later retired and lived in one of the cottages, she came back time and again to fill in as acting matron.

A few years ago, some people at the home were shocked to hear that Sister Perry's husband had died in Queensland. They never knew that she had been married, although it had been no secret to the staff while I worked there. It was common knowledge that Sister Perry was spending her yearly holidays in Queensland with her brother and her husband, with whom she'd stayed good friends. I also knew that she had given birth to a stillborn baby, but I knew nothing about the devastating effect it had on her life until she told me about it on one of my last visits.

"I made the umbilical cord too short and twisted it around her little neck," she said, without showing any emotion.

"How can you blame yourself for that?" I asked.

"It was a beautiful little girl," she said, ignoring my question. "We both loved children but we never dared to have another child."

Thinking about the effect such an experience would have had on me, I offered her my heartfelt sympathy.

"It's all a very long time ago," she said resignedly. "And maybe it was for the best."

Unable to cope with the pain, Sister Perry's husband had refused to take any chances of having to go through such an ordeal again and, thinking that she was to blame, Sister Perry had accepted his decision. She had gone back to nursing in the bush, staying away for long periods at a time. There had never been any reason to get a divorce, she said, as neither of them had any desire to get married again.

I felt very sorry for Sister Perry and her husband who had been torn apart because of ignorance and misunderstanding. They had obviously loved each other very much. What a blessing that people are encouraged to talk openly about their painful losses these days!

Camping at Ayers Rock

During the school holidays, in October 1975, I had five days off in a row. By that time, I had been at Old Timers for six months and we had been in Alice Springs for four years. We had made regular camping trips around town, but this time we planned a trip to the famous Ayers Rock. Very few people who lived or worked at Old Timers had ever been there since it was almost five hundred kilometres away. Only Chris, the English nurse had stayed there for several months in 1969 when she joined her only son David, who had established the first garage near this enormous bare rock, somewhere in the middle of the Australian desert, the previous year.

Like Sister Perry, Hazel and Scottish Ann, Chris was in her early sixties when I met her and she had also been at the home for two years. Chris was a quiet, solidly built lady; her dark hair combed smoothly into a bun at the back of her neck, doing her work at a slow, steady pace. She was always polite and never seemed to lose her temper.

From the day Chris had finished her training as a young girl, she had worked in a hospital near London, which cared for five hundred men and five hundred physically and mentally handicapped women. Her husband, who was a mechanic and bought and sold antique furniture, died after a long illness when David was eleven years old. She had been devastated when David left for Australia as soon as he turned twenty-one in 1965, and he no longer needed her permission. In his sporadic letters, David had been raving on about the beauty of the country, urging her to come too.

"Goodness, gracious me! I could not do that!" Chris said, when we had talked about leaving our countries. "I had my job and would have to leave my lovely old house where I had lived nearly all my life. I could not just go off to such a strange, far away country." Three years later, Chris had changed her mind, realising that David would never come back to England.

"I had to sell all my beautiful antique furniture to pay for that dreadful boat trip," she said sadly, shaking her head.

David had abandoned his garage at The Rock when he met her at the wharf in Adelaide. After many years of drought, it had started to rain on the day he had opened his workshop in 1968 and it had kept on raining cats and dogs for months on end. Records show that the Rock had been shrouded in clouds for four months at the time. With no traffic being able to get through on the dirt road, his business had gone broke.

During the twelve months following her arrival Chris had travelled with David in his old truck up the east coast, then via Townsville to the centre of Australia, camping on the side of the road and picking up supplies for David's hobby of restoring old cars. After staying in Alice Springs for a while, they moved south again, then via the Nullarbor Plain to Carnarvon in Western Australia, where David worked with his uncle for a while. With an eighteen-foot long caravan being dragged behind his over-loaded old Landrover, Chris' hyperactive son had driven the hundreds of miles of the treacherous inland track via Docker River to Ayers Rock, where they finally arrived at the end of 1969. Back in Alice Springs again, David's request to re-open his garage at Ayers Rock was approved.

Apart from a few native families living in 'humpies', there were only a couple of sheds which were called 'Hotels' when Chris came to the now famous Ayers Rock. David's garage, next to the camping grounds was no more then an open tin shed. To comply with government regulations, David had stretched a canvas tarpaulin over the shed, so that it blended in with the environment, and extended it with a veranda where he worked on his vintage cars.

Even though more then fifty thousand tourists visited Ayers Rock each year, a service station was not permitted at the time. David supplied them with fuel from forty-four-gallon drums. The empty drums later provided him with a fence around his property.

When, after a few months, Chris had had enough of the heat and her son's poor living conditions, David took her to Alice Springs where the Uniting Church provided her with a little cottage and a job at Old Timers, nursing during the week and cooking at weekends.

A year before I met Chris, David had been seriously injured in a freak accident. On a rainy Saturday he was adjusting the fuel lines of his old T-Model truck on the side of Gap Road, then the outskirts of town, when a huge scraper veered off the road towards him. The front wheel had hit David, throwing him clear of the rest of the scraper, but he had hit his leg on a corner of the enormous blade, at the front of the earthmover.

"The heavy machine was not responding to the controls," the driver, who was a friend of David's, wrote to me, describing the accident. "If I had followed correct procedure and released the brakes instead of slamming them on, Dave would definitely have gone under the wheel of the scraper."

However, the impact had crushed the lower part of David's body. Doctors had told Chris that it was unlikely that her son would ever walk again, but David would prove them wrong, determined to make a living for himself no matter how crippled he was. Several months after the accident, he was transferred to the hospital in Darwin, suffering a mental breakdown. He hated it there and soon planned his escape. His first attempt failed as the footpath in front of the hospital had been broken up and his wheelchair got stuck in the mud. At five o'clock in the morning a few weeks later, still bound to a wheelchair and dressed only in short pyjama pants, David escaped from the hospital successfully. This time, he had phoned a taxi to pick him up at the entrance. Because of streakers at that time, it had taken a lot of persuasion before the driver accepted his fare and took him into town in his pyjama shorts. On his way to the bank to draw enough money for his airfare, a housepainter working on the Catholic Church had given him an old shirt. After some trouble at the airport, he had flown back to Alice Springs where he arrived completely exhausted, on his shocked mother's doorstep.

When I met him, shortly after I started work at Old Timers, David was living in town with two Aboriginal girls, aged twelve and fourteen, and a little boy of three, who was David's son. The mother of the children had left them. Every day after work, Chris walked to David's place across the Todd River. She spent every spare moment teaching the girls cooking and cleaning, as well as helping David, who walked with great difficulty and was in constant pain, with the upholstering of his vintage cars. I had great admiration for both of them for their courage and their dedication to the children.

The road to Ayers Rock was still only a dirt track when we set out to go camping there for the first time in October 1975. The rain that was forecast, added to the excitement of the children, who protested loudly when Fred wanted to postpone the outing. We had heard stories of cars getting bogged down to the axles in the mud, people having to wait for days for the water to subside so that they could get through, and of them being eaten alive by mosquitoes. We usually went camping with friends and were looking forward to being on our own this time. I was a little worried too, but as Fred had driven the four-wheel drive Nissan Patrol for a few years now, I was quite confident that he could get us safely through the roughest patches we could possibly encounter. It did not seem to matter at Old Timers if I stayed away a bit longer, and Fred was his own boss as a contractor at Panorama Guth, which had been opened to the public two months earlier. Henk was going on a well-earned holiday the following month and Fred had made enough frames for his paintings to last until he would come back after Christmas.

On Friday evening we carefully packed the car and the trailer we had borrowed from a friend, hoping to leave early the following morning. With the children and the dog packed like sardines in the back of the short-wheel based Nissan, we left at six am on the dot, as planned.

By the time Fred pulled up on the side of the road for our first coffee break, about two hundred kilometres out of town, the clouds had disappeared and the sun was shining in the incredible blue sky we had become so used to. Josie, our beloved dog, leaped out of the car the minute Fred opened the door. Before any of us realised what was happening, a dreadful smell drifted our way. A little distance away Josie was having a ball, rolling around and around in a fresh pat of cow dung!

Instead of drinking coffee, we spent the next half hour frantically trying to clean the muck off the dog. We used our only roll of toilet paper, half a bottle of dishwashing detergent, and one of our precious jerry cans of water, but we had no hope of getting rid of the smell. Cursing Josie in turn, we held our noses for the remainder of the trip.

Apart from some rough patches, the road was not as bad as we had expected it to be. The salt lakes near Mt. Ebenezer were a complete surprise to me, as I had never heard about them before. It must have been absolutely horrendous for the early settlers to realise that if there was water in the lakes, it was too salty to drink.

Like most other travellers at the time, we assumed that we were near Ayers Rock when we noticed Mt. Conner in the distance, but the road went on and on. When we spotted the famous monolith, the road twisted and turned for another fifty kilometres. At times it seemed as if we were getting further away instead of getting any closer. When we finally arrived at the camping ground at the base of the Rock, we all had sore necks from trying to see the top of it through the small windows of the Nissan. Yulara, the nearby village, had not even been thought of at that time. The view was truly spectacular, every bit as powerful as I had expected. I wanted to sit there and admire it for a while, but Fred hurried us along as usual, to get the tents erected, the beds made and the evening meal prepared before we sat down and relaxed. The children were given strict instructions not to leave the camp until the work was done and we could all go together.

Up to now, we had only taken the boys' red and blue, barn-shaped tent with us when we went camping for a weekend, but this time we brought the big, green tent we had used for many years in Holland. As our family grew, we had extended it with another compartment and a five by three metre veranda we could close in. In Holland, we usually stayed in a camping ground close to where we lived during the children's long summer vacations, so that I could stay there with the kids when Fred had to go back to work after his three weeks holiday. He then spent most of the nights as well as the weekends at the camp until the children had to go back to school. We were debating selling the tent until Sam's letter arrived, in which he told us that he could not finish the house and we would probably have to sleep in it. We had considered ourselves lucky time and again, that he had borrowed those old caravans for us, because our beautiful tent would never have survived the first storm we had two weeks after we arrived.

A strong wind was blowing while we were setting the big tent up at Ayers Rock that afternoon. The ground was rock-hard. We had no hope of getting the pegs in at half metre intervals, as was required. By the time we finished setting up camp the wind had died down and we took a stroll to the base of the enormous Rock that has a circumference of nine kilometres. As it would be dark at seven there was only time to explore a small section of the various caves and astonishing rock formations. At one point, three Aboriginal children were sitting in a triangular shaped cave, smiling and waving happily. When I asked if I could take their picture, they giggled shyly at first, then posed as if they had their picture taken every day.

Back in the camping area, Fred offered to cook the evening meal. He opened a couple of cans of Irish stew and heated the contents in an open frying pan, above the campfire, while I made 'plastic potatoes' (instant, mashed potatoes) out of a packet. Tired from the long day, we all went to bed early. A little after five-thirty the following morning, we watched in astonishment how the rock turned from a dark brownish-red to bright orange, as the sun came slowly over the horizon; a truly fantastic sight which overwhelmed me.

After an early breakfast of bread toasted on a stick above the campfire, and eggs boiled in a billycan, we set out to climb the Rock. Josie ran with our three eldest children up the steep path followed by Fred with Simone and Richard while I took Regine to look at the seven copper plaques that were screwed onto the rock wall near the start of the climb. When I read the names and dates of the people who had died on the rock while climbing it, I became very concerned about the safety of the children, watching them disappearing over the crest of the Rock.

When I spotted Fred, sitting near the top of the recently installed chain through the binoculars, I realised with a shock that Simone as well as Richard had gone with the others. I panicked when he slowly came down, on his backside. With Regine in tow I climbed up to a low rock-formation, called 'Chicken Rock' for obvious reasons, to meet him, angry with him for letting the kids get further ahead without him. I anxiously waited for their return. My heart was beating wildly when I saw them coming down, step by step, sometimes backwards and resting often, the eldest taking turns helping the little ones. I breathed a sigh of relief when they were all safely on the ground, assured by the children that there was nothing to it.

"You should've come with us," they said enthusiastically, each trying to get a word in. "It's fantastic at the top! There were some Americans who took photographs of us with Josie. They said that she was probably the first dog who had ever been on Ayers Rock. They told us that we should put her name in the book."

"What book?" I asked, and, "Did you?" Breathlessly they told us that there was a visitor's book at the end of the climb and how Eugene had put Josie's name in it. "Josie, the Super-Dog," he said proudly.

Later that day we bought certificates in the souvenir shop at the camping grounds saying that each of the children had climbed the Rock. From their pocket money the boys bought a medal with 'I've climbed Ayers Rock' for Josie, and put it on her collar. The photo I took of her still reminds us of what a lovely and loyal dog she was, the best dog we ever had. It broke our hearts when she died of heartworm three years later.

It wasn't until much later that we learned about the cultural and spiritual significance of Uluru to the Aboriginal people. Had we known this at the time, we would never have allowed Josie to go with the children on the climb.

A strong wind struck up during the night. We had been up several times to tie our big canvas 'home away from home' down and it threatened to collapse on top of us when we woke up in the morning. It was still early when, after securing the tent and having breakfast, the Nissan rattled over the corrugated dirt road to the Olgas, known to the Aboriginal people as Kata Tjuta. This is a splendid group of domes, about thirty kilometres from the Rock. The road, winding around the huge domes to the 'Valley of the Winds' at the back, seemed to take forever, but the reward was well worth the trouble it took to get there. We spent a great day walking, climbing and exploring the high rock formations and relaxing while having a picnic near a lovely, clear water hole. The water was too cold for a swim, but the children had great fun throwing pebbles into the clear stream for Josie to fetch. At times her whole head disappeared under the water, not resting until she could bring the stone back. Even though the stones got bigger and bigger Josie never hesitated for a moment to retrieve them. She still showed no signs of tiring of it when the children had enough.

At the sunset viewing area near the Rock we had another picnic. Along with groups of hotel guests and campers, we sat on an old blanket in the soft red dust on top of a sand dune, waiting for the mighty Rock to change colour according to the pictures we had seen. We were very disappointed with the show. The half dozen photos I took show little difference, apart from it getting darker. We have been to the Rock many times since and know now that the great colour changes are mostly in winter, especially when there are clouds in the sky, at the right place and at the right time.

It rained during the night, but the sun was shining brightly again in the morning. Raymond and Eugene were keen to climb the Rock again and they took Josie with them. After they had left we set off to explore some more caves, but I felt very restless and uneasy.

"We shouldn't have told them that we would time them," I complained to Fred. "Now they're hurrying to be back as quickly as they can." Cold shivers ran down my back and muscles tightened in my chest when I remembered the rain and realised that the path was wet and would be very slippery.

"We'd better get back," Fred said irritably when I told him what I was thinking. "You're spoiling our fun with your whingeing." But he proved to be as anxious as I was. When we returned to the start of the climb, he eagerly searched the top of the Rock through the binoculars, ignoring my pleas for me to have a look through them too. I had shown him the copper plates with the names of people who had died of heart attacks or from an accident. Reading the warning signs not to climb under certain conditions, which included rain, had done nothing to ease my nerves.

When Fred shouted that he had spotted the boys and finally handed me the binoculars, I held my breath watching them coming down on their bottoms, then standing up and walking backwards again. It seemed to take ages, but they had in fact only been away for three-quarters of an hour, which was a very short time to go up and down the Rock, I was told.

Ever since that first visit, I have wanted to climb Ayers Rock, or Uluru - it's traditional Aboriginal name - as it is now universally called. At one stage some years ago, I felt fit enough and determined to do it next time we were there, but by the time I got to the top of Chicken Rock, I 'chickened out' again. Fred climbed to the top of the chain then he came down too.

The next time we were there, a helicopter arrived and we watched a man brought down from the Rock on a stretcher with great difficulty by the rangers and an emergency team. I took a picture, lining up the helicopter above the rescuers with the stretcher halfway up the Rock and the group of copper plates, which had doubled in number in a span of five years. Seeing the photograph has cured me of having any desire, or regrets of being unable to climb Ayers Rock.

It was close to midday when we walked back to the camping ground after the boys had climbed the Rock for the second time. Thick clouds were building up and a strong wind was blowing. We decided to stay in the camp, reading and playing games until the storm had passed. As time went by the sky grew black in the northwest while the sun was still shining in a cloudless sky above us. Lightning flashed through the dark, rolling clouds. While we tied the tent down and locked the car, I anxiously watched the storm draw closer and closer. Fred and the boys were digging a deep gutter around the tent, when suddenly all hell seemed to have broken loose in the distance. As if the heavens had opened a huge door, an enormous mass of hailstones pounded down on one end of the Rock while the sun still shone on the other. The hail bounced up high off the rock, forming a big arch before it showered down to the ground like a bridal veil. It was a spectacular view but, as I was holding the tent while Fred tried to hammer some more pegs into the ground, I had no hope of getting my camera to take a picture. We didn't have the time to stand there, watching the splendid view either, as within minutes we had to seek cover while the rain pelted down on the camping area. Through the windows of the tent I watched the continuous lightning, anxiously covering Regine's ears with my hands to block the terrifying noise of the deafening thunder.

Hundreds of waterfalls still ran down in all directions from the top of the Rock after the rain had stopped and the sun was shining again. Half an hour later most of the water had drained away. Enjoying the beautiful fresh air with a cup of coffee, Fred and I yelled in turn at the kids not to go into the tent or the car with their muddy feet. After a while Fred made a fire with the dry wood he had put in the Nissan before the storm hit, to bake pancakes for tea. Sitting around the campfire, with the mozzies out in full force, we made plans for the one remaining day. Exhausted from the long, eventful day we went to bed early.

The sky was pitch black again in the north when we woke up early the following morning. Not prepared to take any more chances, Fred insisted that we should go back to Alice Springs immediately.

"If that lot comes down, we won't be able to get home for weeks," he predicted as he started to pack up, under loud protests from the children. By the time Lilian and I had made a heap of sandwiches for breakfast, Fred was ready to go.

"We can eat them on the road," he said, hurrying us along.

We were already bouncing along on the road before some of the children were properly awake and they went straight back to sleep. Without stopping, Fred drove on at a steady speed, trying to avoid the many pot-holes and only slowing down at big puddles, which often covered the road from one side to the other. After we passed a few buses stranded on the side of the road, we were astounded to be overtaken by a Morris Minor.

Glad that we were on the bitumen after the turn-off on the road to Adelaide, I asked if I could drive for a while but Fred refused, saying that he was enjoying it himself. I felt disappointed, and sat silently sulking for a while. Being together for those last four days had revived our relationship a bit. It had been a wonderful holiday and I knew that I should not let those minor disappointments upset me so much. Apart from the week we had in Adelaide two years ago, we had not spent much time alone together since we arrived in Australia. We had both worked very hard during that time. There was still another day before I had to go back to work, and I would make the most of it.

On the news in the evening we heard that Ayers Rock had been flooded that afternoon. The road had been closed a few hours after we left and was not likely to be opened for the next couple of days. It drizzled all day on my last day off and heavy showers woke us up several times during the following night. I was expected back at work at six-thirty that morning and, as nobody had to get up for school, I quietly left the house. It was still dark when I set off in my Morris Minor for Old Timers. To get there, I had to get through the Gap, where the road and the railway go side by side with the Todd River, between the steep hills of the McDonnell Ranges. When I got to the turnoff, the lights of the Mini suddenly shone on a big mass of water across the road. As soon as I stopped the car I noticed that the water was rising rapidly. As I backed the car up another car arrived. The driver agreed that it was too dangerous to go through in the Mini.

I went home again and rang Old Timers. We arranged that Fred would take me in the Nissan and if he could not get through either, I would walk along the much higher railway lines and someone would pick me up on the other side. When we got to the Gap, the police had set up a barricade. Several tourists were lugging their heavy suitcases, walking between the railway lines to get to the other side where they would be picked up by the airport staff to meet their plane for the early flight.

The 'oldies' were relieved to see me again, saying they had missed me and that they had been worried that I would not be able to get back for a quite a while after all the rain.

Feeling happy and appreciated, I realised how fond I had grown of all of them in such a short time.

The Good Life

By the time Christmas came around in 1975, we were well settled and content in the small town in the centre of Australia. We had been in Alice Springs for four and a half years and no longer felt isolated and cut off from the rest of the world. Although Fred and I both worked long hours, our social life was better then it had ever been for me in my life. We went dancing regularly at organised balls and fund-raising events at the schools. Through our involvement in the scouting movement, I became close friends with Beth, the new postmaster's wife, who had arrived in town at the beginning of the year. Fred hit it off very well with John too, and I felt free to visit her when I needed someone to talk to.

Because of the circumstances at home while I was growing up, I had never been able to have a close friend for very long. I always envied Jopie, my only sister, her bosom-friend Lenie, who lived a few doors up from us. From the day they could walk Jopie had disappeared to her friend's place whenever she wanted to. I would have loved to have Beth to myself, but with her happy-go-lucky nature, she had many friends with whom I had to share her. Beth and John had four children, three girls and a boy. Their eldest three were the same age as some of our children but the youngest, a beautiful little doll, was only two. With her bright blue eyes, blond hair and her cute manners, she wound her whole family around her little finger. At first, I could not believe that Beth was often up with her for hours during the night, because the little darling did not want to go to sleep when it suited the rest of the family for her to do so. That was unheard of where we were brought up, but times were changing rapidly in all aspects of life...

Together with Beth and John and some of their other friends, we regularly went camping in a creek bed somewhere close to town, and further away on long weekends. John grew up in Victoria and was an experienced bush driver. After they married they had lived in Tasmania, where Beth came from, for ten years. Fred felt a lot safer travelling the rough bush-roads when John was with us, as there had been some hair-raising situations. On our way to Ruby Gorge after we camped at Arltunga, a former gold-mining town, the track was so steep that the road ahead could not be seen at all. I felt sure that we were all on our way to heaven, when all I could see from the passenger's seat in the front of our four-wheel-drive, was the sky.

It seems incredible, given the rocks and rugged country, that hundreds of men visited here in the late 1880's in the hope of finding rubies only to find near-worthless garnets. at the turn of the century there were some three thousand gold-prospectors and miners, most of them staying for a short time. Those early settlers had to make enormous sacrifices and suffered terrible hardships in the hope of striking it rich. But then, of course, at that time people were poor in most parts of the world. Life wasn't much easier for my grandparents, who were living on the land in Holland.

Later in the year, we camped at Palm Valley, a truly unique place; a tropical oasis completely different from the other gaps and gorges we had seen. Hundreds of ancient cycad palms and tall Livingstonias, cabbage palms, believed to be from the time of the dinosaurs, grow there on the huge rocky outcrops of the ancient Finke River. At the time there was no road in at all, we just drove through the dry riverbed behind John, hoping not to get bogged in the deep sand, followed by a treacherous trip over high boulders and steep, slippery slopes. You never knew what to expect around the next corner. I was glad when we came to a flat, sandy spot where we made camp. We had a marvellous time, but as dark clouds were threatening to lock us in, I felt mighty relieved when we were safely on the straight road home again.

On the way into the valley, we had called in at Hermannsburg, an Aboriginal settlement established by the Lutheran Mission. The first missionaries came from Germany in 1877, from a place with the same name. I recalled to Beth how relieved I had been to see the name 'Hermannsburg' on the map, thinking that there was at least one other town where I could go shopping.

About a hundred native people with lots of very scrawny dogs, were living in the settlement, most of them in primitive huts or 'humpies', open shelters made of bits of corrugated iron and twigs. Sitting in large groups in the shade of the big white gum trees, they waved to us. They seemed quite content with their existence. I recently read a book called 'Straight Out Man' by Barbara Hensen, about Pastor Albrecht and the Hermannsburg mission, which increased my admiration for those early pioneers even more. Even if changing the religious beliefs of Indigenous people was not in their best interest, through their incredible dedication, those missionaries had saved many lives, which enabled the offspring of those survivors to make their own choices now.

Numerous events were held in and around Alice during the year especially during the winter months, starting with the Bangtail Muster parade on the first Monday in May. The parade was named after the practice cutting off the tails to count a herd of cattle at mustering time, although the parade itself had nothing to do with that. The parade was always followed by a fun day of sports and games. Nearly every organisation, including the scouts, participated enthusiastically.

By the end of 1975, each one of our six children was in a different group of scouting, which was a unique situation since there were only six groups in the scouting movement, three for boys and three for girls. Richard was a Cub, Eugene a Scout, and Raymond a Venturer in the boy scout group, and Regine was a Brownie, Simone a Guide and Lilian a Ranger, in the different girl scouts sections. I made several pictures of them in their different uniforms, but by the time my film was finally full and developed, there seemed no point in sending a picture to the local paper, because Eugene had moved up and joined the Venturers. Scouting is still very popular in Alice and is now giving some of our grandchildren a good start in life.

While Lilian was with the Rangers, she was also a Cub leader. Going on seventeen, she started to go out on her own. She had worked in the children's ward at the hospital during the holidays since she was fourteen. She loved the Aboriginal children she looked after, but she became disheartened by their endless diarrhoea, vomiting and snotty noses. This time, she wanted to do something else during the Christmas holidays. However, when the matron rang during the first week of the holidays to ask her why she had not applied, she soon felt encouraged and went happily to work at the hospital again for five weeks. From the money she had earned before, she had paid for a holiday in Adelaide with our neighbours from Holland, Dick and Joyce, bought curtains for her own room when we moved into the new house, and she went on a school holiday to Queensland during the Easter break. From the money she earned this time, she went to my brother Henk, who still lived in Sale, in Victoria. Robin's sister Liz, was the same age as Lilian. Together they had taken the train into Melbourne several times, having a marvellous time shopping. We were living in such an isolated place that I was happy for Lilian to spread her wings and, as she was in good company, I did not worry about her. Those worries would come soon enough when she had her first boyfriend.

Not long after her return from Melbourne, Lilian's interest in one of the Venturers was changing. Howard, a Queen's Scout, was a nice fellow from a good family, but my own experiences with boys at that age made me feel very uncomfortable. The idea that she might ruin her future by getting pregnant was my greatest concern, no matter how sensible a girl she was. They usually went to the drive-in on Friday or Saturday nights with a whole group of youngsters. I would go to bed before the movies finished, but like a good mother hen, I could never sleep until all my chicks were home, including the boys. One evening when I had dozed off to sleep, I woke up at twelve-thirty with a start, knowing that something was wrong. Raymond and Eugene were both in bed but Lilian was not home.

"Go back to sleep!" Fred grumbled. "She'll be here soon enough." I tossed and turned, as I could not possibly relax, which irritated Fred even more. After a quarter of an hour, I got up again, restlessly watching the minutes ticking slowly by. Any mother in the same position would know how hollow and loud a clock ticks when you are pacing the floor, anxiously waiting for the safe return of a child, especially during the night.

At one o'clock, I decided to ring Jenny, one of Lilian's best friends. Her father answered the phone with a sleepy voice.

"I don't know if Jenny is home," he said. "What time is it?" No, Jenny was not home either, but her father seemed not in the least worried.

"For goodness sake! They are grown-up girls," he said, annoyed with my concern.

I hesitated, wanting to ring Helene's parents. Maybe I was silly and overprotective, like John had said. I woke Fred up. Pacing the floor together, I argued that Helene's parents might be as worried as we were, and he agreed that I should ring them. They were asleep and did not know that their eldest daughter was not home either. They were not in the least worried, until I reminded them that Howard had boasted about how fast his old car could go on the sharply twisting, single-lane highway that leads through the hills north of town. We promised to ring each other when there was any news.

Fed up listening to my worries and complaints, Fred went back to bed.

'Wake me up when she gets home," he warned; "I'll make sure that she'll never be late again!"

I was now angry with Fred as well as with Lilian. As terrible scenes flashed before my eyes, my anger soon turned to grave concern again, and I prayed fervently for the safe return of my eldest daughter.

The phone rang shortly after two o'clock; Helene had just walked in, very surprised that her parents were still up, and Lilian was on her way. Overjoyed I told Fred, stunned that he had gone straight back to sleep again. He jumped out of bed, ready to give our daughter a piece of his mind. Another half an hour passed and Lilian was still not home. Recalling how we had completely forgotten about the time when we were young ourselves, talking endlessly and wanting to make love, we were both worked up by the time we heard a car pull up in the driveway.

Lilian looked shocked to see us waiting for them. Fred pulled her roughly away from the door, then got stuck into Howard, who had followed her into the hall. Unable to speak English in his rage, Fred scolded him in a flood of Dutch. The poor guy did not know what hit him when Fred pushed him out of the door, yelling at him to never, ever, dare set a foot in our house again.

"I'd better get back to bed before I lose my temper with you young lady!" he snapped at Lilian, who strongly defended Howard.

When he left the room, Lilian told me what happened. After a long drive on the north road when the movies finished, nobody felt like going home. Thinking that we were all asleep, they had gone to Emily Gap, eight kilometres east of town where they went 'skinny dipping' in the moonshine. Seeing the look of horror on my face, my dear daughter went to great lengths to explain to me that she had kept her undies and bra on and, although it was full moon, the water was dark and the others were unable to see anything anyway.

That night I had felt the full responsibilities of motherhood. I knew what we had been like and times were changing fast. I was terrified about the sexual freedom that was displayed in magazines and on television. I finally appreciated Mum's anxiety when I went off to Fred's place on the other side of Holland for the weekend, when I was a little older than Lilian's age. And he was a sailor, nine years older than I was...

Realising that my troubles had only just begun it took me a long time to go to sleep that night.

Two weeks before Christmas 1975, it rained heavily and the Todd was running for the second time in a month. We had spent the previous Sunday afternoon at Wiggly's Waterhole, a popular swimming spot not far out of town. The children had a marvellous time jumping from a tree into the deep water and splashing around on the inner tubes we had taken with us. It was school holidays and my day off, when the boys arranged with their friends to go down the Todd River from 'Wigglys' to the Telegraph Station on their inner tubes. They could not find anybody to drive them there, so they begged me to take them in the Nissan. I had never driven on bush roads before and agreed reluctantly. Expecting them all to sit in the back with empty tubes, I was horrified to see them pull the neighbour's trailer into the driveway, stacked high with already blown-up truck tyre tubes, provided by Brenton, their scoutmaster, who worked at a local tyre-fitting workshop. They had patched them up during the week in their friend's yard. Brenton, who was only four or five years older than our boys, gave them a marvellous youth. It wasn't until recently that I heard about the dangerous situations they got into at the time. I cringed when Eugene showed me pictures of them with only their heads and the handlebars of their motorbikes above water in Wallaby Gap.

At first, I firmly refused to drive with the trailer, worried that I might get bogged, even without it. Raymond assured me that it made no difference driving with a trailer behind the car and that they would all help me. I gave in despite the knot in my stomach. Lilian decided to come too. Raymond sat in the front to show me the way. The others, Lilian and Eugene and the boys' friends Tim, Michael and Bruce all piled in the back. As we had only been to Wiggly's once before, and the narrow tracks through the hills all looked the same, we soon got lost. With my nerves on edge and our eldest son feeling embarrassed by my lousy driving skills, tempers were flaring when I drove straight into a huge puddle at the bottom of a hill.

"I should never have been so stupid to take you!" I shouted, when Ray yelled that his friends' mothers all knew how to drive a four-wheel-drive properly. They all got out of the car, unhooked the trailer and turned it around, the six of them lifting it, bit by bit. Under the boys' instructions, I drove through the puddle, which wasn't as deep as it had seemed to be. With sweat pouring

231

off my face, I tried to turn the heavy vehicle on the narrow track, only being partly successful. When my fifteen-year-old son, who would be starting his apprenticeship as a motor-mechanic after the holidays, said that he could do better, I did not hesitate to let him have a go. He had no problems getting the car in front of the trailer and I happily let him drive to the waterhole where they would unload the big tubes and start their adventure down the fast-flowing Todd River.

Scolding myself for having to drive back with the trailer on my own, and having let them talk me into taking them in the first place, I watched them disappear down the rocky stream on the big tubes, with a heavy heart and a lump in my throat. There were many deep holes and treacherous boulders further on in the river...

Fred wasn't happy at all when I picked him up from the gallery on my way home and told him what I had done. We were both relieved when we watched all six of them coming down the river at the Telegraph Station an hour later. Glowing with excitement, they told us about the fantastic trip. Only one of the tubes had been punctured by a sharp rock. Lilian's body was black and blue everywhere the following day.

One weekend after Christmas, Raymond and Eugene had their heart set on going rabbit hunting with their friends. They were very disappointed when it rained again, seeing their plan literally falling in water. When it stopped raining at noon on Friday, they managed to persuade Fred to take them to their favourite trapping spot, somewhere on the old south road. As usual, they packed everything they needed, including food and their camping gear, in the back of the Nissan.

"I'm crazy!" Fred complained to me time and again before they left later that afternoon. "I should never have given in to them."

Three hours later, when Fred was still not back I started to worry. The boys' usual hunting ground was only twenty kilometres out of town. He should have been home ages ago. Another two hours went by before he turned into the driveway, just before dark. The Nissan was covered with mud and so was Fred. His humour matched his appearance perfectly.

"I should never have listened to them," he said when he told me what happened. The old dirt track, which was seldom used, had a lot of water on it. Time and again the boys had walked into a big puddle to see if it was safe to cross. They'd had to make a lot of detours through the unpredictable soil beside the road and it had been a slow-going, nerve-racking trip for Fred. They had only gone eight kilometres when the Nissan sank to its axles in the mud. I could well imagine how Fred would have been fuming. Lucky for them, there were plenty of mulga bushes in the area to put in front of the wheels of the Nissan. Big rocks put behind the wheels had prevented the heavy vehicle from slipping back into the bog. It had taken them ages to get the car out and Fred refused to go further.

"They didn't want to come back with me, so I just dropped them there," he said, still at boiling point. "I told them that I would pick them up on Sunday afternoon at the same spot, and left them to it."

I woke up when it started to rain softly during the night, picturing our sons and their friends on the soaking wet soil in their makeshift swags. But I did not worry too much about them, thinking what a different, adventurous life they had, compared to what it would have been like for them if we had stayed in Holland.

When Fred went to pick the four boys up on Sunday afternoon, I went with him. What a mess they were! Covered in dirt from top to toe but grinning happily, they proudly showed us the twenty-four rabbits they caught in their traps, twelve for us and twelve for their friends. They had also caught a big feral cat. Like the rabbits, they had become a big problem in the Centre, with its fragile ecology.

The whole process of trapping and killing rabbits turned me off and I refused to skin and clean them right from the start. My mother would have called me a wimp but for once I didn't care. The boys soon had it down to a fine art, skinning a rabbit and cleaning it inside and out in one minute flat. I was very proud of the way they came home with the rabbits in the esky. They would rinse them under the tap in the laundry and prepare them for the freezer, no matter how tired they were. I was not keen on rabbits myself, but I didn't mind cooking them occasionally. At one time there were fifty rabbits in our deepfreeze, most of which were sold by the boys for additional pocket money.

Christmas 1975 we invited several friends to an Australian style lunch at our place for the first time. The smorgasbord of dishes that everybody brought was set out on the patio at the back of our house, including some rabbits that I had fried according to my mother's recipe. When I told our friends about it, one of the fellows immediately dropped his second piece, pulling a face as if he had been eating his own dog. Some of them didn't believe that it was rabbit. They tasted like chicken, they said.

Being no cook to speak of, I proudly gave our guests my mother's simple secret of making rabbits taste like chicken. Cut them in pieces, rub salt and pepper in and fry them brown on all sides in margarine quickly, with a couple of slices of smoked bacon. Turn the heat on low, add a little water and put a lid on the pan. Let them simmer gently, adding a little water and turning them occasionally, until they are cooked thoroughly in about an hour or so.

Although we were all very happy in Australia, that did not prevent me from getting terribly homesick. At those times when the strong emotions of being unable to be with my family overwhelmed me, even their letters did nothing to console me.

"We will be back in five years," Fred had promised when we left. "For a holiday if we are successful, or for good if we are not."

Easily said, but there was no way out either way, that I could see when I felt so miserable. It was far too expensive to go to Holland for a holiday, even for only the two of us, and if things went wrong we could never afford to get back. Even then, where would we live?

A lot had happened at home since we had left. Mum had sold the farm to Wim when he married Gerda in March '74. She now lived in the middle of a row of identical houses in the village, with my youngest brother Ties. My three other brothers, Wout, Wim and Bart, now all had little children. My only sister, Jopie and my brother Bart, who married six months before we left, had a new house, which was of course no big deal but I was 'dying' to see them all again when I was in that unreasonable, black mood called 'homesickness'. The only times Fred felt miserable was when he had to do a job he was not familiar with, and the children seldom talked about Holland at all. A letter from Mum early in November '75 had sent me straight into the 'black hole'.

"I have great news for you," she wrote casually, half way through her letter. "Ties is getting married on the ninth of December."

She went on talking about the everyday happenings in her life, which mainly consisted of visiting friends, playing cards, knitting and embroidering. Then, at the end of the letter she wrote that she was happy that Ties was getting married, as the young couple would live with her. There was no way that they could have a place of their own in over-populated Holland, and that way Mum's happiness was assured, since Elly would relieve her from the housework she hated to do herself.

I was stunned! My little brother, not even twenty-one yet, was getting married! Mum had written to us about his girlfriend only a few months earlier. She was only sixteen, six months younger than Lilian. In her previous letter, Mum said that she was worried about the couple, as Elly was a real girl of this time, doing whatever she wanted to.

"She must be pregnant," Fred said when he read the letter.

"Of course," I replied. "Why else would they get married at that age? But how can Mum be so happy about it? You know how angry and humiliated she was when Bart had to get married, and that is only a few years ago."

"Times have changed," Mum said resignedly when I confronted her about it a year later. "Young people these days do what they like. And you know what Ties' father was like," she added, pulling up her shoulders.

The fact that Ties was getting married brought a lot of memories back. I would rather have kept them buried deep inside me. I was fifteen when Ties was born and I wondered how many people in the village would still think that he was my child instead of my forty-seven-year old mother's. It had been me who had changed his nappies, bathed him and walked proudly behind the hideous old pram to the village, whenever I had a chance to get away from the old house...

There had been a lot of talk in the village about my crude stepfather, whom Mum had married after she had only met him a couple of times. We kids needed a father and an aunt had said that he was a good man. Mum later said that he had made a girl pregnant when he was young and that his father had therefore disinherited him. Pa's dirty talk had made people guess that he would have had his way with me. Thank God, he never went that far! Perhaps due to Mum's endless prayers, which had made me so angry at the time.

"He must be stark raving mad!" our eldest children, aged fourteen, fifteen and seventeen said, when I told them the news. "Now he will never come to Australia."

They had all hoped that Ties, their favourite uncle, would join us when he was eighteen, as Fred had said he could before we left Holland. Raymond and Eugene had already seen their hopes go down the drain when Mum wrote earlier that Ties had a girlfriend.

On the ninth of December, the day of Ties' wedding, I cried all day. I was already suffering for weeks from a sore back and stiff neck, dreadful headaches, nosebleeds and heavy periods, and now I felt worse. After I had an overall check-up, including a blood test that did not reveal anything abnormal, I decided to go to the local chiropractor. He had established a clinic in town recently, which was rapidly becoming very popular with people with back problems. He took an X-ray and said that my neck was completely out of shape, which did not surprise me since I had been holding it at a crooked angle for weeks. After cracking my neck into place a few times, it became impossible for me to relax before the next treatment, making it an even more uncomfortable procedure, and I stopped going.

My old friends at work felt quite sorry for me. They recommended all sorts of remedies that had helped them in similar situations, varying from vinegar compresses, taking hot and cold baths, hanging onto a doorframe, rubbing in goanna, tea-tree and eucalyptus oils, to standing on your head and taking a stiff drink. I don't know which did the trick in the end. Perhaps it was a mixture of feeling loved, a good cry and a stiff drink before retiring at night that pulled me out of the dark hole that time. In any case, I was feeling healthy and happy again by the time the Christmas parties came around.

It's rather sad that even in the mid-seventies, my young brother could still not talk openly about pregnancy before marriage. In a letter, thanking us for our wedding present, Ties did not mention that Elly was pregnant at all. He told me not to worry about him. "If you marry well, you are never too young," he wrote. "I feel good about this one." Not a word about becoming a father for the very first time, something that proved to have been so important to him at the time. Nobody, except Wim's wife Gerda, who was pregnant herself at the time, mentioned it until a few weeks before the wedding.

Ties was right about his positive feelings; after more than twenty-five years they are still a close and happily married couple, dedicated parents to their three now grown-up children. They joined us in Alice Springs in 1981 and, although Elly suffered regularly from homesickness, they too are happy to be in Australia.

One evening, a few weeks into the New Year, 1976, we were surprised to see our Dutch friend Jose's husband, Craig, race into our drive way on his push bike. I quickly opened the door for him but he did not want to come in, distressed and in a great hurry.

"Jose has had a terrible accident," he said, gasping for breath. "She is in hospital."

"What happened?" I asked. "Is she going to be all right?"

"She fell through a window in the passage and cut her throat on the glass; it was awful," Craig shuddered. "We won't know if she'll come good again for a while yet," he said while tears dropped down his cheeks. "Her main artery and her vocal cords were cut; she might never be able to speak again."

My hand had automatically gone to my own neck to protect it from the lump that had suddenly blocked my airways. They had been extremely lucky. A micro-surgeon had been on his way to the airport after a visit in town. He had returned to the hospital and operated on her immediately.

Poor Jose! Craig came to ask me to write to her mother in Holland to let her know what had happened. He had left Sasha, their cute baby girl, with their neighbours. He could look after her himself, he said, when I offered to take care of her, as he had told his boss that he was in no state to work anyway. I promised to visit Jose the following day and he knew where to find me if he needed any help. I had taken care of Sasha for a few weeks when she was four weeks old and Jose had been taken to hospital, bleeding heavily and in terrible pain. Sasha had apparently been part of a twin. The second foetus had died in the early stages of development and Jose had to go through the trauma of giving birth again.

"It was far worse than the first time," she said when she came home, vowing that she would never have another child. Until one of my daughters had a miscarriage, I had no idea that that could be as painful and traumatic as giving birth to a fully-grown baby. I feel terribly sad for all those women who had to go through such an ordeal without something to show for it. At that time they could not even talk about it, without being frowned upon.

236

I was amazed when I found Jose sitting in an armchair in the old hospital, smiling sadly when I visited her the following afternoon. Tubes were attached to her on all sides and bandages held her head in place.

"I can't talk," she wrote on a pad on her lap. "Will you write to my mother?"

"Of course!" I whispered, automatically assuming that I could not produce any sound either. "What would you like me to tell her?"

"Tell her I'm going to be OK," she wrote. "She should not worry! I'll be out in six weeks."

Jose's mother, who had fled to Holland from Indonesia in 1948 along with thousands of her country-folk, lived on a pension in a small apartment in Amsterdam. In her reply, she wrote about her grave concern for her daughter's welfare, and her sorrow that she was not in a position to fly over to Australia to help her in any way. She could not sleep from worrying, as being in hospital for six weeks in Australia was going to ruin the young couple financially and bring Jose and Craig into life-long debt, she wrote. She had rung my mother, who had visited her after her stay with us in the Centre in 1972. Luckily, Mum had been able to reassure her a little.

Like most people in Holland, Jose's mother had no idea what life was like in Australia. Living in a remote area did have its advantages too. It was a great feeling for me to be able to write back to her that Jose's treatment would not cost them a penny. Even the airfares to Adelaide for follow-up treatment were free and her salary would be paid as normal.

With a group of four families we spent Easter 1976 at Kings Canyon, some four hundred kilometres to the south-west of town. Eighty kilometres of the road was still no more than a narrow dirt track, with big potholes all the way. In the evening of Easter Saturday we joined in with the children painting hard-boiled eggs, by the light of a kerosene lamp in our big tent. When the kids were all asleep, the colourful eggs were hidden in the bush. Early the next morning, they happily searched for them while Beth and I prepared food and drinks for the long hike over the top of the magnificent Canyon.

No, life in Australia was not bad at all. I doubted if we could ever live in Holland again after the freedom we enjoyed here.

New Friends

In the second half of 1976 several members of the nursing staff left when their contracts ended. If they wanted to stay for another year, they had to renew their oath of loyalty to the mission. Some of my fellow workers resented the fact that I was never asked to do so.

The two young girls, Kathy and Rhonda were replaced with two married nurses. The two new sisters both came from Melbourne. They were around fifty and lived in town with their husbands. Margaret, the kitchen hand, returned to Victoria to look after her ageing parents and Beryl, also a single country girl who lived with her parents somewhere in Victoria, took her place. She was a small dark-haired girl in her late thirties, very meticulous in her manners and speech, and always out to please everyone. Working for the mission was a great opportunity for these girls to get away from home for a while.

Then, shortly before Christmas, Frances the cook left to look after a widower with two children. We were all sorry to see her go, as she had been so easy to work with. Because no replacement could be found, Sister Perry and Chris shared the cooking again until, at the end of January, a pretty looking twenty-year-old girl with a thick mop of dark, curly hair came in, asking for a job. She was left stranded in town at the end of the tourist season, as a touring coach company no longer needed her service.

"Trish was another God-sent blessing," Sister Perry told me later. "I had just about had it with working day and night.

The only experience Trish had was cooking breakfast, making salads and cooking meat on a barbecue for tourists. Cooking two hot meals a day for the old folks was very frightening for her. Being watched by half a dozen pairs of eyes from the dining room did nothing to ease the poor girl's nerves. On her first day, Chris and I watched in amazement how she cooked potatoes, carrots and peas in huge pots of boiling water, fished them out with a skimmer and dished them straight onto the old folk's plates. After dinner she made several trips to the back fence of the property and threw whatever was left in the pans onto the bank of the Todd River. Chris shook her head over so much waste, screwing her mouth up as she always did when she disapproved of something, saying "That would have made a lovely soup for tea tonight."

Trish learned to cook properly eventually and, because she was willing to listen to their advice, she became very popular with the oldies as well as the staff.

During the first week of January, a married couple, also from Melbourne, joined the staff. Molly, a medium built blonde lady was a trained nurse, and Jim a tall, slim fellow with curly, greying hair and dark brown eyes was employed as a maintenance officer. Jim had been at Old Timers with a working party, a group of men who gave their services to the mission in exchange of food and shelter, for six weeks just after I started there the previous year. I had felt awkward and very shy under the gaze of his dark, penetrating eyes and the special attention he gave me when he asked every day with his deep voice: "How is the little Dutch girl today?"

Jim had been fed up with his job as a salesman-upholsterer. Unable to settle back in Melbourne, he had decided to take more time off. Because Jim had liked it so much at Old Timers, and Molly needed a break too, they had signed up for twelve months with the mission. They lived in a cottage on the far end of the property, overlooking the wide bed of the dry Todd River.

A few weeks after their arrival, Jim and Molly invited us to a staff barbecue at their place one Saturday afternoon. It was the first time Fred had come out to Old Timers for a social event. Normally ill at ease with strangers, I was relieved to see him talking to Jim, looking quite relaxed. He was still not happy with me working there, but it was great for me to see him feeling at home with my new work-mates. Sipping our drinks, we watched the sun go down behind the hills and later admired the millions of stars through the thick branches of the beautiful old gum trees.

Speaking slowly in a southern accent, Molly told me a bit about their family. Like me, Molly was only eighteen when she married Jim, who was not much older than her at the time.

"We were just a couple of kids," she laughed. "Jim was still in the Navy at the time. He looked so handsome in his uniform."

"Oh, you fell in love with a uniform too, did you?" I asked. "Fred was in the Dutch navy when I saw him for the first time."

I told her how my girlfriend and I had waved to the two sailors from a safe distance, when we passed them at a bus stop on our bikes. My friend had gone to work a little later and I had nearly died of shock when I saw Fred and his mate waiting for me at the railway station.

Jim was a few years older than Fred. He had just returned from active service at the end of World War II, when they married. They had four daughters; three of them married. Their youngest daughter nicknamed Jack, was sixteen and would be joining them later in the year. Their eldest daughter, Laura, had four children, ranging from four to ten years, of which three were handicapped with different problems. Laura herself suffered from a liver disease. The children's father had left them before the last child was born. Molly had been taking care of her second family for several years, as well as having her own full-time nursing job. She needed a break badly. When Jim suggested going to Alice Springs for a year their two other married daughters, who had no children, offered to take care of their eldest sister and her family.

Molly had taken up nursing again when her own daughters were all at school. She was a very caring person and I loved working with her. She was just as horrified as I had been when I first had to leave poor, crippled Tessa and old Jack sitting on their commodes in the shade of a tree all morning. She asked me to get a heap of rags out of the storeroom. Watching her making soft padding around the metal bedpan in the open armchair, I felt ashamed. Why hadn't I thought of doing that myself? Molly's care was lost on Sister Perry who could not see the benefits of the soft padding at all. She shook her head when I helped her put Tessa back in bed, later that morning.

"Who's silly idea is this?" she asked with disdain. In her no-nonsense, bush-nurse's eyes, those soft city methods did more harm then good to the tough skin on Tessa and Jack's bottoms. It was far more important that the fresh air could freely circulate around the open chair, which prevented the poor woman from the inevitable bedsores, she said. However, she allowed us to go ahead with the idea because Tessa and Jack loved the extra care. Molly had already shown me how to massage Tessa's pressure areas, getting the blood circulation going, which was the only way to prevent the painful and very difficult to heal bedsores, she said. Because I usually worked in the hostel and Molly was always in the hospital, there were many days that I did not see her at all. But I saw plenty of Jim, who worked around the hostel and shared his tea breaks with us. His dark eyes were disturbing me more every day.

A few weeks after the barbecue at Molly and Jim's place, I invited them to our house for dinner. I had cooked the usual Dutch Sunday meal of soft spicy meat with thick gravy, cauliflower with white sauce, boiled potatoes, applesauce and cucumber in vinegar; the most successful dishes I could cook. When I put the meal on the table, I was painfully aware how plain it looked compared to the colourful meals of huge steaks, baked potatoes, pumpkin, tomatoes, peas, carrots and other mixed vegetables that the Australians dish up every day.

After a dessert of cheap ice-cream with fruit-salad out of a tin, the table was cleared, and when the dishes had been done with the help of our guests, my photo albums came out. They are my pride and joy. As we did not take many photos then, I usually kept them pretty well up to date, trying to let every page in the book tell a story. Molly and Jim were very interested to see how we lived in Holland. Some of our children hung far over the table, putting their own opinions into the stories. When we came to some photographs, taken while I was in hospital shortly before we left for Australia Molly asked: "What were you in hospital for Mien?"

I was putting some cups and saucers on the table for the coffee and stopped dead in my tracks when I heard our ten your old son, Richard, say:

"Oh! That was when Mum got de-sexed!"

It was still for a few seconds, then our guests roared with laughter, joined by Fred and the kids, while I nearly died from the embarrassment, wanting to sink into the ground. I had explained to the children that I could not have any more children when I came home from the hospital after a prolapse operation in 1970. Our cheeky son had obviously drawn his own conclusion as Tanja, our German Shepherd was de-sexed a few weeks earlier. Seeing them all in stitches, I relaxed and joined the chorus.

We soon became good friends with Molly and Jim. One day in April, when we were talking about homesickness, Fred told them about his promise to go back to Holland after five years.

"We're planning to go to Europe for a holiday next year," Molly said. "Why don't you come with us?"

The more we thought about it, the better we liked the idea. Our house was just about finished and, although we had a mortgage to pay off, Fred was earning enough for us to live on so that I could save the money I was earning towards the trip. Lilian would be seventeen by the time we were planning to go and the younger children could stay with their friends for a few weeks. Molly got brochures and flight-plans. The plane fare became a lot dearer when the tourist season started on the first of April, so we decided to travel on the last day of March (1977).

Although they were a little disappointed that we were not coming on our own, both Fred's and my family were ecstatic and started to make plans immediately for our holiday. They would all take time off to take us out and show us around. All we needed was the money for the trip to get there, they said. Fred's favourite sister, Bep, and my mother wrote how they told everybody who cared to listen how proud they were of us, having our own house and being able to afford a trip home so soon. But things did not turn out the way we planned, mainly because of the fact that I had fallen in love with Jim.

Although I often felt embarrassed and uncomfortable with it, I loved the attention he gave me. His long legs would touch mine under the table when we were having morning coffee and afternoon tea, and his lips formed kisses when nobody was looking.

Thinking back on it, I still blush, realising that everybody would have known about it at the time. My face always showed my inner turmoil immediately when something was bothering me.

"Your face is an open book," my mother had said a hundred times.

Feeling mortified, I realised that old Alice surely would have seen it with her sharp eyes. I again saw us sitting around the table, which did not even had a tablecloth on it to protect me from the view from the kitchen or the lounge-room.

One day, Molly suggested going dancing at the R.S.L. club on a Saturday night, with a large group of people. Because Jim had been in the army during the war, he and Molly were members and they could sign us all in as their guests. I asked Sam, my bachelor brother, to come along too, so that I could introduce him to the new cook, Trish, Beryl, her assistant in the kitchen, and Lindsay, a new sister who had also joined the staff. Lindsay was a very attractive, soft-spoken girl, a little younger then I was. She came from London on a working holiday and was gratefully accepted by the A.I.M. to work at Old Timers for a year. Sam was attracted to her immediately.

The happy sounds of a Hammond-organ came toward us when we walked into the R.S.L. building. Allan Terry, a well-known local musician, played merry tunes and sang popular songs all night, while we danced the evening away. Because the meals and drinks were cheap, the outings soon became a regular event, but they could not last. Molly and Fred did not seem to be in the least concerned about me dancing with Jim, which had a disastrous effect on me from the first time he put his arms around me. I was terribly nervous. I'm sure he could feel me trembling while we swirled around the floor. Like Fred, he was a good dancer, but because Jim was tall, I floated in his arms, feeling dizzy when he planted little kisses on my hair, whispering that I was beautiful. I wanted the music to go on forever and did not dare look at him when he took me back to my seat, saying how much he had enjoyed dancing with me. Because there were more girls than men in the group and Jim danced with every one of them, we only had one or two other dances together. Fred was enjoying himself tremendously, hardly missing a dance with so many girls to choose from.

Molly proved to be quite a character. She loved to mix and mingle, talking and dancing with everyone, in and outside the group. We had a lot of fun dressing up before we went out, wearing long frocks, as was the fashion at the time. One nigh,t Molly wore a bright red dress with a large corsage of silk flowers pinned at the front.

"You look marvellous!" I said when I greeted her at the entrance of the club. "That dress looks stunning on you." Molly cracked up laughing.

"Did you hear that Darl?" she asked Jim, repeating what I had said.

"I told you so," Jim chuckled. "Nobody will be able to tell the difference."

Between fits of laughter Molly said she was wearing her sexy low-cut nightie. The flowers she had put at the front were covering her cleavage.

As time went on, it became a standing joke that I always danced with my eyes closed. I was careful to do that whenever I danced with Sam or Fred too, so that I could feel more relaxed when I danced with Jim. I felt in heaven when I was swirling around the floor in his arms. He was the tall man I had dreamt of marrying when I was a young girl.

As the weeks went by, I began to fantasise about Jim and me being together forever, like a teenager in love for the first time. My heart was beating in my throat and my legs turned to jelly, whenever I saw him.

One Sunday evening, I was feeling terribly lonely, longing to see Jim. Nobody seemed to notice me at home. The children had gone to bed as usual, early on Sunday evening, and Fred was content reading newspapers and watching telly until the program finished at eleven o'clock. On an impulse, I slipped out of the house and drove in the Mini to Old Timers in the hope of catching a glimpse of Jim. Parked at the gate waiting in my little car, I did not have the faintest idea what I was going to say to him if he turned up. We had never been together alone or had any conversation other then some fleeting remarks.

Suddenly, it was as if lightening had struck me. I asked myself what on earth I was doing there. Was I prepared to walk out on my family?

Even though it was nothing unusual for me to fall asleep in front of the TV and to go to bed unnoticed, I felt disgusted when Fred had not even noticed that I had been away at all. Tears dripped onto my pillow realising that the only times he paid any attention to me were when he wanted to make love, once or twice a week. I cried myself to sleep that night.

During the following days I tried to stay away from Jim as much as I could. Later in the week, I heard that he and Molly had had a fiery argument. I had not seen Molly for a whole week when I met her in a passage unexpectedly and she turned her head the other way. I felt terribly hurt. Naive as I was, it never entered my head that her reaction had anything to do with Jim's attention for me. He had told me that she was in a bad mood and did not want to go dancing the following Saturday evening as planned. They had been "at each other's throat" my colleagues said.

Molly did not speak to me during the following weeks either, turning her head every time we met. Then one morning Jim told me that Molly had gone back to Melbourne because their eldest daughter had taken a bad turn again. When she came back a fortnight later, she brought two of their grandchildren with her. She was her old self again, and my relationship with her slowly returned to normal but we didn't go dancing anymore, and they never mentioned going to Holland with us either. Their grandchildren often came over to our house to play with our youngest children and, although they were not Catholic, they all went with us to the midnight mass at Christmas that year and enjoyed the candle-lit breakfast afterwards.

Shortly after New Year, Molly and Jim returned to Melbourne, as Molly had the overwhelming feeling that something was about to happen with their eldest daughter. Laura's condition deteriorated quickly and she died a few months later. Molly and Jim took in their four grandchildren, aged six to twelve, and prepared to rear their second family.

My love for Jim had ebbed away in a matter of weeks. I slowly came to see him for what he was, just a nice fellow, like Fred, with some habits I did not like. During the following twenty years, Molly became one of my closest friends. Fred and Jim got on very well too, but for some reason, I never felt at ease with Jim, maybe because we had never talked about the way we had felt for each other.

As I wanted to include this powerful experience in this book, I hoped to be able to bring the subject up with both of them, when we stayed with Molly and Jim for a few days, some time ago. Driving in our minibus on our way to Victoria, I talked casually to Fred about it.

"I knew that Jim was keen on you," he said with a frown on his face. "But I never knew that you had fallen in love with him."

"No, of course not! You were as blind as a bat at the time," I laughed.

I had just about given up hope of having an opportunity to talk about it, when Jim and I were suddenly alone for a few minutes, on the morning of our departure. He was watering the garden when I came out of our camper. Fred was having a shower and Molly was preparing breakfast in the kitchen. With butterflies in my stomach, I made some remarks about the beautiful weather and the plants when Jim said, without looking at me:

"I was just thinking of the different way things would have turned out if you and I had continued our relationship, at the time. You did feel as I think you did about me, didn't you?" he asked. I glanced at him briefly.

"I think I did," I said. "I wasn't sure how you felt about me."

"I thought you knew that I was prepared to run off with you, but then Laura got sick again and everything changed."

"Just as well," I smiled awkwardly. "It would have been a disaster for both our families."

Thinking about it later, I realised that it would not just have had a terrible effect on our immediate families, but also on my mother, our brothers and sisters, their families and friends. Like a stone thrown in still water, it would have had far reaching effects on everybody around us.

With the air cleared between us, I looked forward to preparing a party for Molly and Jim's fiftieth wedding anniversary when they stayed with us again the following winter. Not many couples make it to fifty years these days. Staying together for so long is looked upon as boring. Our marriage has weathered many storms during the forty-four years we have now been together. Working through our differences has made ours into a very rewarding relationship. From observing other couples, I am convinced that it can be just as painful, frustrating, challenging and exciting to work on your existing relationship when there is a complete breakdown in communications, as it is to break up and change partners.

244

New Australians

Because of my lack of training, or so I thought at the time, I often did not know how to cope with particular situations in my nursing job. There was always something going on, happy and sad things, but there was never a dull moment. I would get very frustrated with Liz, the night nurse, for the casual way she treated her job. Liz was a dark-haired, slender girl in her early thirties. She was a qualified sister, but she never wore her uniform. She was the only nurse who wore pants to work, saying that they were much more comfortable and nobody saw her during the night anyway. She ignored the strict regulations about animals and always brought her two dogs with her to work, as they kept her company and let her know when there were strangers around the place. One was a black and white kelpie with a lovely fluffy tail, the other a blue healer with one black eye. They were well behaved, since she took them every Saturday to obedience training. She always took them with her on her rounds around the hostel during the night. George, the manager, hated dogs as well as cats with a passion, but Liz took no notice. She even took the dogs with her when she visited him in the evening while she was supposed to be on duty.

I had been on duty in the hospital until nine o'clock one night and came back at seven in the morning, in time to feed the patients their breakfast. As always, Liz was very talkative and stayed around talking non-stop in her deep voice. She left the hospital when I took a bowl of porridge to Tessa, the little Aboriginal woman who had had a stroke. The strong smell of ammonia made me gasp for breath when I lifted the blankets off her to sit her up a little better. I was horrified to see that she was still lying in exactly the same position as I had put her the night before. The same thick pad of rags I had put between her legs was still there. The poor woman was soaked to her neck. The patients were supposed to be made comfortable and they had to be turned at least twice during the night to prevent bedsores, but Liz had told me at the start that she had no intention of disturbing the patients when they were asleep. Looking at me with those sad eyes, crying softly, Tessa said that she had been awake for hours.

I was not only angry with Liz, but also with the manager, as she spent half the nights at his place when she was on duty and she often went there for breakfast in the morning as well. Sister Perry thought the world of Liz and I could hardly complain to the church's minister either. When I first started work at the hospital, my fellow workers advised me to make sure that there was always a table or a desk between us when I was on my own with that particular minister, saying that he liked to cuddle the nurses. I did not take much notice. Priests and ministers were close to God. They had given their lives to serve Him and would have higher things on their minds, but the rumours made it impossible to go to him to discuss our problems. I was very shy with anybody in such a high position anyway, and Liz was mighty proud that he often came to her place for dinner, at times staying the night, when he was in Alice Springs for a visit.

When I started writing about my experiences, I told a friend at the writers' club about this warning, wondering how I would go about writing these kinds of things. I wanted to write about real people and not leave my most important impressions out. My friend had lived in the bush all her life and was in the process of writing her own story.

"I know exactly whom you are talking about," she laughed. "The women in the bush used to ring each other and say; 'Is your husband home? The minister is on his way for a visit!' Because distances were so great from one station to the next, a visit often meant an overnight stay at the homestead. On my way home, I thought about the other men I had met who were convinced that every woman liked to be kissed and cuddled and touched in private places. I wondered if they, like my stepfather had lacked the natural love and closeness of their mothers when they were little. Or had they been molly-coddled by them and could not live without cuddling? Some men could not bear to see their wife's love for her children, especially for her first born. Feeling left out, he would pay attention to another woman, or take his frustration out on the child. My mother could not love my eldest brother because my grandmother had spoiled her first-born grandson. Maybe it was because her own mother did not care about her, that she had not been able to protect me from my stepfather's interference…

I loved my visits with Nancy, the manager's wife who still lives at Old Timers, sharing my experiences with her. She is a lovely lady, small and slim with an unbelievable amount of energy. I admired her for the way she had put up with things without ever complaining. While I was working there, Nancy suddenly had to go to hospital and she was sick for quite a while. It wasn't until much later that I learned she'd had her second breast removed; the other had been taken off a few years earlier.

In her mid-eighties now, she is still very much the same, always friendly and doing what she can for the home and the people around her. George, her husband, retired at the end of 1978, when the new complex at Old Timers was fully occupied and the Government took over. He suffered a heart attack and passed away in 1981, aged sixty-eight. They never had any children, as that was not to be, Nancy said sadly, when I asked her about it. Nancy was able to put a lot of things in perspective for me and I came to realise how difficult the job of managing the place had been for both of them.

George was a little man of Scottish decent, 'which explained his tight-fisted nature', I was told when I first met him. To give himself an air of importance, he would put his chest out and his bottom lip would go down a little further when he addressed the staff about a very important matter, usually about his frustrations with the dogs and cats the girls kept feeding.

It was difficult to keep a straight face at those meetings, especially after I told Molly and a few other girls that whenever I saw George talking to a group of nurses, I thought about our Bantam rooster among his hens.

"George seemed obsessed with cats," I said, sipping tea with Nancy in her cosy unit one afternoon.

"It wasn't only the cats that drove him mad," Nancy said. "The dogs were just as big a problem. People were not allowed to have dogs or cats when we took over the management. That was hardly fair as those who had been there before we came were allowed to keep their pets."

"And Liz brought her dogs to work with her!" I put in.

"She wouldn't come otherwise," Nancy sighed. "You know what endless problems we had when Nicole came. She had two dogs and three cats. There was just no way she would take the job if she could not bring them." As the name of that matron still gave me the cold shivers, I quickly changed the subject. She had made life unbearable for me, causing me to give up the job I loved. Nancy sadly shook her head when I told her about my experiences with Liz.

"It was awfully hard for us to get her to go back to the hospital," she said. "I would say to her 'Shouldn't you go back to see if the patients are all right', and George would mention that it was time for us to go to bed, but she just kept talking."

"But George was the manager," I protested. "Surely he could have sent her straight back to her duties?"

"It wasn't as simple as that," Nancy explained. "The nurses were not his responsibility and we had no experience in managing a place as big as this."

George and Nancy had been at Old Timers a little over two years when I met them. Before that, they had been the first house-parents at St Phillips, (now St Phillip's College) which, when it was opened in Alice Springs in 1965, was a boarding school for children who lived in the bush. It was only a small place at the time, and they had stayed there for two years. From there they had gone overseas for a year, where they had visited their relatives in Scotland and England, most of whom they had never met before. When they came back from the trip, they were offered a similar position as house-parents and caretakers in Cowen, a small isolated community in the far north of Queensland, where they looked after about twenty Aboriginal children during the following three years.

George was offered the position of manager at Old Timers at the end of

1972, when the manager at the time wished to retire. Most of the fifteen new cottages and seven staff units that were added to the complex that year, were occupied.

"It was extremely hard for George to fill John's (Blakeman) shoes," Nancy said. "John had many years experience in managerial positions and he was such a keen gardener. George was a chef, not a gardener at all."

Mr. Blakeman and his wife Margaret were much admired by the staff of the head office in Sydney, for their dedication to the A.I.M.

"The manager's house, near the entrance of the complex, was built for John in the early sixties," Nancy went on. "When we came, he and Margaret had moved into one of the new cottages at the back. It was not easy for George to have John living at the property. He had done so much to improve the place."

"Poor George!" Nancy said, thoughtfully stirring her tea. "He often had the feeling that John was breathing down his neck."

By talking to Nancy, it slowly dawned on me how people were put into positions they could not handle, simply because there wasn't anybody else available or willing to take on the exhausting, low-paid jobs working for the mission. By employing George, his hard-working wife came free. At the time, there was just no other way. If it hadn't been for the A.I.M., which survived on donations from the public, there would never have been a 'resting place for old people' at that time.

After talking with Nancy and Sister Perry about the responsibilities and demands put upon the matron by head office in Sydney, I felt great empathy for the two sisters who had accepted the position when no matron could be found, while I worked there. The first acting matron tried to cope with her responsibilities by drinking wine and taking too many sleeping pills. Her replacement, a much liked sister-in-charge, changed within a couple of months to a regimental sergeant major, bossing everybody around until she suffered a nervous breakdown. Both were sent on sick leave, well before a year ended. The new matron made life very difficult for the staff too, forcing two nurses to leave and leaving other members of the staff no option but to quit the job they loved.

Until the new hostel for forty-five people and a fifty-bed nursing home had been built in 1977, the home relied heavily on the help of volunteers from town, mostly members of the Uniting Church. Shortly after the official opening by Prince Charles, in October 1978, the running of Old Timers was taken over by the Government. According to the latest polls, the home is now one of the best in Australia. Still, there is no better place than home, if it is at all possible to stay there.

In the early seventies, the manager was responsible for the administration

248

of the whole complex, the upkeep of the extensive gardens, the sale of the citrus fruit and the maintenance of the buildings, as well as looking after the occupation and collection of rent for the cottages. George also took care of transporting patients to and from town in the A.I.M. station wagon. He was called upon at all hours, day and night, to get prescription and other medications for patients from the chemist, or the hospital in town. He also delivered the mail.

Living next to an Aboriginal camp also brought its fair share of problems. Because there was not much of a fence around the property, people strolled in at any time asking for food, a lift into town, the use of the telephone or medical attention, or even just for a match to light a cigarette. They usually brought their families with them, together with half a dozen scrawny dogs, and they regularly camped in the grounds during the night, or on George and Nancy's veranda.

Life became a little easier for them when Jim came in January 1976. While he was there, two young Aboriginal men were taken on to help with the gardening. Not used to any kind of routine, it took them a while to settle into white-man's way which was not as easy as they had expected it to be. Just turning up for work whenever they felt like it had been most frustrating for George as well as for Jim.

When we were naturalised in December 1976, Jim asked if he could bring the boys to the party at our place, which proved to be a real eye-opener for them as well as for us.

"They thought that we were crazy when we took them home at midnight while the party was still going," Jim said later. "The fact that we had to be fit for work in the morning meant nothing to them. They would party on until it was finished, even if it took days, they said."

Some time ago I visited an old friend in hospital, when an Aboriginal man in the next bed asked: "You're Minny, aren't you?" Surprised, I asked him how he knew my name.

"I remember you. You was Jim's friend," he said. "We was at your place when you had a big party."

Graham, in his mid forties, had had a stroke. We talked for a while about the good old days at Old Timers, which he had apparently enjoyed very much, saying that those had been the best years of his life.

With the required five-year waiting time coming to an end in October '76, we applied for Australian citizenship, each for our own reasons. Although Fred said that he would never want to go back to live in Holland, I wanted to be sure that he could not change his mind when things would not be as good as they were for us at that time. Going back to the country they came from, only to find that they no longer belonged there, had had a devastating effect on immigrants. Having an Australian passport would make it very difficult, if not impossible for Fred to go back on his word I thought, which was of course very naive.

Fred reckoned it was only fair that we became Australians, since our children were being educated here and because most Government jobs were only available to Australians at the time, being naturalised was important for our children's future. Fred also wanted to be able to vote, to have a say instead of just criticising the Government that was in power. He was worried about his job. Now that Panorama Guth was finished and Henk planned to take life easier, there wouldn't be enough work for Fred to make a living. When we came back from our trip to Holland, he wanted to apply for a more secure job as a maintenance-handy-man at the Space Base, the Joint Defence Facility, for which he also needed to be an Australian citizen.

Apart from our family, there were another six people being naturalised on the ninth of December 1976. Knowing that we were breaking our ties with Holland, the simple ceremony on the lawn of the Alice Springs Council offices on that beautiful sunny day was a very emotional affair for both of us. Lilian and Raymond were also permitted to swear their oath of allegiance on the Bible to Queen Elizabeth because they were above the age of sixteen. The other four children would automatically become Australian citizens, included on Fred's passport. During the twelve months following their twenty-first birthdays, they would be able to apply for dual-citizenship, if they wanted to. However, by that time, they were all 'true-blue Aussies' and forgot about it. Only Richard, who wanted a working visa at the time, has the benefit of being Australian as well as Dutch. Some of our Dutch friends could not see the need to become Australians. They jokingly called us traitors, but most of them would later take the big step, too.

To mark the happy occasion of becoming 'Aussies', we organised a party at home that night, which was attended by about eighty people. A huge Australian flag, borrowed from Panorama Guth, was hung up in the back yard and was decorated with balloons and streamers in the familiar colours of red, white and blue, the colours of the Dutch as well as the Australian flag. Some Dutchies missed the separate orange *wimpel* (streamer) of the much-loved Dutch Royal Family, which stems from the House of Orange. In true Australian style, our friends, neighbours and colleagues insisted on bringing their own drinks. They also presented us with an array of Australian ornaments and souvenirs, which still remind us of that happy day. Later in the evening, a large trestle table was set up in the middle of the lawn for the food, provided by Pat and John Govers, who had supported us so much in that memorable time of October 1971. They had made a delicious Australian meal, a hearty beef stew with lots of vegetables, baked potatoes and various salads. To make sure that

250

everyone had their fair share, they dished it out themselves, saying that a lot of people turned into bloody pigs when the food was just put on the table. I never fail to think of Pat's words when I see people piling up their plates at a smorgasbord dinner, seemingly without a thought for anybody else.

Pat's gift to us was a big cake, a beautiful map of Australia, red in the centre and green around the coast. A little Australian flag proudly moved in the breeze at the centre of the map where Alice Springs would be.

Before she asked us to cut it, Pat told our guests, in her colourful way of speaking, how we had met on that first day in Alice Springs when we had nothing but twenty kilograms of luggage between the eight of us, and those 'bloody old caravans' to sleep in. After praising us for the way we had adjusted ourselves to the way of life in Central Australia, and wishing us all the best for the future, she asked people to fill their glasses and proposed a toast; "To the new Aussies!"

During those last months of 1976, my relationship with Fred had steadily improved, but he was not happy at all when Jim presented me with his army slouch hat at the party. He insisted that I give it back to him the following day. As I did not want to risk my newly-found friendship with them, I argued that Jim and Molly would probably be offended if I gave it back to them so soon. Jim's hat, hanging on the wall between the many other Australian gifts, reminded me time and again of the easy way a marriage could break up if our partner is taken for granted. I gave it back to him much later.

As often happened when I am under a lot of emotional stress, I had done my back in, just before a German ball was held at the Italian club in October. This time I had bent down to take a tin from the bottom of the store cupboard when a sharp pain in my back made me gasp for breath. After several trips to the chiropractor, I still could hardly walk the day the ball was on, but we had not been out dancing for quite some time so I was as determined as a stubborn child to go anyway. We had a marvellous time, dancing to German and Swiss tunes in the Italian club with our Dutch friends, drinking orange juice and vodka. Because I could not sit at all, I kept on dancing until I became violently ill from the strong liquor. I don't know how I got home that night. The following morning I still felt as sick as a dog, but when I got up, I had the surprise of my life; my backache had disappeared completely!

The birthday party I had organised for Fred in November had been a great surprise for him and our plans to go to Holland the following March also helped to revive our marriage. We only needed to pay for our fares our families wrote enthusiastically, but there was not much work at the Panorama, and I worried about not having any spending money. Because we needed every penny we could spare, Fred could not do the finishing touches on the house either and decided to try his hand at painting instead.

His first painting, a Dutch landscape with a windmill and skaters, was sold before it was finished. My excitement about the extra money was short-lived when my beloved Mini gave up the ghost a week later and needed a new motor. Several weeks went by before another second-hand motor was found and Lilian's boyfriend, Howard, and his mate finally had time to put in. During that time, Fred often had to get up at six o'clock in the morning to take me to work and pick me up at all hours because of my different shifts, which stretched his patience to the limit. There were some very difficult and painful situations at work at the time too, as the second matron was about to be sent on sick-leave. Fred was right. Life would be so much easier for all of us if I would only quit the job and take up sewing again, but the thought alone made me shudder.

As Christmas came and went, our planned trip to Holland became more and more uncertain. We were relieved when a friend asked Fred to make a six metre long wall-unit, which kept him busy for some weeks and enabled us to pay for the tickets.

By the time Fred finished the job at the end of February, Henk (Guth) had returned from his holiday in Europe. There were some four hundred frames waiting for him to fill, and although he had made a huge stock of paintings in all sizes before he left, there was nothing left for sale on the walls, and the season had not even started.

On one of my days off, a couple of weeks before Henk came back, Fred had made a painting at the entrance to Standley Chasm, fifty kilometres out of town; his first attempt at an Australian landscape. Although it was very hot that day, it was great to sit beside him on the narrow path into the chasm, seeing the scene in front of us slowly appear on the canvas while visitors stopped and watched. My heart overflowed with pride for my husband, being able to do such a wonderful thing.

Fred worked on the painting until four in the afternoon. It only needed some finishing touches, which he could do at home when it had dried a little. I proudly carried the easel back to the car when a sudden gust of wind pulled the painting off the easel and it landed face down in the red dust of the path. Needless to say, it broke my heart to see the beautiful picture ruined. Fred wanted me to throw it in the rubbish bin when we came home, but I put it in the shed.

While I was at work the following day, he had picked most of the sand off, finished the picture, and taken it to work. The girls loved it. The sand made it more authentic, they said. As the only paintings from Henk that were left were not for sale, Fred was easily persuaded to put a frame around it and display it in the gallery. It was sold a few days later.

A week earlier Fred had made a small painting of Ayers Rock, a simple picture with a bright blue sky, which hurt my eyes to look at it. A couple of days before Henk came home, Father M, the local priest came into the gallery, wanting to buy a painting of Ayers Rock, but there weren't any. As the priest was very disappointed, the girls had shown him the little one Fred had made. I was as horrified as Fred was when he told me that Father M had taken that awful picture to the hospital to give it to the Archbishop of California, who'd had a heart attack when he was climbing the Rock. Some weeks later, Father M came in the gallery and told Henk that the archbishop was very happy with his painting of Ayers Rock, which now hung above his bureau in the Palace.

"I never paint Ayers Rock. I hate painting it," Henk had said.

The girls then told Henk that Fred had painted the picture. To Fred's relief, Henk never said a word about it.

Because Fred worked at the Panorama for a long time, and he later made a name for himself with his landscape paintings we sold in our own gallery, many people think that Fred was one of the Dutch artists who had helped Henk paint the Panorama in 1975. By writing this story I have put the record straight and hopefully Henk's mind at ease.

Our renewed excitement about being able to go to Holland suffered another setback when our eight-month old German Shepherd, Tanja, needed a hip replacement operation on both sides. Because of in-breeding, displaced hips were a common problem in German Shepherds, the vet said. The cost of one operation was one hundred and seventy-eight dollars, nearly as much as I earned in a month! Our children were heartbroken at our cruel decision to have our beloved Tanja put down. They would save all their pocket money to help pay for the expense they said, which saved Tanja's life. Then, two weeks before we were to leave, we received a hefty tax bill in the mail, more than double we had expected. Because there was no tax taken out of Fred's pay each week, as he was self-employed, he had to pay provisional tax, which had to be paid before we left the country. I was devastated. We also had to leave a substantial amount of money behind for the children to live on and we now had hardly any pocket money left for the trip at all.

Even from before we were married, Fred had paid into a life insurance policy in Holland so that I would be cared for if anything happened to him. His parents had hardly been able to buy food while they were paying into a similar fund for him since the day he was born. The pushbike Fred had bought at twenty-one from their sacrifices had meant little to him, as he was earning enough money himself at the time. We decided to get rid of the dubious fund, even though we would get less than half we had paid into it over the years. In the meantime, I suffered from migraine headaches, a very painful back and excessive monthly bleedings. At the end of January, the doctor sent me to a specialist who advised me to have a hysterectomy the following week, when

253

a surgeon was scheduled to come up from Adelaide. As I would have had to cancel our trip, for which the fares were already paid, the doctor instead booked me in for a curette in February, which might see me through for a while.

We now had a small amount of money at a bank in Holland and Sam could lend us some for the kids while we were away. We were still able to go. No, we were not rich, but at least we had made it this far!

Home Is Where The Heart Is

As the day of our departure came closer, I grew more and more nervous. Torn between my excitement about seeing my family in Holland again and the anguish that something terrible could happen to the children without us being able to get back, made my stomach play havoc with me. Terrible images of the plane crashing, or having an accident on the busy roads in Holland, made me have to rush to the toilet time and again. It was just as well that I was so busy.

Fred patiently pointed out that flying was the safest way of travel and no one in our families had ever had an accident on the road that we could think of, other than having a broken leg. Lilian was eighteen now. She was a real mother hen, taking care of her brothers and sisters. I was about to marry Fred when I was her age. She wanted to become a nurse, maybe a midwife. They would be all right, she said, reminding me that she was only fourteen when we went to Adelaide three and a half years ago. She had now already had her driver's licence for over a year. Yes, they had been fine, but Holland was on the other side of the world and we would be gone for six weeks. Perhaps there was no need for me to worry. Sam's girlfriend Lindsay would call in regularly and she could always call on Margot (Dutchie) next door, who was also a registered nurse. Only the four eldest would be at home, Regine and Richard would be staying at their friends' place. Raymond had started his apprenticeship as a diesel-mechanic, and Eugene worked at Woolworths after school and on Saturdays. There was no need for me to worry about Simone either. She was very keen on ballet and would spend every free moment at the Youth Centre with her best friend Lynne. And Sam would be there. He had no intention of going to Holland. Mum would be very disappointed.

On the morning of our departure, I could hardly swallow my piece of toast because of the lump in my throat and the turmoil in my stomach. Fred urged me to eat at least something, when the news came on. I felt my blood curdle when the newsreader informed us of a plane crash at the airport in Tenerife. A plane from the KLM, the Dutch airline had collided with another aeroplane... There were not expected to be any survivors.

I must have been in shock, as I don't remember saying goodbye to the children, how we went to the airport, or being on the two hour flight to Darwin, where we stayed the night. It was terribly hot and humid when I woke up from a two-hour nap. We were saying at the Asti Hotel, close to the centre of the city. After a shower and something to eat, we decided to go for a walk. It was nearly dark and much cooler, with a salty breeze coming in from the Timor Sea. The air was full of a sweet scent. When I picked up a creamy white flower, I realised that it came from the beautiful frangipani, which lined the street. After admiring the soft, velvety petals, I put my nose close to its yellow heart, feeling more alive as I deeply inhaled the soothing perfume of the lovely flower. We were amazed that only a few houses showed any signs of the cyclone disaster that had hit Darwin two years earlier

Still carrying the flower, we noticed a church a few minutes later, St Mary's Cathedral. The simple building did not resemble anything like the cathedrals I had seen in Holland. The doors were wide open, a soft light was shining and it was lovely and cool inside. We admired and talked about the big arched stained-glass window in the steeple behind the altar, then we sat in silence for a while, praying for a safe trip, our children at home and the poor people who had lost their lives in the air disaster. I felt much better when I left the church, knowing that we were all in God's hands. What was to happen would happen, and He would give us the strength to cope as long as we put our trust in Him. I wondered when and why we had we started to drift so far away from the church.

During the Singapore Airways flight from Darwin to Singapore, I reminded myself time and again that there was nothing we could do but trust that we would be safe, especially when we flew through a terrifying thunderstorm shortly before we were due to land at Singapore Airport. Thunder and lightning followed each other in quick succession. The sky was pitch black and the aircraft shook violently in the turbulence, caused by a strong wind. I sat rigidly in my seat with sweating hands wondering how the plane could possibly avoid being hit by the continuous lightning. It became sweltering hot in the plane, as the air-conditioning wasn't working. Sweat was soon dripping off my face. A sigh of relief went through the plane when the aircraft steadied itself and the air-conditioner came on again. The friendly airhostesses came around with heated towels to wash our faces and hands, as they had done before during the long flight. By the time we arrived in Singapore, my legs were still shaking from the ordeal.

While we tried to find our way among thousands of travellers in the huge brand-new airport, Fred panicked when he realised that we had only ten minutes before the plane would be leaving again for Amsterdam. We still had to be checked in and wondered which way to turn, when we heard some people speaking Dutch. They had made the trip many times before, they said, when we walked with them to the other side of the big hall. While we waited anxiously for our turn, the elderly couple kept their calm. They assured us that the plane would wait until everyone had been checked in. Living in Australia for many years had taught them to be patient, they said.

As soon as we were seated in the big Jumbo, we were handed a thick newspaper full of pictures of the worst air disaster in the history of aviation. Photos of the wreckage... Devastated people... Row upon row of coffins...

Two Boeing 747s, a KLM and a Pan American had collided at the airport in Tenerife in the Canary Islands, killing 582 people. Too anxious to sleep, I stayed awake all night during the twelve-hour flight to Amsterdam. The sun was breaking through the mist when we crossed the German border. It was fascinating to see Holland from the air as Fred pointed out the villages and cities. The country looked like a colourful patchwork of hundreds of tiny paddocks, divided by rivers and channels, and a small forest here and there. Before I realised what was happening, the plane was touching down at Schiphol, Amsterdam's airport, on Wednesday 30th of March 1977, at a quarter to nine in the morning. The passengers applauded.

When we walked into the arrival hall, everybody around us suddenly spoke Dutch. While we waited to go through customs, exhausted from the long journey, we could see our families behind a dark tinted glass wall.

Home, Sweet Home! What a moment! We didn't have arms enough, wanting to hug everybody at once. Mum looked well and happy. She had hardly changed in the six and a half years we had been away. They were nearly all there. Only Wout's wife, Tony, and young Ties' wife, Elly, had stayed at home with the babies. Ties had grown from a young boy of sixteen into a man. Fred's favourite sister, Bep, could not believe how well her brother looked. She had expected Fred to be much skinnier from all the hard work he had done. Before we left I had made a safari-like suit for him from rust-brown rib-cord, which looked great with his greying hair. Bep had brought a thick overcoat for him, borrowed from her son-in-law, and a cardigan she had knitted for him. As I hated to be cold, I had insisted on taking the colourful orange, red and beige checked Harris-tweed overcoat I had made for Bart and Janny's wedding, shortly before we left Holland in 1971.

The sun was shining, but the cold air took our breath away when we walked out of the airport buildings. We had all but forgotten the dreadful air disaster in Tenerife until we reached the car park, where the Dutch flags were flying at half-mast. Fred went in the car with his family, while I went with Wim, Gerda and Mum, for the one hour drive to Hooglanderveen, the village where I grew up. Talking non-stop with my hand in Mum's, I caught glimpses of the beautiful green countryside, the black and white Frisians and the pointed church towers in the many villages we passed through. Before I knew it, we had came to our own village, where we stopped in front of a row of identical houses in the main street; Mum's new abode. A Dutch flag, borrowed from the neighbours, hung out of the window and an arch, made from greenery and bright paper flowers, surrounded the front door. Tears welled up in my eyes again when I read the inscription at the top of the door: "Welcome Home!"

A gulf of warm fluid escaped when I stepped out of the car. Afraid that anyone would notice, I quickly slipped inside. Ties' young wife, Elly, looked shocked when I asked her for a towel. I had disappeared into the toilet beside the front door even before I had said 'Hello' to her. My period had started a few hours before we landed. As I had had a curette two weeks earlier, I had not expected it so soon. I had no choice but to ask the airhostess for a sanitary pad. She gave me a whole pack, which I had nearly used up by the time we landed.

Elly proved to be extremely quick and efficient in whatever she did. As soon as everyone came in, she and Tony served coffee with the traditional *gebakjes*, small, fancy cakes made by the village baker. They had also made a huge pan of fresh vegetable soup with vermicelli and *balletjes*, spicy little meatballs. The delicious soup was served later in the afternoon with a basket full of bread-rolls, dressed with ham, metwurst, cheese and my favourite, the thinly sliced smoked beef we could not get in Alice Springs.

Black stars were dancing before my eyes by the time everyone had left, shortly after six o'clock. Grateful to be able to go to bed at last, I went upstairs. Elly and Ties would sleep in the attic while we were there. I smiled when I read the sign on their bedroom door where we would sleep: 'The Director's Room'.

Before I went to bed, I replaced the second hand-towel Elly had given me with a clean one. I would have loved a shower but I was too tired, and I washed myself at the hand basin in the bedroom instead. Except in summer when it was hot, most people only showered once a week in Holland. Most houses had a hand-basin in every bedroom to have a wash before getting into bed in the evening and to freshen up in the morning. I was still rinsing the towels when Fred came in, shocked to see the colour of the water.

"It looks worse than it is," I said weakly. "I'll write to Lindsay tomorrow and ask her to make an appointment with the doctor."

When I woke up early the following morning, after a long night's sleep I felt like a new person. Unable to stay in bed long, Fred got up early too, a pattern that would take several days to change to normal. I had already written a letter to Lindsay and the children when Mum got up, followed by Ties, who had to go to work, and Elly with little Wendy. Aged twenty-two, Ties operated the largest crane in the district.

During the time we had been away, my family had gained several new members. Until the previous day, I had never met Elly, or Wim's wife, Gerda. The previous spring, four new grandchildren were born within six weeks, three in Holland and one in Australia, Henk and Robin's second son, Richard. When we left, only Jopie, my only sister, had two children, a boy aged five and a girl of seven. Wout and Tony now had two little boys, Bart and Janny had a son and a daughter, and Wim and Ties each had a cute little girl. We talked with Elly and Mum and played with little Wendy, until Wout came to take us to the farm where I grew up, now Wim and Gerda's place, three kilometres out of the village. A few years earlier, Wim had sent us photographs of the old house, where I was born on the living room floor in October 1939, being burned in an exercise by the local fire brigade. It was a very emotional moment for me when we drove onto the property where so much had happened to me. Without the old cottage, Mum's Little Heaven, the place looked awfully bare.

"Don't look so miserable," Wout said. "We don't have many good memories of the *ouwe keet* (old hovel)."

As we walked to the new house that was built shortly after I married Fred and left home, Wout explained that the old house had been in bad disrepair. They'd planned to restore it, but because Wim was not permitted to rent it out to pay for the expense, he had no choice but to burn it.

The new house had changed quite a bit. It took me a while to get used to seeing a strange young woman with a baby in the rooms where Mum, Wim and Ties had lived when we left for Australia. Gerda had written regularly to us from the day Wim asked her to marry him and I soon felt at home with her. She was a lovely, down to earth girl. I could not have wished for a better match for my favourite brother.

Tears are welling up in my eyes while I am writing these sentences. I still find it hard to accept that I shall never see my lovely brother again. Wim died instantly of a heart attack shortly before Easter in 1995, leaving Gerda behind with three teenage daughters.

To our great relief, my excessive bleeding stopped on our second day in Holland. Even though our days were long, being up early and never going to bed before midnight, I felt fit and well most of the time. After two days in Hooglanderveen, Bep and her husband Bert picked us up to stay with them in Arnhem for a couple of days. Bert, who had retired from his job as police inspector the previous year, drove us to Velp, where Fred was born and where we had lived for the first nine years of our marriage. The following day, they showed us around Oosterbeek, where we lived for the last four years before we left for Australia, and where our children had tended the graves of the soldiers who had lost their lives during the Second World War. Nothing much had changed in either of those places, except for the traffic and all the cars parked on both sides of the road in almost every street. Not many ordinary people owned a car when we left in October '71. Being used to the wide spaces between the houses in Alice Springs, everything seemed so small and the roads so narrow.

With Bep and Bert we visited several of Fred's relatives, getting heartily sick of having to tell the same story over and over again. Mum turned sixty-eight on the seventh of April, the Thursday before Easter. During the first two weeks of our stay in Holland, we went to five birthday celebrations, travelling back and forth from Amersfoort to Arnhem. As usual on birthdays, friends and neighbours called in during the day and the entire family was expected in the evening. Until the last minute, Mum still expected Sam to turn up for her birthday. I was happy when Jopie arrived from Arnhem early in the afternoon, but she could not stay for long. She had begged her husband to let her be with our family in the evening but he had refused. He could easily have had dinner at his mother's place, Jopie said, but he did not want to hear of it, saying that it was bad enough that he had to look after the children after school. There were times I envied my sister for marrying a tall, handsome looking man with plenty of money. Now I felt sorry for her.

While we were in Arnhem, Fred's older brother Henk and his cheerful wife Gijsje, booked a trip for us to Paris by bus. They invited their best friends, Tinus and Kelly, to come along too. The trip with a well-known company was very cheap; ninety dollars for the two of us for five days, including hotel with breakfast, excursions and a show. We departed from Rotterdam at eight-thirty on Easter Monday morning, had lunch in Belgium and arrived in Paris at four o'clock in the afternoon. As I had never been outside the border before, I had no idea that it was only five hundred kilometres to go from Amsterdam to Paris, the same distance as from Alice Springs to Tennant Creek, our nearest town!

It did not take us long to get to know several other couples in the bus, most of them people like us, emigrants dying to get away from the family for a couple of days. Of most couples the man was Dutch and his partner had a different nationality, on holiday in Holland but living in Canada, South Africa or Indonesia. There was also a couple from Sydney. Like Sam and John, he had 'escaped' to Australia in the early fifties, showing his Australian wife where he came from. Continuously having to translate what was said was very frustrating and exhausting for them. It was bad enough having to tell the same stories over and over again. We would have been the same if Jim and Molly had been with us.

We were both fascinated with Paris, the romantic old city, with the ancient buildings, the intricate gardens, the chaotic traffic and its multitude of coloured people. Our five-storey hotel was in a narrow street, somewhere on the outskirts of the city. Hundreds of cars were parked on either side of the street, bumper to bumper. Wondering how on earth they would get their cars out, we watched in amazement as a man backed into the car behind him, then forth, bumping into the car in front until he could drive away. Well! What else were bumper-bars for?

We made at least one excursion a day to palaces, cathedrals and churches, soaking up the history of the places and strolling through the gardens afterwards.

We were most impressed by the woodcarvings and stained glass windows everywhere, but especially in the Notre Dame. Fred could not get enough of watching the artists at Mont Martre, as they worked on their different styles of paintings.

The weather was perfect while we were there, such a contrast with Holland where we had snow, hail and rain most of the time. One windy afternoon, we went back to the Eiffel tower, planning to climb it as far as we could, but it was closed. The tower apparently sways dangerously when the wind is strong. We watched the traffic on the roundabout near the Arc De Triomphe instead; nine lanes of endless traffic, going round in circles until they got into the right lane to turn into the direction they wished to go. This was in 1977; I wonder what it is like now!

One afternoon, when we came back from an excursion, our coach could not possibly get through as an 'ugly duck' (Citroen) was parked at the inside of a corner. Most of the men got out to see what could be done. With four at the front and four at the back they bounced the car up and down a couple of times then, at the count of three, they lifted the funny duck-shaped car onto the footpath.

I could sit for hours on a terrace in the sun sipping tea or lemonade, just watching some of the eccentric people, for which Paris is famous. We both loved walking the boulevards along the Seine, especially at night, looking at the many handcrafts, artefacts, paintings and pen and charcoal drawings. Unfortunately we could only afford to buy a few.

We were disappointed with the show that was included in the trip. Instead of going to the famous Moulin Rouge as I had expected, we went to one of the many obscure places, somewhere in the middle of the city. After climbing several steep, narrow wooden stairs we came to a dimly lit room with dozens of small round tables with as many high-backed chairs as they could have possible fitted around them. With the dark-red velvet curtains, the elegant round chairs and the long mauve-coloured tablecloths with a single silk flower in a small crystal vase on the tables, the room looked cosy. While several waitresses struggled among the crowd, serving a complementary glass of champagne, the room was filling quickly. By the time the show started we were packed so tightly that there was no way to get out, not even to go to the toilet. Nobody seemed to mind that we were all trapped like rats in a cage if there should be a fire.

The elaborate costumes of the performers looked old and worn and none of them fitted properly. The dancers were often out of time with the music, especially when a long row of girls danced the famous can-can, and most of the sketches were rather vulgar. When the first part of the show was finished everybody rushed to the door to go to another room, higher up in the building for the second part, which happened to be a cheap strip-show in a dark, timber attic, also with a wooden floor... As they had done at the nightclub in Adelaide, several people in the audience went berserk when a dancer, male or female took the last of their clothes off.

On the last day of our visit, the coach-driver took us to the palace of Louis the fourteenth in Versailles, a mighty castle with fantastic gardens where we spent all day. Because my in-laws and their friends had been to Paris several times before, they could not make up their minds what to do with the last evening. In the end we decided to take the underground metro into the city and back, just to have something to do.

On our way back to Holland, we both looked forward eagerly to getting back to Hooglanderveen, hoping there would be a letter from the children. Lilian had written a long letter to us in perfect Dutch, shortly after we had left. We now had another surprise, as Eugene also wrote to us in nearly faultless Dutch. There was also a letter from Simone and Richard, but those were in English; they were only six and eight when we left Holland. In another long, entertaining letter, this time written in English as that was much quicker, Lilian gave us a day to day account of what was happening at home. So far everything was fine. I became worried when I read in Eugene's letter that he had bought a motorbike, a second-hand, 250cc Honda trail bike. He was only fifteen and did not have a licence... He also wrote how they had gone with Brenton to the fish-hole, some seventy kilometres out of town. The old truck from the scouts had sunk to its axles in the mud. As it was getting dark and they could not get the truck out, they had walked twenty-five kilometres through the hills back to Jay Creek, an Aboriginal settlement. When they had not returned before dark, their friend's parents had come looking for them and it had been well after midnight when they finally got home.

Then I opened the thick envelope with the application forms for the nursing training course, the second one to be held at the Alice Springs Hospital. I was thrilled when I read that Lindsay had made an appointment for me for an interview, which meant that my application had been accepted, despite my lack of education, she said.

A couple of days after our return from Paris, we went with Bep and Bert to Germany for three days, where two of their married daughters lived. We came back via Luxembourg and Belgium. As I had never been across the border before, I had no idea how beautiful those countries were. Coming into Holland from Belgium, it was amazing to see how the farmhouses changed from old run-down places, to large new ones, as soon as we crossed the border. Everything in Holland breathed prosperity and luxury, which made us wonder why we had left. Wages were five times as much as they had been when we had left our country...

262

As the Australian dollar had devalued to less than half everything was very expensive for us, especially meat and clothing. When we went into a butcher's shop to take some meat home, I mentioned to Fred that the prices were not as bad as I thought. To my embarrassment the butcher pointed out that the price advertised on the label, was per hundred grams, not per pound (five hundred grams) or per kilogram as it used to be.

As the weeks sped by, going out day after day became very tiring for us. My brothers and Jopie's husband took turns in taking a day off from work to show us whatever we wanted to see. As we had seen very little of Holland while we lived there, we usually left the choice up to them. To make the most of their day off they would come early in the morning to pick us up and we seldom returned before midnight. Then, early the following morning the next person was there to collect us for their special treat. In between those outings, we would visit our own personal friends and neighbours, who also lived on either side of the country. Our friends Kees and Riet, with whom we had gone camping every year, took us to the fascinating Delta Works in the south of Holland. The project, which started after the sea had claimed nearly two thousand lives on Queen (then Princess) Beatrix's birthday, the 31st of January 1953, was still in progress. It was fantastic what the engineers had achieved to protect the low-lying islands from flooding again.

On a bitterly cold day a few days later, Bart and Janny showed us the new *polders* in Flevoland, reclaimed land from the sea. As a strong wind howled over the endless empty fields, we spent most of our time in the museums in the former islands Urk and Schokland, admiring our country folks again for their ingenuity, hard work and perseverance.

We spent a lovely day with Henk Guth's brother, Jurrian, and his wife Cor. Now that they were getting older, they had moved from their beautiful house in the forest near Arnhem, where they had shown us slides of Alice Springs, back to nearby Putten, where Cor was born and grew up. After the war, Putten became known as 'the village of the widows'. In September 1944 the Germans had taken all their men, between the ages of eighteen and fifty, to work in Germany in reprisal for an attack on a German officer; only seven of them came back.

A few days later we visited Frits Pieters, one of the two well-known artists who helped paint Panorama Guth in Alice Springs. Frits took us to the famous cheese markets in Gouda and Haarlem, where he lived with his wife Molly, restoring antique paintings and clock-faces that had been damaged in a fire. Like Henk, Frits is now in his early eighties and they are both still painting.

Back and forth we travelled between Arnhem and Amersfoort. While we were staying with Jopie and her husband Ben in Arnhem, we visited a magnificent castle in Elthen, just over the border of Germany, which was only twenty kilometres from where they lived. Although the old castle had made a big impression on me, I remember our walk through the Hoge Veluwe, the forest we knew so well, better. It was there that I had a lengthy talk with my only sister, who was four years younger than I was. Even though we lived only seven kilometres away from each other during the last ten years before we left Holland, I hardly knew her. We had drifted apart after she married into a well-to-do business family, who had apparently controlled her every move.

Back in Hooglanderveen, my eldest brother Wout showed us the gardens of the Motherhouse of the Sisters of St Joseph in Amersfoort, where he was a gardener-chauffeur. He introduced us to several of the hundred nuns, aged between sixty and a hundred and one, who were still living in the convent. One lively sister showed us the chapel and their own private hospital, where bedridden nuns and elderly, fragile priests were nursed.

Wout and Tony also took us to the famous Keukenhof, not far from Amsterdam. The sun was shining for a change so we spent a glorious day in those magnificent gardens. Because it was extremely cold that spring, the tulips, narcissus, crocuses and hyacinths were still out in their full glory. On the way home, via a scenic route through Het Gooi, we came across a big windmill, which had been made into a posh restaurant. Lunch in the Keukenhof had been too expensive, so we were starving. Wout was right when he said that the meals in the beautiful windmill would be dear too. I nearly fell over backwards when I read the menu beside the entrance door: they wanted twelve guilders-fifty for a cup of soup!

Tony and I were in stitches when Wout reminded us that we had not been prepared to pay two-fifty for a cup of soup in the Keukenhof. Later that evening we had a delicious meal in a Chinese-Indonesian restaurant in Amersfoort. We ate as many *loempias*, fried rice, satays and stir-fried vegetables as we wanted for the grand total of twenty-four guilders for the four of us, including a glass of beer for the men and house-wine for Tony and me.

As time went on, Mum complained that we were never home. Because there was only room for four people in most cars, she often had to stay home. Sometimes she came with us, when Fred drove a short distance, or with Wim, when Gerda stayed home. The highlight of our visit for her was eating *poffertjes* (tiny pancakes) with rum and lots of fresh cream in Blaricum, a picturesque village near Hilversum, Netherland's radio-city.

It took us a while to get used to the narrow streets and the cramped way of living of most families. Even though it was often bitterly cold, most people still left the curtains open at night; to close them would mean that they had something to hide. When we went for a walk, we could see what programmes were on the television, and who was watching what station in the neighbourhood. It was a pleasant surprise for me that most people now switched the television off when we visited them.

By the time we had been in Holland for a month, we were both ready to go home to Australia. Although we went out almost every day, time dragged on during the last two weeks. We had become very tired the busy schedule and of talking about our lives in Australia, over and over again.

As was the custom, Jopie and her husband celebrated their copper wedding anniversary (twelve and a half years) with a big party, held in the same restaurant in our village as their wedding reception had been in 1964. The actual date had been half a year earlier, but as we were coming to Holland, they had postponed the party.

"Not many couples would dare to celebrate their thirteenth wedding anniversary," Ben joked at the happy event. They separated shortly after. Jopie later married a much younger man with whom she has a happy life.

At the party we met Mum's youngest sister Tante Cor, who was over from Canada for the second time since she had left in 1948. Talking to her made me realise once more how much easier our emigration had been, compared to all those people who had left shortly after the war. But then, times were different. Each in our own way, we took a step back to move two steps forward later. When Ties and Elly came to Australia in 1981, ten years after we had gone, their emigration was a lot easier than ours had been. But they still had just as hard a time, simply because they had enjoyed a much better lifestyle before they left Holland.

We were with Wim and Gerda in Lelystad, a brand-new village in the middle of the empty polders, when I rang the airport to confirm our return trip. Hearing the operator say the airlines in Australia were on strike indefinitely, I burst into tears, heartbroken. It wasn't until I was told that we couldn't get back, that I realised how homesick for Australia - and our children - I was. That night, we rang Alice Springs for the first time. It took hours for the call to be established. Although the line was bad and we spoke only for a few minutes, it had cost Mum a small fortune.

Things were all right at home Lilian said lamely; they could cope another week.

"It may be weeks before we can go home," I sobbed. "You know how long some of those strikes can last!" In a letter we received a couple of days later, Lilian told us that Richard and Regine both had come home as they were homesick, and she and Howard had split up the previous week. Not wanting to spoil our holiday, she did not tell us that she was crying herself to sleep every night... Lilian also informed me that arrangements had been made for me to go into hospital as soon as I came home.

The KLM officer had told me that we could only go as far as Singapore, and she warned us that the hotels were already overflowing with stranded travellers. We decided to stay where we were and ring the airlines every day to see when we could go back to Australia.

To take our minds off things, our families organised more outings to places we had not been, but I often wished they would leave me alone in my misery. My wish came true on the morning of our farewell party, as I was bleeding heavily again. Feeling utterly sorry for myself, I swallowed some aspirins and crawled back under the heavy blankets.

A good cry and a couple of hours of sleep worked wonders for me and I thoroughly enjoyed the unusual dinner in the posh newly furbished restaurant in the village. Our two families had decided to go 'gourmetting', the latest fashion of eating out. There were several sets of four to six small frying pans on spirit burners on long tables when we came in. While we had a drink and waited for Fred's family to arrive, a lot of dishes with pieces of chicken, pork and beef, sliced potatoes and cut up vegetables were brought in by the waitresses, followed by fresh salads and pancake mixture. The idea was that we all cooked our own food in the little frying pans, which proved to be great fun for everyone. We felt rather embarrassed when our families were presented with the bill and divided between them as previously arranged.

"Fifty guilders each and we still had to cook it ourselves!" some of them said rather disgustedly. Fred promised to shout them all a meal when we came back rich, but so far that hasn't happened.

My relief, when we could finally leave Holland a week later, was so great that I felt no need whatsoever to cry when I said goodbye to my family for the second time. Feeling a little ashamed that we had been smiling and waving happily, we disappeared through the big doors at the airport. It wasn't until our arrival at the airport in Frankfort that I suddenly became nervous about flying again. The building had to be vacated as a homemade bomb had supposedly been put in a waste-paper basket somewhere in one of the buildings. When we boarded again, we met up with another Dutch couple who lived in Alice Springs. They, too, were happy to going back to the centre of Australia, where we now felt we belonged. We really felt that we were on our way home when we boarded the Qantas flight to Darwin in Singapore. The journey seemed to have taken twice as long when we finally stepped onto the tarmac in Darwin in the early morning of May the twentieth, greeted by the sun in the familiar blue sky. Australia! Home Sweet Home! How we had missed the sun!

Alice Here We Are Again!

Because we had to wait several hours for the connecting flight from Darwin to Alice Springs, we let other people go to have their luggage checked first. When it was our turn, the customs officer asked what nationality we were.

"We are Australians!" I said, proudly handing him my passport.

"Oh yeah!" the officer grumbled, turning up his eyes. "But where did you come from originally?"

"From Holland," I said, taken aback. "We immigrated six years ago and have been back for a holiday."

"Any cheese or clogs?"

"Why would we bring cheese?" I asked. "We can get plenty of that here." Our hope at not having to open our bulging suitcases vanished when the officer ordered Fred to open one of them, so that he could see for himself that the clogs we had were painted souvenirs, as I said they were. My anger about the unfriendly way we were treated vanished like snow in the sun when Fred opened the first suitcase and lots of little black cats fell all over the officer's desk. At the last minute someone had handed us a large paper bag of those popular sweets for the kids.

"What on earth are they?" the grumpy officer asked.

"*Katjesdrop*, Dutch liquorice," I laughed. "Taste one; they're really nice!" Without a glimmer of a smile he declined and we still had to open the other suitcase.

The two-hour flight to Alice Springs seemed to take forever. Oh! How I looked forward to hug our children one by one! I could picture them all waiting at the airport with Sam, as they had done when we came back from Adelaide four years earlier when we returned from our buying trip for our lovely spacious house. I pictured us getting home. Tanja, our German Shepherd, walking again after her hip-replacement, wagging her tail enthusiastically. A dozen pink and grey galahs screeching in the lemon-scented gumtrees above her head, oranges and grapefruit, the sweetest in the world, ready for picking. The sun shining in the bright blue sky as it had when we left for Holland more than seven weeks earlier. Alice Springs, our home forever no matter what would lay ahead...

How could we have stayed away so long?

The excitement of seeing Sam and all six of our children waving as the plane taxied past them at the old airport is indescribable for me.

Home Sweet Home! What a terrific joy to hug our children, just as I imagined it. Oh, how I had missed them and what a lovely big house we had. The garden looked even better than when we left. As promised, the old Scout truck, on which the boys and their friends had worked for months, had finally been taken somewhere else.

We had not bought many souvenirs, but the family had given us lots of gifts to take home for the kids. During the Christmas holidays Fred, the boys, Lilian and her boyfriend had made a 'train room' in the shed for the train set which had been stored in boxes all those years. They were delighted with the new miniature train and the railway crossings Fred had bought in Germany where they were a lot cheaper than in Holland. The stainless-steel cheese-cutters with wooden handles we bought for our friends for one dollar a piece, proved the best souvenirs we could have given them, as they were not available in Australia at the time.

When I went back to work at Old Timers the following Monday morning, I was greeted enthusiastically by the 'oldies' as well as by my colleagues. It was great to see my postcards from Holland in every room. For most of the residents it was the first private mail they had received in years.

Bulldozers had started on the upgrades and extensions of the A.I.M. complex at the beginning of the year, and great progress had been made while we were away. The little hospital was extended from six to fifty beds, and a row of new rooms was added onto the existing twelve, facing the road. The idea was that the residents would temporarily go to the hospital in town while the building was in progress, but the old 'bushies' decided to stay home. The six people in the little hospital were moved into three former staff flats nearby and a mobile kitchen was put beside the old storeroom. It was quite a balancing act to carry a heavy tray of food, to the hospital patients, dodging the bulldozer and the trucks, which often threw up tons of dust. Little did we know that the winter in 1977 would be the coldest on record; there were more than thirty nights of frost of up to eleven degrees below zero! The old people in the hostel were often shivering in their rooms, as the electricity had to be off frequently during the building works, and the falling debris made it too dangerous for them to sit in the sun to get warm. Half of them never made it into the new building, which was officially opened by the Prime Minister, Malcolm Fraser, in April 1978.

It was just as well that we did not know what lay ahead of us when we came back from Holland. I often wonder how we survived crisis after crisis during the two years that followed.

I was booked in to have a hysterectomy two weeks after we came home from the trip to Holland in May 1977, but the operation was cancelled at the last minute as the surgeon was unable to come to Alice Springs. For different reasons, varying from an outbreak of dysentery and unexpected emergencies, to the surgeon going on holiday two days before I was to be admitted, my appointment was cancelled another seven times; and always at the last minute.

I would say goodbye to my friends at work to go into hospital on Sunday, only to be told late on Friday afternoon that my surgery had been postponed for another three to six weeks. In the meantime, I had to keep my bag packed and the household organised for my three-week stay in hospital. As I was bleeding heavily for a couple of days each month, sometimes having to stay in bed for the first days, I became very run-down. While all this was going on, Matron Black was extremely helpful to me, putting me back on the roster, time and again.

Although I missed her terribly, I was very excited when Lilian went to Melbourne to become the nurse I had never been able to be, shortly after we came home from Holland. As there was an oversupply of nurses at the time, it had been very difficult for Molly to get her a place at Epworth Hospital where she worked. A few weeks after Lilian left, I was told that, because of my pending surgery, I was no longer acceptable for the nursing training course in the Alice Springs hospital, which just about broke my heart. I had so looked forward to making that dream true...

It made it hard for me to accept that nursing was not what my caring daughter wanted, when she came back three months later, homesick and engaged at nineteen. I burst into tears when, at the end of October my surgery was cancelled for the sixth time and I was booked into the hospital in Darwin two days before Christmas. It would be stinking hot and I didn't know a living soul in Darwin. I sobbed when I told Matron Black about it. She took me into the office, where our own doctor was having his weekly consultation that Friday afternoon. As we were not privately insured, he advised me to rush into town before closing time to become a member of a health insurance, as it was the last day of the offer of waiving the waiting time. When he rang me at home later that evening, he had booked me in with his surgeon friend in Adelaide for the following Thursday. Because I had nearly bled to death during previous surgery in Holland, I had to be there two days early to have some 'bleeding' tests. On Sunday afternoon the doctor rang again, very apologetic, as his friend was going on holiday the following morning, he would be away for six weeks and would operate on me as on his first day back at work.

Lilian started work in the kitchen at Old Timers in November, the day before Prince Charles came for a visit. Because we would all be introduced to the Prince, we had to be in full uniform that day. Most of us never wore stockings in summer, and we had to buy white lace-up shoes for the occasion, which we would never wear again. The whole place was buzzing with excitement before the Royal Visitor arrived. By the time he finally walked into the lounge-room of the new hospital, accompanied by the minister and the manager of the A.I M. who flew up from Sydney for the occasion, most of the oldies were tired of waiting. Matron Black, a very energetic and cheerful lady, who had been appointed to supervise the renovations, introduced us one by one to the Prince. George, the manager, looked more important than ever.

When Prince Charles shook hands with Blanche, the little Aboriginal lady, she answered his question about where she came from at length, then she asked; "You gimme a beer now?"

When it was my turn to shake Prince Charles' hand, he asked where I came from too and commented on my still strong accent. Like my colleagues, I was surprised how small he was. Everyone agreed that he was a likeable, down-to-earth guy.

Something went terribly wrong at the formal dinner, which was attended by a hundred people from all walks of life in the community. Nine of them ended up in hospital with food poisoning. Lilian's fiancé, who was invited because he was a Queen's Scout, was one of them. Howard was in hospital for more than a week. It was also a very difficult time for our friends Pat and John, who did the cooking for the Royal visitor. Pat had cooked for every visiting member of the Royal Family for fifteen years. The incident was later blamed on an exhibition of snakes that had been held in the old building the previous week; others said the fish had been off. We all felt terribly sorry for the Prince who suffered from what was later jokingly referred to as the 'Royal Shits'.

I finally left for Adelaide to have surgery at the end of November, on my own, as we could not afford for Fred to come with me. I had never been alone in such a big city before; Adelaide was almost as big as a whole province in Holland. I was nervous about the operation, but at least I would be home for Christmas, if everything went all right, of course...

After being unconscious for almost two days, I came to life in a room full of flowers. Dick and Joyce, our former neighbours in Holland, and their Dutch friends Jan and Coby who had visited us in Alice earlier in the year, took turns in visiting me every day. After the first week when I was no longer in a lot of pain, I thoroughly enjoyed their visits. I enjoyed talking with the nurses and learning about the lives of other women in the ward. I also loved reading a few good books, something I seldom had time for in our busy household. I received a lot of mail, including a huge card from my colleagues and the first love-letters from Fred in twenty years.

Because I nearly died when I had a 'prolapse repair' in Holland in 1970, and Fred's mother had died after a similar operation, Fred could not possibly stay at home when one of my protruding veins became infected two weeks after my surgery. As promised, my brother Henk and Robin drove up from Sale with their two little boys in the third week. Before I left the hospital, the surgeon warned me not to lift anything heavier than a few kilograms for at least six weeks. I was run-down and anaemic, however, so it would take me longer than that to recuperate.

On Saturday afternoon, the day after I came home from Adelaide the phone rang. "Oh my God!" I heard Fred say. "I'll be there immediately."

"Lilian rolled the car on Larapinta Drive," he called out to me when he put the phone down. "The Nissan is a write-off the fellow said."

"What about the kids?" I asked anxiously but he did not hear me anymore as the front door closed behind him. With a pounding heart I listened to the Mini roaring out of the driveway. Lilian had left with Richard to do some shopping when it had stopped raining only moments earlier. After waiting for almost an hour, imagining the worst, Fred rang from the hospital. The kids had been very lucky, he said. The ambulance had already taken them to hospital when he arrived at the scene. Lilian was badly bruised and shaken. She had lost control of the steering on the wet road. A cut in her head required seven stitches and one in Richard's knee needed seven. They were both kept in for observation until eleven o'clock that night. The Nissan was on its side with the roof caved in and the front window smashed. During the following weeks I wished that the damage to the Nissan's body would disappear by itself just as the many black bruises on Lilian and Richard's bodies did. The car was not insured and we had to use it without a top for eight months before we could afford to have it repaired. While the weather was still warm it was fun for most of us to drive the 'naked jeep', but when winter came with temperatures below zero in the morning, the novelty soon wore off, even for Lilian and Ray who both had their licences soon after they turned sixteen. Fred felt most embarrassed at having to drive the roofless Nissan for so long, which did nothing to relieve the tension in the house.

A couple of days after the accident, we received a letter from Holland saying that a motorist had scooped Mum up when she crossed a busy road on her pushbike. An accident was bound to happen; Mum seldom bothered to get off her bike or look around before she crossed the road. Like many older villagers she would simply put her arm out in the direction she was going and go for it, expecting the traffic to give her right of way. But this time she had actually stopped. She had let several cars pass when a motorist suddenly appeared from behind another car and hit her. She had already been in hospital three weeks when she wrote the letter. Her leg was badly broken in several places.

Although Mum was quite happy in the rehabilitation centre where she stayed for eight months, I was often homesick, wanting to be with the rest of the family who doted on her. Because a phone call was still far too expensive, I wrote long letters to her every week. She had kept them all and they were invaluable to me in compiling this story.

Feeling quite good again, I looked forward to going back to work at Old

Timers in the last week of February 1978. Matron Black had promised me light work, but as there was none, she helped me make the beds that morning. Within an hour I was shaking and I looked as white as the sheets we were putting on the beds. After the coffee break she sent home me for another two weeks of rest. When I tried again a fortnight later, the heavy work still proved too much for me. As it was not likely that there would be suitable work for me in the near future, I had no choice but to quit the job I loved so much, going back to sewing to supplement our income. Because we dreamed of Fred having his own business one day, I enrolled in a six-week receptionist course at the Community College (now TAFE) learning to type to the tune of 'the yellow rose of Texas' which was very confusing for me. Because an A sounded like an E and an E like an I to me, I kept mixing up the vowels. In the end I got a certificate that said something like '14 words a minute with 6 errors'. The teacher was obviously embarrassed to send it to me, as I received it in the mail two years later.

Fred was very worried about his future at the Panorama, as an unemployed neighbour had slowly taken over the heavy jobs from the cleaning lady. Henk had also let him paint the boards and make some frames, as he had done when we were away in Holland.

It was a welcome relief for us when, at the end of March '78 Henk and Elizabeth invited us to a local ball. The rest of the staff of the Panorama were also invited, the two girls who served in the gallery, Sady the cleaning lady and the neighbour and his wife. We had not been out for ages and danced the night, and our worries, away. We thoroughly enjoyed ourselves, cheerfully walking back to the car park with Henk and Elizabeth well after midnight, only to find that the Mini, my precious little car, had disappeared.

Stealing cars had become a real problem in town; joy riding by young white fellows as well as Aborigines who had soon learned how to hot-wire a car to drive home to the settlements. Like Sam had said before, up until a few years before we came, nobody bothered to lock the car in town, Henk said, while we walked to the police office to report the missing car. The officer on duty did not give us much hope of getting my beloved Mini back in one piece.

After a frustrating night, too angry to sleep, Fred went out with the boys in the roofless Nissan early on Sunday morning, to look for my little car. The police found it later that morning in a ditch on the road to an Aboriginal settlement twenty kilometres out of town. I was relieved to see that there was no further damage to the car other than it being covered in mud and the wires had been cut. It was a sorry sight for me to see the dirty Mini on a trailer behind the still topless Nissan, but at least it was back.

In the last week of March I had the first of a series of injections to block some of my varicose veins, which had been inflamed while I was in hospital.

272

As I had heard that those injections were extremely painful, it was a pleasant surprise that there was no pain at all apart from the prick of the needle. A few weeks earlier Mrs Higgins, the director of the Youth Centre had asked me to help make Dutch costumes for the yearly Bangtail Muster parade on Mayday, as their theme was Holland that year. Dressing one hundred and eighty children in a variety of realistic-looking Dutch costumes on a small budget was a very time consuming, and at times frustrating job, but I loved being involved and the result was well worth the effort.

Two days before the parade, I had to have my second injection to block off another of my troublesome veins. As the previous injection had given me no problems, I went without Fred. Although this time the treatment hurt and my leg was bandaged up from my foot to my crotch, I felt quite capable of driving home in the Mini. I was not at all prepared for the excruciating pain that welled up in my leg as soon as I drove out of the gate at the hospital. I decided to go straight home instead of calling in at the Panorama for Fred as I had promised. Within a few minutes the pain took my breath away. The feeling in my leg became so heavy that I could not move my foot on the accelerator. Realising that I had no hope of stopping the car, I prayed fervently that I would not have to give way at the coming intersections. Sweat was running off my face when I finally turned into our street and approached our driveway. I somehow managed to stop the Mini with a screeching noise and beeped the horn. Within seconds Fred, who had come home early, came running out of the house.

"What on earth happened?" he asked when he saw me crying with my head on my hands on the steering wheel.

Under a flood of pent-up tears I told him that I could not move my foot from the accelerator. With my arms around his neck, he carried me into the bedroom and laid me down on the bed. Always feeling uncomfortable with illness, he gave me a couple of aspirins and left me to it. The pain eventually subsided and I fell into a deep sleep.

My leg was still hurting when I sat proudly in one of the old-fashioned open buggies during the parade, surrounded by bright paper flowers and wearing the colourful Frisian costume I had made for myself. It was a delight for me to see all those little Dutchies in their bright costumes. The white caps worn by the girls, and the boys' clogs, which were made out of orange hessian donated by Henk Guth, received a lot of comments. My favourite was the group of girls dressed in the costumes of Bunschoten and Spakenburg, former fishing communities close to where I came from. With their typical rolled up hair-do and square shoulder caps they stole the hearts of many of our country-folk who watched the parade. Other people had made a huge windmill, cheese carriers and a street-organ. As usual, the Youth Centre had the biggest float and won the first price in the show.

As winter wore on the boys had straightened out the hood of the Nissan as well as they could, but as Fred felt ashamed to drive it, he took it to the panel beaters in town in August. When it came back as new a few weeks later, the Mini broke down again. As the cost of repairing it was too high, it had to be sold. With little hope for another in the near future, I missed my little car - my independence - terribly.

Another big blow came our way when we received a hefty bill from the hospital in Adelaide. We had expected the medical insurance to pay for everything, but it only covered the hospital bed, not any of the doctors' services and the use of equipment. I wrote to the A.I.M. asking about sickness benefits as my wages had stopped when I went into hospital. It was a great disappointment when they answered that I was not entitled to any compensation as a hysterectomy was classified as 'elective surgery'. Would people just have to let themselves bleed to death?, we wondered.

Then, at the beginning of June, Fred was told that as of the first of July, the start of the new financial year, he was no longer needed to make the frames for Henk so that Louis, his neighbour could have a full-time job. Although we had seen it coming, losing the job he loved after seven years was a very bitter pill for Fred to swallow. However, later on we saw that it had been a blessing, as it had opened the door to owning our own business.

It was a great relief when, a couple of days after the devastating news, an elderly lady in town took Fred on as her new picture framer at her bookshop and art gallery in the main street. After he cleaned out the incredible mess in her tiny workshop the following week, she ordered new guillotines for him to cut mouldings and mats, but she avoided the subject of pay. During the next four weeks, we called in every Sunday after Mass, asking what she was prepared to pay, either per frame or on a weekly wage. After ignoring us for half an hour or more, she would tell Fred to come back the following week, saying that she was still waiting for her accountant to come up with the figures. In the last week of June, Fred was making frames at the Panorama when a tall man in his early forties called in. Introducing himself as the eccentric gallery-owner's new picture framer, he asked Fred for the keys of her workshop. Fuming with rage, Fred went to see the old lady, who calmly told him that there would be plenty of work for both of them. But by that time, Fred had had enough and decided to leave them to it.

It was a sad day for both of us when Fred left Panorama Guth. Within six months we had both lost our jobs while we still had five teenagers living at home to be fed and educated. On top of that, Lilian and Howard planned to get married in September and, according to tradition, we were expected to pay for our daughter's wedding. While all this was going on, I was devastated

274

when a silly misunderstanding cost me my friendship with my closest friend Beth, just when I needed her support so much.

At the beginning of July Fred held his first painting exhibition at home in the back yard, and sold some of the dozen landscape paintings on display. While we were talking to Alison, our neighbour, about the successful day, the phone rang. It was the hospital: our two eldest sons and their friends had rolled their car on the old South Road. Alison, who was a doctor, scolded us for our carelessness; she had seen them leave; five or six of them including Simone and her friend Lynne, in the back of the open tray. Eugene had been working all week on his pride and joy, the old utility he had bought recently. Together with Ray, they had filled the dents with putty and they were preparing it for spray-painting that morning. We had been so busy talking to people that we had not even noticed that the car was gone.

Relieved of our anxiety, we both cried with laughter when we saw all six of them sitting in the waiting room at the hospital, covered in red dust, their hair sticking up in all directions. They had been very lucky that the kids in the back had been thrown free of the car. We were also relieved to hear that Ray was driving; Eugene didn't have a licence. His friend beside him in the cabin had a broken nose. Another lesson none of them would forget easily.

It was about that time Fred had a sudden cramp in his chest while he sat peacefully smoking a cigarette. He put it out until the pain had gone. As the same thing happened when he had another puff a little later, he put the cigarette out again, screwed the packet up and threw it in the rubbish bin in the kitchen. He had tried to retrieve it later but I had taken it immediately to the big bin in the driveway, glad that he had finally decided to give that expensive, foul-smelling habit away. We all hated him smoking, especially in the car. Although he became difficult to live with for a while, he persevered, encouraged by our happiness of the fresh air in our house as well as in the car. Unbeknown to him I later saved up the money that would otherwise have gone up in smoke. It was a very proud moment for me when I could hand him the cash to buy the stereo tower he wished for. Thankfully, none of our children picked up this dangerous habit.

We could surely do with an outing when Pat and John invited us to a 'fishing seminar' a few weeks later, held at their hideout called 'Chitabine Lodge' at Harts Range, seventy kilometres north-east of town. The name, 'sheet-of-iron' came from their Aboriginal friends who guided them into the ranges, looking for gemstones. About a hundred people were staying the night in campervans, tents and swags. Pat only wanted us to bring our own drinks and some fresh bread and lettuce, as there was no shop at the nearby police post. I had a marvellous time talking to some of the Aborigines and station people about their way of life in the bush, and in turn answering their questions about our immigration and what life on the land was like in Holland.

As always, Pat and John cooked a beautiful meal. Apart from lots of different steaks cooked on the barbeque, Pat deep-fried large chunks of fresh fish, caught by John and his mates in Borroloola, in the far north of the Territory, on his latest fishing trip. Later that night, by the light of a torch, we helped them bury cardboard fish in all shapes and sizes deep into the loose sand of the dry creek beside the tin shed they lived in. Early the following morning the children dug them up enthusiastically.

One of the guests, a well-known businessman, had fallen asleep close to the fire the previous night, too drunk to notice burning the inside of his thighs. His wife was not amused when she saw the blisters and he later allowed the kids to bury him up to his neck in the cool sand. He just lay there contentedly smoking a cigarette, encouraging the kids to pile more sand over his body and keep it wet.

After a late breakfast with heaps of bacon, eggs, sausages, tomatoes and onions fried on the barbeque, there was a shooting competition with clay targets. As most of the men had drunk too much the previous night to aim accurately, the prize, a set of beautiful gold-rimmed liqueur glasses was won by our eldest son Ray, who had become a member of the local gun club when he turned eighteen a few weeks earlier.

Another of those family outings that had kept us sane during that difficult time, was a weekend camping at Glen Helen, a hundred and twenty-five kilometres to the west, where we swam in the beautiful gorge. I realised how dangerous those deep waterholes were when I got bad cramp in my legs in the middle of the big pool. I was extremely grateful that Fred was swimming beside me, holding my head above water until the debilitating pain subsided. Come to think of it, he never swam in another waterhole, reluctantly letting me go in after he made me promise him, quite unnecessarily, to stay close to the edge.

Our three youngest children were playing 'shop' with sultanas and other goodies in the back of the Nissan, when two wild donkeys in the area joined them, eating the sweet treats out of their hands. A group of visiting Italians later dared each other to have a ride on one of the docile-looking donkeys. When, after quite some time, a fat, balding man finally sat back to front on one of the animals, another fellow hit the donkey with a branch he had ripped off a nearby gum tree. The donkey did not take much notice when the fellow on its back grabbed its tail, but when his friend hit the donkey again, he screamed and the donkey bolted. Everyone doubled up with laughter as we watched the donkey disappear over a hill, the poor man holding tightly onto its tail, just like Dick Trom in a famous Dutch comic film.

When one door closes another door usually opens...

After Fred left the Panorama, he got some work at the local joinery. Even though a bitterly cold wind blew through the open shed and he had to work with out-dated machinery again, he enjoyed the company of the other men he worked with and the variety of projects he made instead of only picture frames. Because Fred was no real cabinetmaker, a tradesman, he needed a lot more time to make an item. That made him nervous and irritable, especially when he had to quote in advance. Because his English had not improved much over the years, he often felt isolated and 'left out'. He missed the Dutch jokes he had shared with Henk terribly.

When in 1983, six of our family members came over from Holland to celebrate our silver wedding anniversary, Simone, our then twenty-year-old daughter said one day rather surprised:

"Gosh! I haven't heard Papa laugh so much since we left Holland, when I was eight."

In his spare time, Fred continued to paint landscapes. Unfortunately, he needed to be relaxed to be able to paint. The other way around, painting as a form of relaxation, would have saved us a lot of hardship in the future!

Although Fred was home a lot, I felt more and more lonely and isolated after losing my colleagues and my daily contact with the old folks. When, at the beginning of July, Matron Black asked if I would help Lorna in the office two days a week, I was beside myself with joy. It was absolute heaven for me to see the surprised look on the faces of my old friends, when they saw me sitting behind my desk. Although I often came home with a headache from all the new things my rusty brain had to absorb, I loved my job in the new office, which was a hell of a lot easier than nursing had been in the old place!

At the end of August 1978, nine months after my surgery, I was simply bursting with energy. I could not understand how some women complained that having their womb removed made them feel less of a woman. I was surely much better off without it. But then of course, mine had well and truly done its job! Apart from going to the office and to the college two days a week, I did the alterations for my old friend Pat's dress shop in town again and I was busy sewing for Lilian's wedding.

How times have changed! At the time Lilian was working at Old Timers and she lived in a staff unit on the premises. When we recalled the things that happened around the time of her wedding, Lilian reminded me how I had refused to finish her wedding dress shortly before her wedding day. I had been furious, saying that she no longer deserved to wear a white dress. I was dumbfounded at first, then I remembered...

It was one of those painful, humiliating facts I had conveniently forgotten. I had been beside myself with fury when I heard that Howard had spent the night in her flat, a couple of weeks before the wedding. Not only had I been terribly disappointed that my sensible eldest daughter had betrayed my trust in her, but she had broken the rules at Old Timers. Word had spread quickly through the complex and the disapproving looks of my older colleagues and the twinkle in the eyes of others had been too much for me to bear.

I sat staring at the last paragraph for a while. What a hypocrite I was! Had I forgotten that I slept at Fred's place many times when we were courting? At seventeen! Sure, Fred's father was always home, but he slept downstairs. Mum must have been worried sick when I was away for the weekend. Or had she been able to sleep peacefully after handing her concerns for my safety to God, like she always did when something was bothering her? However, I don't remember having any ill feelings towards either of them on the wedding day. Fred would probably have reminded me how near to impossible it had been for us to wait until we were married, only twenty years earlier. My only concern was that Howard was so young. Although she was only nineteen, Lilian was mature enough, but twenty was far too young for any fellow to make such a commitment.

Lilian's simple but elegant satin wedding dress, with a short chiffon cape, was ready in time. I also made the lovely pale-green dresses in the same style for Simone and the other two bridesmaids, Regine's long mauve dress with flowery frills, my own long, dark blue dress as well as a suit for each of our three sons. The result was well worth the effort and frustration to get it all ready in time, as everyone looked great on the day and I had saved a small fortune. Although Fred was reluctant to accept Howard's parents' offer of sharing the cost of the reception and dinner party as it was held at home in the garden, it enabled us to invite all the young couple's family, friends and colleagues.

My brother, Henk, drove up from Sale in Victoria a week before the wedding, with Robin and their two little sons, to help us with the preparations and the cooking. It was a real surprise for us when Jolanda, our Dutch friend we had met on the boat, flew up from Melbourne on the day before the wedding, staying for a week. Apart from the fun and laughter we had with her, Jolanda had also saved us the cost and time of having to go to a hairdresser.

According to tradition, Lilian spent the last night before her wedding day at home. The young couple would go to a hotel for their wedding night, then move into a flat nearby which belonged to Howard's parents. They planned a belated honeymoon in Holland the following spring much to my mother's delight. Unfortunately that would not happen, as they never had any money for such extravagance.

No wedding ever seemed to go without something going wrong. In the evening before the happy event Jolanda and I were struggling for ages to iron out the hems of the circular frills at the bottom of the bridesmaids' satin dresses, which kept twisting.

"Serves me right for being a lazy dressmaker, doing them by machine instead of by hand as I'm taught," I berated myself. While we talked about the fast way things were changing, a blood-curling scream came from Simone's bedroom. The door flew open and Lilian rushed out, crying loudly. Her hand covered her left eye, a trickle of blood dripped down her bare arm. Simone followed, looking ashen.

"Get Alison! Quick!" Lilian yelled. "My eye! My eye!"

I dropped the iron and Jolanda grabbed a packet of frozen strawberries, the first thing she saw, from the freezer.

"What happened?" we asked in unison.

I'll never forget the terrified look in Lilian's eyes when we insisted she take her hand away and let us have a look before we took her to Alison, the doctor next door. Looking as white as a ghost, Simone told us how they had put the desk lamp on a higher shelf so that she could see better and it had tumbled down on Lilian's face while she was plucking her sister's eyebrows. The sharp edge of the cheap metal lamp had made a two centimetre cut in Lilian's cheek, just below her eye. Jolanda assured her that it did not look too bad but the worried look on my face and Fred's impatience to take her to Alison right away did nothing to calm Lilian's nerves. With the packet of frozen strawberries on her face, Fred took her next door a moment later.

Alison had put two 'butterfly' bandages over the wound, which she carefully removed the following afternoon. Fred had been stunned at the doctor's reaction, scolding him about the accident. Alison, a single lady in her early sixties, worked for the Royal Flying Doctor Service. She had seen the most awful cases. A few weeks earlier, she had gone with a rescue-team to treat a man who had fallen into a ravine while climbing at King's Canyon. There had been a picture of her in the paper carrying the patient, whose leg was broken, back to the homestead on a stretcher with a ranger. Alison later apologised for her outburst, saying that she felt sorry for Lilian who would have a black eye on her wedding day and she was sick and tired of the people's carelessness.

Although it was regarded bad luck for the couple to see each other on the night before the wedding, we broke with tradition and called Howard to comfort Lilian, as she was still very distressed. Thanks to the ice, the bandages and the cream Alison had put on her cheek, we did not have a 'bride with a black eye' after all; when Jolanda was finished with her makeup, the wound was hardly visible.

Howard was not a Catholic, therefore they were married in the Uniting Church on the 30th of September, 1978. We had stopped going to church every Sunday quite some time ago, so we had no problem with their 'mixed' marriage.

279

I did not have to worry about Mum's reaction either. Although she had been a nun for four years before she married my father, she had always believed that God was there for everybody, regardless of religion. Like her, I was happy that they wanted to be married in a church and to have God's blessing.

On the day after the wedding we went with Jolanda Simpson's Gap. Because it had rained a lot in August the wildflowers were out in profusion. The large patches of red, blue, yellow and white wildflowers between the flowering bushes and trees at where reminded us of being in the famous 'Keukenhof' in Holland. I don't remember having seen such a mass of colour around 'The Alice' in the springtime since.

Such a pity Sam wasn't there! He had finally gone to Holland the previous November, for the first time since he had left home almost nineteen years earlier. He was obviously enjoying himself, 'gallivanting around Europe in his flash car', Mum wrote. Sam had bought a Triumph TR7 while he was in England, visiting Lindsay. Our hope of Sam marrying her had vanished when he wrote that he was now working for an American base in Germany, where he had a new girlfriend. Mum was very disappointed that Sam was rarely home for more than a couple of days, but he was taking her to Canada before he returned to Australia. As always on important occasions, I had also missed the rest of my family, especially my mother, my only sister and my youngest brothers Wim and Ties: the price we had to pay for leaving Holland.

Shortly after Lilian's wedding our family participated in the Folklorico, which had been held at the Alice Springs High School for the first time the previous year. With the help of our Dutch friends Margot, Tilly and Marianne, a Dutch nurse who had just started work at Old Timers, we prepared several different Dutch specialities to sell in our food stall, my first attempt at cooking for the public at large. Because the first Folklorico had been such a huge success, we made an enormous amount of oliebollen batter and hundreds of little meatballs, to be fried on the spot and served hot with mustard. We also made over a hundred *slaatjes;* individual small potato salads made with ham, carrots, peas, onions, gerkins, raw apple, mustard and mayonnaise. I hardly slept the night before the event worrying about everything that could go wrong and having to throw most of the food out. My worries proved unnecessary, like ninety-nine percent of them usually are. Within two very busy hours the lot was sold out and a nice amount of profit could be handed to the school's fund-raising committee. After we packed up, we had plenty of time to watch the variety of dancers in their colourful costumes, see the many other countries' displays and taste their different dishes; incredible what a splendid job most people had made of their stalls. Wearing the Frisian costume I had made for the Youth Centre's Mayday parade, I felt proud to be involved again.

Tired, but still highly stimulated by the happy event, I decided to call in at

280

Sam's flat, the granny-flat beside the big house where we had started our life in Alice Springs four years earlier. Sam had rung from Germany the previous evening asking us to have a look, as the young fellow who lived in it had not paid him any rent for months.

Memories of the old leaking caravans and having to sleep without any form of air-conditioning in those stinking hot months after our arrival, flooded back to me when I entered the property. How lucky we were that Pat Govers had brought us all those household items, and that Sam's friends Bill and Pat Dooley had let us strangers use their house with everything in it over the Christmas holidays. I remembered the disappointment when we still had to go back into the hot caravans, as Sam's house was still not ready for us to move in.

A dreadful stench nearly knocked me over when I opened the door of the flat and stared at the mess in front of me. Dirty clothes were scattered around everywhere and a mouldy breakfast stood on the table; the guy had obviously left in a hurry weeks ago. When I opened the fridge, the revolting smell of rotting meat took my breath away. I quickly closed the door and ran out of the flat, holding my nose. Suddenly feeling worn-out from the long day on my feet, I went home where Fred had started to clean our own mess from cooking, waiting for me impatiently. He went to the flat and came back with a notice saying that the electricity had been cut off six weeks earlier as the bill had not been paid; so, the flat could wait.

The following morning, a Sunday, we went early to Sam's place to clean the revolting mess. With a clothes peg on my nose and having to run into the fresh air to stop me from throwing up, I helped Fred dump the lot in a hole he had dug in the back yard. When we came home several hours later, Robin rang from Victoria; Henk had had an accident a couple of days earlier, she said. He would be in hospital for quite some time but we should not worry; his condition was now stable. My stomach cringed when Robin told me that a blade of the angle-grinder Henk was working with on the two-story house he was building had exploded. A piece of the blade had hit him in the stomach. Clutching his belly he had jumped off the two-metre high scaffolding and lay crawling in the grass. His work-mate had taken him to the hospital where the nurses had laughed at him for making such a noise over a cut that only required a few stitches. As the excruciating pain persisted they had kept him in for observation during the night, making fun of him when he whined in pain. Because Henk was very ill the next morning an x-ray had been taken which showed that a piece of the blade had severed his bowel from his stomach. He had been rushed to the operating theatre immediately where a drain was put in.

Two weeks later, Henk came out of hospital having to wear a 'bag' for six weeks. By that time, the connection of his intestine would have healed sufficiently to have the bag removed. We had an urgent call from my sister-in law when he was back in hospital shortly after Christmas.

"It's Robin, Mien. Would you please come and see if you can talk some sense into that stubborn brother of yours?" she asked. Her voice broke when she continued in her hurried way of speaking: "Things went terribly wrong. Henk has lost his trust in the doctors… he refuses to eat or drink… he looks like a ghost… the doctor said he'll die if he doesn't start eating soon."

When I talked to Henk earlier he had told me that he firmly believed that his intestine would heal by itself if he let them rest, but you had no say in the matter when you were in a hospital. Shortly after the reconnection, Henk had been 'standing on his head' with pain. When the pain had persisted, his abdomen had been opened again; his bowel had twisted, causing the excruciating pain. As there are some five or six metres of twisting and curling intestines in a human body it seemed amazing to me that it could be joined without that happening.

Henk had already been in intensive care for more than three weeks, when Jolanda picked me up from the airport in Melbourne and drove me straight to the hospital in Sale, some three hundred kilometres further. I'll never forget the terrified look on my brother's face, his dark-rimmed eyes sunken deep into their sockets. Because he had ripped the drip out several times, he was tied to the bed. Holding my hand tightly, he told me of his fear of the hospital. They wanted to open him up again, but Henk refused, and he was afraid to eat, as that would hurt too much.

"If he would only drink, he'll be on his feet in no time," the nurse, who had shown us into his room, said. I was grateful that Jolanda was with me; she worked in a hospital with severely handicapped children, and had a lot more experience with sick people than I had. She patiently explained to Henk that the body could do without food for a while, but as eighty percent of it consisted of water, it needed plenty of nourishing liquid to survive. But Henk was adamant that fasting was the way to go: "If I don't eat, it won't hurt" he kept saying.

Henk doesn't remember any of these details. He was adamant that he had never refused to eat other than in the first week. He had pulled the intravenous tubes out in sympathy with an old man who had pulled his out. Henk had been disgusted seeing how a group of doctors and nurses had jumped on the old fellow forcing the tubes back in. We know now that shortage of fluid affects our brain, which causes electrolyte and salt disturbance to the extent that we can't think clearly. According to a friend, who is a doctor, Henk's story is highly unlikely. The strong drugs he was getting for such a long time would have made him hallucinate, which becomes very real to the patient.

Jolanda stayed the night. Before she went back to Lilydale the following morning, she managed to persuade Henk to take a few sips of milk with a promise to start eating. It was strange for both of us to be with my brother's religious family who did not acknowledge the birth of Christ at Christmas. I wanted to fry oliebollen on New Year's Eve, but Henk asked me not to mention it as it might upset Robin; their religion did not approve of celebrating that either. But Robin loved to try new recipes and we ended up frying some after all. Before I returned to Alice a few days after New Year (1979), Henk was well on his way to recovery, joking about his abdomen looking like a street-map, and happily eating the freshly baked oliebollen I had brought with me.

One of the hospital doctors later apologised for the mistakes that had been made. Although Henk and Robin were angry about it for a while, they never asked for compensation, which they would have had to consider if the hospital had persisted with the eleven-thousand-dollar bill.

Accidents do happen and every one of us makes mistakes. People in power don't seem to realise that the world becomes unliveable when hospitals and doctors are faced with being sued, often for millions of dollars. It makes everybody nervous: the increasing high cost of insurance is already crippling social events, volunteering and fundraising as well as the many sporting groups, which keep our youngsters occupied and off the streets.

In March 1979, Sam finally came back to Alice from his extended trip to Europe and Canada, after showing off his white sports car to his friends in Victoria and Queensland, looking like a tramp with his bald scalp and his fluffy shoulder-length hair. He reluctantly let me cut it after being pestered about it for weeks by everyone who knew him.

At that time, Regine and a friend from school had been to what was referred to as the local zoo, a property owned by a rather eccentric old couple. Roy the owner had asked Regine to bring her sister next time to ride his horses because they needed to be exercised everyday, and he was too old to do it himself. As we would not have to pay for the girls' lessons, I had no trouble persuading Fred to see what it was all about.

Half a dozen big, colourful parrots welcomed us with a cheery 'Hello' when we arrived at the Morgan's property. There were lots of other birds in shabby cages and just flying around the house and kangaroos, rabbits, chickens, ducks and ostriches were all mixing happily together in the untidy yard. In a nearby paddock, a huge white buffalo stood staring at us.

After a while Regine pulled us impatiently to the other side of the old farmhouse where Roy, a slender man in his early seventies, was exercising two beautiful Arabs running in a circle on long ropes, which he held firmly in his hands. He was wearing a suit and tie. When he spotted us he tied the horses on the railing and shook hands with Fred, briefly lifting his hat to us.

While we were talking his wife joined us.

'Auntie Bo' was a big woman. Her nearly white hair, tucked into a dainty white net, her bright red lipstick and her wide flowery skirt were in stark contrast with her beige men's shirt with large pockets, tucked into her skirt and thick socks in heavy workmen's boots. Her left eye was closed permanently and she had little sight in the other. After I introduced myself she looked at Regine and Simone on the horses, then back to me, asking abruptly: "Are you their mother? Do you teach your girls how to cook?"

"They are better cooks than I am," I laughed.

"Oh! Good! When I married Roy I could only cook steak on a barbecue," she replied. "One day my neighbour gave me a handful of peas she grew in her own garden. There were only a few, six or seven, maybe a dozen of them. I didn't have a clue what to do with the funny looking things," she continued, chuckling at the memory. "I made a fire in the backyard, filled the big pot with water and hung it above the fire. While it came to the boil I had another look at the peas, opened them up and took the seeds out. I didn't think Roy would like 'm and gave 'm to the pigs."

When the water boiled Bo had thrown the shells in and watched them "dancing like canoes on a river". Her belly shook with laughter when she told me how she had thrown the shells on the lawn, boiling water and all, then picked them of the ground and gave them to the pigs too.

While the girls were riding, Bo told us about the white buffalo she had reared with a bottle as the mother had rejected it when it was a baby. Saying that it would be a very sad day for them when they had to leave the place, she invited Fred and me to the house for a 'cuppa' and to see the other animals they had accumulated over the years. A five-foot long perentie walked past us when we got inside. The house was no more than a shelter with a dirt floor, divided into a kitchen, a family room and a bedroom. While our eyes adjusted to the dark, another dozen parrots greeted us from their cages in a passage. We admired the beautiful creatures, feeling sorry for them being locked up. We had to be careful not to tread on lizards, rabbits and the little chicks with their mothers, while dodging the many pigeons that were flying around in the living room where cobwebs were left hanging like curtains from the corrugated iron roof to the floor, left there to 'catch mosquitoes'. Some lizards of different shapes and sizes scurried up and down the rough rammed-earth walls and a mouse ran past our feet while Bo chased a hen that was scratching around on the table between beautiful porcelain teacups. A piece of hessian above the table prevented droppings from the chickens roosting on the open rafters from falling on the table. It was no wonder the health department wanted them to get rid of the animals and move into a proper house, but the old couple were clean and content, determined to stay as long as they could.

The girls loved riding Roy's horses and I enjoyed taking them there. It was very humbling for me to learn more about Bo's life; it always made our own troubles melt as snow before the sun. She grew up in some remote part of the South Australian bush, the only girl with eleven brothers. From a very early age, Bo had always worked in the bush with her father and brothers, mustering and driving the cattle to the railway station in Marree from where they were transported to the abattoirs in the cities. Until she married Roy she had never been in a suburban house. When she was twelve, a camel had bitten her nine-year-old brother while they were working close to their house. As her father was working a long way from home, Bo's mother, who just had another baby, had bandaged the boy's leg and sent her to take her brother to the railway station in Marree from where they would travel by train to the nearest doctor in Port Augusta. Blood had seeped through the bandage as soon as they left. Bo had tried to make the two-hour ride on horseback as smooth as possible but her brother had been crying out with pain all the way. While they were waiting for the train he had just about lost consciousness. The attendant had given him a drink and changed the bandage. That was when Bo saw that the camel had ripped a big chunk of meat off the back of her brother's leg. Fearing that he would die, they had to wait for hours for the train that took them from Marree to the hospital in Port Augusta, another three hundred and eighty kilometres further south. Her brother had been in a critical condition when they arrived but he survived the ordeal.

After working for the local joinery for a year, Fred detested having to go into other people's places to do the often difficult and time-consuming jobs. It was a great relief for both of us when he was asked to renovate a cottage for the new matron at Old Timers the following autumn, even though he had instructions to use as many old materials as possible. However, when he finished six weeks later, the architect at 'Head-Office' in Sydney wasn't happy with the result and the mission refused to pay for his wages and the materials he had paid out of his own pocket. It took the temporary manager who had supervised the job three months to ensure Fred was finally paid. As my part-time job had to see our family through, things went from bad to worse at home as well as at work.

After the renovation of the new matron's cottage, she started to avoid me at times, pretending that I was not there at all. By the end of the year I suffered from all sorts of ailments, including a sore stomach, backache and migraine. I had come to hate myself for crying at the drop of a hat, which made Fred angry, saying "Quit the bloody job!" time and again. After some tests in hospital, the specialist advised me that I should leave before I had a total breakdown, as that was obviously the cause of all my trouble.

Apart from the cabinets he made at the joinery, Fred also made frames at home for Carl van Nieuwmans, another well-known Dutch-born artist in Alice Springs. Carl, also called the 'Rembrandt of the Centre' bought lengths of raw timber which Fred 'dressed' (stained, coloured, varnished and lined) before he made them into the required sized frames.

Going into business was a real eye-opener for us. Soon after we started advertising picture framing we were advised by the town council that we were not permitted to run a business from home, we needed a 'home-economic' licence but when I asked for the paperwork at the government office they had never heard of such a thing. Then an inspector of the taxation office called in, followed by a letter from the electricity commission to say that we needed a separate power connection as electricity for business was a lot dearer than for a household. In Holland it was the other way around. On top of that we had the police on our doorstep to inspect the moulding as some had gone missing from the art-gallery owner's workshop in town. As Fred had already sold several paintings at his first exhibition, we decided to take the plunge and start our own gallery and picture-framing business in one of the many new shops that had just been built on the edge of town.

With money borrowed from Sam and a belly full of butterflies, we made another dream come true when 'Bloms' opened on New Year's Day, 1980. We soon found that running a business, having to pay the high cost of renting and other overhead costs, was not as easy as we had expected, but our shop soon flourished. Shortly after opening, Fred was asked to teach leadlighting at the local craft council and to supply the materials.

When, in February 1981, my youngest brother Ties came to Australia with his wife, Elly, and three small children, we extended our business with art-materials and leadlighting supplies, which provided Ties with a job until he found work in his own field of earthmoving. Life has been good to them in Alice Springs too. Their three adult children have no desire to live elsewhere in the near future either.

At the age of forty-eight, Sam married Rita, a lovely lady from Jakarta in May 1986. They have two beautiful teenage daughters. At sixty-four Sam is now building his retirement home on his property in Queensland.

On the 13th of October 1981 we celebrated being in Alice Springs ten years with a delicious dinner in one of the many hotels in town. Towards the end of the evening Eugene, then twenty-one, stood up and raised his glass to us. Our eyes filled with tears when he said: "To Mum and Dad! Coming to Australia is the best thing they could ever have done for us!"

Our other five children applauded; they all agreed with him wholeheartedly.

The Australian Government wasn't particularly interested in Fred, the officer in The Hague said when we applied for emigration; at forty-one he was too old. They wanted our children, Australia's future.

When they were teenagers, our children could not wait to leave Alice, but most of them came back to settle. Lilian, Ray, Eugene and Regine and seven of our eleven grandchildren are still living here, while Simone is happy in Perth and Richard in Darwin with our other four grandchildren.

Retired now, Fred and I are happy to be able to give something back for the privilege of being here in this beautiful country with its variety of cultures, wide open spaces and clear blue skies. Fred is making a lot of people happy with his hobby of building and demonstrating street-organs, teaching a bit of our Dutch culture in the process. I hope to do the same by caring for my elderly friends and writing our stories, thankful for meeting such a variety of weird and wonderful people who have made our immigration to the centre of Australia such a colourful adventure.

Epilogue

Tired, but happy with the progress I had made with my writing one afternoon in 1997, I was sitting in the lounge-room, sipping a cup of tea with my son Eugene and his wife Cindy. Eugene had been helping me for hours, editing the story about our first camping trip to Ayers Rock in 1975 while I was working at Old Timers, correcting spelling mistakes and talking about the logic of the sentences. As always, we had lengthy discussions about the different ways he and I perceived the happenings at the time. Eugene was ten when we came to Australia. I am extremely grateful to his teacher who insisted that he learned the basics of the English language properly. He is very critical about every aspect of my writing and I liked it that way, as it kept me on my toes.

"I'm not looking forward to writing about the time I worked at Old Timers," I said thoughtfully. "I've been putting it off for quite a while but I'll make a new start with it tomorrow."

"Why is that?" Cindy asked, "I always thought you liked it there."

"I did! I loved it very much, but it will bring back a lot of very painful memories too," I replied.

"I'll tell you now, Mum, I will never read, let alone edit anything you write about Old Timers!" Eugene warned me. "I could not bear your crying and complaining all the time. You made us all sick to death with your continuous whingeing about the bloody place."

I looked at him, stunned. I always wanted my children to be honest with me but I felt as if he had stuck a knife into me, which he slowly turned when he continued: "We all hated it. Dad and Ray and I just closed off as soon as you started to complain, when you came home. Why you didn't give the bloody job away, I'll never understand!"

By that time tears were dripping down my face.

"How can you say a thing like that?" Cindy asked angrily. "How can you be so cruel?" I just sat there shaking my head.

"You had no idea what was happening to me at the time, did you?" I asked softly, overwhelmed with all the emotions that came rushing over me. "Just like Fred, you all closed your eyes at the time. It did not make any difference to him that I loved the old people. He just wanted me to quit and have me home all the time. He hated to have to get up a bit earlier in the morning to make sure that the kids got to school in time," I sobbed.

That evening I wrote about the incident in my journal, listing all the things that had happened during those four and a half years I worked there and how I felt at the time. Looking at it all, wondering how we managed to survive, I was stunned when I realised that I had forgotten that I had also lost my best friend, Beth, during that difficult period of time; first by a silly argument and later when she lost her battle with cancer.

When I finished writing the list of all we had been through since our return from Holland, I asked Fred to read it. At first he refused, as my journal is private, but he reluctantly agreed when I said: "It's never easy to communicate verbally, so you might as well read how I feel. We are still wanting to get to know each other better, aren't we?" I challenged him. I had waited till the program on the TV had finished but he did not want to switch it off. While he read the four pages, I tried to concentrate on an article in a magazine. It annoyed me that he was still stopping to smile at the singer on the screen as I had hoped for his undivided attention on something that was so important to me. But the wriggling of his stockinged feet, resting on the coffee table, told me that it was touching him emotionally.

"God, how I hated it all!" he said when he put my journal down. "It was awful for me to see that the job made you so unhappy but I could not make you stay at home no matter how hard I tried."

"But can't you see what it meant to me?" I asked, annoyed at his stubbornness. "I could not just leave because we had trouble with a matron! I loved the old people. They made me feel good about myself and they appreciated every little thing I did for them."

I reminded him that our four eldest children were already in high school when I had started and that I was home at three-thirty in the afternoon whenever I had an early shift. I also pointed out that I was very conscious of keeping the place clean, the sewing under control, which included an endless need for repairs, making curtains for the new house, school uniforms, etc. and I had the evening meal prepared for them when I had an evening shift.

"Have a look through the photo album," I said. "I was amazed at the number of new dresses, ballet costumes and outfits I had made for dress-ups and special events." But Fred remained adamant that I had grossly neglected them as a wife and mother.

He had been quite surprised when I told him a few months earlier how I had fallen in love with Jim, who was still a good family friend.

After all we had talked about, I felt terribly hurt when Fred still insisted that I had made life miserable for everyone at home from the day I had started at Old Timers in May 1975 until the day I could not take any more, in December 1979.

As I didn't want my children to bottle up their feelings as I had always done, I asked them one by one the same question during the week that followed: "Tell me honestly how you felt about me during the time that I worked at the Old Timers Home".

The first one I asked was Ray, the eldest of the boys.

"I don't remember ever feeling bad about it," he said. "I know that you cried a lot as there were always a lot of problems but, as I couldn't do anything about it, I went happily on my own merry way." I told him what Eugene had said.

"Really?" Ray said. "I wonder why he felt like that. But don't let it upset you; Eugene is very critical about everything and everybody anyway. I can truly say that it did not bother me in the least, apart from feeling sorry for you, of course," he added.

When I asked Lilian, she sat looking at her hands for a while, adjusting her rings.

"If anything, I feel terrible that we supported you so little at the time," she said thoughtfully. "I look back on a marvellous youth."

Now it was my time to say: "Really?"

"Yeah, I was always out and about with my friends," she answered.

"Fred reckons that I made you take the responsibility to run the household," I said.

Lilian assured me that she had never felt that way, ever. She knew that my mother had made me look after my brothers and sister from a very early age and that I had hated it so much that I had not wanted that to happen to my eldest daughter. While we were talking, Fred came in and asked Lilian about all those times she had to cook and clean.

"It wasn't like that at all," she replied. "I only cooked an occasional meal of spaghetti or macaroni for the rest I only cooked when I felt like it."

Later on that evening I rang Simone in Queensland.

"Don't worry about me," she laughed when I asked her the same question. "I was such a selfish pig at that time, that I would never have taken any notice of anyone else but me."

"But I remember you being very angry with me, crying that I was never there when you needed me," I reminded her.

"Oh; did I? When was that?" she asked.

"We had been in Holland when you had your first period," I said.

"Oh, yes, I remember," she said. "How could you do that to me? You knew that that was going to happen sooner or later, didn't you? Here I was with the most important thing that was happening in my life and you were on the other side of the world! How dare you!" she laughed.

Richard, our youngest son, who lives in Darwin, assured me that the only problem he had in his young life was the fact that he could never do any good in the eyes of his big brothers. He had only pleasant memories of me working at Old Timers as he often came with me and he liked talking to the old folks.

"No; I don't have any bad feelings at all about you going out to work," he said.

Regine's only sour grapes was the fact that I had let her stay with our strict Catholic friends when we had gone to Holland in 1977, she said.

"But you liked it there; I still have the letter you wrote to us to prove it," I protested.

"Oh, yes! But you don't realise what you had done to me, do you?" she complained. "They made me pray the rosary, every evening on my knees, day after day, for seven weeks! And when Lilian asked me if I wanted to go to the John Denver concert on the council lawns, they wouldn't let me go, which was even more horrible!" she cried, "I'll never forgive you for that as long as I live," she promised laughingly.

In spite of the pain it caused me, I was glad that Eugene had told me about those strong, negative feelings, which were obviously still bothering him now. It explained to me why he always seemed reluctant to help me with the 'oliebollen', a Dutch treat we made every year at the Old Timers Fete, in which our whole family got involved.

But I had it all wrong Eugene said when he apologised later. I had jumped to the conclusion that I had made his life miserable. He had had a wonderful youth. He was not happy about helping with the fete, simply because there were so many other things that needed his attention and I often gave the impression that I was sorry that I had taken it on myself.

He was right of course. As with every other fund-raising group, you make a commitment months ahead, not knowing who is available to help you when the day comes. Eugene knew very well that nothing ever got done if you were not prepared to take those risks.

"The fact that I did not want to edit that particular part of the story, was because I had heard it all so often, and that kind of sob-story was not my cup of tea," he said.

Knowing that my children did not suffer from my 'selfishness' to persevere with my job at Old Timers, I happily finished the story. Writing has opened many doors for me and made me more compassionate towards others, realising that we only see the outside of people, with an occasional glimpse of what goes on inside. Talking openly with Fred, as we did when we were courting, has also been very beneficial for our relationship, which is still blossoming.

We had the shop for nearly ten years when I suffered a nervous breakdown after the death of my mother and Lilian took over. I had just turned fifty and I had no idea what I was going to do with myself, when we met an author while we were on holiday in West Australia in September 1990. Listening to our immigration stories, she encouraged me to write them down, even if it was only for our grandchildren. I happily wrote a list of what to include, only to find that I needed to unburden myself from the baggage I was still carrying from the past. Fred was quite happy to go to Holland with me to find out more about the happenings in my family.

Those four months in Holland and Canada in 1991 became an exhausting, but also a very rewarding, time for me. The idea was that I would collect information for my book while Fred would paint, but that did not happen, mainly because nobody took my writing seriously, and Fred had no inspiration to paint at all. In the end, it has all been worthwhile as my first book 'Father Forgive Us...' has not only given readers of all walks of life 'a pleasant surprise' and freed me from my frequent depressions, but it also brought our family closer together.

What more could I wish for?

During these last ten years Fred and I have become very much 'in tune', admiring and encouraging each other to use our gifts to the best of our capabilities. Through our hobbies, Fred building and demonstrating street-organs and my love for writing, gardening and caring for elderly people, we are reminded time and again that the world is still full of wonderful people. Helping and making others happy is truly bouncing back on us a hundred-fold!

"Father Forgive Us...."

Coming to terms with my tears

My mother's 'Little Heaven' was often Hell for all of us.'

Mien Blom

"Father forgive them, they don't know what they do..." my stepfather always said, no matter whether he was talking about a salesman who was dishonest or Hitler killing the Jews. I in turn, needed to forgive, not only my stepfather for sexually and verbally abusing me, but also my mother for turning a blind eye to what was happening, and the local priest for destroying my belief in a loving God.

Author

I read this manuscript with a great deal of interest and also with great admiration for an author who could master a second language later in life and write so lucidly in it. This is a well-described family history/autobiography, composed in simple language with clarity, honesty and compassion. The Dutch farming family, which figures in it, with all their faults, idiocyncrasies and foibles, come very much alive as people.

The material presented here is written in a clear, well-crafted expository style and it is factual and well organised; one receives a vivid impression of the toughness of life as it is lived, conveyed little affectation, self-pity or complaint. It is also refreshingly unjudgmental.

National Book Council Inc.
Manuscript Assessment
Nr 97/472

The New Farm House

ISBN 0646-41301-5

9 780646 413013